Kuala Lumpur,
Melaka & Penang

"All you've got to do is decide to go
and the hardest part is over.

So go!"

D0271009

Contents

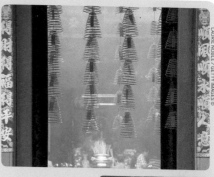

(left) Joggers in KLCC Park (p51)

....

(above) Guandi Temple (p76)

....

(right) Statue of Hindu deity inside Batu Caves (p115)

....

Masjid India, Kampung Baru & Northern KL
p85

Golden Triangle & KLCC
p48

Chinatown, Merdeka Square & Bukit Nanas
p71

Lake Gardens, Brickfields & Bangsar
p95

Welcome to Kuala Lumpur

Imagine a city, its skyline punctuated by minarets, Mogul domes and skyscrapers, its colourful, food-stall-lined streets shaded by banyan and rain trees.

Asian Cybercity

This is Kuala Lumpur (KL), Malaysia's sultry capital, packed with historic monuments, steel-clad skyscrapers, lush parks, megasized shopping malls, bustling street markets and trendy nightspots. Also an essential part of the vibrant mix are incense-wreathed, colourfully adorned mosques and temples of the country's Malay, Chinese and Indian communities. A reverence for these ancient cultures is balanced with a drive to be plugged into the contemporary world, as evidenced by an exciting contemporary art and design scene and a buzzing digital economy.

Historical Canvas

Today's KLites are separated by barely a handful of generations from the tenacious Chinese and Malay tin prospectors who founded the city. By the time the British made it the capital of Peninsular Malaysia in the late 19th century, KL had only been in existence for a couple of decades.

Since then, the city has been the scene of history-defining moments for Malaysia. Stadium Merdeka was where, in 1957, the country's first prime minister Tunku Abdul Rahman punched his fist seven times in the air and declared independence. And the Petronas Towers were officially the tallest buildings in the world when they opened in 1998.

Delicious Diversions

Reach for the sky by all means, but also keep a close eye on what's happening closer to the ground. To fully connect with locals, join them in two of their favourite pastimes: shopping and eating. Malaysian consumer culture achieves its zenith in KL, where you could spend all day browsing glitzy air-conditioned malls such as Pavilion KL and Mid Valley Megamall in search of bargains. Alternatively, explore Central Market for locally made souvenirs, then dive into the culinary melting pots of nearby Chinatown or Masjid India.

Take to the Streets

It won't take you long to realise, despite the heat, this is a city best explored on foot. Walk and you can catch all the action and save yourself the frustration of becoming entangled in one of KL's all-too-frequent traffic jams. To tackle this problem, a new mass rapid transit (MRT) system is under construction. Soaring property values are also causing characterful old buildings to be torn down and replaced with bland new towers. Such disruptions aside, parts of KL retain the laid-back ambience and jungle lushness of the *kampung* (village) it once was.

Why I Love Kuala Lumpur

By Simon Richmond, Author

In KL, it's all about the food – this city offers a mouth-watering mix of Asian culinary traditions. Start with a breakfast of fresh *popiah* and congee at Imbi Market, seguing into a snack of freshly made roti and spicy chicken curry at Jln Belfield's SS Spicy Food stalls. Move onto Chinatown for a must-have bowl of *asam laksa* on Madras Lane. Save room for afternoon tea somewhere nice (Majestic Hotel fits the bill) and for supper on Jln Alor – the perfect end to a KL dining day.

For more about our author, see p264.

Above: Locals dining outdoors in KL

Kuala Lumpur's
Top 10

Street Food *(p26)*

1 White tablecloths? Snooty waiters? A roof? No need to bother with all that! In KL some of your best dining experiences will happen on the street. Freshly cooked meals served from mobile carts, stalls and shophouse *kopitiam* (coffee shops) are the way to go. Jln Alor is the city's most famous eats street, jammed with alfresco tables. The atmosphere and food is good here but prices will be higher than at more locally patronised hawker gourmet destinations such as Lucky Gardens, Imbi Market or the street stalls scattered around Brickfields.

✗ *Eating*

Petronas Towers *(p50)*

2 It's impossible to resist the magnetic allure of the Petronas Towers: the 452m-high structure is beautiful to look at, as well as being the embodiment of Malaysia's transformation into a fully developed nation. Designed by architect Cesar Pelli, this glistening, steel-wrapped structure is the focal point of the Kuala Lumpur City Centre (KLCC), a 40-hectare development that also includes an imaginatively designed tropical park, a fun aquarium, an excellent kids' museum, a world-class concert hall and one of KL's best shopping malls.

⊙ *Golden Triangle & KLCC*

Shopping Malls *(p40)*

3 Come for the air-conditioning, stay for the designer bargains! The roll call of brands in malls Pavilion KL, Suria KLCC and Publika will impress even the most sophisticated of shoppers. Refreshments are never far away, with masses of restaurants and excellent food courts always part of the retail mix, along with everything from doctor-fish spas to luxurious multiplex cinemas and karaoke rooms. It's the unexpected finds – the feng shui stores, art galleries and Hindu temples – that really set these malls apart. RIGHT: BERJAYA TIMES SQUARE (P68)

🛍 *Shopping*

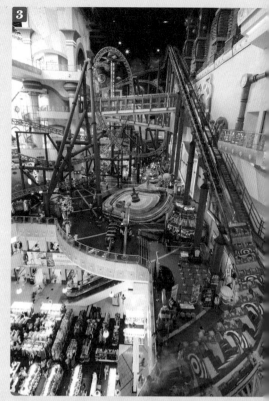

FRIM (p117)

4 The Forest Research Institute of Malaysia (FRIM) is an emerald jewel, a natural escape from KL's urban grind. Feel your soul start to calm as soon as you enter this 600-hectare reserve where hard concrete and traffic pollution give way to soft foliage and fresh air. Get the blood pumping on the steep hike up to the thrilling 200m-long Canopy Walkway that hangs a vertigo-inducing 30m above the forest floor and provides panoramic views back to the city. Down on the ground look for the pond that's home to an arapaima, a giant South American fish.

⊙ Day Trips from Kuala Lumpur

Batu Caves (p115)

5 It's always a very busy and colourful scene at this sacred Hindu shrine but, if you can, time your visit for a holy day, the biggest of which is Thaipusam. Guarding the 272 steps that lead up to the main Temple Cave is the 43m gilded statue of Murugan, assisted by a platoon of lively macaques who show little fear in launching raids on tourists' belongings. A new cable car at the foot of the giant limestone outcrop takes the sweat out of reaching Temple Cave. ABOVE: STATUE OF MURUGAN (P115)

⊙ Day Trips from Kuala Lumpur

Chinatown (p76)

6 Plumes of smoke curl upwards from smouldering coils of incense, flower garlands hang like pearls from the necks of Hindu statues and the call to prayer punctuates the honk of traffic. The temples and mosques of the city's Hindus, Muslims and Chinese Buddhists are crammed shoulder to shoulder in this atmospheric neighbourhood along the Klang river – where KL was born. Don't miss eating at the daytime Madras Lane hawker stalls or savouring the bustle and fun of the night market along Jln Petaling. BELOW: INCENSE AT SZE YA TEMPLE (P76)

⊙ *Chinatown, Merdeka Square & Bukit Nanas*

Merdeka Square (p74)

7 Stand beside the Victorian fountain next to the empty expanse of lawn and take in the impressive scene. When it was called the Padang, members of the Royal Selangor Club would politely clap as another wicket fell in a colonial cricket match. At midnight on 31 August 1957, the flag of the independent nation of Malaya was hoisted on the 95m flagpole. The eastern flank is dominated by the handsome Sultan Abdul Samad Building, decorated with copper-clad domes and barley-sugar-twist columns.

⊙ *Chinatown, Merdeka Square & Bukit Nanas*

8

Tun Abdul Razak Heritage Park *(p98)*

8 What was once known as the Lake Gardens is now KL's major recreation area, named after the country's second prime minister. The botanical garden laid out during British days remains at the park's heart and is flanked by one of the city's top attractions, the KL Bird Park. There are lots of other things to see and do here including visiting the National Planetarium, KL Butterfly Park and the striking National Monument commemorating those who lost their lives fighting communists during the Emergency.

LEFT: MILKY STORK, KL BIRD PARK (P98)

◉ *Lake Gardens, Brickfields & Bangsar*

Islamic Arts Museum *(p97)*

9 The dazzling collection of objects housed in this fine museum prove that religious devotion can be married with exquisite craftsmanship. The building itself – with its Iranian-tiled facade and decorated domes – is a stunner, its galleries filled with natural light and amazing works gathered from around the Islamic world. Don't miss the architecture gallery with models of some of the great Islamic buildings. The museum's gift shop is also one of the best places in KL to buy beautifully designed and expertly made items from across the Islamic world.

◉ *Lake Gardens, Brickfields & Bangsar*

Thean Hou Temple *(p100)*

10 KL has plenty of Buddhist temples but none as visually striking as this one. Rising out of the leafy surrounds of Robson Heights in four terraced levels, this architecture is the stuff of pure Chinese fantasy, with dazzling mosaic dragons and phoenixes flying off the eaves and snaking around columns. It's all built to house effigies of the heavenly mother Thean Hou as well as Kuan Yin, the goddess of mercy, and Shuiwei Shengniang, goddess of the waterfront. Visit on festival days and weekends to see the temple at its most lively.

◉ *Lake Gardens, Brickfields & Bangsar*

What's New

Cycling Kuala Lumpur

Started by Jeffrey Lim and a group of volunteers, the KL Bicycle Map Project (http://studio25.my) has created a map of cycling routes across KL. Together with the rental KL by Cycle operation it's looking as if this automobile-dominated city might be inching towards becoming two-wheel friendly. (p99)

Majestic Hotel

A welcome restoration of a grand KL hotel, updated with a new tower extension, gorgeous Rennie Mackintosh–inspired spa, and orchidarium. (p135)

Troika Sky Dining

The umbrella name for the dining and drinking trio – Cantaloupe (p60), Strato (p59) and Claret (p65) – spread across the 23rd floor of the Foster Partners–designed Troika complex.

Nada Lama

Bodily bliss awaits at this rustically beautiful spa out in the leafy surrounds of Sungai Penchala. (p101)

Private Galleries

Make appointments to view the splendid contemporary-art collections at the private galleries Sekeping Tenggiri (p103) and Ruang Pemula (RuPé; p53).

Secret Bars

Speakeasy-style bars such as Tate (p65) and Omakase + Appreciate (p93) are a hit with the cocktail-quaffing generation.

Coffee Culture

KL's caffeine addicts gather at indie cafes such as RAWcoffee (p65), Typica (p56) and Coffee Stain by Joseph (p61), where the art of the barista and single-origin beans rule.

KLIA2

Replacing the Low Cost Carrier Terminal is this new wing (www.klia2.info) of the International Airport at Sepang. (p216)

KL Sentral

The development of the city's transport hub continues with Aloft Hotel (p134); a new mall, Nu Sentral (p113); and – finally – the monorail linked directly to the main station.

Walking Tours

Sign up for the Visit KL (p226) free guided walking tours of Merdeka Square and Brickfields. Tastier options are the food-themed walking tours offered by Simply Enak (p24) and Food Tour Malaysia (p26).

For more recommendations and reviews, see **lonelyplanet. com/kuala-lumpur**

Need to Know

For more information, see Survival Guide (p215)

Currency
Malaysian ringgit (RM)

Language
Bahasa Malaysia and English

Visas
Generally not required for stays of up to 60 days

Money
ATMs widely available; credit cards accepted in most hotels and restaurants

Mobile Phones
Local SIM cards can be used in most phones; if not, set your phone to roaming

Time
GMT/UTC plus eight hours; no daylight saving

Tourist Information
Visit KL (Map p248; ☑2698 0332; www.visitkl.gov.my; KL City Gallery, Merdeka Square; 🚇Masjid Jamek)

Malaysian Tourism Centre (Map p250; ☑9235 4900; http://matic.gov.my; 109 Jln Ampang; ⊙8am-10pm; monorail Bukit Nanas)

Daily Costs

Budget: less than RM100
➡ Dorm bed RM12–RM35

➡ Hawker stalls and food courts for meals

➡ Use public transport; plan sightseeing around walking tours, free museums and galleries

Midrange: RM100–RM400
➡ Double room in midrange hotel RM100–RM400

➡ Two-course meal in midrange restaurant RM40–RM60

➡ Take taxis and guided tours

Top End: more than RM400
➡ Luxury double room RM450–RM1000

➡ Meal in top restaurant plus bottle of wine RM200

Advance Planning

Two months before Book flights and accommodation.

One month before Plan itinerary, checking to see if there are any events or festivals you may be able to attend.

One week before Book online for tour up Petronas Towers and for foodie walking tour. Make reservations at any top-end restaurants.

Useful Websites

Visit KL (www.visitkl.gov.my) Official city tourism site.

Time Out KL (www.timeoutkl.com) Monthly listing magazine; sign up online for its weekly 'what's going on' digest.

Lonely Planet (www.lonelyplanet.com) Destination information, accommodation bookings, Thorn Tree travel forum and more.

WHEN TO GO?

The city can be busy during Chinese New Year and Ramadan. In July there may be haze due to smoke from field-clearing fires in Indonesia.

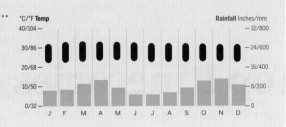

Arriving in Kuala Lumpur

Kuala Lumpur International Airport (KLIA) Trains RM35; every 15 minutes from 5am to 1am; 30 minutes to KL Sentral. Buses RM10; every hour from 5am to 1am; one hour to KL Sentral. Taxis from RM75; one hour to central KL.

KL Sentral Transport hub with train, Light Rail Transit (LRT), monorail, bus and taxi links to rest of city. Taxi is by prepaid coupon to Chinatown/Golden Triangle (RM13).

Pudu Sentral Long-distance buses from many parts of Peninsular Malaysia and Singapore arrive at this station close to Chinatown.

Singapore express buses also arrive at Kuala Lumpur Station, Berjaya Times Square and the Corus Hotel opposite the Kuala Lumpur City Centre (KLCC).

For much more on **arrival** see p216.

Getting Around

Buy the **MyRapid card** (www.myrapid.com.my; RM10), which includes RM8 in credit, at monorail and LRT stations. Tap at the ticket gates or when you get on Rapid KL buses for fare to be deducted.

➡ **Monorail** Stops in mostly convenient locations; gets very crowded during evening rush hours (6pm to 8pm Monday to Friday).

➡ **LRT** Also handy (for Chinatown, Kampung Baru, KLCC) but network is poorly integrated.

➡ **GO KL City Bus** Two free loop services connecting up Chinatown, Golden Triangle and KLCC.

➡ **Taxi** Can be flagged down with metered fares starting at RM3 for first two minutes. Not all taxi drivers will agree to use meter, and at some designated taxi ranks a prepaid coupon system for journeys operates.

For much more on **getting around** see p218.

Sleeping

There are plenty of budget lodges and hotels and five-star properties, but reserve in advance especially if visiting during busy Asian travel seasons such as Chinese New Year and the end of Ramadan. You can often snag great online deals for top-end accommodation, which compensates for the dearth of characterful midrange options. Serviced apartments are also well worth considering, especially for longer stays. Rates at the cheaper places usually include all taxes and service charges, but many midrange and all top-end places quote prices without these added, so reckon on an extra 16% on the bill.

Useful Websites

➡ **Agoda** (www.agoda.com) Deep discounts on hotel rates available at this local site.

➡ **iBilik** (www.ibilik.my) Short-term rental apartments and homestays.

➡ **Cari Homestay** (www.carihomestay.net) More homestay options.

For much more on **sleeping** see p127.

Top Itineraries

Day One

KLCC (p48)

 Breakfast at **Imbi Market** then hop in a taxi to the Kuala Lumpur City Centre (KLCC), where you've prebooked tickets up the **Petronas Towers**. Afterwards, browse the shops in **Suria KLCC**, see a free art exhibition at the excellent **Galeri Petronas** and enjoy the science-related exhibitions at **Petrosains**.

> **Lunch** Suria KLCC (p69) has oodles of dining options including two food courts.

KLCC (p48)

Take a postlunch stroll around **KLCC Park**. At 3pm Tuesday to Thursday head to the **Malaysian Tourism Centre** for its traditional dance and music show. Alternatively, learn about sea and river life at **Aquaria KLCC** or join the 3pm tour of the Malay-style wooden house **Rumah Penghulu** next to **Badan Warisan**.

> **Dinner** Enjoy chicken wings and grilled fish at Wong Ah Wah (p58) on Jln Alor.

Golden Triangle (p48)

 Go mall-hopping along Jln Bukit Bintang until 10pm then head to Changkat Bukit Bintang and Jln Mesui for the bars; **Palate Palette** is a superb choice. Check out **No Black Tie** for its jazz and classical concerts.

Day Two

Merdeka Square (p71)

 Admire the historic buildings of **Merdeka Square**, then either cycle on a hired bike or take a taxi to the **Tun Abdul Razak Heritage Park**. Start at the **National Monument**, then walk through the **Perdana Botanical Gardens** to reach the **National Museum** by 10am in time for the free guided tour.

> **Lunch** *Nasi lemak* at Hornbill (p105) or fish at Kompleks Makan Tanglin (p105).

Lake Gardens (p95)

Continue to enjoy the leafy surrounds of the park at the **KL Bird Park** or **Butterfly Park**. Save at least an hour or more for the splendid **Islamic Arts Museum**, then admire the architecture of **Masjid Negara** and **Kuala Lumpur Railway Station**.

> **Dinner** Old China Cafe (p80) for Nonya food or Jln Hang Lekir street eats.

Chinatown (p71)

 Go souvenir shopping at **Central Market**, then push your way through the crowds at Chinatown's **Jln Petaling night market**.

GREG ELMS / GETTY IMAGES ©

Birdwing butterfly at KL Butterfly Park (p99)

Day Three

Chow Kit & Kampung Baru (p85)

 Have breakfast at **Bazaar Baru Chow Kit**, one of KL's most atmospheric wet markets, then amble through the Malay area of **Kampung Baru** admiring the traditional wooden houses and flower gardens.

 Lunch Go old school at Yut Kee (p91) or colonial at Coliseum Cafe (p92).

Bukit Nanas (p71)

 Walk from **Masjid India** to Bukit Nanas where you can traverse the canopy walkway of **KL Forest Eco Park** and then go much higher up the **Menara KL**, to get your bearings of the city from the revolving restaurant **Atmosphere 360**.

Dinner Enjoy Chinese at Robson Heights (p106) or Indian food in Brickfields.

Brickfields (p95)

For another panoramic perspective of KL stand on the upper terraces of the gloriously decorative **Thean Hou Temple**. Walk around the many religious sites of **Brickfields** in the cool of evening and enjoy a cocktail at the rooftop **MAI Bar** overlooking KL Sentral.

Day Four

Batu Caves (p115)

 Climb the 272 steps at **Batu Caves** to pay your respects at the Hindu **Temple Cave** and learn about bats and other cave dwellers in the **Dark Cave**.

Lunch Tuck into Thai at Samira (p93) in Sentul Park.

Titiwangsa (p89)

Views the city skyline from **Titiwangsa Lake Gardens**. Nearby is the **National Visual Art Gallery**. To see more contemporary works make an appointment to view the private collection at **Ruang Pemula (RuPé)**.

 Dinner Splash out at Acme Bar & Coffee (p60) or Cantaloupe (p60).

Golden Triangle (p48)

Sink a sunset cocktail at **Heli Lounge Bar**. If your budget doesn't stretch to fine dining, a meal at **Jalan Imbi Hawker Stalls** or **Jalan Sayur Stalls** will be equally memorable and delicious.

If You Like...

Historic Buildings

Sultan Abdul Samad Building Glorious brick structure with Moorish architectural influences and 43m clock tower. (p75)

KL Train Station A Mogul fantasy, once the rail hub of the peninsula. (p103)

Stadium Merdeka Sporting venue where independence of the Federation of Malaya was declared in 1957. (p76)

Loke Mansion Restored home of tin tycoon Loke Yew, now a law firm's office. (p87)

Sultan Sulaiman Club City's oldest Malay club in the heart of Kampung Baru. (p89)

Modern Architecture

Petronas Towers Iconic twin towers that lord it over the city. (p50)

Putrajaya Showcase of modern urban planning and vaulting architectural ambition. (p124)

Bank Negara Malaysia Museum & Art Gallery Hijjas Kasturi–designed complex. (p87)

Kompleks Dayabumi Delicately beautiful exterior design featuring Islamic motifs. (p77)

Istana Budaya Traditional Malay design is applied to this performing-arts hall. (p94)

Putrajaya (p124)

Animal Encounters

KL Bird Park Giant aviary that's home to some 200 mostly Asian species. (p98)

Aquaria KLCC Pools swimming with everything from starfish to sand tiger sharks. (p50)

Butterfly Park Hundreds of species of fluttering insects and other critters. (p99)

Zoo Negara Feed elephants, camels and deer; watch orangutans and tigers. (p116)

Forest Research Institute of Malaysia (FRIM) Macaque and langurs (leaf monkeys) hang out in this junglelike reserve. (p117)

Art Galleries

National Visual Arts Gallery KL's top public gallery with a new portraits section. (p89)

Ruang Pemula (RuPé) Appointment-only private gallery with blue-chip contemporary collection. (p53)

Sekeping Tenggiri Another outstanding private collection worth making an appointment to view. (p103)

Publika Mall stacked with commercial art galleries and the MAP exhibition space. (p111)

Galeri Petronas Interesting exhibitions at this great space in Suria KLCC. (p51)

Bank Negara Malaysia Museum & Art Gallery Off-the-beaten-track collection of major Malaysian artists. (p87)

Religious Sites

Masjid Negara The National Mosque is a classic piece of modern architecture. (p102)

Sri Mahamariamman Temple Venerable Hindu shrine in Chinatown. (p76)

Masjid Jamek Recently restored mosque sporting elegant Mogul-influenced design. (p79)

Sze Ya Temple Atmospheric Chinese temple dedicated to one of KL's founding fathers. (p76)

Thean Hou Temple Fabulous Buddhist temple on a leafy hill overlooking city. (p100)

Buddhist Maha Vihara Historic Sinhalese Buddhist temple in Brickfields. (p103)

Museums

Islamic Arts Museum Marvel at gorgeous works of art inspired by Muslim faith. (p97)

National Museum Covering the region's history from prehistoric times to modern day. (p102)

National Textiles Museum Admire skilful weaving, embroidery, knitting and batik printing. (p75)

Petrosains Science-focused discovery centre at KLCC. (p51)

Markets

Pudu Market There's always plenty of activity at KL's biggest wet market. (p56)

Bazaar Baru Chow Kit Heady sensory experience at this long-established wet market. (p87)

Chinatown Wet Market Darkened alleys where locals shop for fresh produce. (p77)

Petaling Street Market Piles of pirated goods alongside the real deal. (p82)

Masjid India Night Market Best of the weekly *pasar malam* (night markets) with added Bollywood factor. (p91)

For more top Kuala Lumpur spots, see the following:

➡ Eating (p25)

➡ Drinking & Nightlife (p35)

➡ Entertainment (p38)

➡ Shopping (p40)

PLAN YOUR TRIP IF YOU LIKE...

Parks & Gardens

Perdana Botanical Garden Also don't miss the nearby Hibiscus and Orchid Gardens. (p99)

KLCC Park Jogging track, great kids' playground, top views of Petronas Towers. (p51)

Titiwangsa Lake Gardens Serene park surrouding a large lake in northern KL. (p91)

KL Forest Eco Park A lowland dipterocarp forest in the heart of the city. (p79)

Taman Botani Landscaped gardens beside the lake in Putrajaya. (p125)

Viewpoints

Menara KL Dine in the revolving restaurant atop this telecom tower. (p73)

Petronas Towers Watch fearless window cleaners from the 86th-floor observation deck. (p50)

Thean Hou Temple City panoramas and decorative dragons and phoenixes. (p100)

Heli Lounge Bar Bottoms up at the cocktail bar on the helipad. (p61)

Chin Woo Stadium Peaceful Chinatown spot to view sunset across the city. (p84)

Month by Month

January

This month can be very busy for travel if Chinese New Year falls within it, so plan ahead. Thaipusam, the other major festival at this time, can also fall in February in some years.

⚜ Chinese New Year

Dragon dances and pedestrian parades mark the start of the new year. Families hold open house and everybody wishes you *kong hee fatt choy* (a happy and prosperous new year). Celebrated on 19 February 2015, 8 February 2016 and 28 January 2017.

⚜ Thaipusam

Enormous crowds converge at Batu Caves north of KL and at Nattukotai Chettiar Temple in Penang for this dramatic Hindu festival involving body piercing. Falls between mid-January and mid-February.

March

⚜ Birthday of the Goddess of Mercy

Offerings are made to the very popular Chinese goddess Kuan Yin at temples across the region; a good one to visit is Thean Hou Temple in KL. The goddess is also honoured three times more during the year, in April/May, July/August and October/November.

⚜ Putrajaya International Hot Air Balloon Fiesta

Held over four days in Putrajaya, this festival has hosted hot-air-balloon pilots from as far afield as New Zealand and Switzerland, and attracts over 100,000 spectators. Find details at www.myballoon-fiesta.com.

April

The end of the light monsoon season on Malaysia's west coast, but not the end of rain, for which you should always be prepared.

☆ Petronas Malaysian Grand Prix

Formula 1's big outing in Southeast Asia is held at the Sepang International Circuit over three days, usually at the start of the month. Associated events and parties are held in KL.

May

This quiet month, prior to the busy school holidays, is a good time to visit, with a couple of big parades.

⚜ Wesak Day (Vesak Day)

In celebration of Buddha's birth, enlightenment and death there's a major procession with illuminated floats and thousands of people carrying candles through KL, starting from the Buddhist Maha Vihara. Celebrated on 1 June 2015, 21 May 2016 and 10 May 2017.

⚜ Colours of 1Malaysia

Merdeka Square is the location for this tourism-focused night parade and entertainment extravaganza, with dancers depicting traditional dances as well as quirky themes of homestays and contemporary art.

June

The first Saturday of June is the official birthday of Malaysia's king, marked by a parade at the national palace, an address to the nation and an award ceremony. From 2014 to 2016 Ramadan will start in June and finish in July.

✾ Cooler Lumpur Festival

In 2013 MAP Publika was the location for the inauguration of the Cooler Lumpur Festival (www.coolerlumpur.com/word). It's planned to be an annual arts fest with a specific media focus, be it literature, film or art.

✾ Putrajaya Floria

This flower and garden festival (www.ppj.gov.my/putrajayafloria) lasts nine days and is a big affair. Expect colourful displays of exotic blooms including orchids and bougainvillea.

August

✾ Festival of the Hungry Ghosts

Chinese Malaysians perform operas, host open-air concerts and lay out food for their ancestors. The ghosts eat the spirit of the food, but thoughtfully leave the substance for mortal celebrants. Celebrated towards the end of the month and early September.

✾ National Day

Join the crowds at midnight on 31 August to celebrate the anniversary of Malaysia's independence in 1957. Events are held in Merdeka Square (Dataran Merdeka) and across KL.

September

Haze from forest and field-clearance fires in Indonesia can create smog in KL, so avoid visiting during this month and the next if you are prone to respiratory complaints and asthma.

☆ KL International Jazz Festival

Apart from hosting major international jazz artists, this festival (www.klinternationaljazz.com), held at University Malaya, has art exhibitions, a hot-air-balloon show and market stalls.

October

The start of the monsoon season on Malaysia's west coast, but rainfall is not so heavy or constant as to affect most travel plans.

✕ Malaysian International Gourmet Festival

Prestigious restaurants and master chefs all pitch in with their best efforts during this month-long celebration of edible creativity in KL that includes food fairs and cooking classes. Full details at www.migf.com.

November

☆ Urbanscapes

Major two-day indie-music and arts culture fest (http://urbanscapes.com.my). Previous artists have included the likes of Sigur Rós and local songstress Yuna.

✾ Deepavali

Tiny oil lamps are lit outside Hindu homes to attract the auspicious gods Rama and Lakshmi. Indian businesses start the new financial year. Happens on 11 November 2015, 31 November 2016 and 19 October 2017.

December

School holidays can see hotels booked up towards the end of the month when many people arrive in the region to holiday over Christmas and New Year.

✾ Winter Solstice Festival

Called Dong Zhi in Mandarin and Tang Chek in Hokkien, this Chinese festival offers thanks for a good harvest and usually occurs between 21 and 23 December. It's celebrated by eating glutinous rice balls served in a clear sugar syrup.

LUNAR CALENDAR

Hindus, Muslims and Chinese follow a lunar calendar, so the dates for religious festivals vary each year. Muslim holidays typically move forward 11 days each year, while Hindu and Chinese festivals change dates but fall roughly within the same months. Dates have been given where they are known, but may be subject to slight change.

With Kids

KL has a lot going for it as a family holiday destination. Its textbook Southeast Asian cultural mix offers chances to watch temple ceremonies and sample an amazing range of food. Nature is also close at hand, along with clean accommodation, modern malls and fun amusement parks.

CHRISTIAN KOBER / GETTY IMAGES ©

Macaque monkeys, Tun Abdul Razak Heritage Park (p98)

Animal & Jungle Attractions

It's not so long ago that tigers and other beasts of the jungle prowled the outskirts of KL. Abundant swaths of greenery within the city and surrounds mean that wildlife is still very much present. At Batu Caves and the Forest Research Institute of Malaysia (FRIM) encountering wild monkeys, such as macaques and langurs, is pretty much guaranteed. Zoo Negara is one of the region's better-managed facilities and offers visitors a chance to become a volunteer for the day.

In the heart of KL there's the Aquaria KLCC with its many sea creatures and touch pools, as well as the excellent KL Bird Park, Butterfly Park and Deer Park, all at the Tun Abdul Razak Heritage Park. Day trips out of KL that are easy to organise include to Kuala Gandah Wildlife Conservation Centre to view rescued elephants, and Genting Highlands and Fraser's Hill (Bukit Fraser), both top birdwatching locations.

Parks & Theme Parks

For small kids, the following parks have top-grade playgrounds with slides, splash pools and the like: Perdana Botanical Gardens, KLCC Park and Titiwangsa Lake Gardens.

Brave kids and teens will be thrilled by the chance to make like a monkey in the tree tops by traversing the canopy walkways at the KL Forest Eco Park and FRIM.

When the weather turns too hot or rainy, the Berjaya Times Square Theme Park provides an indoor energy-burning and fun-injecting experience, as does the indoor theme park at Genting Highlands.

Pack your swimsuits and suncream and head to Sunway Lagoon for a brilliant water theme park with water slides and a surfing beach, along with other attractions including a mall and ice rink. There's also a water park at the City of Digital Lights at i-City outside Shah Alam.

Museums, Temples & Heritage Buildings

At the National Museum engage your kid's imagination by introducing them to the 11,000-year-old skeleton 'Perak Man' and finding out what activities are scheduled for the discovery room. Heading up the Petronas Towers is not just an opportunity to gawk from high at the city but also to learn about the tower's construction and, afterwards, visit the hands-on science museum Petrosains within the Suria KLCC mall.

Batu Caves, with its Hindu temples, colourful tableaux of Hindu tales and legends, monkeys, and natural Dark Cave, holds much to capture a child's imagination. The dazzlingly decorated Thean Hou Temple likewise, for photo ops of Chinese zodiac statues, flying dragons and a pool teeming with scores of tortoises.

Dining Out

KL's myriad dining outlets offer meals that will appeal to the fussiest of kids. Although you may not think it, a busy food stall is usually the safest place to eat – you can see the food being prepared, the ingredients are often fresh and if the wok stays hot there's little chance of bacteria. Grown ups can also try more adventurous dishes while the kids get something more familiar.

If outdoor eating is something you're not comfortable with, then there are plenty of indoor food courts – all the major malls have them and choice and standards are universally fantastic. Many restaurants attached to hotels and guesthouses will serve familiar Western food, while international fast food is ubiquitous. Midrange and upscale restaurants often have high chairs but most budget places don't.

Malaysian drinks are very sweet and even fresh juices usually have sugar added. To cut down on sugar ask for drinks

without sugar or order bottled water. It's not a bad idea to carry a Steripen (www.steripen.com), a battery-run water filter about the size of a small screwdriver that can purify tap water as well as ice cubes in any kind of drink.

Markets & Malls

KL's crowded wet markets and street markets are no place to be pushing a buggy around. The butchering stalls can also be the stuff of a child's nightmares. But if you have curious older kids then markets can also be a great opportunity for learning about and tasting new tropical fruits and veggies.

Some shopping malls go overboard to embrace the family. Publika has a particularly good selection of shops for kids and parents including ones offering clothing, toys, crafts and books, as well as a play area and, on Sundays, free bikes to cycle around the complex. Plays spaces and crèches are available at Megakids in Mid Valley Megamall and Kidzsports & Gym in Bangsar Village.

Older kids and teens will love exploring Sungei Wang Plaza's warren of youth-oriented outlets. The Tokyo Street section of Pavilion KL and Parkmaya section of Farenheit88 are also a dream for those into Japanese fashion and comic cultures.

On the ground floor of the annex at Central Market you'll find a stall where you and your kids can try your hand at painting batik; the same company offers this course at Kompleks Kraf Kuala Lumpur.

Like a Local

In KL, the traditional greeting is not 'How are you?' but 'Sudah makan?' (Have you eaten yet?), underlining the national obsession with food. Hawker stalls, kopitiam (coffee shops) and mamaks (Indian Muslim hawker stalls) are where locals catch up on news and gossip with their friends and family.

Devotee at the Thaipusam festival, Batu Caves (p115)

Food Tours & Supper Clubs

Tap into what truly makes this city tick: the search for the next great meal. There are many online blogs and sites (p26) devoted to the local dining scene and a couple of great food tours (p26) that get you walking the streets, grazing along the way.

For a unique food experience there's the option of dining in a local home. Simply Enak (www.simplyenak.com) can arrange this, as can Plate Culture (www.plateculture.com), which matches people who love cooking with those searching for a home-cooked meal. Home-based 'underground supper clubs' and 'private kitchens', such as Jen's Underground Supper Club (http://jensundergroundsupperclub.com), are popular among locals; search online for dates when dinners are offered.

Join the Celebration

Being a multicultural, multifaith city there's seldom a week that goes by in KL without some kind of religious or cultural celebration. As well as ceremonies at mosques, shrines and temples, this often this means special things to eat and drink.

Securing a reservation at popular restaurants in the weeks leading to Chinese New Year can be tricky, as friends, colleagues and family gather over endless banquets. Ramadan bazaars and buffets are reason enough to visit KL during the Muslim holy month. For weeks before Deepavali, KL's Little Indias are awash in stalls selling clothing, textiles and household goods as well as special sweets and savoury snacks.

Shopping Culture

Next to eating, KLites' favourite pastime has to be shopping. These two obsessions dovetail in the city's multiplicity of malls. More local shopping experiences can be had at classic Southeast Asian fresh produce day markets, such as Pudu Market and Bazaar Baru Chow Kit, and at several atmospheric night markets, the most famous of which is the one along Jln Petaling. Craft markets are becoming popular, with monthly ones to attend at Bangsar Shopping Centre and Publika.

PAUL KENNEDY / GETTY IMAGES ©

Malaysian seafood laksa

Eating

KL is a nonstop feast. You can dine in incredible elegance or mingle with locals at street stalls, taking your pick from a global array of cuisines. Ingredients are fresh, the cooking high quality and hygiene standards are excellent. Most vendors speak English and the final bill is seldom heavy on the pocket.

NEED TO KNOW

Price Ranges

For one meal including a soft drink:

$ less than RM15

$$ RM15–60

$$$ more than RM60

Business Hours

➡ Cafes & food stalls: 7.30am–midnight

➡ Restaurants: noon–2.30pm & 6–10.30pm

Blogs & Online Resources

➡ A Whiff of Lemongrass (www.awhiffoflemongrass.com)

➡ CC Food Travel (www.cumidanciki.com)

➡ FriedChillies (www.friedchillies.com)

➡ KYspeaks.com (http://kyspeaks.com)

➡ Masak Masak (www.masak-masak. blogspot.com)

Language

See the Food Glossary on p233.

Reservations

Only recommended for top-end places or if you are a large group.

Smoking

Banned in air-conditioned cafes and restaurants.

Tipping & Service Charges

At some mid-range and all top-end places prices will be '++' meaning 6% government tax and 10% service charge will be added to the bill. Tipping is not expected but leaving small change will be appreciated.

Courses

Available at the following:

➡ Bayan Indah (p101)

➡ LaZat Malaysian Home Cooking Class (p124)

➡ Nathalie's Gourmet Studio (p111)

➡ Rebung (p107)

➡ Starhill Culinary Studio (p70)

Food Tours

➡ Food Tour Malaysia (www.foodtour malaysia.com)

➡ Simply Enak (www.simplyenak.com)

Assorted dishes at a restaurant in KL's Little India

Where to Eat

HAWKER STALLS, MARKETS & FOOD COURTS

The tastiest and best-value food is found at hawker stalls, and locals are fiercely loyal to their favourite vendors. Many hawkers have been in business for decades or operate a business inherited from their parents or even grandparents; the best enjoy reputations that exceed their geographical reach. To sample Malaysian hawker food, simply head to a stand-alone streetside kitchen-on-wheels, a *kopitiam* (coffee shop) or food court. Place your order with one or multiple vendors, find a seat (shared tables are common) and pay for each dish as it's delivered to your table. You'll be approached by someone taking drink orders after you've sat down – pay for these separately as well.

Intrepid eaters shouldn't overlook *pasar* (markets). Morning markets include stalls selling coffee and other beverages, as well as vendors preparing foods such as freshly griddled roti and curry and *chee cheong fun* (rice noodle roll). *Ta pao* (takeaway) or eat in – most can offer at least a stool. *Pasar malam* (night markets) are also excellent places to graze.

There's little to fear about eating from outdoor hawker stalls or food markets but if you want some air-conditioning and a little more comfort, there's no shortage of indoor food courts in KL's malls.

COFFEE SHOPS & RESTAURANTS

While some *kopitiam* operate like food courts, with different vendors under one roof, others are single-owner establishments. Expect to be served noodle and

Above: Sticky rice in grilled banana leaves

Right: *Popiah* (Malaysian-style spring rolls)

Eating by Neighbourhood

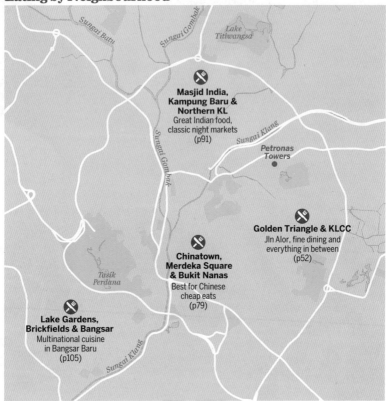

Masjid India, Kampung Baru & Northern KL
Great Indian food, classic night markets
(p91)

Golden Triangle & KLCC
Jln Alor, fine dining and everything in between
(p52)

Chinatown, Merdeka Square & Bukit Nanas
Best for Chinese cheap eats
(p79)

Lake Gardens, Brickfields & Bangsar
Multinational cuisine in Bangsar Baru
(p105)

rice dishes, strong coffee and other drinks, and all-day breakfast fare such as half-boiled eggs and toast spread with *kaya* (coconut jam).

Restoran (restaurants) range from casual, decades-old Chinese or Malay restaurants to upscale establishments boasting international fare, slick decor and a full bar.

VEGETARIANS & VEGANS

Given the inclusion of prawn paste and fish in many dishes, vegetarians and vegans will find it difficult to negotiate their way around most menus. Chinese vegetarian restaurants and hawker stalls (signage will include the words *'sayur-sayuran'*) are safe bets – they are especially busy on the 1st and 15th of the lunar month, when many Buddhists adopt a vegetarian diet for 24 hours.

Indian vegetarian restaurants are another haven for snacks such as steamed *idli* (rice cakes) served with dhal and *dosa,* as well as *thali* (full set meals consisting of rice or bread with numerous side dishes). Look also for Chinese eateries displaying rows of stainless-steel pans and advertising 'economy rice'; this type of restaurant will have several pure vegetarian dishes.

What to Eat

CHINESE

Thanks to generations of immigrants from all parts of China, KL boasts a notable range of regional Chinese cuisines including Cantonese, Sichuanese, Teowchew, Hokkien and Hakka.

Home-grown Chinese dishes that the city is famous for include *pan mee*. Literally 'board noodles', these are substantial hand-cut or hand-torn wheat noodles tossed with dark soy sauce and garlic oil, garnished with chopped pork and crispy *ikan bilis* (dried sardines or anchovies), and served

TOP TASTES

Don't even think about leaving KL without sampling these much-loved specialities:

➡ *Asam laksa* – hailing from Penang, this is a sour and chilli-hot bowlful of round rice noodles in a fish-based soup, garnished with slivered torch ginger flower, chopped pineapple and mint.

➡ *Cendol* – a wonderfully refreshing sweet of shaved ice mounded over toothsome mung bean noodles, all doused in fresh coconut milk and luscious palm-sugar syrup.

➡ *Char kway teow* – wide rice noodles stir-fried with prawns, cockles, bean sprouts and egg; it vies with *nasi lemak* for the title of 'national dish'.

➡ *Nasi lemak* – rice steamed in coconut milk and served with *ikan bilis*, fried pea-nuts, half a hard-boiled egg, *sambal* (chilli sauce) and a selection of curries; often eaten for breakfast.

➡ *Roti canai* – flaky unleavened bread griddled with ghee until crisp and eaten with curry or dhal; it's another breakfast favourite.

with soup on the side. Some versions include a poached egg.

More expensive than your average noodle dish but well worth it are *sang har mee* (literally 'fresh sea noodles'): huge freshwater prawns in gravy flavoured with Chinese rice wine and the fat from the shellfish heads, served over *yee mee* (crispy fried noodles).

Hainanese immigrants were the private cooks of the British during colonial rule which has led to a hybrid style of Western cuisine still served in old-school places such as Yut Kee, Colliseum Cafe and, in a much more fancy version, the Colonial Cafe at the Majestic Hotel.

MALAY & NONYA

Head to Kampung Baru to sample the specialities of Malaysia's eastern states, such as Kelantanese *nasi kerabu* and *ayam percik* (barbecued chicken smothered in chilli-coconut sauce) and, from Terengganu, *nasi dagang* (nutty, coconut milk–cooked red rice).

Also look out across the city for restaurants serving Nonya (also spelled Nyonya), or Peranakan, cuisine, a fusion of Chinese and Malay ingredients and cooking techniques.

INDIAN

KL's two Little Indias – the official one in Brickfields and the other around Masjid India – are the places to sample Indian cooking, although you'll find the cuisine of the subcontinent served right across the city. Further afield, Klang's Little India also has an excellent array of Indian eateries.

A very KL experience is taking supper late at night at an Indian Muslim eatery known as a *mamak;* these typically run 24 hours,

serve comfort food dishes such as *roti canai, mee goreng* (fried noodles) and *murtabak* (pancakes stuffed with meat).

OTHER CUISINES

KL's dining scene is fully international and you needn't look far to find – thanks to Malaysia's huge immigrant workforce – inexpensive Thai, Burmese, Nepalese, Indonesian, Bangladeshi and Pakistani fare.

SCE HWAI PHANG / GETTY IMAGES ©

Salt-and-pepper fried tofu

Among the more upmarket dining options are restaurants serving Italian, French, fusion, Japanese and pan-Asian cuisine, ranging in style from casual chic to white tablecloth.

When to Eat

To those of us used to 'three square meals', it might seem as if Malays are always eating. In fact, five or six meals or snacks is more the order of the day than strict adherence to the breakfast-lunch-dinner trilogy. Breakfast is often something that can be grabbed on the run: *nasi lemak* wrapped to go *(bungkus)* in a banana leaf or brown waxed paper, a quick bowl of noodles, toast and eggs, or griddled Indian bread.

Come late morning a snack might be in order, perhaps a *karipap* (deep-fried pastry filled with spiced meat or fish and potatoes). Lunch generally starts from 12.30pm, something to keep in mind if you plan to eat at a popular establishment.

The British left behind a strong attachment to afternoon tea, consumed here in the form of tea or coffee and a sweet or savoury snack such as *tong sui,* various

Indian fritters, battered and fried slices of cassava, sweet potato, banana and – of course – *kueh* (traditional cakes often made from glutinous rice).

Mamak and hawker stalls see a jump in business a few hours after dinner (which is eaten around 6.30pm or 7pm) when Malays head out in search of a treat to tide them over until morning.

Festivals & Celebrations

It's no surprise that a people as consumed with food and its pleasures as Malays mark every occasion with edible delights.

At Chinese New Year banquets each table is sure to be graced with *yee sang* (literally 'fresh fish'; a Cantonese raw-fish dish believed to bring luck in the coming year). Other foods special to this time of the year (look for them in Chinese supermarkets) include pineapple tarts, *kueh bangkit* (snow-white, melt-in-the-mouth cookies), *nga ku* (deep-fried Chinese arrowroot chips) and *ti kueh* (glutinous rice cakes wrapped in banana leaf).

The Ramadan bazaars are reason in themselves to visit KL during the Muslim holy month. Vendors compete to secure a

Rice-cake desserts at Central Market (p77)

EATING HABITS

➡ You'll rarely find a knife on the Malaysian table – fork and spoon are the cutlery of choice. Forks aren't used to carry food to the mouth, but to nudge food onto the spoon.

➡ Chinese food is usually eaten with chopsticks (Westerners may be offered a fork and a spoon as a courtesy).

➡ Malays and Indians eat rice-based meals with their right hand (the left is reserved for unclean tasks), using their thumbs to manoeuvre rice onto the balls of their fingers and then transferring the lot to their mouth. Moistening your rice with curries and side dishes helps things along and, as with any new skill, practice makes perfect.

➡ Before and after eating, wash your hands with water from the teapot-like container on your table (Malaysian eateries) or at a communal sink to the rear or side of the room.

➡ Napkins on the table (and a towel to wipe your wet hands) aren't a given, so it's always a good idea to carry a pack of tissues when heading out to graze.

➡ In some Chinese eateries, after you've placed your order a server will bring a basin of hot water containing saucers, chopsticks, bowls and cutlery to the table. This is meant to allay hygiene concerns – remove the items from the water and dry them off with a napkin (or shake them dry).

➡ Restaurants adhering to Muslim dietary rules are classed as *halal* and will not serve alcohol. Restaurants advertising themselves as pork-free don't use pig products in any of their dishes.

Top: Coffee and *kaya* (coconut-jam) toast

Middle: Preparation of rice and meat dish

Bottom: Chicken and beef satay from a vendor on Jln Alor (p58)

lucrative spot at one of the city's Ramadan markets, which swing into action late in the afternoon to serve those breaking the fast at sunset. They offer an excellent opportunity to sample home-cooked, otherwise hard-to-find Malay dishes.

For the Indian festival Deepavali, special foodstuffs are shipped from the subcontinent, such as hand-patted pappadams and *kulfi* (a frozen, milk-based dessert).

Above: Mangosteen and prawn salad
Left: Rambutans at a street market

Lonely Planet's Top Choices

Jalan Alor (p58) KL's premier eats street is an unmissable culinary experience.

Imbi Market (p52) Wake up early and dive into this hawker heaven.

Robson Heights (p106) Dig into delicious Chinese food.

Rebung (p107) Feast on a buffet of expertly made Malay dishes.

Sushi Hinata (p58) Extra-ordinarily good sushi prepared by expert Japanese chefs.

Best by Budget

$

Madras Lane Hawkers (p79) Sample the best *asam laksa* and *yong tau fu* in Chinatown.

Jalan Imbi Hawker Stalls (p52) Head to Imbi in the evening for this great set of stalls.

Capital Café (p91) A truly Malaysian cafe serving Malay, Chinese and Indian food.

$$

Kedai Makanan Dan Minuman TKS (p52) Feel the heat at this Sichaunese joint on Jln Alor.

Thai-la (p91) Lovely Thai food on the fringe of Little India.

Coliseum Cafe (p92) Sample sizzling steaks in a classic colonial-era haunt.

$$$

Bijan (p58) Malay cuisine with fine-dining flair in a relaxed atmosphere.

Cantaloupe (p60) Jaw-dropping views, designer decor, fancy French cuisine.

Hit & Mrs (p108) Hidden gem with experimental cooking and cool vibe.

Best by Cuisine

Malay & Peranakan

Old China Café (p80) Chinatown standby serving Nonya dishes in atmospheric old building.

Limablas (p53) Retro cafe offering home-style cooking.

Baba Low's 486 Bangsar (p107) Melaka-style Nonya cuisine in an off-the-radar location.

Wondermama (p107) Contemporary twists on Malaysian classics.

Chinese

Sek Yuen (p56) Pudu landmark with dishes made in a wood-fired kitchen.

Yut Kee (p91) Classic Hainanese *kopitiam* known also for its Western-style dishes.

Fei Por (p56) Luscious chicken rice and barbecued pork served into the early hours.

Kin Kin (p92) Dry *pan mee* specialist; they also offer a vegetarian version.

Indian

Sri Nirwana Maju (p107) Banana leaf heaven in Bangsar.

Saravanaa Bhavan (p92) Several outlets for this famous vegetarian operation.

Authentic Chapati Hut (p105) Freshly made Indian breads and curries at this popular outdoor stall.

International & Fusion

Acme Bar & Coffee (p60) Super stylish, great for a lazy brunch or leisurely dinner.

Twenty One Kitchen & Bar (p58) Chic pit stop rising above the hullaballoo of Changkat Bukit Bintang.

Peter Hoe Beyond (p80) A haven of peace, healthy salads, quiches and sinful cakes.

French

Cuisine Gourmet by Nathalie (p82) Sophisticated dining experience at the foot of Menara KL.

Yeast Bistronomy (p107) Brilliant bistro/bakery in the heart of Bangsar Baru.

La Vie En Rose (p81) Fish soup, duck confit and coq au vin are all on the menu.

Italian

Strato (p59) Tasty pasta and pizza high up the Norman Foster Troika building.

Il Lido (p60) Elegant fine dining in the shadow of the Petronas Towers.

Nerovivo (p59) Classy Italian eatery in a bungalow close by Changkat Bukit Bintang.

Hawker

Madras Lane Hawker Stalls (p79) A treasure hidden behind Chinatown's wet market.

Jalan Sayur Stalls (p56) Pudu alleyway crammed with delicious hawker food.

Jalan Imbi Hawker Stalls (p52) A great alternative to touristy Jln Alor – and much cheaper.

Japanese

Sushi Hinata (p58) Sublime sushi, sashimi and other haute-Japanese creations.

Santouka (p57) Rich pork-broth ramen noodles in Pavilion KL.

Fukuya (p59) Full range of Japanese dishes served in an elegant bamboo-surrounded bungalow.

Vegetarian

Dharma Realm Guan Yin Sagely Monastery Canteen (p59) Join office workers for a healthy breakfast or lunch.

Blue Boy Vegetarian Food Centre (p53) Friendly stall holders craft tasty veg dishes.

Woods Macrobiotics (p57) Offering organic, vegan and wholefood edibles.

Bakery & Patisserie

Tommy Le Baker (p93) Top-grade sourdough bread, pastries, sandwiches and quiches.

Bisou (p59) Cupcake delights served in Bangsar Village and Suria KLCC.

Les Deux Garcons (p108) Its wasabi macarons are a flavour sensation.

Best Market Food

Bazaar Baru Chow Kit (p87) Sample noodles in a rich cow's liver soup and array of Malay desserts.

Masjid India Pasar Malam (p91) A wide range of excellent food stalls at this Saturday night market.

Bangsar Sunday Market (p106) Noodles, satay and fresh juices at this lively and mainly daytime market.

Best Local Breakfast

Imbi Market (p52) Try the *popiah*, congee and egg tarts. Closed Monday.

Chee Cheong Fun Stall (p79) Best rice noodles in Chinatown.

LOKL (p81) Choose between delicious dessert toasties or a full English.

Best of the Chain Gang

Ben's (p57) Tempting range of Western and Malay comfort foods.

Little Penang Kafé (p60) Offering excellent versions of Nonya specialities.

Delicious (p108) Reliable, elegant restaurant with something for everyone.

Nasi Kandar Pelita (p59) Flash *mamak* with branches next to the KLCC and in Bangsar.

Best Afternoon Tea

Carcosa Seri Negara (p135) Grand colonial hotel serves a lovely afternoon spread.

Atmosphere 360 (p81) Gorge on the buffet in Menara KL's revolving restaurant.

Smokehouse Restaurant (p108) Bargain blow-out tea including scones, apple pie, sandwiches and brownies.

Market in Chinatown, KL (p71)

Drinking & Nightlife

Bubble tea, iced kopi-o, a frosty beer, or a flaming Lamborghini – KL's cafes, teahouses and bars offer a multitude of ways to whet your whistle. Muslim mores push coffee and tea culture to the fore, but there's no shortage of alcohol-fuelled venues where you can party the night away with abandon.

Time for Tea

British colonial rule left Malaysians with a taste for tea. The leaf is grown on the peninsula in the Cameron Highlands, with BOH the largest producer of black tea; there's also plenty of tea imported from China, India and Sri Lanka.

One of the best shows at hawker stalls and *kopitiam* is watching the tea wallah toss-pour an order of *teh tarik* (literally 'pulled' tea) from one pitcher to another. The result is one very frothy cuppa. A true *teh tarik* is made using condensed milk, but this ingredient has largely been replaced by condensed creamer made from palm oil.

Other tea drinks of note are *teh halia* (tea flavoured with ginger), *teh ais* (milky iced tea), *teh-o-ais* (iced tea without milk) and *teh limau* (tea with lime juice). For an especially rich cuppa, ask for *teh susu kerabau* (hot tea with boiled fresh milk).

Chinese restaurants and cafes invariably serve green tea or pale-yellow chrysanthemum tea, often sweetened with sugar.

Coffee Culture

Traditional Malaysian *kopi* (coffee) is also popular. This dark, bitter brew is served in Chinese coffee shops and is an excellent antidote to a case of jetlag. Another unique-to-Malaysia caffeinated drink is *cham* – a blend of milky coffee and tea.

There's no need to go without your daily dose of latte or espresso, though. Recently the *kopitiam* and their contemporary counterparts – chains such as Coffee Bean & Tea Leaf (www.coffeebean.com), PappaRich (www.papparich.com.my) and Old Town White Coffee (www.oldtown.com.my) – are being challenged by independent cafes that deal in single origin beans and employ baristas trained to use classic coffee-making machines.

Juices & Other Nonalcoholic Drinks

Caffeine-free alternatives include freshly blended fruit and vegetable juices; sticky-sweet, green, sugar-cane juice; and coconut water, drunk straight from the fruit with a straw. More unusual drinks include *barley peng* or *ee bee chui* (barley boiled with water, pandan leaf and rock sugar served over ice); *air mata kucing* (a sweet dried longan beverage); and *cincau* (a herbal grass-jelly drink; to add a splash of soy milk ask for a 'Michael Jackson').

Sweetened kalamansi juice and Chinese salted plums may sound a strange combination but make for a thoroughly refreshing potion called *asam boi*. There's also a whole range of bubble teas, drinks which come with various sago pearls, jellies and other edible additives floating in them.

Wine, Beer & Spirits

Sky-high duties on alcohol can make a boozy night out awfully expensive. The cheapest beers are those brewed locally, such as Tiger and Carlsberg; they're best enjoyed alfresco

NEED TO KNOW

Business Hours

➡ Bars: 5pm to 1am Sunday to Thursday, to 3am Friday and Saturday. Happy Hours offering two for one drinks and other deals typically run from opening until around 8pm.

➡ Clubs: 9pm to 3am Tuesday to Saturday; Zouk is the only club open until 5am.

How Much?

➡ Local beer: RM15

➡ Imported beer: RM25

➡ Cocktail: RM30

➡ Coffee: RM5

➡ Tea: RM5

Drinking Water

➡ Drink bottled water rather than tap.

➡ Avoid ice if a place looks dodgy.

Cover Charges

Club admission ranges from RM30 to RM60 depending on the venue and event.

Bar Crawl

The **Original Drinkdeals KL Pub Crawl** (without/with flyer RM70/65) meets at 8.45pm every Friday at 47 Changkat Bukit Bintang and every Saturday in the lobby of Office Tower1 Jln Nagasari (next to Lust). The charge for the crawl covers five drinks at five local bars.

Information

➡ **Time Out KL** (www.timeoutkl.com) Latest info on cafes and bars.

➡ **Utopia Asia** (www.utopia-asia.com) For local GLBT info.

➡ **Life for Beginners/Cafe Stories** (http://lifeforbeginners.com/cafe stories) Blog on local coffee scene.

while watching the streetside theatre of Jln Alor or Chinatown's Jln Hang Lekir.

Clubbing

Wednesday to Saturday are the main clubbing nights with plenty of different events happening to suit all music tastes. What's in and out is fairly fluid so it's best to check local media listings before heading out. Be prepared for cover charges, which typically include your first drink.

GLBT Scene

There's a fairly open GLBT scene in KL with several established gay dance nights, the main ones being at Frangipani Bar and Marketplace. A great new addition to the scene is the monthly Rainbow Rojak (www.facebook.com/RainbowRojak); this laid-back and inclusive event for all sexual persuasions is upstairs at Palate Palette.

Drinking & Nightlife by Neighbourhood

➡ **Golden Triangle & KLCC** Home to Changkat Bukit Bintang, KL's busiest drink strip, and several classy sky-high bars.

➡ **Chinatown, Merdeka Square & Bukit Nanas** Mainly backpacker bars in Chinatown, several with rooftop views.

➡ **Masjid India, Kampung Baru & Northern KL** Masjid India is where you'll find the most drinking options, though they're still thin on the ground.

➡ **Lake Gardens, Brickfields & Bangsar** Bangsar is the place for classy cocktail bars and cool cafes.

Lonely Planet's Top Choices

Palate Palette (p61) Board games, fun events and a cool inclusive attitude.

Marini's on 57 (p65) Toast the close-up views of the Petronas Towers.

Heli Lounge Bar (p61) Amazing city views from the helicopter-pad-turned-cocktail-lounge.

Coliseum Cafe (p93) Colonial charmer where Somerset Maugham enjoyed a stiff one.

Typica (p56) Offering a creative mix of caffeinated drinks and sweet things.

Best Clubs

Zouk (p66) Multizoned dance space that keeps on pumping till 5am.

Vertigo (p112) Party with a flash crowd out in Mid Valley.

Butter Factory KL (p66) Another reliable brand on the KL clubbing scene.

Best for Coffee

RAWcoffee (p65) Lovingly prepared coffees with vegan food.

Coffea Coffee (p109) Slick Bangsar operation by a Korean Barista champ.

Coffee Stain by Joseph (p61) Intense espresso blends and single origin coffees.

Best Cocktail Bars

Omakase + Appreciate (p93) Speakeasy joint on edge of Masjid India.

Tate (p65) The hat's the clue to the entrance to this secret drinking hole.

Ril's Bangsar (p109) Sophisticated assignation spot with inventive mixologists.

Best for Views

Marini's on 57 (p65) Book a seat for a bird's-eye view of the KLCC.

Heli Lounge Bar (p61) Thrilling rooftop drinks in the heart of the Golden Triangle.

MAI Bar (p109) Fun poolside bar overlooking KL Sentral.

Best for Tea

Starhill Tea Salon (p64) Nibble macarons with your lapsang sousong.

TWG Tea (p64) Classy tea emporium in Pavilion KL.

Purple Cane Tea House (p82) Learn the art of the Chinese tea ceremony.

Best GLBT Friendly

Palate Palette (p61) Mark your calendar for the monthly Rainbow Rojak party.

Frangipani Bar (p61) Friday is Frisky night for the boys.

Marketplace (p66) Sweat it out on the dance floor, cool off on the roof.

PLAN YOUR TRIP DRINKING & NIGHTLIFE

eahouse in Chinatown

☆ Entertainment

KL has plenty of entertainment options, but you have to keep your ear to the ground to discover the best of what's going on. Conservative tastes and censorship mean that quite a lot of what is on offer is bland and inoffensive, but occasionally controversial and boundary-pushing performances and events are staged.

On the Stage

Major international popular music artists often add KL to their Asia tours, but sometimes have to adapt their stage shows to accommodate devout Muslim sensibilities.

To see and hear traditional Malaysian dances and music, there's the regular shows at Malaysian Tourism Centre (p226) during the day, as well as every night at the nearby restaurant Saloma (p66). Central Market's Kasturi Walk is the stage for free music and dance events at the weekends.

Various restaurants and bars, including Circus, have live music and dance performance. Al-Amar offers belly dancing (Saturday night and Sunday brunch). Jazz is also popular and the accomplished Malaysian Philharmonic Orchestra is well worth catching in concert at the Dewan Filharmonik Petronas.

At the Movies

KL's many multiplexes screen major international and local movies. The venues are generally top class. Tickets, which range from RM15 to RM30, are cheaper the earlier in the day the screening is and can be booked online.

Cultural centres including **Alliance Française** (✆2694 7880; http://kl.alliancefrancaise.org.my; 15 Lg Gurney; ⊕Ampang Park) and **Goethe Institut** (✆2164 2011; www.goethe.de/ins/my/kua/deindex.htm; 374 Jln Tun Razak, 6th fl Menara See Hoy Chan; ⊕Ampang Park) screen foreign movies with subtitles; check the websites for details.

Spoken Word & Spectator Sports

Monthly spoken word events include Readings@Seksan (http://thebookaholic.blogspot.co.uk/p/readings-events.html) and Ceritaku@No Black Tie at No Black Tie. There's also the less regular Pecha Kucha nights staged by the British Council usually at Publika.

KLites are fans of football (soccer) and basketball, and the city also gets caught up in the Petronas Malaysian Formula 1 Grand Prix held at the Sepang International Circuit (p125).

Entertainment by Neighbourhood

➡ **Golden Triangle & KLCC** Orchestral classical music, intimate jazz and pop performances all get a showing at venues in these central areas.

➡ **Chinatown, Merdeka Square & Bukit Nanas** Free dance and martial arts performances at Central Market on the weekend.

➡ **Masjid India, Kampung Baru & Northern KL** Istana Budaya and Kuala Lumpur Performing Arts Centre are two of the city's major performing arts venues.

➡ **Lake Gardens, Brickfields & Bangsar** Performing arts events at Publika or classical Indian dance shows in Brickfields.

Lonely Planet's Top Choices

No Black Tie (p66) Intimate space hosting jazz and classical music concerts.

Dewan Filharmonik Petronas (p66) Gorgeous classical concert hall at the foot of the Petronas Towers.

Kuala Lumpur Performing Arts Centre (p94) Progressive theatre and dance venue set in a beautiful park.

Publika (p111) Events at the MAP performance spaces; free movies in the central courtyard.

Panggung Bandaraya (p82) The old City Hall transformed into an elegant theatrical venue.

Best for Movies

GSC Pavilion KL (p67) Treat yourself to the Gold Class section.

TGV Cineplex, Suria KLCC (p67) Get your Hollywood fix at this multiplex.

Coliseum Theatre (p94) Go Bollywood at this historic Masjid India theatre.

Best Spectator Sports Venues

Bukit Jalil National Stadium (p67) Soccer matches and major music concerts are held here.

Selangor Turf Club (p67) Lay your bets at the racecourse.

MABA Stadium (p82) Catch a basketball match.

Best Dance Venues

Temple of Fine Arts (p110) Brickfields home of classical Indian dance.

Sutra Dance Theatre (p94) Shows choreographed by a Malaysian dance legend.

Istana Budaya (p94) Major venue for dance and theatre performances.

Best for Jazz

No Black Tie (p66) Discover some of the best talents on the local scene.

Sino The Bar Upstairs (p109) First Monday of month is its jazz jamming event.

The Venue (p66) Classy joint to enjoy local and international artists.

NEED TO KNOW

Tickets
➡ **Ticketpro** (www.ticketpro.com.my)
➡ **TicketCharge** (www.ticketcharge.com.my)

Info
➡ **KL Dance Watch** (http://kldancewatch.wordpress.com) Blog with info and reviews on local contemporary dance scene.
➡ **Kakiseni** (http://kakiseni.com) Events listings and more.
➡ **Football Association of Malaysia** (www.fam.org.my) Details of soccer matches.

Courses
➡ **Kuala Lumpur Performing Arts Centre** (p94) Acting, dance and courses in traditional instruments.
➡ **Sutra Dance Theatre** (p94) Courses in Odissi and other forms of classical Indian dance.
➡ **Temple of Fine Arts** (p110) Courses in classical Indian dance, song and music.

Arts & Music Festivals
➡ **Urbanscapes** (p21) Festival held in November that combines art, music and design.
➡ **KL International Jazz Festival** (p21) Held in September at the University Malaya.
➡ **Cooler Lumpur Festival** (p21) Publika is the venue for this cultural fest that focuses on a different artistic genre each year.

PLAN YOUR TRIP ENTERTAINMENT

Vendor in Little India, KL

Shopping

Kuala Lumpur is a prize fighter on the Asian shopping parade, a serious contender to retail heavyweights Singapore, Bangkok and Hong Kong. On offer are appealing handicrafts, major international brands (both legit and fake versions), masses of malls and decent sale prices. The city's traditional markets are hugely enjoyable and atmospheric experiences regardless of whether you have a purchase in mind.

Where to Shop

MALLS & DEPARTMENT STORES

KL and the Klang Valley are liberally peppered with air-conditioned malls, some so big it would take several days to do them justice – Mid Valley Megamall and Sunway Pyramid, for example, are communities unto themselves with hotels, entertainment facilities and, in the former, a one-hundred-year-old Hindu temple!

Anchoring the malls are department stores:

AEON At Mid Valley Megamall (p112).

Metrojaya (p68) At Mid Valley Megamall and BB Plaza.

Parkson At Pavilion KL (p67).

Isetan At Suria KLCC (p69), Lot 10 (p68) and Gardens Mall (p112).

MARKETS

Day markets focused around fresh produce include Pudu, Chow Kit and Chinatown. Vendors at *pasar malam* (night markets) sell prepared food, clothing, accessories, DVDs and CDs and the like. Some occur daily, such as the one along Jln Petaling in KL's Chinatown; others, once or twice a week.

Look out for flea, fashion and craft markets, such as the monthly events at Publika and Bangsar Shopping Centre, and the more occasional Super Stylish Shopping (www.superstylishshopping.com) which started in Penang but has branched out to KL.

What to Buy

Skilled artisans may be a dying breed, but you can still find great handmade craft items for sale in KL. Fashion, contemporary-art galleries, antique stores and interior-design shops are also worth a look.

There are bargain buys, but Malaysia is too affluent to offer dirt-cheap prices. Counterfeit goods are a problem – not just Prada handbags and Rolex watches, but also software and electronics. Buyer beware!

FASHION
The area around KWC Fashion Mall (p56) is home to KL's rag trade, importing the latest looks from factories and designers across Asia. Local major labels include:

British India (http://britishindia.com.my) For high-quality linen and cotton pieces at Suria KLCC, Pavilion KL, Mid Valley Megamall, Bangsar Shopping Centre and Publika; its cheaper brand Just B has outlets in Publika and Gardens Mall.

Padini (www.padini.com) Offering many different brands, several of which – such as Seed, Padini Authentics and Vincci (for shoes and accessories) – can be spotted at all the major malls.

Bonia (www.bonia.com) Quality Italian-style leather fashions and accessories for men and women.

If you're wanting to snap up some designer brand bargains, visit **MO Outlet** (www.mo-outlet.com; 63 Jln Tasik Utama 3, The Trillium, Lake Fields, Sungai Besi; ⊙10am-7.30pm; 🚇Sungai Besi, then taxi), the end-of-line and bargain sale outlet for luxury brand retailer Melium; its 50-plus labels include D&G and Hugo Boss, as well as Malaysian and Asian designer ready-to-wear garments.

TEXTILES
Batik is produced by drawing or printing a pattern on fabric with wax, then dyeing the material. The wax contains the various colours and, when washed away, leaves the pattern. Batik can be made into clothes,

NEED TO KNOW

Business Hours

Variable, but most places open from around 9.30am to 7pm Monday to Saturday. Department stores and malls are open 10am to 10pm daily.

Sale Times
➡ **Malaysia Grand Prix Sale** March to early April
➡ **Malaysia Mega Sale Carnival** Mid-July to mid-September
➡ **Malaysia Year-End Sale** End November to early January

Refunds

Policies vary from shop to shop; as a rule you'll find more flexible, consumer-friendly service at international brand stores.

Handicrafts Courses
➡ **Aziz Ma'as** (p68) Learn traditional and innovative batik from master artist Aziz Ma'as at his studio at the foot of Bukit Nanas.
➡ **C Woks Design** (http://batikcwok.blogspot.com) Paint your own batik panel from RM20. Either choose a readily prepared design or create your own.
➡ **Kompleks Kraf Kuala Lumpur** (p69) Try your hand at traditional Malay crafts such as batik at the craft village in the grounds of this one-stop crafts complex.
➡ **School of Hard Knocks** (p93) Entertaining classes (RM60; 30 minutes) where you make your own pewter bowl; advance booking required.

homewares or simply displayed as works of art.

Another textile to look out for is *kain songket,* a luxurious fabric with gold and silver threads woven throughout the material.

BASKETRY & MENGKUANG
All sorts of useful household items are made using rattan, bamboo, swamp nipah grass and pandanus leaves. *Mengkuang* (a local form of weaving) uses pandanus leaves and strips of bamboo to make baskets, bags and mats. Look in Central Market and around Chinatown for these items.

Shopping by Neighbourhood

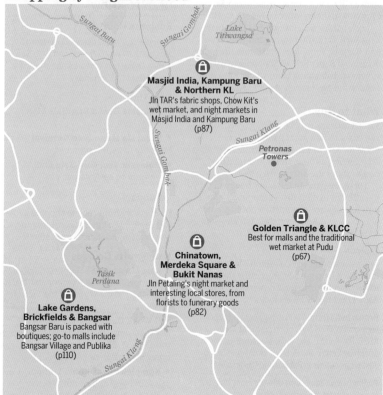

Masjid India, Kampung Baru & Northern KL
Jln TAR's fabric shops, Chow Kit's wet market, and night markets in Masjid India and Kampung Baru
(p87)

Golden Triangle & KLCC
Best for malls and the traditional wet market at Pudu
(p67)

Chinatown, Merdeka Square & Bukit Nanas
Jln Petaling's night market and interesting local stores, from florists to funerary goods
(p82)

Lake Gardens, Brickfields & Bangsar
Bangsar Baru is packed with boutiques; go-to malls include Bangsar Village and Publika
(p110)

KITES & PUPPETS

Eye-catching *wayang kulit* (shadow puppets) are made from buffalo hide to portray characters from epic Hindu legends, while kites are made from paper and bamboo strips in a variety of traditional designs. The crescent-shaped *wau bulan* (moon kite) can reach 3m in length and breadth, while the *wau kucing* (cat kite) is the logo of Malaysia Airlines. You can find kites and puppets in Central Market.

METALWORK

Malaysia's skilled silversmiths specialise in filigree and repoussé work, where designs are hammered through the silver from the underside. Objects crafted out of pewter are synonymous with Selangor. Royal Selangor has several outlets in major malls including Suria KLCC and Pavilion KL.

WOODCARVING

The Hma' Meri tribe from Pulau Carey off the coast of Selangor are particularly renowned for their sinuous carvings of animist spirits. You can find these Orang Asli crafts at a stall in Central Market.

Lonely Planet's Top Choices

Publika (p111) Innovative complex combining culture, art and great food with retail.

Peter Hoe Evolution (p83) Colourful, well-made homewares and decorative pieces.

Central Market (p77) Best selection of local arts and crafts.

Wei-Ling Gallery (p110) Invest in a piece of contemporary art.

Best Batik Buys

iKARRTiNi (p70) Wearable batik in contemporary designs.

Pink Jambu (p111) Bright colours and attractive designs at this Publika outlet.

Kompleks Kraf Kuala Lumpur (p69) The Karakenya section is stacked with all kinds of prints.

Best Bookshops

Kinokuniya (p70) KL's best printed-matter pit stop.

Silverfish Books (p113) Local publisher with its own small bookshop.

Best Fashion Designers

Khoon Hooi (p68) Luxury with an edge from award-winning designer.

Nurita Harith (p110) Bangsar-based designer; her NH brand offers affordable style.

Aseana (p70) Plenty of bling-tastic frocks and resort wear at this KLCC outlet.

Best Boutiques

Never Follow Suit (p110) Quirky and inventive shop with original pieces by Joe Chia and upcycled vintage picks.

Seethrough Concept Store (p110) One of the best selections of local designers for men and women.

Lonely Dream (p113) Offering own-label clothing and other designers' wares.

Best Malls

Publika (p111) Schedule a day to browse the shops, art galleries and the many great places to eat.

Pavilion KL (p67) Setting the gold standard for Bukit Bintang's gaggle of malls.

Sungei Wang (p67) Who knows what you'll discover in this multilevel warren of youth cool and fashion.

Suria KLCC (p69) A retail nirvana at the base of the Petronas Towers.

Best Museum Shops

Islamic Arts Museum (p97) Top-notch range of arts and crafts and design and art books.

National Textiles Museum (p75) For quality batik and local designer goods.

Explore
Kuala Lumpur

KL'S TOP SIGHTS

Neighbourhoods at a Glance

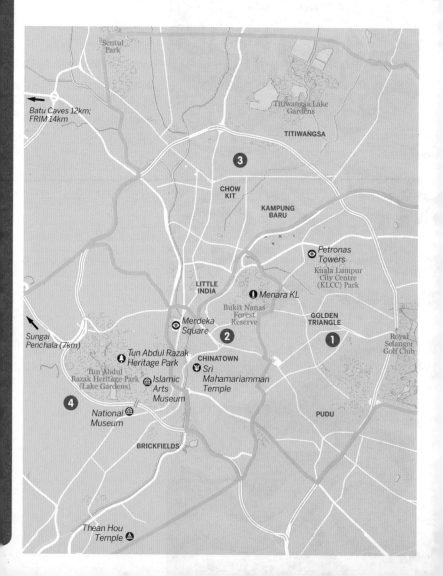

❶ Golden Triangle & KLCC (p48)

Centred on Bukit Bintang (Star Hill), the Golden Triangle is roughly the area bounded by Jln Raja Chulan, Jln Bukit Bintang and Jln Sultan Ismail. It's home to a cluster of major shopping malls and many excellent places to eat and drink, not least of which is Jln Alor, Kuala Lumpur's most famous food street. Kuala Lumpur City Centre (KLCC) is the vast development anchored by the Petronas Towers. East of here are places of interest along Jln Tun Razak and Jln Ampang. South of Bukit Bintang is the distinctly Chinese district of Pudu, home to the inner city's largest wet market and a giant wholesale clothing market.

❷ Chinatown, Merdeka Square & Bukit Nanas (p71)

You don't have to look too hard to find traces of old KL in Chinatown's shophouse-lined streets, which border the confluence of the Klang and Gombak rivers. This is where the city was born, reached its teenage years with the development of Chinatown, and celebrated its late 20s with the establishment of the British colonial ensemble around Merdeka Square. The Malay fort that once topped the jungle-clad hill Bukit Nanas has long gone, replaced by one of the city's most recognisable landmarks, the Menara KL telecommunications tower.

❸ Masjid India, Kampung Baru & Northern KL (p85)

Surrounding the mosque of the same name, Masjid India is KL's second Little India area, teeming with fabric and clothing shops and not to be missed for its Saturday night market. To the east are the traditional wooden houses of Kampung Baru, a Malay village within the heart of the modern city. Chow Kit, north along Jln TAR, has an infamous reputation for drugs and vice, but by day it also hosts a wonderful wet market packed with tempting hawker stalls. Further north are the leafy surrounds of Lake Titiwangsa and Sentul, both providing respite from the city with parks and the chance to watch performing arts.

❹ Lake Gardens, Brickfields & Bangsar (p95)

Born of the British desire to conquer the teeming jungle and fashion it into a pleasant park, the Lake Gardens remains a lush breathing space in the heart of KL. It's mainly covered by the Tun Abdul Razak Heritage Park and includes major institutions such as the Islamic Arts Museum, National Museum and National Mosque. KL Sentral and neighbouring Brickfields (location of KL's official Little India) are immediately south of here, while the upscale residential area of Bangsar – one of the top locations in the city in which to shop and eat – is to the southwest.

Golden Triangle & KLCC

Neighbourhood Top Five

1 Getting the most out of the **KLCC** (p50), by heading to the Petronas Towers observation deck, dropping by Galeri Petronas, Petrosains and Aquaria KLCC, and exploring the imaginatively designed KLCC Park.

2 Enjoying the great eats of **Jalan Alor** (p58) and the bars of **Changkat Bukit Bintang** (p61).

3 Creating your own batik print at **Kompleks Kraf Kuala Lumpur** (p69) and **My Batik** (p70).

4 Shopping for international and local brand bargains at **Pavilion KL** (p67) and the other malls of Bukit Bitang.

5 Making an appointment to view the private art gallery **Ruang Pemula** (RuPé; p53).

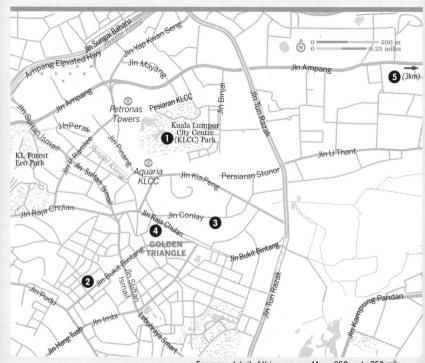

For more detail of this area, see Map p250 and p252 ➡

Explore: Golden Triangle & KLCC

The intersection of Jln Sultan Ismail and Jln Bukit Bintang marks the heart of the Golden Triangle, Kuala Lumpur's premier shopping, dining and nightlife district. Studded with office towers, condominiums and glitzy shopping malls, such as Pavilion KL where you could spend all day, the district actively courts Middle Eastern visitors with its sidewalk cafes at which patrons puff on *shisha* pipes.

Changat Bukit Bintang is the city's most raucous nightlife area and has several good restaurants, while nearby Jln Mesui is more laid-back. The icing on the Golden Triangle's edible cake remains the food street Jln Alor and – our favourite reason for getting up early – the breakfast stalls at Imbi Market.

An elevated, covered walkway links Bukit Bintang with Kuala Lumpur City Centre (KLCC), anchored by the iconic Petronas Towers. Also here is a spacious landscaped park, huge convention centre, aquarium, excellent children's museum, world-class concert hall and Suria KLCC, another of KL's great shopping malls.

Out towards Jln Tun Razak you'll find a few interesting things to see and do, as well as in the Imbi and Pudu areas, the former the location of major construction projects for Mass Rapid Transit (MRT) stations and the city's new financial district, Tun Razak Exchange.

Local Life

⇒**Hawker heaven** Having breakfast at Imbi Market (p52) and returning at night for the great selection and outdoor atmosphere of Jln Imbi Hawker Stalls (p52).

⇒**Massage and reflexology** Bukit Bintang is peppered with places offering to rub your tired feet and muscles. You can also try dipping your feet in a pool of doctor fish (p69).

⇒**Discover Pudu** Rise early to pick through Pudu Market (p56) and stick around for great eats at the hawker stalls on Jalan Sayur (p56).

Getting There & Away

⇒**Monorail** The best way to access the area with stops along Jln Imbi and Jln Sultan Ismail. Avoid the evening weekday rush hour, 6pm to 8pm.

⇒**Bus** There are two free GO KL City Bus loop services, but they can get snarled in traffic.

⇒**Walking** The fastest way to get around during rush hour. Take advantage of the partly air-con covered walkway between KLCC and Pavilion KL.

Lonely Planet's Top Tip

Go to concierge desks in each of the major malls to sign up for free discount shopping cards that may entitle you to free gifts and often save you 10% or more on prices at many outlets.

Best Places to Eat

⇒ Imbi Market (p52)
⇒ Kedai Makanan Dan Minuman TKS (p52)
⇒ Cantaloupe (p60)
⇒ Acme Bar & Coffee (p60)
⇒ Limablas (p53)
⇒ Sushi Hinata (p58)

For reviews, see p52 ⇒

Best Places to Drink

⇒ Palate Palette (p61)
⇒ Heli Lounge Bar (p61)
⇒ Marini's on 57 (p65)
⇒ Taps Beer Bar (p61)
⇒ Pisco Bar (p61)
⇒ Tate (p65)

For reviews, see p61 ⇒

Best Places to Shop

⇒ Pavilion KL (p67)
⇒ Sungei Wang Plaza (p67)
⇒ Suria KLCC (p69)
⇒ Fahrenheit88 (p67)
⇒ Kompleks Kraf Kuala Lumpur (p69)

For reviews, see p67 ⇒

TOP SIGHT
PETRONAS TOWERS & KLCC

Resembling twin silver rockets plucked from an episode of *Flash Gordon*, the Petronas Towers are the perfect allegory for the meteoric rise of the city, from tin miners' hovel to 21st-century metropolis. They are the crowning glory of Kuala Lumpur City Centre (KLCC), which covers 40 hectares of land that was once the Selangor Turf Club.

Petronas Towers

Opened in 1998, the Petronas Towers reach up nearly 452m; for six years they were the tallest structure in the world and they remain the world's tallest twin towers. The design for the 88-storeys-high tower blocks, by Argentinian architect Cesar Pelli, is based on an eight-sided star that echoes arabesque patterns. Islamic influences are also evident in each tower's five tiers – representing the five pillars of Islam – and in the 63m masts that crown them, calling to mind the minarets of a mosque and the Star of Islam.

Get in line around 8.30am to be sure of securing one of the 960 tickets issued daily (half of which are sold in advance online) for the guided 45-minute tour of the towers. The ticket office is in the towers' basement. First stop is the **Skybridge** connection on the 41st floors of the towers at 170m. Having walked across this you'll then take the lift up to the 86th floor **observation deck** at 370m.

Aquaria KLCC

The highlight of this impressive **aquarium** (Map p250; ☏2333 1888; www.aquariaklcc.com; Concourse, KL Convention Centre; adult/child/senior aquarium RM50/40/30; ⊙10.30am-8pm, last admission 7pm; ☒KLCC) in the basement of the KL Convention Centre is its 90m underwater tunnel which you walk through to view sinister-looking sand tiger sharks and

DON'T MISS...

➡ Petronas Towers
➡ Aquaria KLCC
➡ KLCC Park
➡ Galeri Petronas

PRACTICALITIES

➡ Map p250
➡ www.petronas twintowers.com.my, www.klcc.com.my
➡ Jln Ampang
➡ adult/child RM80/30
➡ ⊙9am-9pm Tue-Sun
➡ ☒KLCC

giant gropers. A guided tour (RM199) will clue you in on all the fishy details. Daily feeding sessions for a variety of fish and otters are complemented by ones for arapaima, electric eel and sharks on Monday, Wednesday and Saturday (2.30pm and 3pm).

Certified divers can get into the tanks with the sharks (RM400); if you're not certified, you can opt to be lowered into the tank in a protective cage (RM199). If you have kids aged 6 to 13, they can take part in sleepovers at the aquarium.

KLCC Park

Brazilian park designer Roberto Burle Marx never lived to see the completion of the imaginatively landscaped **KLCC Park** (Map p250; ⊙7am-10pm; ⊡KLCC) planted with 127 trees, some of them saved from the Selangor Turf Club. A 1.3km soft-surface jogging track winds its way around the park past the children's playground, paddling pool and Masjid Asy-Syakirin.

Naturally, the park is the best vantage point for photos of the Petronas Towers. In the early evening, it can seem like everyone in town has come down here to watch the glowing towers punching up into the night sky. Every night at 8pm, 9pm and 10pm, the **Lake Symphony Fountains** play in front of the Suria KLCC.

Galeri Petronas

Swap consumerism for culture at the excellent **Galeri Petronas** (Map p250; ☑2051 7770; www.galeripetronas. com.my; 3rd fl, Suria KLCC; ⊙10am-8pm Tue-Sun; ⊡KLCC) **FREE**. This corporate art gallery showcases a wide range of contemporary photography and paintings. It's a bright, modern space with interesting, professionally curated shows that change every few months.

Petrosains

Kids and kidults can fill an educational few hours at **Petrosains** (Map p250; ☑2331 8181; www.petro-sains.com.my; Level 4, Suria KLCC; adult/child/youth RM25/15/20; ⊙9.30am-4pm Tue-Fri, to 5pm Sat & Sun; ⊡KLCC). This interactive science museum in Suria KLCC is packed with all sorts of buttons to press and levers to pull. Many of the activities and displays focus on the wonderful things that fuel has bought to Malaysia – no prizes for guessing who sponsors the museum.

SHOPPING

Amid the usual plethora of international labels at Suria KLCC, look out for the following local buys:

➡ **Pucuk Rebung** (p70) Upmarket arts, crafts and antiques.

➡ **iKARRTini** (p70) Batik design fashions with separate men's and women's outlets.

➡ **Aseana** (p70) Fancy party frocks.

➡ **Tenmoku Pottery** (p70) Ceramic art.

➡ **Kinokuniya** (p70) Books, stationery and art supplies.

There are scores of different dining options in Suria KLCC, plus two food courts: Signatures, on Level 2, specialises in international food; and Rasa Food Arena, on Level 4, offers local dishes. Our picks include Little Penang Kafe (p60) and Melur & Thyme (p60). Several places offer outdoor dining facing onto KLCC Park.

GOLDEN TRIANGLE & KLCC PETRONAS TOWERS & KLCC

◉ SIGHTS

PETRONAS TOWERS & KLCC
BUILDING, NEIGHBOURHOOD

See p50.

BADAN WARISAN MALAYSIA
TRADITIONAL ARCHITECTURE

Map p250 (Heritage of Malaysia Trust; ☎2144 9273; www.badanwarisan.org.my; 2 Jln Stonor; ⊘10am-5.30pm Mon-Sat; monorail Raja Chulan) 🏷 Find out about the work of this built heritage preservation society at its head office in a 1925 colonial bungalow in the shadow of the Petronas Towers. The property's grounds contain the **Rumah Penghulu Abu Seman** (Map p250; 2 Jln Stonor; suggested donation RM10; ⊘tours 11am & 3pm Mon-Sat), a handsome example of a restored Malay-style wooden house built in stages between 1910 and the 1930s in the state of Kedah. The trust also holds exhibitions in the bungalow, where there's a shop stocking interesting pieces of wooden antique furniture, local handcrafted items and books.

DHARMA REALM GUAN YIN SAGELY MONASTERY
BUDDHIST TEMPLE

Map p250 (www.drba.org; 161 Jln Ampang; ⊘7am-4pm; 🚇Ampang Park) The calm spaces, potted plants, mandala ceilings and gilded statues create an appropriately contemplative mood for quiet meditation at this colourful modern temple. The complex is dedicated to Guan Yin, the Buddhist goddess of compassion, represented by the central statue in the main building. There's an excellent vegan canteen (p59) behind the complex staffed by volunteers and monks.

TABUNG HAJI
MODERN ARCHITECTURE

Map p250 (201 Jln Tun Razak; 🚇Ampang Park) Designed by celebrated Malay architect Hijjas Kasturi, this tower houses the hajj funding body. The five main exterior columns represent the five pillars of Islam while the overall structure recalls the drum used to summon pilgrims to the hajj and the shape of a traditional Arabic perfume vessel.

MUSLIM CEMETERY
CEMETERY

Map p250 (off Jln Ampang; ⊘7am-6pm; monorail Bukit Nanas) Tucked away off Jln Ampang behind Hotel Maya and split from Kampung Baru by a highway is one of KL's oldest Muslim burial grounds shaded by trees, some of which are over a century old. The famous film director, actor and singer P Ramlee,

two of his former wives and his co-star AR Tompel are buried here. In March 2013 a storm uprooted seven trees in the cemetery damaging 30 graves including Ramlee's.

✗ EATING

✗ Golden Triangle

★KEDAI MAKANAN DAN MINUMAN TKS
CHINESE $$

Map p252 (Jln Alor; mains RM15-30; ⊘5pm-4am; monorail Bukit Bintang) Our favourite place to eat on KL's busiest food street is this non-touristy Sichuan joint that has a menu only in Chinese (don't panic, there are pictures and the friendly staff speak English). It's all good, from the chilli oil fried fish to the gunpowder chicken buried in a pile of mouth-numbing fried chillies.

★IMBI MARKET
HAWKER $

Map p252 (Pasar Baru Bukit Bintang; Jln Kampung; meal RM10; ⊘6.30am-12.30pm Tue-Sun; monorail Bukit Bintang) The official name is Pasar Baru Bukit Bintang, but everyone knows it simply as Imbi Market. Breakfast is like a party here with all the friendly and curious locals happily recommending their favourite stalls. We like Sisters Crispy Popiah; Teluk Intan Chee Cheung Fun, where Amy Ong serves a lovely oyster-and-peanut congee and egg puddings; and Bunn Choon for the creamy mini egg tarts.

The market is slated to move as the area is developed into the Tun Razak Exchange financial district over the next few years.

JALAN IMBI HAWKER STALLS
HAWKER $

Map p252 (cnr Jln Imbi & Jln Barat; dishes RM6; ⊘5pm-midnight; monorail Bukit Bintang) A car park by day turns into a great open-air hawker-stall area by night. All the usual hawker favourites are here: we enjoyed the dried chilli *lajioa pan mee* topped with mushrooms and anchovies and the *asam laksa*. There's a popular Thai food stall and an aunty and uncle who always have a long line for their *kuih* (traditional desserts).

NGAU KEE BEEF BALL NOODLES
CHINESE $

Map p252 (Tengkat Tong Shin; noodles RM5; ⊘24hr; monorail Bukit Bintang) The dish at this venerable street stall comes in two parts: dry, steamed noodles topped with a thick soy-sauce mince, and the chunky beef balls in a clear soup – delicious! Refresh your palate with the salty-sweet lime drink *asam boi*.

FOOD REPUBLIC
FOOD COURT $

Map p252 (Level 1, Pavilion KL, 168 Jln Bukit Bintang; meals RM10-20; ☉10am-10pm; monorail Bukit Bintang) Outstanding choice and slick design make this probably the best shopping mall food court in KL. It's also surrounded by scores of proper restaurants.

BLUE BOY VEGETARIAN FOOD CENTRE
CHINESE, MALAY $

Map p252 (☎2144 9011; Jln Tong Shin; mains RM3-10; ☉8am-6pm; �; monorail Imbi) It's hard to believe that everything prepared at this spotless hawker-style cafe at the base of a backstreet apartment block is vegetarian, but it's true – in fact, if you bypass the stall using egg, it's all vegan. The *char kway teow* (broad noodles fried in chilli and black-bean sauce) is highly recommended.

RESTORAN NAGANSARI CURRY HOUSE
MALAY, INDIAN $

Map p252 (Jln Nagansari; meals RM5-10; ☉7am-midnight; monorail Raja Chulan) This simple hawker-style restaurant serves a good selection of Malay dishes – soup *mee,* tom yum and so on – with a few Indian favourites thrown in for good measure. Fans blow moist air around the dining hall to keep diners cool.

★LIMABLAS
MALAY $$

Map p252 (☎2110 1289; www.facebook.com/pages/Lima-Blas/576054345757434; 15 Jln Mesui; mains RM10-28; ☉noon-3pm & 5-10pm Mon-Sat; ☎; monorail Raja Chulan) You can tell one of the partners in this appealing Nonya restaurant is an interior designer – the look of the place channels old Malaya combined with hipster chic (check those oversize Tretchikoff prints on the wall). Try the chicken curry, aubergine in sambal sauce and the *sago gula melaka* (sago pearls in a brown sugar sauce).

LOAF
BAKERY $$

Map p252 (☎2145 3036; www.theloaf.net; Levels 3 & 4, Pavilion KL, 168 Jln Bukit Bintang; meals RM10-20; ☉10am-10pm; monorail Bukit Bintang) This bakery cafe and bistro (which has ex-PM Dr Mahathir as an investor) is a Malaysian take on a Japanese baked goods shop. Its big range of baked goods is uniformly divine and we love the mini cheesecakes for a quick snack. There are other branches around the city.

PINCHOS TAPAS BAR
SPANISH $$

Map p252 (☎03-2145 8482; www.pinchos.com.my; 18 Changat Bukit Bintang; tapas RM13-30; ☉5-11pm food, until 3am bar; monorail Bukit Bintang) This is the real deal for tapas, run by a Spaniard and packed with KL's approving Spanish-speaking community. A great place for a solo meal and drink or fun with a group when you can munch your way through the wide-ranging menu.

WORTH A DETOUR

RUANG PEMULA (RUPÉ)

Below the offices of lawyer Pakhruddin Sulaiman, in a shophouse block in Ampang, lies the captivating private gallery **Ruang Pemula** (RuPé; ☎4279 7720; www.rupe.com.my; Block 1, Pusat Perdagangan Taman Dagang, Jln Dagang Besar, Ampang; ☉by appointment) FREE. Pakhruddin and his wife Fatimah have been amassing one of Malaysia's top private art collections since around 1996 when they bought two major works, *Brothers* and *Does History Change?*, in the first solo exhibition of Bayu Utmo Radjikin. These works by the now-prominent contemporary Malaysian artist are among hundreds displayed and stored in the gallery nicknamed RuPé and meaning 'beginner's space'.

Other established and up-and-coming artists with works here include many from the art collective Matahati, Fuad Osman, Shukri Mohammed, Amron Omar and Fadilah Karim. Forged metal sculptures by Raja Shahrima, a cross between ancient Malay warriors and manga robots, are dotted among the gallery spaces, which are arranged to resemble living rooms with designer chairs and Pakhruddin's extensive art and design library.

For anyone interested in Malaysian art, this, along with the private collection at Sekeping Tenggiri (p103), is an absolute must-see. Call to arrange a time to visit and to get directions from the nearest LRT station which is Ampang.

Architecture

From the Moorish Mogul–inspired civic buildings of the late 19th century to the millennial splendour of the Petronas Towers, KL's architecture is nothing if not eye-catching. Explore the city to also find traditional wooden Malay homes, various styles of shophouses in Chinatown and the bold modernist style of buildings such as Masjid Negara and the National Parliament.

TUAH ROSLAN / GETTY IMAGES ©

LAURIE NOBLE / GETTY IMAGES ©

1. Masjid Asy-Syakirin backed by the Petronas Towers (p50)

The 452m-high twin towers are the crowning glory of the KLCC area.

2. Putrajaya (p124)

Only in its second decade of existence, this planned city has an eclectic mix of buildings and bridges.

3. Sultan Abdul Samad Building (p75)

The Moorish domes and 43m clocktower of this building grace the east side of Merdeka Square.

4. Guandi Temple (p76)

This colourful Taoist temple dates back to 1886.

PAUL KENNEDY / GETTY IMAGES ©

WORTH A DETOUR

PUDU

Once a Chinese village on the edge of the city, Pudu is now firmly part of Kuala Lumpur, hosting a lively fresh produce market, a street of wonderful hawker stalls and one of the city's best Chinese restaurants. Its most famous landmark, **Pudu Jail**, was demolished in 2010; only the entrance gate remains.

Sights

Pudu Market (Jln Pasar Baru; ⊙4am-2pm; 🚇Pudu) KL's biggest wet and dry market is a frenetic place, full of squawking chickens, frantic shoppers and porters forcing their way through the crowds with outrageous loads. Stalls here sell everything from goldfish to pigs' heads, cows' tongues and durians in baskets. Arrive early in the morning to experience the market at full throttle. From Pudu Light Rail Transit (LRT) station, go south along Jln Pudu, right onto Jln Pasar, then right down Jln Pasar Baharu, passing the colourful **Choon Wan Kong**, a Chinese temple dating from 1879.

Eating & Drinking

Jalan Sayur Stalls (Jln Sayur; noodles RM5; ⊙11am-midnight; 🚇Pudu) Visit this atmospheric street of hawker stalls during the day to try the famous *hakka mee* stall on the corner with Jln Pudu: order these egg noodles with chopped dry pork, with a side of 'white sauce' (aka melted lard) rather than 'black sauce' (all soy, no lard). Evening grazing could include a luscious *chee cheong fun* (broad ribbons of rice noodles) with curry sauce or the rich and peppery *sup kambing* (mutton broth).

Sek Yuen (☎9222 9457; 313-315 Jln Pudu; mains RM20-40; ⊙noon-3pm & 6-10pm Tue-Sun; 🚇Pudu) Occupying the same beautiful, time-worn, art deco building for the past 60 years, Sek Yuen serves up meals that offer an experience of KL food history. There's no written menu but you can trust the aged chefs toiling in the wood-fired kitchen to make something delicious. Their *kau yoke* (belly pork), *char siew* (barbecued pork) and fried rice are all classics, as is their sweet-and-sour fish.

Fei Por (Map p252; ☎9926 1004; 211 & 213 Jln Pudu; ⊙6pm-4am Fri-Wed; 🚇Pudu) Famous for its chicken rice served into the early hours, this long-running operation in an art deco shophouse also serves rice congee and *cha siew* pork that's well worth the journey.

Wong Kee (Map p252; ☎2145 2512; www.food-journey.com; 30 Jln Nyonya; pork plate RM30; ⊙12.30-2.30pm; monorail Imbi) Get here early as there's only a two-hour window of opportunity to sample chef Wong Peng Hui's famous roasted pork. Chicken rice is also on then menu.

Typica (Map p252; www.typicacafe.blogspot.com; GL-08, Shaw Pde, Changkat Thambi Dollah; ⊙11am-9pm Sun-Thu, to 10pm Fri & Sat) Sit at old wooden desks and savour excellent drip and siphon-brewed coffees, and lovely homemade cakes – try the yam-coconut cake if it's available. There are also other interesting drinks such as pandan latte.

Shopping

Eu Yan Sang (Map p252; www.euyansang.com.my; Lot GL-01 Shaw Pde, Changkat Thambi Dollah; monorail Imbi) Eu Kong opened his first Yang Sang (meaning 'caring for mankind') Chinese medicine shop in 1879 in Malaysia. There are now scores of outlets carrying the company's herbal remedies across the globe, including this impressive one, which also has a herbal restaurant using some of the ingredients.

Purple Cane Tea Square (Map p252; ☎2145 1200; www.purplecane.my; 1st floor, Shaw Pde, Changkat Thambi Dollah; ⊙11am-9pm; monorail Imbi) All things to do with tea are catered for at the main branch of this tea retailer. Tea-appreciation courses are held here and it also sells recycled paper baskets and bags made by **Salaam Wanita** (www.ehomemakers.net), an organisation helping less fortunate women.

KWC Fashion Mall (☎9221 8081; www.kenangacity.com.my; 28 Jln Gelugor, off Jln Kenanga; ⊙10am-8pm; 🚇Hang Tuah, monorail Hang Tuah) This complex in a strikingly modern high-rise block offers head-to-toe fashion items from some 800 wholesale dealers. The Kenanga Food Court on Level 7 has some good outlets and an outdoor seating area with awesome views across the train tracks back to Bukit Bintang. There's a free shuttle bus between here and Central Market.

BEN'S
INTERNATIONAL $$

Map p252 (☎03-2141 5290; www.thebiggroup.co/
bens; Level 6, Pavilion KL, 168 Bukit Bintang; mains
RM10-40; ⊗11am-10pm Sun-Thu, to midnight Fri
& Sat; ☎; monorail Bukit Bintang) The flagship
brand of the BIG group of dining outlets
(which include the Plan B cafes) delivers on
both style and substance. There's a tempt-
ing range of Eastern and Western comfort
foods, appealing, trendy living-room design
and nice touches such as a box of cards with
recipes and talk topics on each table. Other
branches are in Suria KLCC, Publika and
Bangsar Shopping Centre.

SISTERS KITCHEN
MALAY, NONYA $$

Map p250 (☎2142 6988; www.sisterscrispy-
popiah.com.my; 1st fl, Menara Hap Seng, Jln P
Ramlee; set lunch RM15; ⊗7.30am-5pm Mon-Fri,
8am-4pm Sat; monorail Bukit Nanas) Nobody in
KL makes *popiah* (similar to spring rolls
but not fried) quite like the sisters; at the
franchise's main outlet you can try several
different versions as well as a good range of
other Malay dishes. Their set lunch – including drink, dessert and snack of the day –
is good value. The original stall can be
found in Imbi Market.

SANTOUKA
JAPANESE $$

Map p252 (☎03-2143 8878; www.santouka.co.jp;
Level 6, Pavilion Kuala Lumpur, 168 Jln Bukit Bin-
tang; mains RM 30-40; ⊗11am-9.45pm; monorail
Bukit Bintang) Slurp tasty ramen noodles in
a pork broth at this joint in Pavilion's Tokyo
Street, an outlet of a famous stall originat-
ing from the Japanese island of Hokkaido.

RESTORAN OVERSEA
CHINESE $$

Map p252 (☎2144 7567; www.oversea.com.my;
84-88 Jln Imbi; mains RM15-50; monorail Bukit
Bintang) The main branch of this unpretentious banquet restaurant has been pleasing
locals for more than 30 years. Specialities
include pork belly, fish cooked in various
styles and streaky bacon cooked in a pot
with dried chillies.

SAO NAM
VIETNAMESE $$

Map p252 (☎2144 1225; www.saonam.com.my;
25 Tengkat Tong Shin; mains RM30-70; ⊗noon-
2.30pm & 7.30-10.30pm Tue-Sun; monorail Bukit
Bintang) This reliable place is decorated
with colourful propaganda posters and has
a courtyard for dining outside. The kitchen
turns out huge plates of delicious Vietnam-
ese food, garnished with basil, mint, lettuce
and sweet dips. The starter *banh xeo* (a

huge Vietnamese pancake with meat, sea-
food or vegetables) is a meal all by itself.

DRAGON-I
CHINESE $$

Map p252 (☎2143 7688; www.dragon-i.com.my;
Level 1, Pavilion KL, 168 Jln Bukit Bintang; meals
RM40-50; ⊗10am-10pm; monorail Bukit Bintang)
Very popular outlet of this chain serving Shanghaiese food, including steaming
dumplings and its signature dish, a multi-
layer sandwich of braised pork belly and
sheets of tofu soaked in a delicious sauce.

T-BOWL CONCEPT RESTAURANT
ASIAN $$

Map p252 (☎2141 1606; t-bowl.com; 3F-41 & 42,
3rd fl, Sungai Wang Plaza, Jln Sultan Ismail; mains
RM13-16; ⊗10am-10pm; ☎; monorail Bukit Bin-
tang) The owner of this uniquely decorated
Asian comfort-food cafe came up with the
concept while sitting on the toilet – hence
an interior that doubles as a lavatory show
room. Thankfully, the toilet-bowl seats
are nonfunctioning. Fun, but we make no
promises for the quality of the food which
includes such memorable dishes such as
'big poo rice'.

RESTORAN SAHARA TENT
MIDDLE EASTERN $$

Map p252 (☎2144 8310; www.saharatent.com;
Jln Sultan Ismail; mains RM10-30; ⊗11am-2am;
monorail Bukit Bintang) A long-established
favourite serving value-for-money Middle
Eastern cuisine. Come here for Turkish coffee, meaty kebabs and couscous, then sit
back with a bubbling *shisha*.

WOODS MACROBIOTICS
VEGETARIAN $$

Map p252 (Woods Bio Marche; ☎6201 0726;
www.macrobiotics-malaysia.com; Wisma Bukit
Bintang, Jln Bukit Bintang; mains RM11-20;
⊗11am-9.30pm; ☎; monorail Bukit Bintang) An
air of calm hangs over this worthy oper-
ation that ticks all the organic, vegan and
wholefood boxes. Even its brownies are
organic. It also sells groceries and holds
cooking classes at its cooking academy in
Petaling Jaya – check out the website for
details.

LOT 10 HUTONG
FOOD COURT $$

Map p252 (Basement, Lot 10, 50 Jln Sultan Ismail;
mains RM3-20; ⊗10am-10pm; monorail Bukit Bintang) The concept is a collection of greatest
hits from around Malaysia's culinary map
made by experienced vendors. In the warren-
like set-up you can dine on classic rendi-
tions of dishes such as *bak kut the* (pork-rib
soup), chicken rice and Hokkien mee.

DIN TAI FUNG
CHINESE $$

Map p252 (http://dintaifungmalaysia.com; Level 6, Pavilion KL, 168 Jln Bukit Bintang; mains RM10-20; ⊙10am-10pm; monorail Bukit Bintang) Fantastic Taiwan-style soup dumplings and noodles. There's also a branch in Mid Valley Megamall.

RESTAURANT MUAR
MALAY, NONYA $$

Map p252 (☑2144 2072; 6G Tengkat Tong Shin; mains RM10-20; ⊙11am-3pm & 6-10pm Tue-Sun; monorail Bukit Bintang) Ever-reliable home cooking at this unpretentious place with some outdoor tables. Try the *petai* squid and prawns, crispy fried eggs and *cendol* (shaved ice, coconut milk and jelly noodle dessert).

MARCO POLO
CHINESE $$

Map p250 (☑2141 2233; 1st fl, Wisma Lim Foo Yong, 86 Jln Raja Chulan; dim sum RM5-15; ⊙11am-3pm & 6.30-11pm Mon-Sat, 9.30am-11pm Sun; monorail Raja Chulan) At lunch, pick from the steamed baskets of quality dim sum being wheeled in carts at this classy Chinese joint. It also offers a buffet on Sunday.

★ SUSHI HINATA
JAPANESE $$$

Map p250 (☑2022 1349; www.shin-hinata.com; St Mary Residence, 1 Jln Tengah; lunch/dinner set meals from RM50/138; ⊙noon-3pm & 6-11pm Mon-Sat; monorail Raja Chulan) It's quite acceptable to use your fingers to savour the sublime sushi, served at the counter one piece at a time, by expert Japanese chefs

from Nagoya. There are also private booths for more intimate dinners.

★ BIJAN
MALAY $$$

Map p252 (☑2031 3575; www.bijanrestaurant.com; 3 Jln Ceylon; mains RM60-100; ⊙noon-2.30pm & 6.30-10.30pm Mon-Sat, 4.30-10.30pm Sun; monorail Raja Chulan) One of KL's best Malay restaurants, Bijan offers skilfully cooked traditional dishes in a sophisticated dining room that spills out into a tropical garden. Must-try dishes include *rendang daging* (dry beef curry with lemongrass), *masak lemak ikan* (Penang-style fish curry with turmeric) and *ikan panggang* (grilled skate with tamarind).

TWENTY ONE KITCHEN & BAR
FUSION $$$

Map p252 (☑2142 0021; www.drbar.asia; 20-1 Changkat Bukit Bintang; meals RM60-80; ⊙noon-3am; ☎; monorail Raja Chulan) Lots of interesting choices on the menu here, several of which you can sample together on tasting plates. The bar upstairs, with a deck overlooking the street, gets cranking at weekends when a DJ spins chill and dance tunes.

FRANGIPANI
MEDITERRANEAN $$$

Map p252 (☑2144 3001; www.frangipani.com.my; 25 Changkat Bukit Bintang; mains RM60-120; ⊙6.30-10.30pm Tue-Sun; monorail Raja Chulan) A new Spanish chef has injected Mediterranean seafood flavours into this classy, long-running restaurant. There's ambitious combinations of flavours and textures but not everything works – choose carefully! The beautiful dining room has tables sur-

---

JALAN ALOR

The collection of roadside restaurants and stalls lining Jln Alor is the great common denominator of KL's food scene, hauling in everyone from sequined society babes to penny-strapped backpackers. From around 5pm till late every evening, the street transforms into a continuous open-air dining space with hundreds of plastic tables and chairs and rival caterers shouting out to passers-by to drum up business (avoid the pushiest ones!). Most places serve alcohol and you can sample pretty much every Malay Chinese dish imaginable, from grilled fish and satay to *kai-lan* (Chinese greens) in oyster sauce and fried noodles with frogs' legs. Thai food is also popular.

Recommended options:

➡ **Kedai Makanan Dan Minuman TKS** (p52) for mouth-tingling Sichuan dishes.

➡ **Restoran Beh Brothers** (Map p252; 21A Jln Alor; meals R10-15; ⊙24hr, Sisters Noodle 7am-4pm), one of the few places open from 7am for breakfast, where Sisters Noodle serve delicious 'drunken' chicken *mee* (noodles) with rice wine, and there's also a good Hong Kong–style dim sum stall.

➡ **Wong Ah Wah** (Map p252; Jln Alor; dishes RM10-20; ⊙4pm-4am) is unbeatable for addictive spicy chicken wings, as well as grilled seafood, tofu and satay.

rounding a reflecting pool. There's an equally stylish bar upstairs and a newer, partially open-air bar out front serving a tapas menu.

AL-AMAR
MIDDLE EASTERN $$$

Map p252 (2166 1011; www.al-amar.com; Level 6, Pavilion KL, 168 Jln Bukit Bintang; noon-midnight; monorail Bukit Bintang) There's no shortage of restaurants in Bukit Bintang serving Middle Eastern food but few as classy or consistently good as Al-Amar. Choose from a tasty range of *mezze* and grilled meats or go simple with a *shawarma* sandwich. There's belly dancing on Friday and Saturday night and a Sunday lunch buffet (RM87).

For a more casual experience there's **Al-Amar Express** (Map p252; www.al-amar.com; Jln Bukit Bintang; 8am-3am; monorail Bukit Bintang) outside Fahrenheit 88.

HAKKA
CHINESE $$$

Map p252 (2143 1908; 90 Jln Raja Chulan; meals RM80-100; monorail Raja Chulan) Long-running restaurant specialising in Hakka-style Chinese cuisine; try the stuffed crabs and tofu dishes. The outdoor area – the most atmospheric, hung with fairy lights that complement the view of the illuminated Petronas Towers – is open only in the evening.

TOP HAT
NONYA, BRITISH $$$

Map p250 (2142 8611; www.top-hat-restaurants. com; 3 Jln Stonor; meals RM60-110; noon-10.30pm; monorail Raja Chulan, then taxi) Top Hat is set in a spacious bungalow surrounded by peaceful gardens and serves both traditional British – think oxtail stew and bread-and-butter pudding – and local dishes, such as Nonya laksa (RM28). All come with signature 'top hats' (pastry shells filled with sliced veggies) and choice of local dessert.

ENAK
MALAY $$$

Map p252 (2141 8973; www.enakkl.com; Feast fl, Starhill Gallery, 181 Jln Bukit Bintang; meals RM70-100; noon-1am; monorail Bukit Bintang) Althought it gets lost a bit amid the glitzy restaurants of Starhill's Feast floor, Enak is worth sampling for its finely presented Malay cuisine with a sophisticated twist.

NEROVIVO
ITALIAN $$$

Map p252 (2070 3120; www.nerovivo.com; 3A Jln Ceylon; mains RM50-100; monorail Raja Chulan) Tasty Italian food, including crispy

pizza and freshly made pastas, are served at this chic, partly open-air restaurant. Down the hill on the ground floor of the Somerset serviced residences is its cosy stable-mate, **Neroteca** (Map p252; 2070 0530; www.neroteca.com; Somerset, 8 Lg Ceylon; meals RM50-100; 10am-midnight Wed-Mon, 6pm-midnight Tue; monorail Raja Chulan), an equally appealing place.

FUKUYA
JAPANESE $$$

Map p252 (2144 1022; www.fukuya.com.my; 9 Jln Delima; set lunch/dinner from R40/100; noon-2.30pm & 6.30-10.30pm Mon-Sat, 6-10pm Sun; monorail Bukit Bintang, then taxi) In an elegant bungalow surrounded by stands of bamboo, Fukuya conjures the right tone for upmarket Japanese. Lunch deals are best with bento boxes (RM46 or RM58) and mini-*kaiseki* banquets.

✕ KLCC & Around

NASI KANDAR PELITA
MALAY-INDIAN $

Map p250 (www.pelita.com.my; 149 Jln Ampang; mains RM8; 24hr; KLCC) The swish, fan-cooled pavilion near the KLCC is probably the flashiest of all the *mamak* (Indian Muslim) canteens in KL. It serves exquisite Indian Muslim food, including magnificent *roti canai* and *hariyali tikka* (spiced chicken with mint, cooked in the tandoor).

DHARMA REALM GUAN YIN SAGELY MONASTERY CANTEEN
CHINESE, VEGAN $

Map p250 (161 Jln Ampang; meal RM4-6; 7.30-9.30am & 10.30am-3pm Mon-Fri; Ampang Park) Join office workers for a tasty vegan breakfast or lunch at this airy self-service canteen behind the monastery. The food contains no onions or garlic and there are drinks and fruit, too.

BISOU
BAKERY $

Map p250 (www.bisou.com.my; Level 3, Suria KLCC; cupcakes from RM6; 10am-10pm; KLCC) Offers many irresistible flavours of cupcake, plus a monthly special, and other light snacks. There's another outlet on the first floor of **Bangsar Village I** (Map p262; www.bangsarvillage.com/; Jln Terasek).

★STRATO
ITALIAN $$

Map p250 (2162 0886; www.troikaskydining. com/strato.html; Level 23A, Tower B, The Troika, Persiaran KLCC; mains RM25-50; noon-11pm

Mon-Fri, 5-11pm Sat & Sun; 🚇Ampang Park) Climb the shaky spiral staircase to reach this most affordable section of the Troika Sky Dining empire. The menu is packed with appealing, freshly made pasta and pizza that will leave you plenty of cash to enjoy a cocktail or two downstairs in Claret (p65).

LITTLE PENANG KAFÉ   MALAY, NONYA $$

Map p250 (📞2163 0215; Level 4, Suria KLCC; mains from RM15; ⏱11.30am-9.30pm; 🚇KLCC) At peak meal times expect a long line outside this mall joint serving authentic food from Penang, including specialities such as curry *mee* (spicy soup noodles with prawns) and spicy Thai *lemak* (curry) laksa available only from Friday to Sunday. There's also a branch at Mid Valley Megamall (p112).

LIVINGFOOD   INTERNATIONAL $$

Map p250 (📞2181 2778; www.livingfoodmy.com; Menara Tan & Tan, Jln Tun Razak; mains RM20-30; ⏱8am-6pm Mon-Wed, 8am-10pm Thu-Sat, 9am-3pm Sun; 🚲🍴; 🚇Ampang Park) Vegan and raw food is showcased at this appealing cafe, but there's plenty on the menu for the less virtuous, such as turkey burgers and a laksa from Sarawak where the owners hail from. Local artists' works are hung on the walls. The cafe also sells some organic foods.

MELUR & THYME   FUSION $$

Map p250 (📞2181 8001; www.melurandthyme.com; Ground fl, Suria KLCC, Jln Ampang; ⏱8am-10pm; 🚇KLCC) This appealingly designed restaurant's name, conjoining Malay and Western ingredients, hints at its game plan: offering Malay dishes alongside Western standbys such as a Caesar salad. For breakfast the coconut pancakes with caramelised honeydew melon is a very tasty way to kick off a day's shopping in Suria KLCC.

★CANTALOUPE   FRENCH $$$

Map p250 (📞2162 0886; www.troikaskydining.com/cantaloupe.html; Level 23A, Tower B, The Troika, Persiaran KLCC; mains RM100-200, set menus from RM120, lunch RM65; ⏱noon-2.30pm & 6.30-10.30pm; 🍴; 🚇Ampang Park) Who cares about the prices, or what the food is like, if you can dine with this amazing view of the city skyline! Fortunately chef Chris Bauer's imaginative dishes, all lovingly detailed on the menu, generally hit the mark. Watch you don't step off the carpet into the reflecting pools as you totter on your Manolos to your seat!

The three-course set lunch is an affordable way to experience the space; or you could try Strato (p59) and Claret (p65) which are also up here.

★ACME BAR & COFFEE   INTERNATIONAL $$$

Map p250 (📞03-2162 2288; www.acmebarcoffee.com; Troika, Ground fl, 19 Persiaran KLCC; mains RM30-60; ⏱11am-midnight Mon-Thu, 11am-1am Fri, 9.30am-1am Sat, 9.30am-5pm Sun; 🚇Ampang Park) Blink and you might be in a chic bistro in New York, Paris or Sydney. There are tasty nibbles such as root vegetable truffled fries and chilled sugar snap peas if you're not so hungry, and bigger dishes such as lamb shoulder marinated in *kicap* (a type of soy sauce) for larger appetites. It's a great choice for a lazy weekend brunch.

The outdoor section is kept cool by a clever system of under-table air-conditioning.

LEVAIN   CAFE $$

Map p252 (www.levain.com.my; 7 Jln Delima; pastries from RM5, mains RM15-20; ⏱8am-8pm; monorail Bukit Bintang) Appealing bakery, cake shop and cafe in a quiet part of the city centre. The outdoor patio is a pleasant spot for a Western-style breakfast, light lunch or tea-time treat, and the pastries are very good.

IL LIDO   ITALIAN $$$

Map p250 (📞2161 2291; Jln Mayang; mains RM45-70; ⏱noon-2.30pm & 6.30-10.30pm Mon-Fri, dinner only Sat; 🚇KLCC) If it's fine dining Italian-style you're after, then il Lido delivers handsomely with lovely homemade pasta, fish and meat dishes. There's an exclusive club feel to the sophisticated dining room and a bar upstairs for lingering over a nightcap of grappa. A three-course set lunch is RM50.

CILANTRO   FRENCH, JAPANESE $$$

Map p250 (📞2179 8082; www.cilantrokl.com; Micasa All Suite Hotel, 68B Jln Tun Razak; set lunch/dinner RM150/270; ⏱noon-2pm Fri, 6pm-1am Mon-Sat; 🚇Ampang Park) Takashi Kimura is often lauded as one of KL's most accomplished chefs. The ecclectic range of Japanese-French-cuisine inspired dishes might include the likes of *unagi* paired with foie gras and mesclun, confit of Loire poussin with truffle, with a vintage rum baba for dessert.

🍷 DRINKING & 🍸 NIGHTLIFE

Bar-hopping along Changat Bukit Bintang is a must. No Black Tie (p66) is a sophisticated place for a drink, usually with live music. If you just want to chill with a beer or iced coffee and watch the passing parade, then settle into a sidewalk seat on Jln Alor.

🍷 Golden Triangle

⭐PALATE PALETTE
CAFE

Map p252 (www.palatepalette.com; 21 Jln Mesui; ⊙noon-midnight Tue-Thu, to 2am Fri & Sat; 🛜; monorail Raja Chulan) Colourful, creative, quirky and supercool this cafe-bar is our favourite place to eat, drink, play board games and mingle with KL's boho crowd. The menu (mains RM10 to RM30) features dishes as diverse as shepherd's pie and teriyaki salmon. Check the website for details of events such as free indie movie nights and the queer community party organised by Rainbow Rojak (www.facebook.com/RainbowRojak) on the first Friday of the month, which includes musical and spoken-word performances.

⭐HELI LOUNGE BAR
COCKTAIL BAR

Map p250 (📞2110 5034; www.facebook.com/Heliloungebar; Level 34, Menara KH, Jln Sultan Ishmail; ⊙6pm-midnight Mon-Wed, to 2am Fri, to 3am Sat; 🛜; monorail Raja Chulan) Nothing besides your lychee martini and the cocktail waiter stands between you and the edge of the helipad at KL's most thrilling rooftop bar. The interior, a couple of flights of stairs down, is cheesy to the max so only come if the weather's fine when the unsheltered rooftop is open and the view simply amazing.

⭐TAPS BEER BAR
CRAFT BEER

Map p252 (www.tapsbeerbar.my; One Residency, 1 Jln Nagansari; ⊙5pm-1am; 🛜; monorail Raja Chulan) A very welcome addition to KL's drinking scene, Taps specialises in real ale from around the world with some 80 different microbrews on rotation, 14 of them on tap. Sample three for RM30. It has live accoustic music, too, Thursday to Saturday at 9.30pm.

⭐PISCO BAR
BAR

Map p252 (📞2142 2900; www.piscobarkl.com; 29 Jln Mesui; ⊙5pm-late Tue-Sun; monorail Raja Chulan) Although they've used recycled wood palettes – the cheap decorative material of choice for several KL hostelries – other parts of this Peruvian Pisco bar show some imagination, such as the bare-brick walls hung with movie-themed art. A young Paul Newman is handsome company while sinking your drink and nibbling on snacks including *cebiche* (a salad of marinated raw fish).

NEGABA
BAR

Map p252 (📞032-110 1654; www.facebook.com/theestablishmentkl; 31 Jln Mesui; ⊙5pm-midnight Mon-Tue, to 3am Wed-Sat; monorail Raja Chulan) QEII puffing on a ciggie is one of several famous faces painted onto the outside walls of this three-level bar and club. On the ground floor the Industrial Lounge kitchen and bar is a nice place to relax in comfy leather chairs; mix it up with the DJ and glamour crowd at the middle floor, while the rooftop is good for sunset cocktails.

FRANGIPANI BAR
GAY

Map p252 (📞2144 3001; 25 Changkat Bukit Bintang; cover Fri RM30; ⊙5pm-1am Tue-Thu & Sun, 5pm-3am Fri & Sat; monorail Raja Chulan) Friday is the official 'Frisky' gay night at this chic DJ bar, above the restaurant of the same name, but on other nights of the week you'll find a gay-friendly crowd here, too.

CIRCUS
BAR

Map p252 (📞2141 6151; http://circus.com.my; Level 3, Connection, Pavilion KL, 168 Jln Bukit Bintang; ⊙noon-midnight, 2am Fri & Sat; 🛜; monorail Raja Chulan) There's fairly good food at this pop-art decorated restaurant and bar serving an international menu of dishes, but Circus is best visited for its cocktail happy hours (4pm to 8pm) and live-music shows on Friday and Saturday around 9pm. Among the artists who regularly perform here is fab drag diva Roz.

COFFEE STAIN BY JOSEPH
CAFE

Map p252 (www.facebook.com/coffeestainbyjoseph#sthash.bcGq8wQ6.dpuf; Level 3, Fahrenheit88, Jln Bukit Bintang; ⊙10am-10pm; monorail Bukit Bintang) Take your pick from around 10 different single-origin beans for your coffee, which can be prepared by siphon, hand-dripped or brewed in the Heath Robinson–like Chemex contraption. Barista Ang Yee Siang is known for his 3D latte art, sculpting the milky froth into fun cup-top creations.

Markets

Although Western-style supermarkets have become the norm, Kuala Lumpur still sustains several traditional wet and dry food markets as found across Southeast Asia. Arrive around dawn to experience them at full throttle. *Pasar malam* (night markets) are also very popular and fun to explore for their street-food offerings.

1. Masjid India Pasar Malam (p91)
Sample Malay, Indian and Chinese snacks at this Saturday-night market.

2. Petaling Street Market (p82)
Bargain hunt or browse through this popular market.

3. Hawker stalls (p26)
Don't miss trying some of KL's tasiest and best-value food.

4. Durians at a fruit stand
Taste test the 'king of tropical fruits'.

5. Headscarf and shawl stall in Masjid India (p88)
Shop among locals in the markets and arcades of Masjid India.

PAPER + TOAST
CAFE

Map p252 (☎03-2141 6752; www.paperandtoast. com; One Residency, 1 Jln Nagansari; 🖥; monorail Raja Chulan) 🍴 Decent coffee and snacks plus space for digital nomads to park their laptops, work and host meetings. Plus we like that the cafe encourages customers to bring their own containers for takeaway drinks and food.

VILLAGE BAR
BAR

Map p252 (Feast fl, Starhill Gallery, 181 Jln Bukit Bintang; ⊙noon-1am; monorail Bukit Bintang) Columns of glasses and bottles and cascades of dangling lanterns lend an *Alice in Wonderland* quality to this basement bar.

NEO TAMARIND
BAR

Map p250 (www.samadhiretreats.com; 19 Jln Sultan Ismail; ⊙11.30am-2.30pm & 6.30-10.30pm; monorail Raja Chulan) Next to its sister operation, Burmese-Thai restaurant Tamarind Hill, this sophisticated restaurant-bar feels like a slice of Bali smuggled into the heart of KL. Sip cocktails by flickering tealights and a waterfall running the length of the long bar.

TEEQ BRASSERIE
CAFE

Map p252 (☎2782 3555; www.teeq.com.my; 50 Jln Sultan Ismail, Level 8, Lot 10; ⊙6.30-10.30pm, bar open to 1am Tue-Sun; monorail Bukit Bintang) Beside the rooftop garden of Lot 10 is this contemporary-styled brasserie with a relaxed alfresco bar from which you can observe the commercial frenzy of Bintang Walk at a calm distance.

LUK YU TEA HOUSE
TEAHOUSE

Map p252 (☎03-2782 3850; Feast fl, Starhill Gallery, 181 Jln Bukit Bintang; ⊙10am-1am; monorail Bukit Bintang) Enjoy a premium brew inside a charming traditional Chinese teahouse along with dim sum and other dainty snacks.

SIXTY NINE BISTRO
CAFE

Map p252 (14 Jln Kampung Dollah; ⊙5pm-1.30am; monorail Imbi) A very funky youth venue that has a junk-shop chic vibe to its decor, a fun menu of bubble teas and the like, and resident fortune tellers.

WINGS
CAFE, BAR

Map p252 (www.wingsmusicafe.com; 16 Jln Kampung Dollah; ⊙6.30am-1am, to 2am Fri & Sat; 🖥; monorail Imbi) Located a few doors down from Sixty Nine Bistro, this cheerful student hang-out has regular live music, though most drinkers prefer to chill out on the front terrace.

GREEN MAN
PUB

Map p252 (www.greenman.com.my; 40 Changkat Bukit Bintang; ⊙noon-1am, to 2am Fri-Sun; monorail Raja Chulan) There are several Irish-style pubs situated along Changkat Bukit Bintang these days, but this is the original one and it has a very loyal crowd. It's calmer indoors than on the busy terrace. Join in the regular Thursday-night quiz at 8pm for RM15.

J CO DONUTS & COFFEE
CAFE

Map p252 (www.jcodonuts.com; Basement, Pavilion KL, 168 Jln Bukit Bintang; ⊙10am-10pm;

TEA SALON SHOWDOWN

They say imitation is the sincerest form of flattery – perhaps a comforting thought for venerable Parisienne tea emporium Mariage Frères which appears to be the blueprint for a pair of fancy tea salons squaring it off on Bukit Bintang.

In the bowels of Starhill Gallery is local contender **Starhill Tea Salon** (Map p252; ☎03-2719 8550; www.starhillgallery.com/dining_sub.asp?tenantID=248; Starhill Gallery, 181 Jln Bukit Bintang; ⊙10am-1am; monorail Bukit Bintang). Grand columns created from colour-coded tea caddies and luxurious sofas set an elegant tone in which to enjoy a sybratic afternoon tea (RM70 for two; 3pm or 5pm) or nibble at the macarons or handmade chocolates. The salon's 1am closing makes it a good choice for those who fancy a late-night cuppa.

Over in Pavilion KL, the Singapore-based **TWG Tea** (Map p252; www.twgtea.com; Level 2, Pavilion KL, 168 Jln Bukit Bintang; ⊙10am-10pm; monorail Bukit Bintang) has set up its elegant stall. This luxury operation has a mind-boggling range of over 450 varieties of teas and infusions, starting around RM18 a pot. Many are beautifully packaged in pots and boxes as gifts. Afternoon tea is served 3pm to 6pm and starts at RM26.50. It also serves breakfast up until noon for RM28.50.

monorail Bukit Bintang) Its wacky donut creations may have cheesy names (Tira Miss U or Mona Pisa anyone?) but they look so damn tasty that it's difficult to pass by this fried-dough and coffee operation.

SNOWFLAKE
CAFE

Map p252 (http://snowflake.com.my; Sungai Wang Plaza, Jln Sultan Ismail; ⊙10am-10pm, to 11pm Fri & Sat; monorail Bukit Bintang) We're prepared to believe the cute marketing blurb saying that Jimmy learned how to make these refreshing jelly-based drinks and desserts from his Taiwanese gran – they make you realise how much more there is to soft drinks in Asia than canned pop.

BAKITA
BAR

Map p252 (33 Jln Berangan; monorail Raja Chulan) This multilevel, partly alfresco bar, taking up a good-sized chunk of the corner of Jln Berangan and Jln Nagansari, offers maximum people-watching potential, big-screen-TV action and chilled DJ mixes.

WHISKY BAR KUALA LUMPUR
BAR

Map p252 (www.thewhiskybarkl.com; Changat Bukit Bintang; monorail Raja Chulan) Part of the Werner's empire of restaurants and watering holes that have colonised this end of Changat Bukit Bintang – if you don't fancy a dram of the amber nectar then there's his wine bar next door, while upstairs there's the KL version of **Dining in the Dark** (Map p252; ☑2143 2268; www.dininginthedarkkl.com; 1st floor, 46 Changkat Bukit Bintang; 12 sampling plates RM100; ⊙6.30-10.30pm Tue-Sun; monorail Raja Chulan), where blind waiters assist you to eat a meal in a pitch-black room.

BLUE BOY
GAY

Map p252 (☑2142 1067; www.facebook.com/groups/blueboyPLU; 54 Jln Sultan Ismail; ⊙8.30pm-2am; monorail Bukit Bintang) The skanky workhorse of the KL gay scene just keeps on going. Come before 11pm if you wish to sing karaoke with the winking lady boys. Later it gets packed with rent boys and their admirers.

ROOTZ
CLUB

Map p252 (www.rootz.com.my; Rooftop, Lot 10, 50 Jln Sultan Ismail; ⊙10pm-3am Wed-Sat; monorail Bukit Bintang) Golden and glitzy like a Russian oligarch's dream boudoir, this gaudy-to-the-max club sits pretty and aloof atop Lot 10. The entry passage is hung with reproductions of Russian old masters, while

inside you can take your pick from, allegedly, KL's best selection of champagnes.

⚑ KLCC & Around

★ MARINI'S ON 57
BAR

Map p250 (☑2161 2880; www.marinis57.com; Level 57, Menara 3, Petronas KLCC; ⊙5pm-1am; ⊠KLCC) This is about as close as you can get to eyeballing the upper levels of the Petronas Towers from a bar. The sky-high vibe is complemented by superfriendly service that makes sure the cocktails and bar snacks keep flowing. Check the website for its dress code before heading over.

When booking (advised) be aware that it's the lively bar not the laid-back lounge that has the view of the towers.

CLARET
WINE BAR

Map p250 (☑2162 0886; www.troikaskydining.com/claret.html; Level 23A, Tower B, The Troika, Persiaran KLCC; ⊙4pm-1am; ⊠Ampang Park) Whether or not you're dining at Cantaloupe or Strato in the same complex, a visit to Claret is recommended for the same sophisticated ambience and jaw-dropping views across the KLCC park supplemented by a fine wine and cocktail menu. If you're lucky someone may be playing the grand piano.

★ TATE
COCKTAIL BAR

Map p250 (Ground fl, The Intermark, 182 Jln Tun Razak; ☎; ⊠Ampang Park) One of the first of the 'secret' speakeasy cocktails bars in the city, Tate keeps a low profile in the mall-like surroundings of The Intermark. Find your way inside and you'll be surprised by the gentleman's club–like atmosphere, complete with leather lounge chairs and a suit of armour, contrasting against the sophisticated cocktail menu.

RAWCOFFEE
CAFE

Map p250 (www.rawcoffee.my; Wisma Equity Bldg, 150 Jln Ampang; ⊙7.30am-7.30pm Mon-Fri, 9am-6pm Sat; ⊠KLCC) They take coffee making very seriously at this operation in an office building lobby, where the name RAW stands for Real And Wholesome. Beans are sourced from small cooperatives and award-winning estates from around the world and prepared by baristas on top-quality machines. The mainly vegan food selection is great too for those looking for a healthy snack or lunch.

SKY BAR BAR

Map p250 (📞2332 9888; www.skybar.com.my; Level 33, Traders Hotel; ⊙10am-1am, to 3am Fri & Sat; 🚇KLCC) Head to the rooftop pool area of this hotel for a grand circle view across to the Petronas Towers – it's the perfect spot for sundowner cocktails or late-night flutes of bubbly.

APARTMENT DOWNTOWN CAFE

Map p250 (www.atheapartment.com; Jln Ampang, 1st fl, Suria KLCC; ⊙11am-10pm; 🚇KLCC) Imagine you actually live at KLCC at this convivial loungelike cafe-bar with outdoor seating overlooking the park – a lovely spot to revive after a hard day's shopping at the mall.

MARKETPLACE GAY

Map p250 (📞2166 0750; www.marketplacekl. com; 4A Lg Yap Kwan Seng; cover RM35; ⊙10pm-3am Sat; 🚇KLCC) As Saturday night turns into Sunday morning at this restaurant, with a superb rooftop view of the Petronas Towers, KL's gay community dances and drinks like there's no tomorrow. There's a super-relaxed vibe, which is just as well since it's body to body on the dance floor. Friday nights are also gay friendly.

★ZOUK CLUB

Map p250 (www.zoukclub.com.my; 113 Jln Ampang; admission RM60; ⊙9pm-3am Tue-Sun; monorail Bukit Nanas) KL's top club offers spaces to suit everyone and a line-up of top local and international DJs. As well as the two-level main venue, there's the more sophisticated Velvet Underground with a dance floor that's glitter-ball heaven, Phuture for hip hop, the cutting-edge Bar Sonic and the rooftop bar Aristo which is open

---

LOCAL KNOWLEDGE

DANCE & CULTURAL SHOWS

If you'd like to see and hear traditional Malaysian dances and music, there are good shows at the Malaysian Tourism Centre (p226) at 3pm Tuesday to Thursday and 8.30pm Saturday. There's also an evening dance show at 8.30pm daily in the attached restaurant **Saloma** (Map p250; 📞2161 0122; www.saloma.com.my/main.cfm; 139 Jln Ampang; show only RM50, buffet & show RM90; ⊙show 8.30-9.30pm; monorail Bukit Nanas).

---

from 6pm. Word on the street at the time of research is that Zouk will have to move out of its current location in the near future; check the website for updates.

BUTTER FACTORY KL CLUB

Map p250 (📞2141 9998; www.facebook.com/ thebutterfactorykl; 1 Jln Kia Peng; ⊙9pm-3am Tue-Sat; monorail Raja Chulan) Another successful Singaporean clubbing operation has set up shop in KL, offering the usual range of genre nights and special guest DJs.

RUM JUNGLE BAR

Map p250 (http://rumjunglekl.blogspot.co.uk; 1 Jln P Ramlee; ⊙5pm-3am; 🚇KLCC) This long-running and always-raucous bar is one of numerous watering holes along Jln P Ramlee with live music, DJs and happy-hour specials. Note, these places tend to attract lots of sex workers and sexpats.

☆ ENTERTAINMENT

★DEWAN FILHARMONIK PETRONAS CONCERT VENUE

Map p250 (📞2051 7007; www.dfp.com.my; Box Office, Tower 2, Petronas Towers, KLCC; tickets RM10-210; ⊙box office 10am-6pm Mon-Sat; 🚇KLCC) Don't miss the chance to attend a concert at this gorgeous concert hall situated at the base of the Petronas Towers. The polished Malaysian Philharmonic Orchestra plays here (usually Friday and Saturday evenings and Sunday matinees, but also other times) as well as other local and international ensembles. There is a dress code.

★NO BLACK TIE LIVE MUSIC

Map p252 (📞2142 3737; www.noblacktie.com. my; 17 Jln Mesui; cover RM20-50; ⊙5pm-2am Tue-Sun; monorail Raja Chulan) Blink and you'd miss this small, chic live-music venue, bar and Japanese bistro, as it's hidden behind a grove of bamboo. NBT, as it's known to its fans, is owned by Malaysian concert pianist Evelyn Hii who has a knack for finding talented singer-songwriters, jazz bands and classical-music ensembles who play here from around 9.30pm.

THE VENUE LIVE MUSIC

Map p252 (📞2143 3022; www.thevenue.com. my; Level 4, Connection, Pavilion KL, 168 Jln Bukit Bintang; ⊙6.30pm-12.30am; monorail Bukit

WORTH A DETOUR

SELANGOR TURF CLUB & BUKIT JALIL NATIONAL STADIUM

Attend the sport of kings at **Selangor Turf Club** (☏9058 3888; www.selangorturfclub. com; Sungei Besi; admission RM6), a KL institution dating back to 1896 and originally sited where KLCC is now. The grandstand holds up to 25,000 fans and on race days there's a free shuttle bus from Serdang Komuter Train Station and Sungai Besi LRT Station.

Bukit Jalil National Stadium (☏8992 0888; www.stadium.gov.my; National Sports Complex, Sri Petaling; ⊠Bukit Jalil), 16km south of the city centre, is a 100,000-seater venue that's at the heart of the sporting complex built to host the 1998 Commonwealth Games. Soccer matches are often held here, including international games and the Malaysian FA cup final. It's also used for concerts by major local and international pop stars.

Bintang) Specialising mainly in jazz, this new spot in the Pavilion provides a classy performance space for artists from around the region.

KUALA LUMPUR
CONVENTION CENTRE   CONVENTION CENTRE
Map p250 (☏2333 2888; www.klcccconvention-centre.com; Jln Pinang; ⊠KLCC)

GSC PAVILION KL   CINEMA
Map p252 (☏8312 3456; www.gsc.com.my; Level 6, Pavilion KL, 168 Jln Bukit Bintang; monorail Bukit Bintang) Expect lines for hit movies at this multiplex in the popular mall. This one of the few mulitplexes in the GSC chain that has an International Screens program showing art-house and foreign movies.

There's another central GSC multiplex at **Berjaya Times Square** (Map p252; ☏8312 3456; 3rd fl, Berjaya Times Square, 1 Jln Imbi; monorail Imbi).

KL LIVE   LIVE MUSIC
Map p250 (www.kl-live.com.my; 1st fl, Life Centre, 20 Jln Sultan Ismail; monorail Raja Chulan) One of the best things to happen to KL's live-music scene in a while has been the opening of this spacious venue, which has been packing in rock and pop fans with an impressive line-up of overseas and local big-name artists and DJs.

TGV CINEPLEX, SURIA KLCC   CINEMA
Map p250 (☏7492 2929; www.tgv.com.my; Level 3, Suria KLCC) Take your pick from the mainstream offerings at this 12-screen multiplex. Book in advance or be prepared to queue, particularly at weekends.

 SHOPPING

Golden Triangle

★**PAVILION KL**   MALL
Map p252 (www.pavilion-kl.com; 168 Jln Bukit Bintang; ⊙10am-10pm; monorail Bukit Bintang) Pavilion sets the gold standard in KL's shopping scene. Amid the many familiar international luxury labels, there are some good local retail options, including branches of the fashion houses British India, MS Read for larger-sized gals, Salabianca and Philosophy for Men for fun casual wear. Its basement food court is excellent and for a quick trip to Japan head to Tokyo Street on the 6th floor.

★**SUNGEI WANG PLAZA**   MALL
Map p252 (www.sungeiwang.com; Jln Sultan Ismail; ⊙10am-10pm; monrail Bukit Bintang) This ragbag of retail fun promises 'all kinds of everything' and you'd better believe it. Connected with BB Plaza, Sungei Wan is confusing to navigate but jam-packed with youth-oriented fashions and accessories. Anchoring one corner is the Parkson Grand department store, and you'll find a post office, various fast-food outlets and a hawker centre on the 4th floor.

Teens and youthful fashionistas should hunt out HK Station on the 6th floor.

★**FAHRENHEIT88**   MALL
Map p252 (www.fahrenheit88.com; 179 Jln Bukit Bintang; ⊙10am-10pm; monorail Bukit Bintang) Managed by Pavilion KL, this youth-orientated mall is anchored by KL's main branch of Japanese fast-fashion sensation Uniqlo. More Tokyo-cool style is on display

TAMAN CONNAUGHT NIGHT MARKET

In the southeast of the city, stretching along Jln Cerdas, the longest *pasar malam* (night market) in Malaysia happens every Wednesday from 7pm to 1am. It stetches for around 2km with over 500 stalls selling mainly clothing, household goods and food. At the western end near Jln Pantas, fuel up on *kway teow mee goreng* (noodles), fresh juices and baked birds' eggs on a stick.

To reach the market, take the Light Rail Transit (LRT) or Komuter Train to Bandar Tasik Selatan, then hop in a taxi (around RM7).

in the 3rd-floor Parkamaya concept store. Local fashion legend **Bernard Chandran** (Map p252; www.bernardchandran.com) also has his boutique here.

LOT 10   MALL

Map p252 (☑03-2716 8615; www.lot10.com.my; 50 Jln Bukit Bintang; ☺10am-10pm; monorail Bukit Bintang) Fronted by a megabranch of fashion retailer H&M, Lot 10 is yet another of the Bukit Bintang malls worth a browse. There's an interesting National Geographic concept store; the Thai silk and silver jewellery shop **Sakun Silver & Silk** (Map p252; www.sakunsilk.com; 4th fl); Sonny San's very wearable clothes at **Eclipse** (Map p252; www.eclipse.com.my); Lot 10 Hutong (p57), its fine basement food court and the rooftop garden with a gym and nighlife hang-outs Rootz and Teeq Brasserie (p64).

STARHILL GALLERY   MALL

Map p252 (www.starhillgallery.com; 181 Jln Bukit Bintang; monorail Bukit Bintang) Break out the platinum charge card – this glitzy mall is the domain of exclusive fashion brands including Louis Vuitton, Salvatore Ferragamo, Alfred Dunhill and – hmm – British department store Debenhams. The basement is a virtual village of upmarket restaurants and the 'Pamper' floor offers up a good selection of spas and beauty parlours.

KHOON HOOI   FASHION

Map p252 (www.khoonhooi.com; Explore fl, Starhill Gallery, 181 Jln Bukit Bintang; monorail Bukit Bintang) Interesting fabric textures are a signature of this up-and-coming designer's work. What sets his clothes apart is attention to detail, such as pleated belts made from zips or shifts sewn from lace.

BERJAYA TIMES SQUARE   MALL

Map p252 (☑2117 3081; www.timesquarekl.com; 1 Jln Imbi; ☺10am-10pm; monorail Imbi) Lacking the glitz of rival malls, Berjaya's mammoth effort is located just south of Bukit Bintang. The Metrojaya department store has good deals on clothes and there's a small branch of Borders bookstore located in the basement. The centre also has a bowling alley, karaoke, cinema and an indoor theme park.

PLAZA LOW YAT   ELECTRONICS

Map p252 (www.plazalowyat.com; 7 Jln Bintang; ☺10am-10pm; monorail Imbi) KL's best IT mall, packed with six floors of retailers big and small offering deals on laptops, digital cameras, mobile phones, computer peripherals and accessories. Digital-camera memory cards, card-readers and portable hard drives are particularly good value. If you can't find what you need here (particularly electronic parts) then scout around the stalls in nearby **Imbi Plaza** (Map p252; Jln Imbi; ☺11am-9pm; monorail Imbi).

JADI BATEK CENTRE   BATIK, HANDICRAFTS

Map p252 (☑2145 1133; www.jadibatek.com; 30 Jln Inai; ☺9am-5.30pm; monorail Bukit Bintang) On the tour-bus circuit, this batik goods and Malaysian handicrafts showroom and workshop offers plenty of handmade pieces – colourful and pretty things, but no extraordinary designs. Watch artists at work and have a go yourself.

HERITAGE ART & GRAPHICS   ART & CRAFTS

(☑2070 5213; Wariseni, Lot 231 Bukit Nanas, Jln Ampang; ☺10am-6.30pm Mon-Sat, noon-6.30pm Sun; monorail Bukit Nanas) Apart from art supplies, postcards and prints, this gallery-shop on the side of Bukit Nanas stocks the works of batik artist **Aziz Ma'as** (☑012-314 0443; a2zstone@yahoo.com; Wariseni, Lot 231 Bukit Nenas, Jln Ampang; 3-session course RM380; monorail Bukit Nanas): check out his pretty wooden clogs (from RM120) decorated with original designs, each piece unique.

🔒 KLCC & Around

★SURIA KLCC
MALL

Map p250 (www.suriaklcc.com.my; KLCC, Jln Ampang; ◷10am-10pm; 🚇KLCC) Even if shopping bores you to tears, you're sure to find something to interest you at this fine shopping complex situated at the foot of the Petronas Towers. It is strong on both local and international brands such as Jimmy Choo (who as every Carrie Bradshaw knows was born in Penang even if the company is British) and British India (which is actually Malaysian).

★KOMPLEKS KRAF KUALA LUMPUR
ARTS & CRAFTS

Map p250 (✆2162 7533; www.kraftangan.com. my/101/main/content/68; Jln Conlay; ◷9am-8pm Mon-Fri, to 7pm Sat & Sun, museum 9am-5pm; monorail Raja Chulan, then taxi) A government enterprise, this huge complex mainly caters to coach tours, but it's worth a visit to browse the shops and stalls selling wood carvings, pewter, basketware, glassware and ceramics; the best section is the Karyaneka Boutique stocking items made from batik and Malaysian woven cloth. A few craftspeople and artists work in the surrounding Art Colony where you can also try your hand at batik painting. The complex also has a small **museum** (adult/child RM3/1).

SPAS, REFLEXOLOGY & FISH SPAS

The Golden Triangle is stacked with spas and massage parlours offering all manner of pampering, from luxurious treatments with exotic potions to simple salons for foot reflexology or a nibble from the doctor fish.

Practically all KL's five-star hotels offer a luxurious spa experience. One of the best is the Ritz Carlton's **Spa Village** (Map p252; ✆2782 9090; www.spavillageresort.org; Ritz Carlton, 168 Jln Imbi; treatments RM350-850; ◷9am-9pm; monorail Bukit Bintang), with its resortlike atmosphere and wide-ranging menu of Chinese, Indian and Southeast Asian healing and toning therapies.

The 'Pamper' floor of swish shopping mall Starhill Gallery is dedicated to exclusive spa and beauty treatments. Among the less pricey options (ie treatments from around RM240) here are **Asianel Reflexology Spa** (Map p252; ✆2142 1397; www. asianel.com; Pamper Floor, Starhill Gallery, 182 Jln Bukit Bintang; ◷10am-9pm; monorail Bukit Bintang) and the Balinese-style **Donna Spa** (Map p252; ✆2141 8999; www.don-naspa.net; Pamper Floor, Starhill Gallery, 182 Jln Bukit Bintang; ◷10am-midnight; monorail Bukit Bintang). Another sybaritic possibility over at Berjaya Times Square is **JoJoBa Spa** (Map p252; ✆2141 7766; www.jojoba.com.my; 15th fl, East Wing, Berjaya Times Square Hotel, 1 Jln Imbi; ◷11am-midnight; monorail Imbi), which claims to be Malaysia's largest tourist spa – come for seaweed wraps, coffee scrubs and ginger tea.

If the top-end spas are beyond your budget, there are numerous Chinese massage and reflexology centres strung along Jln Bukit Bintang. Pricing is fairly consistent – around RM80 per hour for a full body massage and RM30 for 30 minutes of foot reflexology, though you can bargain down – but standards vary and some places are slightly seedy. A reliable option on the strip is **Reborn** (Map p252; ✆2144 1288; www. reborn.com.my; 18 Jln Bukit Bintang; ◷11am-3am; monorail Bukit Bintang), which like many places offers a fish spa. Be prepared: a good foot massage can be rather painful, but the results will be remarkable.

Often combined with foot reflexology, KL's popular fish spas bring a new meaning to feeding the fish. Immerse your feet in a tank filled with the small *Garra rufa* and *Cyprinion macrostomus*, also known as doctor fish, and allow the flapping podiatrists to gently nibble away at the dead skin. It's an initially ticklish but not wholly unpleasant experience lasting 30 minutes (or as long as you can stand it!). Among the conveniently located places you can sample this service, which costs around RM30, are **Kenko** (Map p252; ✆2141 6651; www.kenko.com.sg; Level 5, Pavilion KL, 169 Jln Bukit Bintang; ◷10am-10pm; monorail Bukit Bintang) and **Morino Kaze** (Map p252; ✆2141 1916; www.morinokaze.com.my; 2nd fl, Piccolo Galleria, 101 Jln Bukit Bintang; ◷noon-midnight; monorail Bukit Bintang).

MY BATIK
BATIK

(☑03-4251 5164; http://mybatik.org.my/; 333 Persiaran Ritchie, off Jln Ritchie; ⊙9am-6pm Mon-Sat) Founded by artist Emilia Tan and set in a leafy compound a five-minute taxi ride east of the KLCC, My Batik sells batik print fashions and homewares in an explosion of colours and patterns. There's also a cafe here, you can meet the artists and arrange to take batik painting courses (from RM50 per person).

PUCUK REBUNG
ANTIQUES, CRAFTS

Map p250 (Level 3, Suria KLCC, Jln Ampang; ⊙10am-10pm; ⊠KLCC) Half museum, half shop, this upmarket arts-and-craft store offers genuine antiques and Malay ethnological items. Only some of the items are for sale – it's worth popping in for a browse around the treasures, and there are some affordable, contemporary craft and art pieces among the antiques.

KINOKUNIYA
BOOKS

Map p250 (www.kinokuniya.com/my; Level 4, Suria KLCC, Jln Ampang; ⊙10am-10pm; ⊠KLCC) Remember when there were huge bookshops that you could spend hours in? Standing against the online-shopping tide is Kinokuniya, which has an excellent English-language selection alongside titles in all the other major languages of Malaysia.

ASEANA
FASHION

Map p250 (www.melium.com; Ground level, Suria KLCC, Jln Ampang; ⊙10am-10pm; ⊠KLCC) Stylish and extensive selection of fashion from local luminaries such as **Farah Khan** (www.farahkhan.com), who specialises in beaded and sequined glamour-wear, and the more casual **Melinda Looi** (www.melindalooi.com.my). Next door its cafe serves pricey Malay food and drinks and has outdoor seating.

IKARRTINI
BATIK, FASHION

Map p250 (www.ikarrtini.com; Level 2, Suria KLCC, Jln Ampang; ⊙10am-10pm; ⊠KLCC) Penang-born Kartini Illias is the designer behind these contemporary batik fashions – supercolourful clothing on fine silk and cotton for men and women.

TENMOKU POTTERY
CERAMICS

Map p250 (www.tenmokupottery.com.my; Level 3, Suria KLCC, Jln Ampang; ⊙10am-10pm; ⊠KLCC) With their kilns based near Batu Caves, Tenmoku Pottery specialises in vases, bowls and other ceramics inspired by natural forms. As well as this outlet there are branches in Central Market (p77) and Mid Valley Megamall (p112).

COCOA BOUTIQUE
FOOD

Map p250 (www.cocoaboutique.com.my; 139 Jln Ampang; ⊙10am-8pm; monorail Bukit Nanas) Brave the tour groups being pushed through this chocolate emporium and small-scale production line to sample unusual local variations such as durian-filled chocolates, or have a favourite photo embossed on chocolate for a unique souvenir.

SPORTS & ACTIVITIES

★STARHILL CULINARY STUDIO
COOKING COURSE

Map p252 (☑2782 3810; www.starhillculinarystudio.com; Starhill Gallery Muse fl, 181 Jln Bukit Bintang; classes RM188; monorail Bukit Bintang) You will not leave hungry after the three-hour-long classes in a variety of cuisines, including local Malay and Peranakan styles, that are offered at this well-designed new culinary-arts institute atop Starhill Gallery.

BERJAYA TIMES SQUARE THEME PARK
AMUSEMENT PARK

Map p252 (☑2117 3118; www.timessquarekl.com/themepark; Berjaya Times Sq, 1 Jln Imbi; adult/child RM48/38; ⊙noon-10pm Mon-Fri, 11am-10pm Sat & Sun; monorail Imbi) Despite the mall location, there's a full-sized looping coaster plus a good selection of thrill rides for teenagers and gentler rides for families. (Avoid the DNA Mixer unless you want to see your *nasi lemak* a second time.)

Chinatown, Merdeka Square & Bukit Nanas

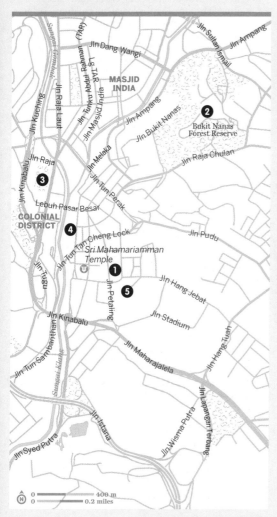

Neighbourhood Top Five

1 Exploring the cultural mash-up of **Chinatown** (p78) on our walking tour, which takes you past venerable Indian and Taoist temples and atmospheric markets.

2 Ascending **Menara KL** (p73) for a panoramic view of the city at the restaurant **Atmosphere 360** (p81).

3 Admiring the colonial architectural ensemble around **Merdeka Square** (p74).

4 Shopping for souvenirs and viewing cultural performances in **Central Market** (p77).

5 Going for a swim at **Chin Woo Stadium** (p84) and sticking around for the sunset view of the city.

For more detail of this area, see Map p248 ➡

Lonely Planet's Top Tip

Gain access to the exclusive members-only Royal Selangor Club (p79) by joining a free two-and-a-half hour walking tour around Merdeka Square, laid on by Visit KL (p226) every Monday, Wednesday and Saturday at 9am.

Best Places to Eat

→ Madras Lane Hawkers (p79)

→ Old China Café (p80)

→ La Vie En Rose (p81)

→ LOKL (p81)

→ Peter Hoe Beyond (p80)

For reviews, see p79 →

Best Places to Drink

→ Aku Cafe & Gallery (p82)

→ Luna (p82)

→ Reggae Bar (p82)

For reviews, see p82 →

Best Shopping

→ Central Market (p77)

→ Petaling Street Market (p82)

→ Peter Hoe Evolution (p83)

→ Junk Bookstore (p83)

For reviews, see p82 →

Explore: Chinatown, Merdeka Square & Bukit Nanas

If there's one part of Kuala Lumpur (KL) that's a microcosm of Malaysia's ethnic and historic mix, it's Chinatown, home and workplace not just to the scions of the original Chinese, Indian and Malay settlers but also to more recent arrivals from Bangladesh, Nepal and Mynamar. Jln Petaling is its central spine, hosting a bustling night market and bracketed by Chinese arch gates. Explore the surrounding streets and alleys and you'll find all manner of businesses, from traditional medicine shops to barbers and songbird sellers, not to mention some of KL's best street eats.

Ringed by impressive colonial-era buildings, Dataran Merdeka (Independence Square, but commonly called Merdeka Square) is a hugely symbolic location: this is where the British handed over control of Malaya to its citizens in 1957. Nearby, the graceful Masjid Jamek, the city's oldest surviving mosque, is shaded by swaying palms at the muddy confluence of the Klang and Gombak rivers that bequeathed the city its name.

East of here rise up the wooded slopes of Bukit Nanas (Pineapple Hill), the oldest protected piece of jungle in Malaysia, atop which stands Menara KL. The tower's observation deck provides fabulous views of the city while at the base are a handful of other attractions.

Local Life

→**Market life** Join locals shopping for fresh fish, meat, fruit and vegetables at the Chinatown Wet Market (p77). There's a flea market on the alley running between Jln Petaling and Jln Sultan early each morning, while from 4pm to midnight Petaling Street Market (p82) becomes one of KL's best night markets.

→**Daily worship** Light joss sticks, have your fortune told and heed the call to prayer at the area's historic temples, shrines and mosques.

→**Raising the flag** Stand to attention at the flag-raising ceremony held from 9.45am to 10am every Monday on Merdeka Square, complete with horseback cavalry, marching soldiers and the major's brash band.

Getting There & Away

→**LRT** Pasar Seni and Masjid Jamek LRT stations are the most convenient for the area. Plaza Rakyat station connects to Pudu Sentral bus terminal (p217).

→**Bus** Free **GO-KL City Buses** (www.facebook.com/goklcitybus) ease connection between Chinatown, Bukit Nanas and the Golden Triangle areas.

→**Walking** These compact areas are easy to explore on foot.

TOP SIGHT
MENARA KL

Located within the KL Forest Eco Park, this 421m telecommunications tower, the tallest in Southeast Asia and seventh tallest in the world, offers an observation deck with exceptional views. Come to appreciate the phenomenal growth of the city while enjoying a Malay banquet or afternoon tea at its sky-high revolving restaurant; or to explore the park's tree tops on the new canopy walkway.

Observation Deck

Although the Petronas Towers are taller structures, the Menara KL (KL Tower) provides a higher viewpoint as its base is already nearly 100m above sea level atop Bukit Nanas. A lift whisks you up to the observation deck in the bulb at the top of the tower, its shape inspired by a Malaysian spinning toy. One floor above is the revolving restaurant Atmosphere 360 (p81); having a meal here is a great deal since the view comes along with the food.

Other Attractions & Events

There's plenty of touristy hoopla at the tower base including pony rides, an F1 simulator and a small aquarium. Look out too for the 150-year-old **Jelutong tree** that was saved during the tower's construction – find it to the left of the tower lobby. Construction of a **canopy walkway** through KL Forest Eco Park (p79) should also be completed in 2014.

Events staged at the tower include the **KL Tower International Night Towerthon Challenge**, a footrace up the 2058 steps of the tower in May; and the **KL Tower International Jump Malaysia** (www.kltowerjump.com), in September, the only time you'll be able to see base jumpers legally flinging themselves off Menara KL.

DON'T MISS...

➡ Observation Deck
➡ Canopy Walkway in KL Forest Eco Park

PRACTICALITIES

➡ KL Tower
➡ Map p248
➡ ☎2020 5448
➡ www.kltower.com.my
➡ 2 Jln Punchak
➡ observation deck adult/child RM47/27, shuttle bus every 15min free
➡ ⊙observation deck 9am-10pm, last tickets 9.30pm, shuttle bus 9am-9.30pm
➡ 🚇KL Tower

TOP SIGHT
MERDEKA SQUARE

The grassy square where Malaysian independence was declared in 1957 is ringed by heritage buildings and dominated by an enormous flagpole and fluttering Malaysian flag. Come here to learn about the city's history and to admire the grand colonial architecture. Join the free walking tour offered by Visit KL (p226) and you'll also gain access to one of KL's most exclusive private member clubs.

History of the Square

Back at KL's founding in the mid-19th century, this patch of land was used to grow fruit and vegetables by the tin prospectors and other settlers. In 1884, after the founding of the Selangor Club, the land was transformed into a games pitch and was called the Padang (meaning 'field').

For the next 70-odd years the Padang remained the green nucleus of colonial power on the Malay peninsula, a place for cricket, parades and civic celebrations. It became cemented in the national consciousness at midnight on 31 August 1957 when the Union flag was lowered and the Malayan States' flag hoisted on the Padang's 95m flagpole.

In 1989, a year after the city took over the Pandang from the Royal Selangor Club, the square was renamed Dataran Merdeka (Independence Square), although it's commonly called Merdeka Square. It was during this era that a giant underground car park and shopping complex was built beneath the square. However a flood in 2003 (similar to catastrophic ones that had submerged the area in 1926 and 1971) put paid to the project.

Raising the Flag

Apart from New Year's Eve, National Day and occasional special events, such as the Colours of Malaysia parade, crowds rarely gather at Merdeka Square. Don't miss the **ceremonial flag-raising ceremony** held 9.45am to 10am every Monday on the square. Around the

DON'T MISS...

→ KL City Gallery
→ National Textiles Museum
→ Sultan Abdul Samad Building
→ St Mary's Anglican Cathedral

PRACTICALITIES

→ Dataran Merdeka
→ Map p248
→ 🚇Masjid Jamek

base of the flagpole (at 102m, it's the tallest in the world) are mosaics depicting the famous scenes of independence from 1957.

KL City Gallery

Get a quick overview of the city's history at the **KL City Gallery** (Map p248; ✆2691 1382; www.klcitygallery.com; 27 Jln Raja, Dataran Merdeka; ⊗8am-6pm; ☎; ⊠Masjid Jamek) **FREE**, which, as well as housing the offices of Visit KL and its tourist information desk, has a huge scale model of the city created by **Arch Kuala Lumpur** (www.archcollection.com). You can see the modellers at work before exiting through a gift shop selling the art works of Arch as well as a good selection of books about KL and Malaysia.

National Textiles Museum

On the square's southeast corner and entered off Lebuh Pasar Besar is the engaging **National Textiles Museum** (Muzium Tekstil Negara; Map p248; ✆2694 3457; www.muziumtekstilnegara.gov.my; Jln Sultan Hishamuddin; ⊗9am-6pm; ⊠Masjid Jamek) **FREE**, which occupies an elegant Mogul-Islamic building designed by the India-obsessed architect AC Norman. Darkened exhibition spaces help preserve the delicate textiles on display – there are some beautiful pieces and plenty of explanation of how they are made. The sad thing is that many of the time-consuming skills necessary for the production of such textiles are dying out, making these pieces increasingly rare. The museum's shop showcases work by young Malaysian designers, and there's a small cafe serving Malay snacks.

Sultan Abdul Samad Building

Gracing the east side of the square are the Moorish domes and 43m clocktower of the **Sultan Abdul Samad Building** (Map p248; Jln Raja; ⊠Masjid Jamek). This glorious brick building, dramatically illuminated at night, was constructed as the secretariat for the colonial administration in 1897. It's another of AC Norman's designs and was named after the Sultan of Selangor at the time. It now houses the national Ministry of Information, Communications and Culture.

St Mary's Anglican Cathedral

When it came to **St Mary's Anglican Cathedral** (Map p248; ✆2692 8672; www.stmaryscathedral.org.my; Jln Raja; ⊠Masjid Jamek), AC Norman ditched the Moorish and Mogul influences and stuck with the traditional blueprint of an English country church. Built in 1894, the Anglican cathedral has beautiful stained-glass windows and a fine pipe organ dedicated to Sir Henry Gurney, the British high commissioner to Malaya, assassinated in 1951 during the Emergency.

FORMER STANDARD CHARTERED BANK

Dating from 1891 and designed by AC Norman, the building that was originally the Standard Chartered Bank was later used to house the National History Museum and was, until recently, a restaurant. There are now plans to turn it into a music museum.

Mosaic portraits of all of Malaysia's prime ministers line a wall next to the Victorian Fountain (1904) said to be have been built in memory of an inspector of the Selangor Miltary; at one time horses would have lapped water here.

CHINATOWN, MERDEKA SQUARE & BUKIT NANAS MERDEKA SQUARE

⊙ SIGHTS

⊙ Chinatown

SRI MAHAMARIAMMAN TEMPLE   HINDU TEMPLE
See p76.

SZE YA TEMPLE   CHINESE TEMPLE
Map p248 (Jln Tun HS Lee; ⊘7am-5pm; ⊞Pasar Seni) This Taoist temple, one of the most atmospheric in Chinatown, was constructed in 1864 on the instructions of 'Kapitan Cina' Yap Ah Loy. You can see a small statue of the man just left of the main altar. Its odd position, squished between rows of shophouses, was determined by feng shui. You can enter the temple through the stucco gatehouse on Jln Tun HS Lee or the back gate on the next alley west.

Fortune-telling sticks are provided for devotees; just rattle the pot until a stick falls out, then find the paper slip corresponding to the number on the stick. Staff will translate the fortune on the slip for RM1. On your way out, note the two gilded sedan chairs used to carry the deity statues during religious processions.

GUANDI TEMPLE   CHINESE TEMPLE
Map p248 (Jln Tun HS Lee; ⊘7am-5pm; ⊞Pasar Seni) Similar in atmosphere to the Sze Ya Temple is the 1886 Guandi Temple. The main hall is hung with fragrant coils of spiral incense, paper clothes and money that are burned to bring good fortune to the ancestors. The temple is dedicated to Kwan Ti, a historical Chinese general revered by Taoists as the god of war. It is also known as Kwong Siew Free School after the clan association who originally built it.

STADIUM MERDEKA   HISTORIC BUILDING
Map p248 (Jln Stadium; monorail Maharajalela) Built for the declaration of independence in 1957, this open-air stadium is where Malaysia's first prime minister, Tunku Abdul Rahman, punched his fist seven times in the air shouting 'Merdeka!' (Independence!). Other big events during its history include a boxing match between Muhammad Ali and Joe Bugner and a concert by Michael Jackson. There are panoramic views of the city from

---

⊙ TOP SIGHT
SRI MAHAMARIAMMAN TEMPLE

This venerable Hindu shrine – the oldest in Malaysia and rumoured to be the richest – was founded by the Pillai family from the Indian state of Tamil Nadu in 1873. For 50 years it was their private shrine until opening to the public in the 1920s.

Flower-garland vendors crowd the entrance and the temple is crowned by a five-tiered **gopuram** (temple tower), built in 1972 and covered in riotously colourful statues of Hindu deities. Passing through the gate symbolises the move from the material to the spiritual world.

The **main prayer hall** has several shrines to different Hindu deities. The main shrine, found at the rear of the complex is for Mariamman, the South Indian mother goddess, an incarnation of Durga, also known as Parvati. On the left side of the complex is a shrine to Ganesh, the elephant-headed god, and on the right is the shrine where Lord Murugan is worshipped.

The temple also houses the **silver chariot** in which statuettes of Lord Murugan and his consorts are transported to Batu Caves during the Thaipusam festival (p202) in January or February each year. Non-Hindus are welcome to visit, but leave your shoes at the entrance.

DON'T MISS...
➡ Gopuram
➡ Main Prayer Hall

PRACTICALITIES
➡ Map p248
➡ http://batucaves-muruga.org
➡ 163 Jln Tun HS Lee
➡ ⊘6am-8.30pm
➡ ⊞Pasar Seni

the grandstands and a couple of evocative photographic murals in the entrance hall.

Though not officially open outside event times, if you turn up between 9am and 5pm the guards are likely to let you take a peek inside. Land around the stadium is slated to be developed as part of the construction of the 118-storey Warisan Merdeka tower as well as a new Mass Rapid Transit (MRT) station.

STADIUM NEGARA   HISTORIC BUILDING

Map p248 (Jln Hang Jebat; ⊡Hang Tuah, monorail Hang Tuah) Officially opened in 1962, this was Malaysia's first indoor stadium and is another heritage building that has been recently given a facelift. Concerts and events are occasionally held here. Murals in the entrance lobby depict the cultural dances of Malaysia's various races and the country's main industries back in the 1960s.

It's not officially open outside event times but between 9am and 5pm the guards will likely let you look inside.

CHAN SHE SHU
YUEN TEMPLE   BUDDHIST TEMPLE

Map p248 (☎20781461; Jln Petaling; ⊙9am-6pm; monorail Maharajalela) Also known as the Green Temple after the colour of its plastered walls, this clan temple features KL's finest example of a Kwangtung pottery-shard-decorated roof, with dioramas of celestial scenes and dramatic woodcarvings inside the main shrine. Completed in 1906 it is modelled after the Chan Family ancestral temple in Guangzhou, China.

GUAN YIN TEMPLE   BUDDHIST TEMPLE

Map p248 (cnr Jln Stadium & Jln Maharajalela; ⊙7am-5pm; monorail Maharajalela) Dedicated to the goddess of mercy, this pretty temple was originally built by Hokkien Chinese in the 1890s and served as a place to say prayers for those buried in the graveyard that was once located on the hill. On the first and 15th day of the month in the Chinese calendar a free vegetarian meal is served here.

CENTRAL MARKET   MARKET

Map p248 (www.centralmarket.com.my; Jln Hang Kasturi; ⊙10am-9pm; ⊡Pasar Seni) The 1930s art deco building that used to house KL's main wet market was rescued from demolition in the 1980s and is now an arts, crafts and souvenir market aimed at tourists. An annex to the rear houses the **Annexe Gallery** (Map p248; ☎2070 1137; www.annexegallery.com; 1st & 2nd fl, Annexe, Central Market, Jln Hang Kas-

turi; ⊙11am-8pm; ⊡Masjid Jamek), a nonprofit centre for contemporary arts that also hosts occasional film screenings, theatre and dance workshops, talks and launches.

Jln Hang Kasturi beside the east side of the market is now called **Kasturi Walk** and has outdoor stalls (open 10.30am to 10.30pm daily). Thirty-minute dance or martial arts performances occur nightly at 9pm.

KOMPLEKS DAYABUMI   LANDMARK

Map p248 (Jln Sultan Hishamuddin; ⊡Pasar Seni) The former headquarters of Petronas, Kompleks Dayabumi was designed by Nik Mohammed and built in 1981. In profile, the 35-storey marble-clad tower, cloaked in delicate fretwork screens, forms a four-pointed star intersected by a square, a recurring symbol in Islamic art. To get here, walk over the footbridge behind Central Market.

CHINATOWN WET MARKET   MARKET

Map p248 (⊙7am-3pm; ⊡Pasar Seni) If you want your chicken freshly killed and plucked this is where to get it! Squished in darkened alleys between Jln Petaling and Jln Tun HS Lee is Chinatown Wet Market, where locals shop for their groceries.

MEDAN PASAR   SQUARE

Map p248 (Medan Pasar; ⊡Masjid Jamek) Recently made into a pedestrian square, this was once the heart of Chinatown, a place of brothels and illegal gambling dens. Yap Ah Loy used to live on the square and a market was held here – hence its name which translates as Market Square. In the centre stands an art deco clock tower built in 1937 to commemorate the coronation of King George IV.

COURT HILL GANESH TEMPLE   HINDU TEMPLE

Map p248 (9 Jln Pudu Lama; ⊙6am-8.30pm; ⊡Plaza Rakyat) There's always a lively scene outside this small temple, dedicated to the elephant-headed god Ganesh, as worshippers buy garlands, light ghee candles and smash coconuts for good fortune.

◉ Merdeka Square & Bukit Nanas

MENARA KL   OBSERVATION TOWER

See p73.

MERDEKA SQUARE   SQUARE

See p74.

🚶 Neighbourhood Walk
Chinatown Architecture

START MASJID JAMEK LRT STATION
END PETALING STREET MARKET
LENGTH 1.6KM; 1½ HOURS

From the station head south down Jln Benteng across which you'll get a great view of ① **Masjid Jamek**. At the junction with Lr Ampang is ② **Medan Pasar**, site of KL's original market square.

Where Medan Pasar meets Lr Pasar Besar you'll see the ③ **OCBC Building**, a graceful art deco structure built in 1938 for the Overseas Chinese Banking Company. Around the corner with Jln Tun HS Lee is ④ **MS Ally Company**, a pharmacy in business since 1909.

Cross Lr Pudu, turn right and, after 25m, duck left into an alleyway leading to the atmospheric ⑤ **Sze Ya Temple** (p76). Exit the way you came in, cross the street and walk through the alley opposite to hit ⑥ **Central Market** (p77).

Exit the market, turn left onto Jln Tun Tan Cheng Lock, then right onto Jln Tun HS Lee. The shophouses along here are among Chinatown's oldest; note the unique feature of a five-foot way (pavement) lower than the road level.

On the south corner is the pale-yellow-painted art deco ⑦ **Lee Rubber Building**; on the 2nd floor is Peter Hoe Beyond where you can pause for refreshments.

Opposite, next to the bright-red, incense-wreathed ⑧ **Guandi Temple** (p76) is Jln Sang Guna, a covered arcade housing Chinatown's atmospheric ⑨ **wet market** (p77). Back on Jln Tun HS Lee pause to admire the ⑩ **Sri Mahamariamman Temple** (p76) and to breathe in the sweet jasmine of the flower sellers outside.

At the junction with Jln Sultan turn left, then right onto Jln Petaling. Further south, around the busy traffic roundabout of Bulatan Merdeka, you find the ornate ancestral ⑪ **Chan She Shu Yuen Temple** (p77) and, across Jln Stadium, the ⑫ **Guan Yin Temple** (p77), dedicated to the goddess of mercy.

Finish at ⑬ **Maharajalela MRT station** or return to Jln Petaling to browse the ⑭ **Petaling Street Market** (p82).

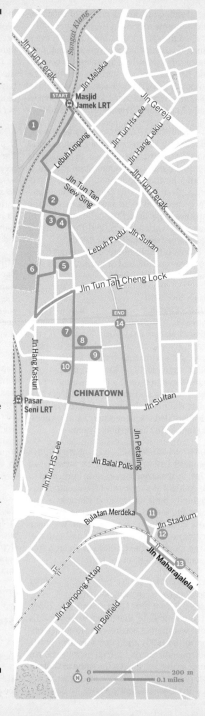

KL FOREST ECO PARK NATURE RESERVE

Map p248 (www.forestry.gov.my; 🕒7am-6pm; 🚇KL Tower) 🏃 If you fancy a bit of a workout on your way to Menara KL, an alternative to the shuttle bus is to climb the short and well-labelled nature trails through the Bukit Nanas Forest Eco Park. This lowland dipterocarp forest reserve covering 9.37 hectares was gazetted in 1906, making it the oldest protected piece of jungle in Malaysia. Explore it alone, or on a free guided tour starting from the entrance to Menara KL at 11am, 12.30pm, 2.30pm and 4.30pm daily and lasting about 45 minutes. By the time you read this, the new canopy walkway should also be completed. There are good displays and leaflets in the **Forest Information Centre** (Map p248; 📋2026 4741; www.forestry.gov.my; Jln Raja Chulan; 🕒9am-5pm) at the base of the hill.

ROYAL SELANGOR CLUB HISTORIC BUILDING

Map p248 (www.rscweb.my; Jln Raja; 🚇Masjid Jamek) Built in mock Tudor style and founded in 1884, this exclusive social club for the KL elite is where the running-and-drinking club, the Hash House Harriers, kicked off in 1938. Women are still said to be barred from its long bar, which has a view of the former playing fields.

MASJID JAMEK MOSQUE

Map p248 (Friday Mosque; off Jln Tun Perak; 🕒8.30am-12.30pm & 2.30-4pm Sat-Thu, 8.30-11am & 2.30-4pm Fri; 🚇Masjid Jamek) Chinatown's Muslim population prays at this beautiful onion-domed mosque which has recently undergone a restoration. Constructed in 1907 at the confluence of the Klang and Gombak rivers, the mosque is an island of serenity, with airy open pavilions shaded by palm trees. The designer was British architect AB Hubbock, who sought inspiration from the Mughal mosques of northern India.

Visitors are welcome outside prayer times, but please dress appropriately and remove your shoes before entering the mosque.

🍴 EATING

🍴 Chinatown & Around

⭐MADRAS LANE HAWKERS HAWKER $

Map p248 (Madras Lane; noodles RM5; 🕒8am-4pm Tue-Sun; 🚇Pasar Seni) Weave your way through Chinatown Wet Market to find this alley of hawker stalls. It's best visited for breakfast or lunch, with standout operators including the one offering 10 types of *yong tau fu* (tofu pockets stuffed with a fish and pork paste) in a fish broth (9.30am to 3.30pm) and, at the far end of the strip, the stall serving *asam* (tamarind) and curry laksa (8am to 2pm).

SS SPICY FOOD HAWKER $

Map p248 (Jln Belfield; meals RM5-8; 🕒6am-6pm Mon-Sat; monorail Maharajalela) On the edge of leafy Kampung Attap, this roadside hawker-stall complex is an ideal breakfast spot for its freshly made roti and onion omlettes. The Indian family who runs the place is very friendly and serves up a tempting selection of meat and veg dishes which can be enjoyed under the shade of rain trees.

CHEE CHEONG FUN STALL CHINESE $

Map p248 (Cnr Jln Petaling & Jln Hang Lekir; noodles RM4; 🕒Thu-Tue 7am-4pm; 🍴; 🚇Kota Raya) One of the best breakfasts in Chinatown can be had at this unprepossessing, decades-old stall tucked away just off the street. All it serves are melt-in-the-mouth *chee cheong fun* (rice noodles) doused with sweet and spicy sauces and a sprinkle of sesame seeds.

Further down Jln Hang Lekir, is the equally good congee (rice porridge) stall **Hon Kee** (Map p248; 93 Jln Hang Lekir; congee RM5; 🕒4.30am-3pm); try the rice porridge with frogs legs in a ginger and spring onion sauce.

KEDAI KOPI LAI FOONG HAWKER $

Map p248 (Jln Tun Tan Cheng Lock; noodles RM6; 🕒6.30am-10pm; 🚇Kota Raya) This old-school hawker-style cafe offers several excellent stalls under one roof on a prominent corner. The anchor is **Lai Foong** (Map p248; 138 Jln Tun Tan Cheng Lok; noodles RM7; 🕒7am-3.30pm), dishing up beef ball noodles since 1956; on Mondays you can ask for its special 'steak and balls' soup made with beef penis and testicles. Far less challenging are the creamy egg tarts and flaky pastries of Tony Kee.

RESTORAN YUSOOF DAN ZAKHIR INDIAN $

Map p248 (Jln Hang Kasturi; roti RM2; 🕒24hr; 🚇Pasar Seni) This huge banana-yellow and palm-tree-green canteen opposite Central Market serves huge portions of delicious *mamak* (Indian Muslim) food; perfect for a roti and curry sauce snack.

TANG CITY FOOD COURT $
Map p248 (Jln Hang Lekir; dishes RM5-10; ⏰8am-midnight; 🚇Kota Raya) Set back from the open-air tables on the main drag, this food court serves a good variety of inexpensive dishes.

⭐**PETER HOE BEYOND** INTERNATIONAL $$
Map p248 (2nd fl, Lee Rubber Bldg, 145 Jln Tun HS Lee; mains RM20; ⏰10am-7pm; 🚇Pasar Seni) You may find the affable Mr Hoe himself serving at this supremely relaxing cafe, where you can tuck into a great lunch of delicious quiche with masses of fresh salad, or just enjoy a cake and coffee in between forays around his stylishly merchandised retail space.

⭐**OLD CHINA CAFÉ** MALAY, NONYA $$
Map p248 (📞2072 5915; www.oldchina.com.my; 11 Jln Balai Polis; mains RM40-50; ⏰11.30am-10pm; 🚇Pasar Seni) Housed in the old guild hall of the Selangor & Federal Territory Laundry Association, this atmospheric cafe captures some of the charm of old KL. The walls are huge and covered with old bric-a-brac, and the cook prepares Nonya dishes from Melaka and Penang, including a fine beef rendang (coconut and lime-leaf curry) with coconut rice and fiery Nonya laksa soup with seafood.

IKAN PANGGANG HAWKER $$
Map p248 (📞019-315 9448; spicy seafood RM12; ⏰5-11pm Tue-Sun; 🚇Kota Raya) Tuck into spicy fish and seafood dishes and luscious chicken wings from this unsigned stall outside Hong Leong Bank, tucked behind the stalls on the corner of Jln Petaling and Jln Hang Lekir. Order ahead – it generally takes 20 minutes for your foil-wrapped pouch of seafood to cook, which allows time to explore the market. Wash the meal down with a glass of *mata kucing* (meaning 'cat's eye'), a refreshing Asian fruit drink, also bought from a stall on the same corner.

LOCAL KNOWLEDGE

TRADITIONAL CHINESE MEDICINE

Ng Chee Yat is the second-generation owner of Kien Fatt Medical Store (p224), a family pharmacy that has been operating in Chinatown since 1943. In 1997 Ng Chee Yat, along with some friends, started the **KL Academy of Traditional Chinese Medicine** (Map p248; 📞2026 5273; www.klatcm.com; 138-140 Jln Petaling; ⏰7-10pm Mon-Fri, 2-10pm Sat, 9am-6pm Sun; 🚇Pasar Seni), which provides training for those wanting to learn the ancient practices of traditional Chinese medicine (TCM). It runs year-long courses in English and operates as a drop-in clinic for patients.

What kind of ailments do patients bring to you for treatment? A variety of things, but mainly aches and pains, soft-tissue injuries and spinal diseases.

What's the fundamental difference between Western medicine and TCM? I could write a dissertation for you about that! Essentially, though, Chinese medicine is more holistic – a TCM doctor may talk about your body's fire, for example, and prescribe a course of treatment to reduce the heat, to cool your system. That may involve acupuncture, cupping, reflexology or a course of herbal remedies.

How much does a consultation cost? It's RM10 to see the doctor and RM20 if that's followed by a session of acupuncture.

How safe is acupuncture? Very safe. The needles are only used once and they are swabbed with alcohol before being used, too.

What kind of training do TCM doctors go through? The majority of students here are working adults, so they come three or four times a week in the evenings to study for three hours each session over five years. To graduate they then have to spend six months on practical training at the Heilongjiang University of Chinese medicine in Harbin, China.

What regulatory control is there of TCM in Malaysia? A bill on TCM is under consideration by the government currently.

PURPLE CANE TEA RESTAURANT
CHINESE $$

Map p248 (☑2272 3090; www.purplecane.com. my; 1 Jln Maharajalela; mains RM10-20; ⊗11am-10pm; monorail Maharajalela) Tucked behind the Chinese Assembly Hall, this laid-back place uses tea as an ingredient in most of its dishes. Intriguing specials include chicken soup with tea and ginseng, and beef simmered in lychee tea. There are also branches in Mid Valley Megamall (p112) and the Shaw Centre in Pudu.

KHUKRI
NEPALESE $$

Map p248 (☑2072 0663; http://thekhukri.blog spot.co.uk/; 1st fl, 26 Jln Tun Tan Siew Sing; meals RM20; ⊗9am-9pm; ⬚Kota Raya) A gathering point for Nepalis in KL, this simple restaurant serves authentic Nepalese cuisine including great *momo* (dumplings), steamed or fried, and spicy chicken and mutton dishes.

CAFÉ CAFÉ
FRENCH, ITALIAN $$$

(☑2141 8141; www.cafecafe.com.my; 175 Jln Maharajalela; mains RM80-100; ⊗6pm-midnight; ⬚Hang Tuah, monorail Hang Tuah) Flickering candles and twinkling crystal decorations conjure a romantic atmosphere at this quirky restaurant a short walk south of Chinatown. Avoid the fancy foie gras dishes; stick to simpler concoctions and you'll do fine.

PRECIOUS OLD CHINA
MALAY, NONYA $$$

Map p248 (☑2273 7372; www.oldchina.com.my; Mezzanine fl, Central Market, Jln Hang Kasturi; mains RM40-60; ⊗11.30am-10pm; ⬚Pasar Seni) The owners of Old China Café also run this upmarket place in Central Market. The menu and ambience is similar but not quite as good as its sibling.

Bukit Nanas & Around

HONG NGEK
CHINESE $

Map p248 (50 Jln Tun HS Lee; noodles RM5; ⊗10.30am-7pm Mon-Thu & Sat, to 5pm Fri, closed Sun; ⬚Masjid Jamek) This long-running Hokkien coffee shop serves expertly made fried *bee hoon* (vermicelli noodles), crab balls and succulent pork ribs stewed in Guinness. It has air-con upstairs, but it's more interesting to watch the world go by at a table on the naturally ventilated street level.

RESTORAN SANDO CHAPATI HOUSE
INDIAN $

Map p248 (11 Jln Tun HS Lee; chapati RM1.20; ⊗6.30am-6.30pm Mon-Sat; ⬚Masjid Jamek) Chapatis are freshly made at the entrance to this no-frills, self-serve cafe that offers one of the cheapest places to snack in the area.

SANGEETHA
INDIAN $

Map p248 (☑03-2032 3333; 65 Lr Ampang; meals RM10; ⊗8am-11pm; ☑; ⬚Masjid Jamek) This well-run vegetarian restaurant serves lots of South Indian delights such as *idli* (savoury, soft, fermented-rice-and-lentil cakes) and *masala dosa* (rice-and-lentil crepes stuffed with spiced potatoes).

★LOKL
INTERNATIONAL, MALAY $$

Map p248 (http://loklcoffee.com; 30 Jln Tun HS Lee; mains RM14-20; ☎; ⬚Masjid Jamek) From its clever name (local, geddit?) and slick design to its tasty twists on, well, local comfort foods, such as its cholesterol-bomb deep-fried Hainanese-meatloaf sandwich and dessert toasties, LOKL ticks all of the right boxes. Its local coffee comes from Kluang, and its Western-style brew is Illy.

★LA VIE EN ROSE
FRENCH $$$

Map p248 (☑03-2078 3883; www.cuisine-stu dio.net/; 39 Jln Raja Chulan; mains RM40-80; ⊗noon-2.30pm & 6.30-10.30pm Tue-Fri, 10am-10.30pm Sat & Sun; ☎; ⬚KL Tower) Based in an airy bungalow with terrace overlooking Bukit Nanas and KL Tower, this stylish place is best for a lazy weekend brunch (from RM50) when there's free flow of breads and pasteries from the restaurant's own bakery.

ATMOSPHERE 360
MALAY, INTERNATIONAL $$$

Map p248 (☑2020 2020; www.atmosphere360. com.my; Menara KL, 2 Jln Puncak; buffet lunch/afternoon tea/dinner RM88/58/198; ⊗noon-2.30pm & 6.30-11pm; ⬚KL Tower) Watch KL pass by from this revolving restaurant atop Menara KL (KL Tower). The lunch and dinner buffets feature a wide range of Malay dishes and are consistently good. Book for evening meals, especially sunset dining. There's a dress code but the staff will provide men wearing shorts with a sarong (to cover the legs).

CHINATOWN, MERDEKA SQUARE & BUKIT NANAS EATING

LOCAL KNOWLEDGE

CHINATOWN BARS

Chinatown has few formal bars, and sinking cold beers at the open-air restaurants around Jln Petaling night market is what many visitors quite rightly prefer to do. Many of the backpacker lodges also have bars, some such as Reggae Mansion (p132), on their roofs.

CUISINE GOURMET
BY NATHALIE
FRENCH $$$

Map p248 (☑03-2072 4452; www.cuisinegourmetbynathalie.com; Menara Taipan, Jln Punchak; mains RM45-90; ☎; ☐KL Tower) Having made her mark with a smaller outlet in Publika (p111), Nathalie gets more creative in this fine-dining space, elegantly decked out in mauve and grey. The bento-style lunches are a bargain and the desserts sublime.

DRINKING & NIGHTLIFE

★AKU CAFE & GALLERY
CAFE

Map p248 (☑03-2857 6887; www.facebook.com/akucafegallery; 1st fl, 8 Jln Panggong; ☎; ☐Pasir Seni) An Asian contemporary chic vibe pervades this gourmet coffee haunt serving beans roasted using hi-tech Japanese technology in Taiwan. Tempting cake treats supplement the drinks which include mint and lemon iced coffees. Exhibitions change on a monthly basis and there are some nice local craft souvenirs for sale.

★LUNA
BAR

Map p248 (☑2332 7777; Menara PanGlobal, Jln Punchak; ☺3pm-1am, to 3am Fri & Sat; ☐KL Tower) A twinkling view of KL's skyline is guaranteed at this sophisticated rooftop bar surrounding a swimming pool. Also up here, inside and facing towards KL Tower, is the smoke-free Cristallo, a playboy-esque bar lined with silver velour sofas and draped with strings of glittering crystals.

★REGGAE BAR
BAR

Map p248 (www.reggaebarkl.com; 158 Jln Tun HS Lee; ☺noon-late; ☐Pasar Seni) Travellers gather in droves at this pumping bar in the thick of Chinatown, which has out-door seats if you'd like to catch the passing parade. There are beer promos, pool tables and pub grub served till late. Reggae Mansion (p132) also has a stylish bar and there's another **Reggae Bar** (Map p252; www.reggaebarkl.com; 31 Changat Bukit Bintang; ☺noon-late; monorail Raja Chulan) in the Golden Triangle.

MOONTREE HOUSE
CAFE

Map p248 (www.moontree-house.blogspot.com; 1st fl, 6 Jln Panggong; ☺10am-8pm Wed-Mon; ☎; ☐Pasar Seni) A quiet space for a coffee, also selling cute handicrafts and feminist literature.

PURPLE CANE TEA HOUSE
TEAHOUSE

Map p248 (www.purplecane.my; 3rd fl, 6 Jln Panggong; ☺11am-8pm; ☐Pasar Seni) Serves a broad range of Chinese green and jasmine teas in a relaxing setting.

☆ ENTERTAINMENT

PANGGUNG BANDARAYA
THEATRE

Map p248 (DBKL City Theatre; Jln Tun Perak; ☐Masjid Jamek) Orginally designed as the City Hall by AB Hubback, this handsome 1896 building has been refitted inside to become one of KL's most beautiful theatrical spaces. The intimate auditorium's design is based on the shape of a Malaysian kite. Join Visit KL's walking tour of Merdeka Square to gain access to the building and see a short Malaysian dance performance here.

The venue has been used as the stage for reality-TV shows *Malaysian Idol* and *So You Think You Can Dance*.

MABA STADIUM
SPECTATOR SPORTS

Map p248 (☑2078 0055; www.malaysia-basketball.com; 6 Jln Hang Jebat; ☐Pasar Seni) Check its website to find out about matches held at the headquarters of the Malaysian Basketball Association. There's also a training court on the roof.

SHOPPING

★PETALING STREET MARKET
MARKET

Map p248 (Jln Petaling; ☺noon-11pm; ☐Kota Raya) Malaysia's relaxed attitude towards counterfeit goods is well illustrated at this heavily hyped night market bracketed by traditional Chinese gateways. In fact, traders start to fill Jln Petaling from midmorning until the whole street is jam-packed with market stalls selling everything from fake Gucci handbags and pirate DVDs to bunches of lychees.

⭐**PETER HOE EVOLUTION**   HOMEWARES
Map p248 (2 Jln Hang Lekir; ⊘10am-7pm; 🚇Pasar Seni) Both here and at the much bigger Peter Hoe Beyond (p80) around the corner you can satisfy practically all your gift- and souvenir-buying needs, with selections from the KL-based designer's creative and affordable range of original batik designs on sarongs, shirts, dresses and home furnishings. The shops also stock an impressive range of Asian home-decor items as well as silver jewellery. The Beyond branch has a cafe that's worth visiting in its own right.

⭐**JUNK BOOKSTORE**   BOOKS
Map p248 (☑03-2078 3822; 78 Jln Tun HS Lee; ⊘8.30am-5pm Mon-Fri, 8.30am-2pm Sat; 🚇Masjid Jamek) One of KL's best second-hand bookstores with thousands of titles piled

high on a couple of floors. Ask staff to show you its selection of antique local titles but don't expect to get them for bargain prices!

JUSTIN YAP   FASHION
Map p248 (www.justinyap.com; 2nd fl, Lee Rubber Bldg, 145 Jln Tun HS Lee; ⊘10am-7pm; 🚇Pasar Seni) The atelier of one of Malaysian fashion's rising young stars is tucked away inside his uncle Peter Hoe's shop. Come here for elegant custom-made gowns and pretty shoes, as well as some off-the-peg items.

BASKET SHOP   HANDICRAFTS
Map p248 (www.thebasketshop.com.my; 10 Jln Panggong; ⊘9.30am-5.30pm Mon-Sat; 🚇Pasar Seni) All kinds of bamboo and woven straw baskets and decorative boxes – lots of ribbons too – are to be found here, perfect for perfectionist present wrappers!

KWONG YIK SENG   ARTS & CRAFTS
Map p248 (☑03-2078 3620; 144 Jln Tun HS Lee; ⊘9am-5pm Mon-Sat; 🚇Pasar Seni) Looking for traditional Chinese teapots, bowls or a kitsch ornament to put on your mantlepiece? Your search is over at this shop that

---

CENTRAL MARKET

Based in an historically significant building, Central Market (p77) offers KL's best selection of souvenirs, gifts and traditional crafts such as batik and kites. The complex is divided between the old market hall and the newer Annexe – at the back of the former you'll find several Asian artefacts and antiques dealers, but you'll need to bargain hard to get good deals. Among our favourite stalls are the following:

Art House Gallery Museum of Ethnic Arts (Map p248; 1st fl, Annexe; 🚇Masjid Jamek) Like stumbling into Indiana Jones' closet. Even if you're not interested in buying, it's fascinating to browse this impressive collection of ethnographic arts from the region and as far afield as Tibet.

Eco Warna & Fine Batik (Map p248; www.finebatik.com; G45 ground fl & MS04 mezzanine fl, Main Bldg; 🚇Pasar Seni) Offers a good selection of modern batik cloth paintings (many of them by Indonesian artists) as well as organically dyed batik clothing and material.

Rhino (Map p248; KB17 ground fl, Main Bldg; 🚇Pasar Seni) Charming hand-painted clogs and handicrafts. The soles of the shoes are made from the wood of the durian tree.

Songket Sutera Asli (Map p248; M53 mezzanine fl, Main Bldg; 🚇Pasar Seni) Fine-quality decorative weavings and embroidery in silver and gold thread.

Tanamera (Map p248; www.tanamera.com.my; G25 ground fl, Main Bldg; 🚇Pasar Seni) Malaysian-brand spa products made from 100% natural materials, including detox infusions, essential oils and various balms.

Wau Tradisi (Map p248; M51 mezzanine fl, Main Bldg; 🚇Pasar Seni) Eye-catching selection of traditional paper and bamboo kites, including the giant *wau bulan* (moon kites) from Kelantan.

specialises in new and antique-style china and porcelain.

SANG KEE
HANDICRAFTS

Map p248 (64 Jln Tun Perak; ☉9.30am-3.30pm Mon-Fri, to 1.30pm Sat; 🚇Masjid Jamek) Back in 1920 when Sang Kee started, all its rattan cane and bamboo baskets and furnishings were made locally. Now, the aged uncles who run this atmospheric emporium will tell you most items come from China.

SPORTS & ACTIVITIES

CHIN WOO STADIUM
SWIMMING

Map p248 (☏2072 4602; www.chinwoo.org.my; Jln Hang Jebat , Chinatown; swimming adult/child RM4/1.50; ☉2-8pm Mon-Fri, 9am-8pm Sat & Sun; 🚇Pasar Seni) The highlight of this historic sports stadium atop a hill overlooking Chinatown is its 50m outdoor pool. All swimsuits must be tight fitting, ie no baggy shorts. In the stadium itself yoga classes are held every Monday at 7.30pm and there are badminton courts to rent.

Masjid India, Kampung Baru & Northern KL

MASJID INDIA | CHOW KIT | KAMPUNG BARU | TITIWANGSA | SENTUL

Neighbourhood Top Five

❶ Meandering around **Kampung Baru** (p90), a low-rise Malay village in the heart of the high-rise city where many residents live in traditional wooden houses fronted by flower gardens.

❷ Stimulating your senses at the market **Bazaar Baru Chow Kit** (p87), pausing to sample local delicacies.

❸ Immersing yourself in the Saturday **night market** (p91) around Masjid India, Kuala Lumpur's other Little India.

❹ Viewing works by Malaysia's top modern and contemporary artists at the **National Visual Arts Gallery** (p89).

❺ Jogging or strolling around **Lake Titiwangsa** (p91) and admiring the panoramic view of the city skyline.

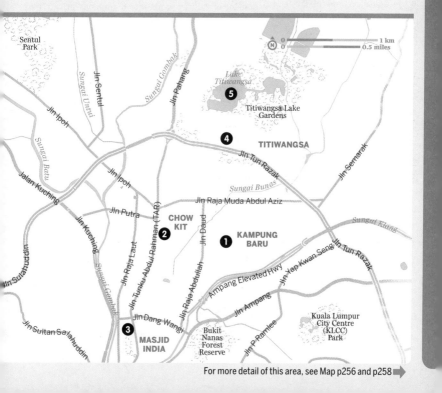

For more detail of this area, see Map p256 and p258 ➡

Lonely Planet's Top Tip

If you're in town over the weekend, don't miss the Saturday pasar malam (night market; p91) on Lg Tuanku Abdul Rahman, held from around 3pm until late.

Best Places to Eat

➡ Yut Kee (p91)

➡ Kin Kin (p92)

➡ Capital Café (p91)

➡ Thai-la (p91)

➡ Mungo Jerry (p92)

For reviews, see p91 ➡

Best Places to Drink

➡ Omakase + Appreciate (p93)

➡ Coliseum Cafe (p93)

➡ Bistro Richard (p93)

For reviews, see p93 ➡

Best Entertainment

➡ Kuala Lumpur Performing Arts Centre (p94)

➡ Istana Budaya (p94)

➡ Sutra Dance Theatre (p94)

For reviews, see p94 ➡

Explore: Masjid India, Kampung Baru & Northern KL

For decades the area around Masjid India had been known as 'Little India'. However, in 2010 part of Brickfields was dubbed KL's 'official' Little India. Being stripped of its title has done nothing to alter the essential subcontinental impact of Masjid India, sandwiched between Jln TAR and Jln Munshi Abdullah. Visit during the bustling *pasar malam* (night market) on Saturday for maximum India-meets-Malaysia atmosphere.

Mostly northeast of Jln Sultan Ismail is Kampung Baru, meaning 'new village'. The land here was reserved for Malays by the colonial administration in the 1890s, and the leafy residential streets are still lined with charming wooden houses. It's a lovely area for casual strolls and for marvelling at the contrast with the skyscrapers of the KLCC and Golden Triangle in the background. Spread around the northern end of Jln TAR, Chow Kit is named after tin miner and city councillor Loke Chow Kit. The zone's rep for sex and drugs mean it's not a good idea to explore this area by night, but don't miss it by day for its magnificent wet and dry market and tasty places to eat.

North of here are a couple of green spaces that also merit exploration: Lake Titiwangsa for the park and the National Visual Arts Gallery; and Sentul West, a redevelopment of railway yards into a gorgeous private park, home to the excellent Kuala Lumpur Performing Arts Centre and a couple of pleasant places to eat and drink.

Local Life

➡**Performing arts** Catch local drama, dance shows and movies at the Kuala Lumpur Performing Arts Centre (p94), based in the leafy surrounds of Sentul West.

➡**Markets** Shop for cheap clothes and fresh food at the Kampung Baru Pasar Minggu (Sunday Market; p90), which starts on Saturday night and finishes in the small hours of Sunday morning.

➡**Movies** Enjoy Indian movies at the retro Coliseum Cinema (p94) or take in the latest blockbuster at Cap Square's multiplex.

Getting There & Away

➡**Monorail** Convenient stops for this area are Medan Tuanku, Chow Kit and Titiwangsa.

➡**LRT** The Ampang–Sentul Timur line and Gombak–Kelana Jaya have stations in these areas.

➡**KTM Komuter** Take the Batu Caves line to Bank Negara and Sentul.

➡**Walking** Masjid India and Kampung Baru are easily and best explored on foot.

⊙ SIGHTS

are fact-laden exhibitions on the region's currency and Malaysia's economic history.

⊙ Masjid India & Around

LOKE MANSION   HISTORIC BUILDING
Map p256 (☎2691 0803; 273A Jln Medan Tuanku; monorail Medan Tuanku) Rescued from the brink of dereliction by the law firm Cheang & Ariff, Loke Mansion was once the home of self-made tin tycoon Loke Yew, although the original part of the structure was built in the 1860s by another rich merchant, Cheow Ah Yeok. The Japanese high command also set up base here in 1942. After years of neglect, the mansion has been beautifully restored; access to the interior is by appointment only, but you're welcome anytime to pause in the driveway and admire the whitewashed exterior.

BANK NEGARA
MALAYSIA MUSEUM
& ART GALLERY   MUSEUM, ART GALLERY
Map p256 (http://museum.bnm.gov.my; 2 Jln Dato Onn, ☺10am 6pm; ⊠Bank Negara) `FREE`
The national bank's conservatively chosen but attractive art collection is housed in a futuristic, metal-clad complex (designed by top Malaysian architect Hijjas Kasturi) uphill from Bank Negara train station in a leafy area. Also in the monetary complex

MASJID INDIA   MOSQUE
Map p256 (http://masjidindia.com; Jln Masjid India; ⊠Masjid Jamek) Clad with polished red granite, fronted by a busy market and surrounded by stalls selling religious items and traditional Malay costumes, this is the mosque that now lends its name to the area. The original wooden mosque was built here in 1883 and replaced by the current structure in 1963. The area's famous Saturday *pasar malam* runs along Lg TAR behind the mosque.

⊙ Chow Kit & Kampung Baru

★**BAZAAR BARU CHOW KIT**   MARKET
Map p256 (Chow Kit Market; 469-473 Jln TAR; ☺8am-9pm; monorail Chow Kit) Middle- and upper-class KLites give this chaotic wet market a wide berth but tourists and the less moneyed locals love it. Apart from freshly butchered meat and filleted fish, there's a staggering array of weird and wonderful tropical fruit and vegetables on sale here, as well as clothes, toys, buckets, stationery, noodles, spices and other commodities. Pushing through the narrow

---

KAMPUNG BARU PAST & PRESENT

Worried about the declining number of Malay residents in the capital, the British set aside 224 hectares of land in the late 1890s on what was then the outskirts of Kuala Lumpur as protected Malay agricultural land. Settlers were encouraged to plant crops in this new village – Kampung Baru. In what seems like a miracle in 21st-century KL, Kampung Baru continues to look very much like a Malay village – albeit minus the vegetable patches and rice paddies. This also means that alongside well-maintained traditional wooden homes you also have unsightly shanty shacks. Apart from Malays, immigrant Indonesians and Thai Muslims also live here.

With an estimated 4200 beneficiaries across 880 separate lots, overnight changes for Kampung Baru were never on the cards. In 2011 the government set up the Kampung Baru Development Corporation (KBDC) to help manage the area's redevelopment by matching landowners with potential investors. Many local residents fought against this move and remain suspicious of the government's overall intentions even though they recognise that development is needed and will likely happen. It's easy to understand the residents' position when Khai Ibrahim, a board member of KBDC, has said, 'There's never been a concrete plan for the development of Kampung Baru.'

In the meantime, Visit KL (p226) at least is hoping that the area's distinct Malay traditional architecture doesn't evaporate overnight: it has plans to start a guided walking tour of the area similar to the ones it also offers around Merdeka Square and Brickfields.

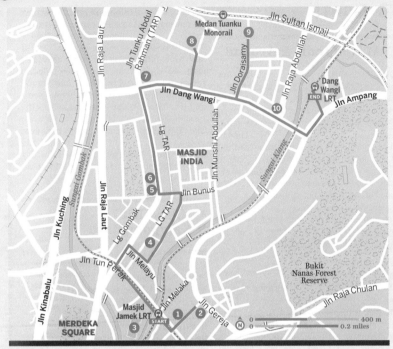

Neighbourhood Walk
Masjid India Ramble

START MASJID JAMEK LRT STATION
END DANG WANGI LRT STATION
LENGTH 1.5KM; 1½ HOURS

From the LRT station walk one block south-east to Lebuh Ampang. Lined with money changers, Indian cafes, and street vendors selling sweets and flower garlands, this street has long been the preserve of the Chettiars from south India. Note the **1 old shophouses** at Nos 16 to 18 and 24 to 30, and the ceramic peacock tiles on the **2 Chettiar House**.

Return to the station, next to which is the venerable **3 Masjid Jamek** (p79). Opposite, Jln Melayu curves around to the covered arcade of market stalls at the pedestrianised end of Jln Masjid India. Pick your way through the tightly packed stalls to find the Indian Muslim mosque **4 Masjid India** (p87). The area is a riot of sari stalls, gold jewellers and DVD and CD shops playing Bollywood soundtracks at full blast. The atmosphere is enhanced on Saturday after-noon when a *pasar malam* (night market) sets up along Lg TAR, the lane sandwiched between Jln TAR and Jln Masjid India.

Next door to the **5 Coliseum Thea-tre** (p94), at the south end of Jln TAR, is another colonial relic – the **6 Coliseum Cafe** (p92), where Somerset Maugham once drank. Stop here for a reviving beer or meal, then continue north along Jln TAR past scores of colourful fabric shops.

Barely recognisable beneath huge ban-ner ads, another art deco movie house, the **7 Odeon**, is on the corner at the cross-roads of Jln Dang Wangi and Jln TAR. Head east along Jln Dang Wangi, taking the first road on the left: on the next corner, oppo-site the car park, is the grand colonial era **8 Loke Mansion** (p87).

The parallel street to the east is Jln Do-raisamy, a strip of restored shophouses turned into bars, clubs and restaurants and rebranded **9 Asian Heritage Row**. Con-tinue down Jln Dang Wangi to the venerable *kopitiam* (coffee shop) **10 Yut Kee** (p91). Dang Wangi LRT is nearby.

aisles is a heady sensory experience. It's also a great place to sample local hawker food and drinks.

TATT KHALSA
DIWAN GURDWARA   SIKH TEMPLE

Map p256 (24 Jln Raja Alang; monorail Chow Kit) A short stroll east along Jln Raja Alang behind Bazaar Baru Chow Kit brings you to the largest Sikh temple in Southeast Asia, spiritual home of KL's 75,000 Sikhs. There's been a temple and school here since 1924 – the present building dates from the 1990s and is open to visitors.

MASJID JAMEK KAMPUNG BARU   MOSQUE

Map p258 (Jln Raja Alang; 🚇Kampung Baru) Built in 1924, Kampung Baru's principal mosque sports a handsome gateway decorated with eye-catching tiles in traditional Islamic patterns. Stalls around the mosque sell religious paraphernalia, including white *kopia* and black *songkok,* the traditional head coverings for Malay Muslim men. Outside the mosque look for the map that shows the seven smaller villages that make up Kampung Baru.

SULTAN SULAIMAN CLUB   HISTORIC BUILDING

Map p258 (Bangunan Warisan Kelab Sultan Suleiman; Jln Datuk Abdul Razak; 🚇Kampung Baru) Dating back to 1909, this is the oldest Malay club in KL and is said to be where the meetings that led to the establishment of the political party United Malays National Organisation (UMNO; the lead party in the ruling coalition) took place. The white-washed wooden club building with a steeply pitched Malay-style roof was restored and reopened with much ceremony in 2007. The building is closed to the general public but you can admire it across the football field or walk up for a closer look.

◉ Titiwangsa & Sentul

NATIONAL VISUAL
ARTS GALLERY   ART GALLERY

Map p258 (Balai Seni Lukis Negara; 📞4026 7000; www.artgallery.gov.my; 2 Jln Temerloh; ◷10am-6pm; monorail Titiwangsa) **FREE** Occupying a pyramid-shaped block, the NVAG showcases modern and contemporary Malaysian art. There are often interesting temporary shows of local and regional artists, as well as pieces from the gallery's permanent collection of 4000 pieces, including paintings by Zulkifi Moh'd Dohalan, Wong Hoi Cheong, Ahad Osman and the renowned batik artist Chuah Than Teng. Overall though, the gallery lacks a wow factor.

The interior is dominated by a swirly Guggenheim Museum–style staircase that provides access to the main galleries. The side staircases also are used to showcase artworks. A new addition on the ground floor is the **National Portrait Gallery**.

MASJID INDIA, KAMPUNG BARU & NORTHERN KL SIGHTS

WORTH A DETOUR

P RAMLEE MEMORIAL

In the 1950s and early '60s there was no bigger star in Malaysia than P Ramlee. The brief life of the charismatic singer, actor and movie director, who died in 1973 from a heart attack aged only 44, is chronicled at the **P Ramlee Memorial** (Pustaka Peringatan P Ramlee; www.arkib.gov.my; 2 Jln Dedap, Taman P Ramlee, Setapak; ◷10am-5pm Tue-Sun, closed noon-3pm Fri; monorail Titiwangsa, then taxi) **FREE**, a short taxi ride north of Titiwangsa.

The modest bungalow Ramlee shared with his wife Saloma, also a famous singer, has been remodelled to incorporate displays about the some 250-plus songs and 66 movies he starred in, along with the personal ephemera such as handwritten lyrics and his piano. For RM3 you can dress up in copies of costumes worn by Ramlee and Saloma, who had previously been married to Ramlee's costar and best friend AR Tompel.

Ramlee may be a legend today, with a road named after him in Kuala Lumpur, but when he died he was reportedly penniless, his style of music and movies having gone out of vogue. His final song, and title of an unmade movie, was *Tears of Kuala Lumpur (Air Mata di Kuala Lumpur)*, its melancholic lyrics reflecting Ramlee's feelings of failure and loss. His grave lies beside those of Saloma and Tompel in the Islamic Cemetery on Jln Ampang.

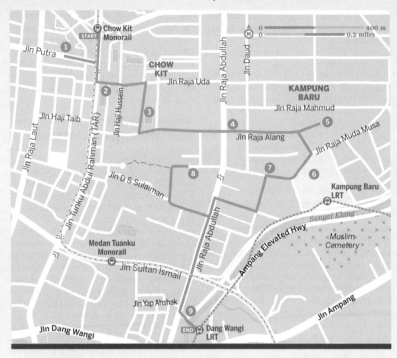

Neighbourhood Walk
Architecture of Chow Kit & Kampung Baru

START CHOW KIT MONORAIL STATION
END DANG WANGI LRT STATION
LENGTH 3.5KM; TWO HOURS

Walk south on Jln TAR, turn right into Jln Putra and continue to **1 No 41**, 1 a tiny wooden house squashed between a pink-painted shoe shop and a mobile phone outlet – this solitary survivor of old Chow Kit is a foretaste of the many traditional houses in Kampung Baru.

Return to Jln TAR and cross over to the entrance to **2 Bazaar Baru Chow Kit** (p87). Explore the market's shaded alleys and hangars, pausing for a snack or a drink along the way. Emerge, blinking into the bright light, on Jln Raja Alang, heading east past the Sikh temple **3 Tatt Khalsa Diwan Gurdwara** (p89). Further along is **4 Masjid Jamek Kampung Baru** (p89), the area's principal mosque.

Where Jln Raja Alang turns south, continue on the smaller road ahead to the end where you'll turn right at a two-level apart-ment block: **5 two palms** in a small field perfectly frame the Petronas Towers. South of here is the **6 Pasar Minggu**, one of the most attractive areas of Kampung Baru with a community stage and small wooden houses surrounding an open area where the Saturday night market is held.

At the junction of Jln Raja Muda Musa and Jln Raja Mahadi stands a photogenic **7 turquoise and white painted house**; explore Jln Raja Mahadi and the cross streets to see more such traditional wooden houses. Cross Jln Raja Abdullah to Jln Dewan Sultan Sulaiman. At the end of a playing field is the handsome black-and-white painted **8 Sultan Sulaiman Club** (p89); approach via the entrance by RHC Healthcare for a closer look.

South along Jln Raja Abdullah you'll pass more wooden homes as the concrete city starts to resume. Just before the end of this walk, at the footbridge across to Dang Wangi LRT station look carefully for one more **9 wooden yellow house** nestling behind the Jumaat Special Nasi Briani food stall.

★**TITIWANGSA LAKE GARDENS**   PARK
Map p258 (Taman Tasik Titiwangsa; Jln Tembeling; monorail Titiwangsa) This relaxing recreational park, a 10-minute walk east of the Titiwangsa monorail station, surrounds Lake Titiwangsa. As well as walking and jogging paths and jolly boating on the lake (from RM3 per hour), there are tennis courts (8am to 7pm/7pm to 11pm RM5/10 per hour), squash courts (8am to 11pm RM6 per hour) and table tennis (RM2 per hour).

With its picture-postcard view of the city skyline, the park is a favourite spot for courting Malaysian couples – and the religious police on the lookout for improper behaviour.

SENTUL WEST   PARK
(www.sentul-lifestyle.com/sentul_west.htm; Jln Strachan, Sentul; 🚇Sentul) This private park is meant for the residents of the development's condos and those that work in the former railway shed buildings converted into modern offices. That said, KLPAC (p94) is here and if you're coming for a show or to patronise the restaurants and cafes in the park, save some time to also partially explore the area (security guards are likely to stop you going too far).

✗ EATING

✗ Masjid India

★**MASJID INDIA PASAR MALAM (NIGHT MARKET)**   MARKET $
Map p256 (Lg TAR; ⊙3pm-midnight Sat; 🚇Masjid Jamek) If you're in town on Saturday, don't miss the *pasar malam* (night market) that runs the length of Lg Tuanku Abdul Rahman, the alley between the Jln TAR and Masjid India from around 3pm until late. There are plenty of stalls serving excellent Malay, Indian and Chinese snacks and drinks.

CAPITAL CAFÉ   MALAY $
Map p256 (213 Jln TAR; dishes RM3.50-5; ⊙7am-8.30pm Mon-Sat; 🚇Bandaraya) Since it opened in 1956 this truly Malaysian cafe has had Chinese, Malays and Indians all working together in the same space. Try its excellent mee goreng or *rojak* (salad doused in a peanut-sauce dressing) or satay (only available in the evenings).

ⓘ RAMADAN MARKETS

Kampung Baru is a great area to visit during Ramadan when street markets offer delicacies prepared specially to break the daily fast. Just remember not to start eating until after sundown.

SAGAR   INDIAN $
Map p256 (☎2691 3088; Semua House, Jln Masjid India; meals RM10; ⊙8am-8pm; 🚇Masjid Jamek) Enjoy the good-value *thali* meals (rice or bread served with assorted vegetables and curries for under RM10) at this footpath cafe, and soak up the street life of Masjid India. There's air-con inside.

MASJID INDIA HAWKER COURT   HAWKER $
Map p256 (Jln Masjid India; meals RM2-10; ⊙8am-9pm; 🚇Masjid Jamek) A bustling covered hawker court serving all the usual Malay, Indian and Chinese favourites. Good to visit if you can't visit the Saturday *pasar malam*.

RESTORAN BUHARRY   INDIAN MUSLIM $
Map p256 (22-24 Jln Doriaswamy; meals RM10-15; ⊙6am-late Mon-Sat, 8.30am-1am Sun; monorail Medan Tuanku) Popular hang-out for office workers during the day and late-night clubbers on Asian Heritage Row. All the usual *mamak* (Indian Muslim) favourites are on offer, plus excellent tom yum soup and delicious mango smoothies.

★**YUT KEE**   CHINESE, WESTERN $$
Map p256 (☎2698 8108; 35 Jln Dang Wangi; meals RM10-15; ⊙7.30am-4.45pm; 🚇Dang Wangi) It doesn't matter how busy it gets at this beloved Hainanese *kopitiam*, the staff remain calm and polite. Skip the Western dishes and go for the house specialities such as toast with homemade *kaya* (coconut-cream jam), *roti babi* (deep-fried bread filled with shredded pork and onions) or the fried Hokkien mee noodles. Its roast rolled pork with apple sauce, available from Friday to Sunday, usually sells out by 2.30pm.

★**THAI-LA**   THAI $$
Map p256 (☎2698 4933; Ground fl, CapSquare; meals RM20-30; ⊙noon-10pm Mon-Sat; 🚇Dang Wangi) One of the best dining options at the CapSquare complex. The food's tasty

LOCAL KNOWLEDGE

BAZAAR BARU CHOW KIT EATS

Great hawker food is found inside Bazaar Baru Chow Kit (p87); the atmosphere is lively, the food tasty and cheap and you can pick up an astonishing variety of tropical fruit for dessert. Look out for the following:

Pak Ngah Bihun Sup (noodles RM5; ☻10am-7pm) Not for the fainthearted: the intensely flavoursome broth for these noodles is drawn from a cauldron in which cows' livers bubble ominously. Ask for it spicy and pay a little more if you want an extra topping of offal. At the north end of the market on the main cooked-food alley.

Nazri (cakes from 40 sen; ☻9am-7pm) Nearby to Pak Ngah Bihun Sup is this stall serving an excellent selection of *kueh* – traditional Malay cakes.

Nam Kee (☻7am-9pm) Buried at the eastern back of the market, this is one of a series of tiny coffee stalls that are like time capsules transporting you back decades to old Kuala Lumpur.

and made by Thai chefs, the decor has a chic charm, and Zaki, the entertainingly camp owner, can talk the hind legs off a donkey.

COLISEUM CAFE INTERNATIONAL **$$**
Map p256 (☏2692 6270; 100 Jln TAR; meals RM15-60; ☻10am-10pm; ᵯMasjid Jamek) Little seems to have changed here – including the aged waiters! – since Somsert Maugham tucked into its famous sizzling steaks and downed a G'n'T in the bar next door. A colonial KL classic, not to be missed, it also serves Chinese food.

SARAVANAA BHAVAN INDIAN VEGETARIAN **$$**
(www.saravanabhavan.com; 1007 Selangor Mansion, Jln Masjid India; meals RM10-20; ☻8am-10.30pm; ☏; ᵯMasjid Jamek) This global chain of restaurants offers some of the best quality Indian food you'll find in KL. Their banana-leaf and mini-tiffin feasts are supremely tasty and you can also sample southern Indian classics such as *masala dosa*. There's also branches in Brickfields and Bangsar Baru.

✗ Chow Kit & Kampung Baru

★**KIN KIN** CHINESE **$**
Map p256 (40 Jln Dewan Sultan Sulaiman; noodles RM6.30; ☻7am-6.30pm; monorail Medan Tuanku) These 'dry' noodles, topped with a soft boiled egg, minced pork, *ikan bilis* (small, deep-fried anchovies), fried onion and a special spicy chilli sauce, are one of KL's great taste sensations. They come with a side of clear soup made from potato leaves and egg. If you don't eat pork, staff do a version topped with mushrooms.

There's also a branch in the EAT food court at Publika.

IKAN BAKAR BEREMPAH HAWKER **$**
Map p258 (Gerak Pak Lang, Jln Raja Muda Musa; meals RM5-10; ☻24hr; ᵯKampung Baru) If you can't make it to Kampung Baru for its Saturday *pasar malam*, head to this excellent barbecued-fish stall, within a hawker-stall market covered by a zinc roof. Once you've picked your fish off the grill there's a long buffet of great Malay *kampung*-style side dishes you can add to it.

KAK SOM MALAY **$**
Map p258 (Jln Raja Muda Musa; meals RM7; ☻8am-3am; ᵯKampung Baru) Specialising in some east coast peninsular Malaysian dishes such as *nasi kerabu* (blue rice), this is the place to dine inexpensively on the main Kampung Baru restaurant strip. Take your pick of items from the buffet along with rice, sit down and the waitstaff will come to take a drink order and tally up your bill.

It also serves BBQ cockles and *kueh*, traditional Malay cakes.

★**MUNGO JERRY** CHINESE **$$**
Map p256 (292 Jln Raja Laut; Bak kut-teh RM10; ☻7pm-6am; ᵯSultan Ismail) This late-night supper hot spot on the edge of Chow Kit is a bare-bones joint that's famous for its chilli-infused pork curry stew, *bak kut-teh*, as well as the original more soupy version. The bequiffed old rocker owner, who is nicknamed Mungo (his brother is Jerry), will likely entertain you with his life story.

✕ Titiwangsa & Sentul

🍷 DRINKING & NIGHTLIFE

D'ISTANA JALAMAS CAFÉ MALAY $

Map p258 (☎4025 3161; Jln Tun Razak, Titiwangsa; mains from RM5; ◉7am-8pm Mon-Fri; monorail Titiwangsa) The cafe at Istana Budaya offers a serve-yourself buffet of Malay and *mamak* favourites such as fish-head curry, salads, snacks and fresh fruit in classier-than-average surroundings. Balcony seats overlook nearby Titiwangsa Park. It's open at weekends if there's a show on at the theatre.

★TOMMY LE BAKER BAKERY, CAFE $$

(☎4043 2546; www.tommylebaker.com; B-LG-7 Viva Residency, 378 Jln Ipoh, Sentul; quiche & sandwiches RM9-20; ◉10am-4pm Tue-Sun; 🚈KTM Sentul) You're not going to meet anyone as passionate about sourdough and baking in KL as Tommy Lee, aka Tommy Le Baker. Trained in Paris, Tommy now bakes amazing breads and pastries at this tiny Sentul outlet tucked around the back of the Viva Residency complex. It also serves good coffee, hearty sandwiches and lovely quiches.

SAMIRA THAI $$

(☎012-921 3880; www.samiraasianterrace.com; Sentul Park, Jln Strachan; mains RM30-60; ◉noon-10.30pm; 🚈Sentul) Overlooking the koi pond and lake at Sentul Park, and very romantic at night when lit by flickering candles. It serves decent Thai and Vietnamese food, with set lunches (served Monday to Friday, around RM25) a good deal.

There are also several bars and cafes at CapSquare (p94) and Asian Heritage Row (Map p256) but neither location has managed to consistently attract the party crowd.

★OMAKASE + APPRECIATE COCKTAIL BAR

Map p248 (www.facebook.com/OmakaseAppreciate; Basement, Bangunan Ming Annexe, 9 Jln Ampang; ◉5pm-1am Wed-Sun; 🚈Masjid Jamek) Shawn Chong and Karl Too are the expert mixologists at this cosy, retro cocktail bar that's one of KL's top secret drinking spots. Sip sophisticated concoctions such as an Earl Grey Mar-tea-ni. Part of the fun is finding the entrance: look for the sign saying 'no admittance'.

★COLISEUM CAFE BAR

Map p256 (http://colseumcafe2012.blogspot.co.uk; 100 Jln TAR; ◉10am-10pm; 🚈Masjid Jamek) The kind of bar in which colonial planters and clerks would have knocked back stouts and G'n'Ts while moaning about the natives. This 1921-era watering hole oozes nostalgia and is worthy of a visit even if you don't eat a meal at the adjoining grill room.

★BISTRO RICHARD CAFE, BAR

(☎4041 3277; www.bistrorichard.com; Lot 268 Jln Strachan, Sentul West; ◉2-11pm Tue-Fri, noon-11pm Sat & Sun; 🚈Sentul) A French style cafe-bar complete with checked red tablecloths in the surrounds of a Japanese Zen rock garden is slightly culturally confusing. Nonetheless, this bistro is a very pleasant

MASJID INDIA, KAMPUNG BARU & NORTHERN KL DRINKING & NIGHTLIFE

WORTH A DETOUR

ROYAL SELANGOR VISITOR CENTRE

Located 8km northeast of the city centre is the **Royal Selangor Visitor Centre** (☎4145 6122; http://visitorcentre.royalselangor.com; 4 Jln Usahawan Enam, Setepak Jaya; ◉9am-5pm; 🚈Wangsa Maju, then taxi), the main factory of the world's largest pewter manufacturer. On sale in the centre's galleries are some very appealing souvenirs made from this malleable alloy of lead and silver, as well as the company's silver pieces under the Comyns brand and its Selberam jewellery.

You can tour the factory and try your own hand at creating a pewter dish at the **School of Hard Knocks** (☎4145 6122; http://visitorcentre.royalselangor.com/vc; 4 Jln Usahawan 6, Setepak Jaya; 30-min classes RM60; ◉9am-5pm; 🚈Wangsa Maju, then taxi). The centre is fronted by a nearly 2m-tall pewter tankard and has an appealing cafe. If you don't make it out here, Selangor's products are sold at its retail outlets in Kuala Lumpur's malls including Suria KLCC (p69) and Pavilion KL (p67).

place for a drink whether or not you happen to be attending a show at adjacent KLPAC.

ENTERTAINMENT

★KUALA LUMPUR PERFORMING ARTS CENTRE
PERFORMING ARTS

(KLPAC; ☑4047 9000; www.klpac.org; Jln Strachan, Sentul Park; tickets RM20-300; ⓡSentul) Part of the Sentul West regeneration project, this modernist performing-arts complex puts on a wide range of progressive theatrical events including dramas, musicals and dance. Also on offer are performing-arts courses and free screenings of art-house movies (usually on Sunday). Combine a show with a stroll in the peaceful grounds and dinner at Samira, beside the Sentul Park Koi Centre.

★ISTANA BUDAYA
PERFORMING ARTS

Map p258 (National Theatre; ☑4026 5555; www.istanabudaya.gov.my; Jln Tun Razak, Titiwangsa; tickets RM100-300; monorail Titiwangsa) Big-scale drama and dance shows are staged here, as well as music performances by the National Symphony Orchestra and National Choir. Designed by Mohammed Kamar Ya'akub, the building's soaring roof is based on a traditional Malay floral decoration of betel leaves, while its footprint resembles a *wau bulan* (Malay moon kite). There's a dress code of no shorts, and men must wear long-sleeved shirts.

★SUTRA DANCE THEATRE
DANCE

Map p258 (☑4021 1092; www.sutrafoundation.org.my; 12 Persiaran Titiwangsa 3, Titiwangsa; monorail Titiwangsa) The home of Malaysian dance legend Ramli Ibrahim has been turned into a showcase for Indian classical dance as well as a dance studio, gallery and cultural centre near Lake Titiwangsa. See the website for upcoming shows.

COLISEUM THEATRE
CINEMA

Map p256 (94 Jln TAR; ⓡMasjid Jamek) One of KL's oldest, still functioning cinemas, this art deco–style building dates back to 1920 and screens Indian-language movies.

CAPSQUARE
ENTERTAINMENT COMPLEX

Map p256 (www.capsquare.com.my; cnr Jln Munshi Abdullah & Jln Dang Wangi; ⓡDang Wangi) On the area's eastern flank is this attractive business, residential and entertainment complex that rests on the bank of the muddy Klang river – it's not taken off as hoped since it opened in 2009 but there's still some decent places to eat and drink here as well as a TGV multiplex cinema.

🏃 SPORTS & ACTIVITIES

TITIWANGSA GOLF CLUB PDRM
GOLF

Map p258 (☑2693 4964; Jln Temerloh, Taman Tasik Titiwangsa; 9 holes RM60; ⊙7am-6pm Tue-Sun, 2-6pm Mon; monorail Titiwangsa) This nine-hole course is located behind Taman Tasik Titiwangsa.

TANAMERA WELLNESS SPA
SPA

Map p256 (☑2694 6260; www.tanameraspa.com.my; Pertama Kompleks, Jln TAR; ⊙noon-10pm; LRT Bandaraya) Discover a wide variety of Malay beauty treatments using indigenous herbs and flowers; the company also has a stall in Central Market selling its spa products. A holistic massage is RM99, a massage plus a body scrub RM150.

Lake Gardens, Brickfields & Bangsar

Neighbourhood Top Five

1 Admiring the beautiful objects and art works gathered from around the world in the **Islamic Arts Museum** (p97), which occupies an impressive building embellished with decorative domes and mosaic tiles.

2 Enveloping yourself in greenery at the **Tun Abdul Razak Heritage Park** (p98), home to KL Bird Park.

3 Exploring multicultural **Brickfields** (p103), home to temples, churches and Kuala Lumpur's official Little India.

4 Marvelling at the architectural detail of the **Thean Hou Temple** (p100) and the views from its elevated terraces.

5 Sampling some of KL's top food and fashion picks in **Bangsar Baru** (p106 and p110).

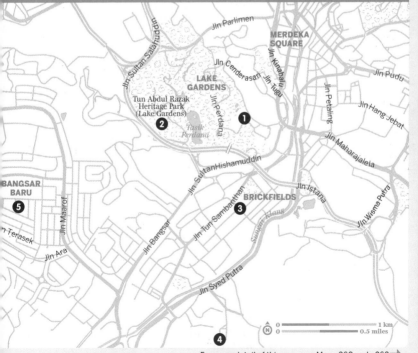

For more detail of this area, see Map p260 and p262

Lonely Planet's Top Tip

Visit KL (p226) runs a free guided walking tour of Brickfields every Saturday, starting from Vivekananda Ashram at 9am and lasting around 2½ hours. You can just turn up, but advance booking is recommended.

 ### Best Places to Eat

➡ Robson Heights (p106)
➡ Rebung (p107)
➡ Lucky Gardens (p108)
➡ Sri Nirwana Maju (p107)
➡ Wondermama (p107)

For reviews, see p105 ➡

 ### Best Places to Drink

➡ MAI Bar (p109)
➡ Hit & Mrs (p108)
➡ Plan b (p109)
➡ Ril's Bangsar (p109)
➡ Coffea Coffee (p109)

For reviews, see p109 ➡

 ### Best for Fashion

➡ Never Follow Suit (p110)
➡ Seethrough Concept Store (p110)
➡ 17A Select Store (p110)
➡ Nurita Harith (p110)
➡ Publika (p111)

For reviews, see p110 ➡

Explore: Lake Gardens, Brickfields & Bangsar

The Lake Gardens were created in the late 19th century as an urban retreat for the colonial Brits to escape the hurly burly of downtown. Recently renamed the Tun Abdul Razak Heritage Park after Malaysia's second prime minister, this lush, landscaped area continues to act as KL's green relaxation zone and includes three museums, six themed parks and other monuments and sights.

Following devastating fires in the late 19th century, KL's colonial administration decreed that bricks would henceforth be used to construct the city's buildings. The area where they were manufactured became known as Brickfields. Many Indian labourers, mainly Tamils from southern India and Sri Lanka, settled here, giving the area its still-predominant Indian atmosphere – that's why it's KL's official Little India. However, in this ethnically diverse 'burb you'll also find a Chinese temple and various Christian churches alongside the Hindu and Buddhist shrines. All are overshadowed by the skyscrapers of KL Sentral, the city's transportation hub around which several new shopping complexes and offices towers have sprouted.

To the south ripple the green hills that are home to KL's main Chinese Cemetery as well as the spectacular Thean Hou Temple and the old Istana Negara. North of here is Bangsar, a century ago a rubber plantation, now an upscale residential area of luxury bungalows and condominiums. Its commercial hub, Bangsar Baru, is one of KL's most pleasant places to eat and shop.

Local Life

➡ **Tugu Drum Circle** (http://tugudrumcircle.blogspot .com) Bang out a beat with the drum circle, who meet beneath the National Monument (p102) every Sunday eve.

➡ **Market life** Go grocery shopping and enjoy great hawker food at the Bangsar Sunday Market (p106).

➡ **Creative mall** Check out the varied weekend events and gallery showings at Publika (p111).

Getting There & Away

➡ **Train, monorail and LRT** KL Sentral, the city's transport hub, is close to both Brickfields and the Lake Gardens; Bangsar is one stop southwest on the LRT.

➡ **Walking** The Lake Gardens can easily be accessed by foot from Chinatown.

➡ **Bus** The KL Hop-On-Hop-Off bus stops at Masjid Negara, KL Bird Park, the National Monument and the National Museum.

➡ **Bicycle** Pedal around the Lake Gardens area with a rental bike from KL By Cycle (p99).

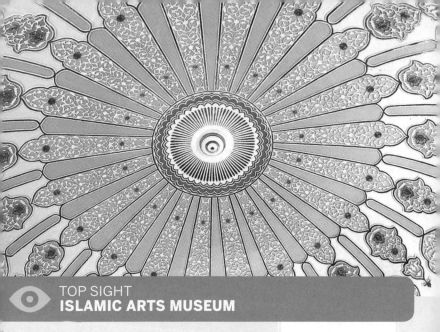

ISLAMIC ARTS MUSEUM

On the southern edge of the Tun Abdul Razak Heritage Park, this museum houses one of best collections of Islamic decorative arts in the world. Aside from the quality of the exhibits, which include fabulous textiles, carpets, jewellery, pottery and scale architectural models, the building itself is a stunner, with beautifully decorated domes and glazed tilework on its facade.

The Galleries

Spread over four levels, the museum has 12 permanent galleries and two galleries for special exhibitions. Start on the 3rd floor in the **Architecture Gallery**, which has scale models of important Islamic buildings, including the Masjid al-Haram in Mecca. There's also a re-creation of a mosque interior. On the same floor in the **Quran and Manuscripts Gallery** look for the 19th-century Qurans from Malaysia's east coast decorated in red, gold and black, as well as a full *kiswah,* an embroidered door panel from the holy Ka'aba in Mecca. 'It's very rare to see such an object,' says Adine binti Abdul Ghani, a curator of the museum, 'as it is usually cut into small pieces to be distributed to pilgrims.' Other favourites of Abdul Ghani include the **Ottoman Room**, a magnificent reconstruction of an 1820s decorative room from Syria; **Chinese calligraphy scrolls**; the weft silk ikat **limar**, a fabric patterned with Islamic calligraphy and now no longer made as the tradition has died out; and **Uzbek pectoral plates**.

Restaurant & Gift Shop

The museum has a good Middle Eastern restaurant (set lunch RM43, Friday buffet RM28) and one of KL's best museum gift shops.

DON'T MISS...

→ Ottoman Room
→ Architecture Gallery
→ Quran & Manuscripts Gallery
→ China Gallery
→ Textiles Gallery
→ Gift Shop

PRACTICALITIES

→ Muzium Kesenian Islam Malaysia
→ Map p260
→ ☑2274 2020
→ www.iamm.org.my
→ Jln Lembah Perdana
→ adult/child RM10/5, with special exhibitions RM12/6
→ ⊙10am-6pm, restaurant closed Mon
→ Ⓡ Kuala Lumpur

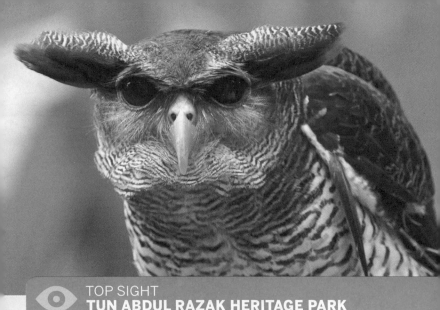

TUN ABDUL RAZAK HERITAGE PARK

Covering 70 hectares, KL's major recreational park is better known by its colonial moniker of the Lake Gardens. Ranging over undulating, landscaped hills, it's a park with something for practically everyone, the main attractions being the KL Bird Park and Perdana Botanical Garden. The Islamic Arts Museum (p97), National Museum (p102), Masjid Negara (p102) and National Monument (p102) also fall within the park's boundaries.

Park History

In 1888 Alfred Venning, Selangor State Treasurer, secured permission from British Resident Frank Swettenham to create a botanical garden around the small stream Sungai Bras Bras. It took more than a decade to clear and landscape the area which today stretches from Parliament House to the National Museum. The stream was dammed to give the park Sydney Lake (Tasik Perdana) – hence the Lake Gardens. In 2011 the park was renamed after Abdul Razak, Malaysia's second prime minister (1970–76). Abdul Razak lived in a house in the park between 1962 when he was deputy PM and 1976 when he died; the home is now the **Memorial Tun Abdul Razak** (Jln Perdana; ☺9am-6.30pm) FREE.

KL Bird Park

This fabulous **aviary** (☎2272 1010; www.klbirdpark.com; Jln Cenderawasih; adult/child RM48/38; ☺9am-6pm) brings together some 200 species of (mostly) Asian birds flying free beneath an enormous canopy. Star attractions include ostriches, hornbills, eagles, flamingos and parrots. It's worth getting to the park for feeding times (hornbills 11.30am, eagles 2.30pm) or the bird shows (12.30pm and 3.30pm), which feature plenty of parrot tricks to keep youngsters amused.

DON'T MISS...

→ KL Bird Park
→ Perdana Botanical Garden
→ KL Butterfly Park
→ National Planetarium
→ Royal Malaysia Police Museum

PRACTICALITIES

→ Lake Gardens
→ Map p260
→ www.visitkl.gov.my/tarheritagepark
→ ☺7am-8pm
→ ▣KL Hop-On, Hop-Off Bus Tour, ▣Kuala Lumpur

Perdana Botanical Garden & Around

The vast **Perdana Botanical Garden** (☏2021 0812; www.klbotanicalgarden.gov.my; Persiaran Mahameru; ⊘7am-8pm) 🛈 FREE is planted with a wide variety of native and overseas plants, trees and shrubs. Sections are dedicated to rare fruit trees, herbs, heliconias, ferns and cycads among other species. At the park's north end there's an excellent children's playground and near the lake is a **deer park**, home to mouse deer and spotted deer. Contact the park to book onto a free guided **walk** (8am and 10am Sunday).

The park is halfway through a major renovation. New features such as an ornamental waterfall and a rebuilt ampitheatre have been added and there are plans for a visitors centre and more specialised gardens.

The **Hibiscus** (Taman Bunga Raya; Jln Cenderawasih; ⊘9am-6.30pm) FREE and **Orchid** (Taman Orkid; Jln Cenderawasih; ⊘9am-6.30pm) FREE gardens are adjacent to the Botanical Garden. Among the 800-odd species of orchid are Vandas and exotic hybrids. There's also a stall where you can buy orchids. The hibiscus is Malaysia's national flower and the garden has more than 200 colourful hybrids with names such as Miniskirt and Hawaiian Girl that flower year-round.

Other Attractions

Looking more like a mosque than a centre for scientific research, the **National Planetarium** (☏2273 4303; www2.angkasa.gov.my/planetarium/; 53 Jln Perdana; gallery free, planetarium adult/child RM12/8; ⊘9am-4.30pm Tue-Sun) is part of the National Space Agency. Parts of the rocket that launched Malaysia's first satellite are displayed in the main gallery. Planetarium shows take place throughout the day in English and Bahasa Malaysia. In the grounds are small-scale models of famous historic observatories, including Jai Singh's Delhi observatory and Stonehenge.

A short walk north of the KL Bird Park is the **KL Butterfly Park** (Taman Rama Rama; ☏2693 4799; www.klbutterflypark.com/; Jln Cenderasari; adult/child RM20/10; ⊘9am-6pm). Among the 101 different species of colourful butterflies fluttering around the covered grounds are real monsters, and there's a bug gallery where you can shudder at the size of Malaysia's giant centipedes and spiders.

Between the Islamic Arts Museum and the Planetarium is the surprisingly interesting **Royal Malaysia Police Museum** (5 Jln Perdana; ⊘10am-6pm Tue-Sun, closed 12.30-2.30pm Fri) FREE. Inside you can watch videos, see police uniforms and vehicles, and peruse a collection of old swords, cannons and kris. There are also some handmade guns and knives seized from members of criminal Chinese 'secret societies' and communists during the Emergency (see p188).

EATING IN THE PARK

KL Bird Park's Hornbill Restaurant (p105), outside the aviary's entrance, is one of the best places to eat if you seek air-conditioning (it also has an outdoor terrace). For tasty hawker food there's Kompleks Makan Tanglin (p105) uphill behind the National Mosque. There are more hawker stalls on Jln Cenderasari near the ampitheatre and a kiosk cafe, open 9am to 6pm, in the boathouse in Perdana Botanical Garden.

A hop-on, hop-off electric tram (adult/ child RM2/1) shuttles around the park's major attractions from 9.30am to 5pm daily; there are stops beside the Masjid Negara and Islamic Arts Museum, and the tram also stops at Dataran Merdeka (but not between 11.30am and 2pm or after 4pm Monday to Friday).

Rent bicycles (and a helmet and lock) and pick up a route map from KL By Cycle (Map p248; KL City Gallery, 27 Jln Raja, Datran Merdeka; per four hours RM30, per additional hour RM5, deposit RM250; ⊘9am-6pm; 🚇Masjid Jamek). Take care crossing busy roads at the start of the route to get to the park.

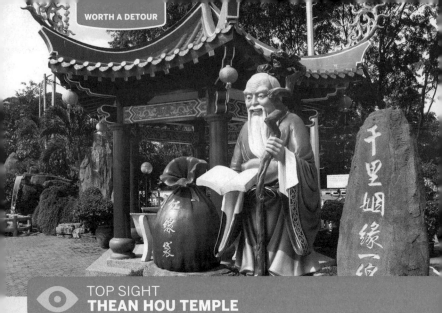

TOP SIGHT
THEAN HOU TEMPLE

Sitting atop Robson Heights, this multilayered, ornate temple is one of the most visually impressive in Malaysia. Dedicated to the heavenly mother, Thean Hou, it provides wonderful views of KL and is a great place to visit on a Buddhist festival such as Wesak Day or during Chinese New Year.

DON'T MISS...

➜ Main Prayer Hall
➜ Chinese Zodiac Statues

PRACTICALITIES

➜ ☑2274 7088
➜ off Jln Syed Putra
➜ ⏲9am-6pm
➜ monorail Tun Sambanthan

History & Design

The temple was officially opened in 1989 and cost the Selangor and Federal Territory Hainan Association RM7 million to build. You can see pretty much every ringgit in its rich architectural detail which includes decorative balustrades, beams, eaves, murals, and flying dragons and phoenixes. Arranged on four levels, the temple is fronted by a statue of Thean Hou beside a wishing well and a garden studded with large statues of the signs of the Chinese zodiac. On the ground floor there are souvenir stalls, a canteen and marriage registration office – this is a very popular spot for weddings. The 1st floor has a large hall where religious and cultural events are held while the 2nd has the temple's administrative offices.

Main Prayer Hall

Thean Hou's statue takes centre stage in the main hall on the 3rd floor with Kuan Yin (the Buddhist goddess of mercy) on her right and Shuiwei Shengniang (goddess of the waterfront) to her left. Smaller statues of Milefo (the laughing Buddha), Weituo and Guandi contribute to this Taoist–Buddhist hodgepodge. Look for the fortune-telling sticks: pick up the bunch of sticks, drop them back in their jar so that one sticks up the tallest. The number on it will correspond to a drawer containing a slip of paper with your fortune on it. Climb to the terrace above for wonderful views and then go back down behind the temple past a medicinal herb garden and a pond packed with tortoises.

PAMELA LAO / GETTY IMAGES ©

TOP SIGHT
SUNGAI PENCHALA

In the city's far northwest, this Malay village, located in a hilly, jungly landscape, seems a million miles from urban KL even though it's less than a 30-minute taxi drive from Chinatown. Come to relax at a rustic Balinese-style spa, eat delicious food or take a Malay cookery course. There's also a couple of great homestays (see p133).

DON'T MISS...

- Nada Lama
- Bayan Indah

PRACTICALITIES

- 11km northwest of central KL
- taxi RM20

Nada Lama

There's no better way to de-stress than booking a spa session at **Nada Lama** (☎017-616 4924, 016-308 0356; www.wix.com/nadalama/org; Lot 3197, Jln Penchala Indah, Bukit Lanjan Damanasara; massages from RM60; ⏲11am-10pm). Surrounded by a forest of durian trees, this eco-spa is rustic. The masseurs are highly professional and skilled in a variety of treatments using organic ingredients. Pampering aside, the cafe alone is worth the trip for its delicious Indonesian food at bargain prices – a meal is unlikely to cost over RM30.

Cooking Classes

A visit to the market followed by learning to cook several Malaysian dishes is the format of **LaZat Malaysian Home Cooking Class** (☎019-238 1198; www.malaysia-klcookingclass.com; Malay House at Penchala Hills, Lot 3196, Jalan Seri Penchala, Kampong Sg; ⏲10am-2pm Mon-Sat). Also worth looking into is the culinary retreat **Bayan Indah** (☎7729 0122; www.bayanindah.com; 3343 Kg Palimbayan Indah; house sleeping 8 RM5200). It's often booked up with corporate events and team-building exercises, but check its online calendar or email about booking a private class or joining a shared group class. Staying overnight here is also a lovely experience.

Other Dining Options

On the main road before the turn-off to Nada Lama, **Subak** (☎7729 9030; www.subak.com.my; Lot 3213 Jln Penchala Indah, Bukit Lanjan; mains RM40; ⏲11am-11pm) serves Indonesian, Malaysian and international dishes in a leafy, relaxed setting. **Muhibbah Seafood Restaurant** (☎7727 3153; Laman, 2851 Jln Seri Penchala, Sungai Penchala; mains RM10-30; ⏲noon-2.30pm & 6.30-10pm) is renowned for its halal Chinese food, including succulent deep-fried *sotong* (squid).

◉ SIGHTS

◉ Lake Gardens

The Lake Gardens area is mainly covered by the Tun Abdul Razak Heritage Park. Atop the tallest hill, the official residence of British government representative Frank Swettenham in the late 19th century is now the luxury hotel Carcosa Seri Negara (p135), while on the park's northern fringes is the Malaysian National Parliament.

ISLAMIC ARTS MUSEUM   MUSEUM
See p97.

TUN ABDUL RAZAK HERITAGE PARK   PARK
See p98.

MASJID NEGARA   MOSQUE
Map p260 (National Mosque; www.masjidnegara. gov.my/v2/; Jln Lembah Perdana; ⊙9am-noon, 3-4pm & 5.30-6.30pm, closed Fri morning; ⬛Kuala Lumpur) The main place of worship for KL's Malay Muslim population is this gigantic mosque, inspired by Mecca's Grand Mosque and able to accommodate 15,000 worshippers. Its umbrella-like blue-tile roof has 18 points symbolising the 13 states of Malaysia and the five pillars of Islam. Rising above the mosque, a 74m-high minaret issues the call to prayer, which can be heard across Chinatown.

Non-Muslims are welcome to visit outside prayer times; robes are available for those who are not dressed appropriately.

NATIONAL MONUMENT   MONUMENT
Map p260 (Plaza Tugu Negara, Jln Parlimen; ⊙7am-6pm; ⬛Masjid Jamek, then taxi) **FREE** This impressive monument commemorates the defeat of the Communists in 1950 and provides fine views across the park and city. Framing the militaristic bronze sculpture – created in 1966 by Felix de Weldon, the artist behind the Iwo Jima monument in Washington, DC – is a reflecting pool and curved pavilion.

Nearby is a cenotaph to the Malay fighters who died in WWI and WWII and at the foot of the hill a sculpture garden commemorating the 20th anniversary of the founding of the Association of South East Asian Nations (ASEAN). The forested hills behind the monument are slated for development into the **Malaysia Truly Asia Centre** over the coming years.

◉ TOP SIGHT
NATIONAL MUSEUM

Housed in a building with a distinctive Minangkabau-style roof, this museum is one of the city's best. A major renovation has resulted in four main galleries with interesting, well-organised displays: Early History, where you'll find the bones of Perak Man; Malay Kingdoms, including the history of the Melakans; Colonial Era, from the Portuguese through to the Japanese occupation; and Malaysia Today, which charts the country's post-WWII development.

There are more things to see outside, including a regularly changing exhibition (extra charge) and a couple of small free galleries: the **Orang Asli Craft Museum** and **Malay World Ethnology Museum**, which has good displays of batik and other fabrics.

Time your visit to coincide with one of the free **tours** (⊙10am Mon-Thu & Sat in English; Tue & Thu in French, Thu in Japanese) given by enthusiastic volunteer guides. Also don't miss admiring the pair of giant **friezes** flanking the front entrance. Designed by Cheong Lai Tong and made of Italian mosaic glass, they depict scenes from Malaysian life and history.

DON'T MISS...
➡ Exterior friezes
➡ Orang Asli Craft Museum
➡ Malay World Ethnology Museum

PRACTICALITIES
➡ Muzium Negara
➡ Map p260
➡ ☑2282 6255
➡ www.muzium negara.gov.my
➡ Jln Damansara
➡ adult/child RM5/2
➡ ⊙9am-6pm
➡ ⬛Hop-On-Hop-Off Bus Tour, ⬛KL Sentral, then taxi

KL TRAIN STATION
HISTORIC BUILDING

Map p260 (Jln Sultan Hishamuddin; 🚉Kuala Lumpur) Opened with much pomp and circumstance in 1911 to receive trains from Butterworth and Singapore, KL's old train station, another of AB Hubbock's Moorish-inspired fantasies, is a wonderful confection of turrets and towers. In 2001 the station was replaced as the city's main transport hub by KL Sentral. Today the platforms are mainly used for KTM Komuter trains to the suburbs and further afield to Seremban and Ipoh. It's looking dishevelled and forlorn, but it's still worth coming here to imagine the glory days. The station's fanciful architecture is mirrored by the Malayan Railway Administration Building across the road.

NATIONAL PARLIAMENT
LANDMARK

Map p260 (www.parlimen.gov.my; Jln Parlimen; closed to public; 🚉KL Sentral, then taxi) Opened on 2 November 1963, the William Ivor Shipley–designed National Parliament creates a striking impression. Sometimes nicknamed the 'toast rack', the complex's rectilinear design features a debate chamber crowned with a modern interpretation of a Malay house roof, crafted in concrete rather than wood.

◎ Brickfields, Bangsar & Around

Brickfields is a compact, multicultural area easily explored on foot; there's also a **free guided tour** offered by Visit KL (p226). The Malaysian Association for the Blind is here, so you'll see many blind people on the streets, some of who work in the area's massage parlours.

South of Brickfields across the Klang river are located the Royal Museum (in the old Istana Negara) and, atop Robson Heights, the spectacular Thean Hou Temple. Bangsar's major sight is the private contemporary-art gallery attached to Sekeping Tenggiri.

THEAN HOU TEMPLE
BUDDHIST TEMPLE

See p100.

SRI KANDASWAMY KOVIL
HINDU TEMPLE

Map p260 (📞2274 2987; www.srikandaswamy kovil.org; 3 Lg Scott; ⊙5.30am-9pm; monorail Tun Sambanthan) Founded by the Jaffna Sri Lankan community in 1909, Brickfield's major Hindu temple is dedicated to Lord Murgan and the mother goddess Sri Raja Rajeswary. It's marked by an elaborate *gopuram* (gateway), flanked by banana trees and is a riot of colourful Hindu gods and goddesses inside. One of the temple's major events is the 10-day **Mahotchava Festival** held around May with celebrations including processions of the wooden deities.

BUDDHIST MAHA VIHARA
BUDDHIST TEMPLE

Map p260 (📞2274 1141; www.buddhistmahavi hara.com; 123 Jln Berhala; 🚉KL Sentral) Founded in 1894 by Sinhalese settlers in Brickfields, this is one of KL's major Theravada Buddhist temples. You'll pass over a half-moonstone to enter the polychromatic main shrine hall which includes a large reclining Buddha. Meditation classes take place on Monday and Thursday at 8pm, chanting classes on Tuesday and Friday at 7.30pm. The Friday session is followed by a dharma talk at 8pm. Classes and longer courses are run on a donation basis. The temple is a hive of activity around Wesak Day when a massive torchlight parade with multiple floats starts from here and works its way around the city.

SEKEPING TENGGIRI
ART GALLERY

(📞017-207 5977; www.tenggiri.com; 48 Jln Tenggiri, Taman Weng Lock; ⊙by appointment; 🚉Bangsar) If you're not a guest at the adjoining guesthouse (p134) you'll need to make an appointment to view landscape architect Ng Seksan's superb collection of Malaysian contemporary art, so large that he's turned over a whole house to store and display it. View pieces by top talents including Phuan Thai Meng, Samsudin Wahab, Justin Lim and Rajinder Singh.

LITTLE INDIA FOUNTAIN
FOUNTAIN

Map p260 (cnr Jln Tun Sambanthan & Jln Travers; 🚉KL Sentral) A focal point of the revamp of Jln Sambanthan as KL's official 'Little India', this eye-catching fountain is billed as the tallest in the country. Symbolic elements in the fountain's design include elephants, swans, lotuses and seven different colours. Flanking the fountain are two abstract metal sculptures of Bharata Natyam dancers created by the **Sculpture at Work** (http://sculptureatwork.com).

SREE VEERA HANUMAN TEMPLE
HINDU TEMPLE

Map p260 (www.veerahanuman.com; Jln Scott; ⊙7am-9pm; monorail Tun Sambanthan) Honouring Hanuman, this temple has been undergoing several years of restoration and

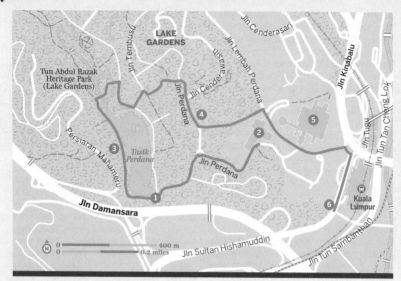

Local Life
A Day in Tun Abdul Razak Heritage Park

The Lake Gardens, now called Tun Abdul Razak Heritage Park, is where the brick, concrete and steel of KL is replaced by lush greenery. Spend a day joining locals as they do early-morning t'ai chi, stroll in the park, eat at hawker stalls, visit the mosque and take afternoon tea at the Majestic Hotel.

❶ Early-Morning Exercise
Set your alarm so you can make it to the park around opening time at 7am; if you're up for it join the joggers and those practicing t'ai chi around Tasik Perdana.

❷ Learn about Islamic Art
If you need to, freshen up back at your hotel before returning to explore the Islamic Arts Museum (p97), where you can check out the excellent collection and any classes or lectures being given. The shop here is an interesting one to browse for gifts, souvenirs and books.

❸ Explore the Gardens
Join garden lovers by exploring the Perdana Botanical Garden (p99). Consider booking a private guided walk around the sections, which include a deer park, hibiscus, orchid and herb gardens as well as many heritage trees predating the establishment of the park. If you have kids, the adventure playground will enable them to burn off energy and meet local children.

❹ Feed the Birds (and Yourself)
Locals have a soft spot for the *nasi lemak* (rice boiled in coconut milk, served with fried anchovies and peanuts) at the Hornbill Restaurant (p105) – you'd be wise to join them here for lunch. Afterwards wander through the free-flight zones of the KL Bird Park (p98), check out the eagles being fed at 2.30pm and perhaps chat with a warden about the park's successful breeding programs.

❺ Admire the National Mosque
You can only visit the Masjid Negara (p102) outside of main prayer times, so time your visit here for between 3pm and 4pm. Don't worry if you're not dressed appropriately – there are voluminous purple robes for non-Muslim men and women to cover up their bare arms and legs (and women's heads).

❻ Afternoon Tea at the Majestic Hotel
Walk around the corner from the grand buildings of the old KL train station to take afternoon tea in the plush heritage wing of the Majestic Hotel (p135) alongside manicured and bejewelled *datins* and *tai tais* (wealthy society Malay and Chinese women).

should be a grand sight when its completed *gopuram* is revealed: it's made up of a coiled tower of the tail of the monkey god. There are often puja (special prayer) services going on here – check the website for details.

ROYAL MUSEUM
MUSEUM

Map p260 (Muzium Diraja; www.jmm.gov.my; Jln Istana; adult/child RM10/5; ☉9am-5pm; monorail Tun Sambanthan) Since 2011, when Yang di-Pertuan Agong, Malaysia's King, received a larger and more opulent set of digs on Jln Duta, the former Istana Negara (National Palace) has been made into a museum. You'll only be able to enter one of the former palace's rooms to see the exhibition on the Malay royals. It's also possible to have your photo taken dressed in traditional Malay costume (RM50).

Built in 1928 by Chinese millionaire Chang Wing, this grand building was used as the residence of the Japanese Governor during KL's WWII occupation. It was requisitioned by the government in 1957 and turned into the National Palace.

SAM KOW TONG TEMPLE
BUDDHIST TEMPLE

Map p260 (16 Jln Thambapillai; ☉7am-5pm; ☒KL Sentral) Established in 1916 by the Heng Hua clan, the 'three teachings' temple has a dragon-decorated roof that contrasts with the soaring towers above KL Sentral. Look for the paintings that show filial piety.

HUNDRED QUARTERS
HISTORIC BUILDINGS

Map p260 (Jln Rozario & Jln Chan Ah Tong; ☒KL Sentral) The parallel rows of concrete houses known as the Hundred Quarters were built in 1905 to house railway employees and other civil servants. These multi-ethnic two roads, Jln Rozario and Jln Chan Ah Tong, are named after former chief clerks of the colonial civil service. The ongoing redevelopment of the area has put these heritage buildings under threat; residents have been given notice to vacate, with an assurance that no one will be moved until suitable alternative accommodation is found.

HOLY ROSARY CHURCH
CHURCH

Map p260 (☎2274 2747; www.rc.net/kuala-lumpur/holyrosary/home_files/index.html; 10 Jln Tun Sambanathan; ☉Mass in English 5pm Sat, 8.30am Sun; ☒KL Sentral) Cut off from the bulk of Brickfields by Jln Damansara, this Catholic church built in 1903 is worth a look for its French Gothic Revival style. It serves mainly a Chinese Catholic congregation.

✕ EATING

✕ Lake Gardens

KOMPLEKS MAKAN TANGLIN
HAWKER $

Map p260 (Jln Cendarasari; meals RM10; ☉7am-4pm Mon-Sat; ☒Kuala Lumpur) The stall named Ikan Bakar Pak Din serves a variety of freshly barbecued fish and is a popular option at this hawker complex up the hill behind Masjid Negara.

HORNBILL RESTAURANT
MALAY, INTERNATIONAL $$

Map p260 (☎2693 8086; www.klbirdpark.com; KL Bird Park, 920 Jln Cenderawashi; mains RM40-60; ☉9am-8pm; ☎; ☒Kuala Lumpur) Providing a ringside view of the inhabitants of KL Bird Park, this slick restaurant and cafe offers very good food without gouging the tourists too much. Go local with its *nasi lemak* (rice boiled in coconut milk, served with fried anchovies and peanuts) and fried noodles or please the kids with fish and chips or the homemade chicken or beef burgers.

COLONIAL CAFE
MALAY, INTERNATIONAL $$$

Map p260 (☎2785 8000; www.majestickl.com/dining.html; Majestic Hotel, 5 Jln Sultan Hishamuddin; mains RM55-130; ☉11.30am-10.30pm; ☎; ☒Kuala Lumpur) British Malay cuisine, as interpreted by Hainanese chefs of yore, is on the menu at this pukka restaurant in the heritage wing of the Majestic. Dishes such as chicken rice served Melaka style with rice balls and mulligatawny soup are served with aplomb – followed by the thud of a hefty bill. The attached tea lounge is where you can enjoy a very fancy afternoon tea – from RM78 for two – that can also be served in the luscious orchidarium.

✕ Brickfields & Around

AUTHENTIC CHAPATI HUT
INDIAN $

Map p260 (Lot 635 Jln Scott; mains RM7; ☉10.30am-11pm; monorail Tun Sambanthan) This bona fide hut at the end of a car park strewn with plastic tables and chairs becomes packed every evening when locals arrive to scoff the freshly made chapatis, other Indian breads and spicy dishes.

ANNALAKSHMI
INDIAN $

Map p260 (☎2272 3799; Temple of Fine Arts, 116 Jln Berhala; ☉11.30am-3pm & 6.30-10pm Tue-Sun;

LOCAL KNOWLEDGE

BRICKFIELDS STREET EATS

Brickfields offers several street vendors serving tasty snacks well worth sampling as you explore the area:

Ammars (Map p260; Asia Parking, Jln Berhala; vadai RM1; ⊙7am-7pm; ⊠KL Sentral) In a parking lot across the road from KL Sentral, the family who run this stall fry up tasty Indian snacks, such as lentil *vadai* (fritters) flavoured with fennel seeds, in giant woks.

Brickfields Pisang Goreng (Map p260; cnr Jln Thambapillai & Jln Tun Sambanthan 4; fritters RM1.20; ⊙10am-6pm; monorail Tun Sambanthan) Offering banana fritters so tasty that it can get away with charging a bit more for them than other vendors. The stall also sells curry puffs.

ABC Stall (Map p260; Jln Tun Sambanthan 4, outside 7-Eleven store; cendol RM1.70; ⊙10am-6pm; monorail Tun Sambathan) Cool your throat with fresh coconut juice, some *ais cendol* (shaved ice) and other desserts.

Little India Fountain Hawker Stalls Great for cheap eats, open around the clock, and a far more pleasant option than the streetside tables down the Little India section of Jln Tun Sambanthan, where your ears will be assaulted by Hindi and Tamil pop songs.

⊠; ⊠KL Sentral) The fancy main restaurant inside the Temple of Fine Arts has set prices for its tasty vegetarian cuisine with a daily lunch buffet (a good deal for RM12). Next to the car park beneath the building, it's still 'eat as you wish, give as you feel' at the simpler Annalakshmi Riverside operation.

VISHAL INDIAN $
Map p260 (☏2274 0502; 15 Jln Scott; meals RM5; ⊙7am-10.30pm; ⊠; monorail Tun Sambanthan) Punters sit at two long rows of tables for the great banana-leaf meals served up at this long-running Brickfields favourite. Good for tiffin snacks and a refreshing lassi, too. If this place is busy it's a very similar deal at Vishalatchi further along the road and run by the same family.

★**ROBSON HEIGHTS** CHINESE $$
Map p260 (☏2274 1633; www.robsonheights. com; 10B Jln Permai, off Jln Syed Putra; mains RM30-60; ⊙10.30am-2.30pm & 5.30-11.30pm; monorail Tun Sambanthan) Folks drive from far and wide to feast on the top-class food served at this rickety hillside joint. While its specialities such as stir-fried pig intestines with dried prawn and chilli, braised terrapin, or Marmite crab may not appeal to all, we can vouch for the delicious baked spare ribs in honey sauce and stir-fried udon noodles in black pepper sauce (RM8).

SIU SIU CHINESE $$
Map p260 (☏016-370 8555; 15-11 Lg Syed Putra Kiri; mains RM40-60; ⊙11am-11pm Tue-Sun;

monorail Tun Sambathan) On the way to Thean How Temple, this is a very good no-frills, partly alfresco place. Order the milk curry prawns with buns to soak up the tasty gravy, or any type of fish.

KELANTAN DELIGHTS MALAY $$
Map p260 (☏2785 1945; www.kelantandelights. com; 1-5 Level 1, Sooka Sentral, Jln Stesen Sentral; mains RM20-25; ⊙11am-9.30pm; ⊠KL Sentral) A rare chance in the capital to sample famous dishes from the east-coast Malaysian state of Kelantan. Order the blue-rice *nasi kerabu* or *nasi tumpung,* a cone of sticky rice layered with seafood and spices. The set meals including drink and dessert are great value at RM31.90.

IKAN BAKAR JALAN BELLAMY HAWKER $$
(Jln Bellamy; meals RM10; ⊙11am-11pm Mon-Sat; monorail Tun Sambanthan) When the king lived nearby it was said he occasionally sent his minions to get an order of grilled stingray from one of the justifiably popular barbecued-fish hawker stalls on the hill behind the former royal palace – there's little to choose between the three of them. Wander around and see what takes your fancy.

✕ Bangsar

BANGSAR SUNDAY MARKET HAWKER $
Map p262 (Pasar Malam; carpark east of Jln Telawi 2; noodles RM4; ⊙1-9pm Sun; ⊠Bangsar) This weekly market is a not only a good place to

pick up fresh fruit, veg and fish, but also a top-class hawker food-grazing zone. There are stalls selling a variety of noodles such as *asam laksa* (a version of laksa that has a prawn paste and tamarind-flavoured gravy), *cheo cheong fun* (rice noodles) or *kway teow* (wide rice noodles stir-fried with prawns, cockles, bean sprouts and egg). Also look for the satay stall where you can sample regular bits of fowl and mutton alongside the more challenging 'bishops nose' (ie chicken bum).

CHAWAN
MALAY $
Map p262 (☑2287 5507; 69G Jln Telawi 3; mains RM5-10; ☺8am-midnight; ⑤Bangsar) A chic contemporary take on a *kopitiam* (coffee shop), offering megastrength coffees from all of the country's states to wash down dishes such as beef rendang and a brown-paper-wrapped *nasi lemak*. There's also a branch in Publika.

BABA LOW'S 486 BANGSAR
NONYA $
Map p262 (☑2284 8486; 1 Lg Kurau; mains RM4-7; ☺7am-10.30pm; ⑤Bangsar) Local foodies drool over this casual cafe serving tasty Melakan-style Nonya food including *popiah*, chicken curry and a luscious laksa. It's also open for breakfast if you fancy a savoury-spicy start to the day.

DEVI'S CORNER
FOOD COURT $
Map p262 (14 Jln Telawi 2; meals RM10; ☺24hr; ⑤Bangsar) A pavement-cafe mood prevails at this food court facing the Bangsar Village II mall. The tray curries are excellent, with plenty of fish, prawns and other seafood. You can get *dosa* (crispy pancakes), biryani and great satay here.

★SRI NIRWANA MAJU
INDIAN $$
Map p262 (☑2287 8445; 43 Jln Telawi 3; meals RM10-20; ☺7am-2am; ⑤Bangsar) There are far flashier Indian restaurants in Bangsar, but who cares about the decor when you can tuck into food this good and cheap? Serves it all from roti for breakfast to banana-leaf curries throughout the day.

★REBUNG
MALAY $$
Map p262 (☑2283 2119; www.rebung.com.my; 4-2 Lg Maarof; buffet RM50; ☺11am-11pm; ✳☎; ⑤Bangsar) The flamboyant celebrity chef Ismail runs the show at this excellent Malay restaurant, one of KL's best, respected for its authenticity and consistency. The buffet spread is splendid with all kinds of

dishes that you'd typically only be served in a Malay home, several such as *onde onde* (glutinous rice balls filled with jaggery) made freshly. Check the website for details of cooking classes on offer.

★WONDERMAMA
MALAY, ASIAN $$
Map p262 (☑2284 9821; www.facebook.com/mywondermama; Bangsar Village I, 1 Jln Telawi 1; mains RM14-24; ☺9am-10.30pm; ☎; ⑤Bangsar) Traditional meets contemporary at this appealing two-level space serving Malay staples such as laksa and *nasi lemak* with a contemporary twist. Live jazz is also performed on Wednesday 8pm to 10pm.

YEAST BISTRONOMY
FRENCH $$
Map p262 (☑2282 0118; www.yeastbistronomy.com; 24G Jln Telawi 2; mains RM25-65; ☺8am-10pm Tue-Sun; ⑤Bangsar) One of KL's best bistros, Yeast performs at the top of its game from breakfast of croque-monsieurs and -madams through sandwiches and savoury tarts for lunch and steaks and stews for dinner. Watch the chefs work at the open kitchen and peruse the freshly baked goods counter before leaving.

NUTMEG
INTERNATIONAL $$
Map p262 (☑2201 3663; www.facebook.com/nutmegkl; Bangsar Village II, 2 Jln Telawi 1; mains RM16-30; ☺10am-10pm; ☎; ⑤Bangsar) The closest thing you're going to get to a Jewish deli in KL is this attractive newcomer that's taking on the big culinary guns of Bangsar and making an impression with its home-made gravlax and salt beef as well as other comfort foods and cakes. And who doesn't love a joint that offers all-day breakfast and has friendly staff?

HOUSE+CO KITCHEN
MALAY, INTERNATIONAL $$
Map p262 (☑2094 3139; www.houseandco.com.my; Bangsar Shopping Centre, 285 Jln Maarof; mains RM20; ☺11am-10pm; ☎; ⑤Bangsar) One of the best places to eat if you're at the Bangsar Shopping Centre mall, this laid-back cafe really can make great local dishes – try the delicious *kway teow* soup or the spicy *mee hoon kerabu* salad, and come hungry as the portions are huge.

FIERCE CURRY HOUSE
INDIAN $$
Map p260 (☑2202 3456; www.facebook.com/FierceCurryHouse; 16 Jln Kemuja, Bangsar Utama; ☺10am-10pm; ☎; ⑤Bangsar) 'Yo bro, this curry is fierce!' Translation: I really like the curry here. Actually it's the fragrant, moist

Hyderabad-style dum biryani rice, with mutton or chicken, that forms part of the restaurant's standard banana-leaf platter that is the real draw. Book ahead for exotic lobster, crab and cod versions.

RESTAURANT MAHBUB
INDIAN $$

Map p262 (☑2095 5382; www.restoranmahbub. com; 17 Lg Ara Kiri 1; mains RM6-12; ⊙7am-2am; ⓐBangsar) Tables spill out onto the street from this long-running operation famous for its fragrant biryani rice and luscious honey chicken.

LES DEUX GARCONS
PATISSERIE $$

Map p262 (☑2284 7833; www.lesdeuxgarcons. com.my; 36 Jln Telawi; macarons & cakes RM5-20; ⊙11am-8pm; ⓐBangsar) Divine *macarons* (try the amazing wasabi or jasmine flavours) and beautiful cakes are served at this tiny, pristine patisserie, along with coffee.

LUCKY GARDENS

South of Jln Ara, Lucky Gardens may not be as ritzy as the grid of Telawis, but locals love to hit the morning fruit-and-veg market here and it is blessed with some delicious and inexpensive dining options.

Visit the **Nam Chuan Coffee Shop** (Map p262; Lg Ara Kiri 2; ⊙7am-10pm; ⓐBangsar), a busy, no-frills food court, so that you can enjoy a bowl of Christina Jong's fantastic Sarawak laksa (RM5) or Ah Mun's *kuih* (rice cakes; RM1) – his *onde onde* (glutinous rice balls filled with palm sugar) are flavoured with real pandan and are considered the best in Kuala Lumpur.

There's also a fantastic strip of outdoor hawker stalls along Lg Ara Kiri: sample vegan Indian delights at **Chelo's Appam Stall** (RM5; ⊙7am-10pm Mon-Sat; ✐); more vegetarian food at **Poomy's** (RM5; ⊙3-11pm Mon-Sat; ✐), including the sweet *appam* (coconut milk pancakes); and the tastebud explosion of **Bangsar Fish Head Corner** (meals RM10-30; ⊙7am-7pm Mon-Sat), where if you don't fancy the actual fish head you can still get the curry sauce poured over rice along with delicious fried chicken.

ALEXIS BISTRO
MALAY, INTERNATIONAL $$

Map p262 (☑2284 2880; www.alexis.com.my; 29 Jln Telawi 3; mains from RM30; ⊙noon-midnight Sun-Thu, to 1am Fri & Sat; ⓐBangsar) Consistently good food is delivered at this Bangsar stalwart where Asian favourites such as Sarawak laksa (the owner is originally from this Malaysian state) mix it up with European fare. After your meal, move on to its ultrasmooth Sino the Bar Upstairs.

DELICIOUS
INTERNATIONAL $$

Map p262 (☑2287 1554; www.delicious.com.my; ground fl, Bangsar Village II, Jln Telawi 1; mains from RM40; ⊙11am-midnight Sun-Thu, to 1am Fri & Sat; ⓐBangsar) Serving healthy salads, pasta, sandwiches and pies (among many other things) in a contemporary setting. It's worth dropping by for the afternoon teas. There are other branches, including one located at the E&O Residences Kuala Lumpur (p131).

LA BODEGA
SPANISH $$

Map p262 (☑2287 8318; www.bodega.com.my; 14 & 16 Jln Telawi 2; mains RM10-40; ⊙8am-1am; ⓐBangsar) This long-running place is four venues in one: an all-day deli-cafe serving good sandwiches; a chilled-out tapas bar; a formal dining room; and a lively lounge bar. Good wine and authentic tapas and paella complete the Spanish mood. It also has big outlets at Bangsar Shopping Centre (p113) and Pavilion KL (p67).

SMOKEHOUSE RESTAURANT
BRITISH, THAI $$

Map p262 (☑2288 1510; www.thesmokehouse. my; 67G Jln Telawi 3; mains RM30-50; ⊙noon-11pm, bar closes at 1am; ⓐBangsar) Half-timbered, Surrey-meets-KL decor signals that this is traditional English cooking territory, with such dishes as fish and chips with mushy peas and beef Wellington on the menu as well as Thai food. Its traditional afternoon tea (RM18) is just the kind of pick-me-up you'll need after trawling the Bangsar Village malls across the street.

HIT & MRS
CONTEMPORARY $$$

Map p262 (☑2282 3571; 15 Lg Kurau; mains RM65, 8-course tasting menu RM175; ⊙7-11pm Tue-Fri, 9am-3pm & 7-11pm Sat & Sun; ☎; ⓐBangsar) Expect inventive (but not always successful) food combinations such as foie gras, milk jam and gingerbread, or steak with manchego, dates and brussel sprouts at this retro-Malaya-meets-Manhattan-chic restaurant.

PRESSROOM
FRENCH $$$

Map p262 (☑2095 8098; www.pressroom.com.my; Lot G110, ground fl, Bangsar Shopping Centre, 285 Jln Maarof; mains RM45-75; ☺8am-midnight; ☜; ☐Bangsar) The La Bodega group is behind this classy modern bistro out the front of this gourmet destination mall. The copper-plated open-air dining space is sophisticated but relaxed and the menu of reliable items, such as steak *frittes* and lamb chops, are supplemented by blackboard specials. There's also a branch at Pavilion KL (p67).

REUNION
CHINESE $$$

Map p262 (☑2287 3770; www.reunion-restaurant.com/; 2nd fl, Bangsar Village II, Jln Telawi 1; meals RM80-100; ☺noon-3pm & 6-10.30pm; ☐Bangsar) The Delicious group brings its restaurant know-how to bear at this elegantly designed contemporary Chinese restaurant that's ideal for a business dinner or intimate date. It's affordable for a lunch treat with most dishes under RM20.

🍷🍸 DRINKING & NIGHTLIFE

🍸 Brickfields

★MAI BAR
COCKTAIL BAR

Map p260 (Aloft Kuala Lumpur Sentral, 5 Jln Stesen Sentral; ☺3pm-midnight; ☜; ☐KL Sentral) On the hotel's roof next to the infinity pool, this Polynesian tiki-themed bar is a dreamy addition to KL's growing band of high-rise bars with panoramic city views. The scarlet bean bags outside are a great place to chill and take in the urban KL scene. There is also a separate lounge for cigar smokers.

🍸 Bangsar

★HIT & MRS
COCKTAIL BAR

Map p262 (☑2282 3571; 15 Lg Kurau; ☺5pm-1am Tue-Fri, 3pm-1am Sat & Sun; ☜; ☐Bangsar) One of KL's most sophisticated places to canoodle and confide over cocktails (RM30 to RM40) or pitchers of punch (RM90 to RM150), this retro-chic bar is an ideal place to arrange an intimate assignation away from the crowds.

★RIL'S BANGSAR
COCKTAIL BAR

Map p262 (☑2201 3846; www.facebook.com/RilsBangsar; 30 Jln Telawi 5; ☺10am-2am; ☜; ☐Bangsar) There's a premium-grade steak restaurant downstairs, but the main action is happening at the dark and decadently decorated cocktail bar upstairs where the mixologists get creative with things such as a candy-floss machine and tropical fruit. Sometimes there's live jazz or a pianist tinkling the ivories.

★COFFEA COFFEE
CAFE

Map p262 (http://coffea.my; 8 Jln Telawi 2; ☺9am-midnight Sun-Thu, to 2am Fri & Sat; ☜; ☐Bangsar) The first in what is sure to be many more outlets of this Korean gourmet-coffee franchise has landed in Bangsar to rave reviews for its single-origin bean drinks and expert barista methods. The look is industrial-chic yet also the kind of cosy that makes you happy to linger.

★PLAN B
CAFE

Map p262 (www.thebiggroup.co/planb; Bangsar Village 1, Jln Talawi 1; ☜; ☐Bangsar) The BIG Group successfully clones the sophisticated Melbourne-look cafe-bar at several locations around town including this one on the ground floor of Bangsar Village. Handy for a latte, a light meal or something more substantial.

SINO THE BAR UPSTAIRS
BAR

Map p262 (☑2284 2880; www.alexis.com.my; 29 Jln Telawi 3; ☺6pm-1am, to 2am Fri & Sat; ☐Bangsar) Above the popular Alexis Bistro and probably the most chilled-out drinking spot in Bangsar Baru. Sink into comfortable chairs and relax to the soothing sounds on the decks. The first Monday of the month this venue hosts a Jazz Jam Session that gives you a chance to catch the best jazz talents in KL.

WIP
BAR

Map p262 (☑2094 1789; www.wip.com.my; G111 ground fl, Bangsar Shopping Centre, 285 Jln Maarof; ☺noon-2am; ☐Bangsar) Standing for 'whipped into place', this partly alfresco restaurant-bar attracts a stylish crowd who prefer to hang in the suburbs rather than shuffle into town.

POCO HOMEMADE
CAFE

(pocohomemade.blogspot.co.uk; Lg Kurau; ☺noon-9.30pm Tue-Sun; ☐Bangsar) Supercute cafe that specialises in the homemade and rustically crafty. Its tofu cheesecake is a creamy delight and there are some pretty handbags, accessories, local-music CDs and simple artworks to buy.

SOCIAL
CAFE, BAR

Map p262 (www.thesocial.com.my; 57-59 Jln Telawi 3; ⏲10am-2am; 🚇Bangsar) A classy sports bar offering pool tables and good food as well as the booze, including a good wine list. The Changkat Bukit Bintang **branch** (Map p252; ☑2142 7021; www.thesocial.com.my; Changkat Bukit Bintang, Golden Triangle) is super popular as is the one at Publika.

ENTERTAINMENT

TEMPLE OF FINE ARTS
THEATRE

Map p260 (☑2274 3709; www.tfa.org.my; 114-116 Jln Berhala, Brickfields; 🚇KL Sentral, monorail KL Sentral) Classical Indian dance and music shows happen here throughout the year. The centre also runs performing-arts courses.

SHOPPING

★NEVER FOLLOW SUIT
FASHION

Map p262 (☑2284 7316; 28-2, Jln Telawi 2, Bangsar Baru; 🚇Bangsar) You're guaranteed to find something special at this extraordinary boutique hidden away on the 2nd floor. New and upcycled clothes and accessories are displayed like art works in a hipster, shabby-chic gallery.

★BANGSAR VILLAGE I & II
MALLS

Map p262 (www.bangsarvillage.com; cnr Jln Telawi 1 & Jln Telawi 2; ⏲10am-10pm; 🚇Bangsar) These twin malls – linked by a covered bridge – offer upmarket fashions, including international brands such as Ted Baker and Zara, and local Malaysian designers such Richard Tsen at **Dude & the Duchess** (Map p262; Upper ground fl, Bangsar Village II), which marries tailored fits and design to interesting fabric choices, or the chic shoes and bags of **Vinci+** (Map p262; Ground fl, Bangsar Village II). Multibrand boutique **Actually** (Map p262; www.facebook.com/ActuallyKL; Bangsar Village II; 🚇Bangsar) offers more on-trend clothing.

Asian interior-design shop **Lasting Impressions** (Map p262; www.lasting-impressions. com.my; 2nd fl, Bangsar Village II) has great decorative pieces. Also here are some shops

and play centres for kids, a decent Western-style supermarket, several good restaurants and cafes and the Moroccan-style spa Hammam (p113).

★SEETHROUGH CONCEPT STORE
FASHION

Map p262 (www.facebook.com/SeethroughConceptStore; 1st fl, 25 Jln Telawi 2, Bangsar Baru; ⏲11am-9pm Tue-Sun; 🚇Bangsar) As well as its own brand of clothes, there's a wide selection of local designers on display at this appealing unisex boutique. Labels to look for include Pearly Wong, Joe Chia, Kazami Homme and When Our Eyes Met.

★17A SELECT STORE
FASHION, VINTAGE

Map p262 (☑2201 7513; www.facebook.com/The OffDay; 17A Jln Telawi 3, Bangsar Bar; ⏲noon-7pm Tue-Sun; 🚇Bangsar) Two businesses harmonise nicely in this former gallery space. Snackfood specialises in kitsch interior decor and vintage collectables, while The Off Day offers a great line in vintage-style denims and workwear. Look for Ceremony and Off Day Cheese Denim jeans, made in Malaysia by an uncle who used to work for Levis (so he knows his denim).

★NURITA HARITH
FASHION

Map p262 (www.nuritaharith.com; 10-2 Jln Telawi 3; ⏲10am-7.30pm Tue-Sun; 🚇Bangsar) Darling frocks and accessories from one of KL's top young designers.

WEI-LING GALLERY
ART

Map p260 (www.weiling-gallery.com; 8 Jln Scott, Brickfields; ⏲noon-7pm Mon-Fri, 10am-5pm Sat; 🚇KL Sentral) The top two floors of this old shophouse have been imaginatively turned into a contemporary gallery to showcase local artists. Note the artwork covering the metal security gate in front of the shophouse next door. The gallery has a second branch at Gardens Mall.

LAVANYA
ARTS & CRAFTS

Map p260 (Temple of Fine Arts, 114-116 Jln Berhala, Brickfields; ⏲10am-9.30pm Tue-Sat, to 3pm Sun; 🚇KL Sentral) 🌿 Lavanya sells craft goods made by single women working at the charitable Shiva Shukthi Trust in Coimbatore, India, including adorable kids' and adults' clothes, home decorations and furniture.

SONALI
FASHION

Map p260 (www.sonali.com.my; 67A Lg Scott, Brickfields; ⏲10am-7pm Mon-Sat; 🚇Tun Sambanthan) Sequins, silks, filigree patterns

PUBLIKA

Art, shopping, dining and social life are all in harmony at **Publika** (www.publika.com.my; 1 Jln Dutamas, Solaris Dutamas; ☺10am-9pm), a forward-thinking retail and residential development less than 10 minutes' drive north of Bangsar. Dazzling murals, quirky themes for the toilets and a fun kids' playground all add to Publika's visual interest and point up a liberal vibe that's in striking contrast to the conservative Islamic high court, the giant mosque and Istana Negara (National Palace) that are the complex's neighbours.

Galleries & Events
Contemporary art is fostered at several independent galleries at Publika with **MAP** (☏6207 9732; www.facebook.com/mapkl; Publika, 1 Jln Dutamas; ⬚KL Sentral) acting as the cultural anchor with a wide variety of performances, talks and art exhibitions held in its White and Black Box spaces – everything from Malaysian death-metal bands to major public events and product launches. Free films are screened each Monday in the central square and there's a handicrafts market held on the last Sunday of the month. MAP's and Publika's Facebook pages list up-to-date details of all events.

Eating & Drinking
There are two good food courts: EAT and Made in Malaysia; the former includes an outlet of Kin Kin where you can sample supremely tasty *pan mee* ('dry' noodles). Other good places to eat and drink include the following:

Bee (☏6201 8577; www.thebee.com.my; 36B, Level G2, Publika, 1 Jln Dutamas 1, Solaris Dutamas; mains RM15-20; ☺9am-midnight Mon-Thu, 9am-1am Fri, 10am-1am Sat, 10am-midnight Sun; ☎) A happening cafe-bar serving burgers, sandwiches, salads and fine coffee and hosting events including live music, film screenings and open-mic nights.

Nathalie's Gourmet Studio (☏6207 9572; www.nathaliegourmetstudio.com; 1 Jln Dutamas, Solaris Dutamas; mains RM25-35; ☺9am-6pm Tue-Wed, to 11pm Thu-Sat) For delicious nouvelle cuisine and melting macaroons. It also runs cooking classes.

Journal by Plan b (http://www.thebiggroup.co/planb; Level G2 Publika, 1 Jln Dutamas 1, Solaris Dutamas; mains RM20-40; ☺10am-10pm) A pile of chairs hanging from the ceiling and an old TV screening P Ramlee movies are part of the quirky decor at this upmarket branch of cafe-bar Plan b. It's a very pleasant place for a lazy breakfast/brunch at weekends.

There are also branches of reliable chains Ben's, The Social, Chawan and +Wondermilk; the latter sells sells cupcakes, milky drinks, comfort food and handcrafty items.

Shopping
Rents are kept low to encourage new talents and retail ideas – look out for pop-up shops on the Level G2 Art Row. **Ben's Independent Grocer** (BIG; www.thebiggroup.co/BIG; Lot 1A, 83-95, Level UG, Publika, 1 Jln Dutamas, Solaris Dutamas; ☺10am-9pm) is a huge and creatively designed supermarket. There's a particularly good section of shops for children including the arts and crafts workshop **Artis Kids Store** (http://artiskidsstore.my; 48, Level G3, Publika, 1 Jln Dutamas, Solaris Dutamas; ☺10am-9pm).

Fashionistas are well served by a good range of small boutiques, as well as major fashion retailer British India and **Elegantology** (www.elegantology.com.my; 35, Level G2, Publika, 1 Jln Dutamas, Solaris Dutamas; ☺10am-9pm), combining local designer wares with fine dining. **Pink Jambu** (www.pinkjambu.com; A4, Level G1-05, Publika, Jln Dutamas 1, Solaris Dutamas; ☺10am-9pm) has great contemporary batik designs for fashion and homewares. **thirtyfour.bespoke** (www.facebook.com/thirtyfour.net; Level G2, Publika, 1 Jln Dutamas, Solaris Dutamas; ☺10am-9pm) makes beautiful leather goods in vivid colours. Browse **It's Freshly Old** (www.facebook.com/freshlyold; 10, Level 3, Publika, Solaris Dutamas, Jln Dutamas 1; ☺10am-9pm) for retro knick-knacks and furnishings.

Getting There & Away
A taxi to Publika from Sentral KL/Bangsar should cost no more than RM10/5 on the meter.

MID VALLEY

Like a fortress island surrounded by concentric moats of highways and rail tracks, Mid Valley is a two-tower complex anchored by two giant malls: **Mid Valley Megamall** (www.midvalley.com.my; Lingkaran Syed Putra; ⊘10am-10pm; 🚇Mid Valley) and its luxe sibling **Gardens Mall** (www.thegardensmall.com.my/; Mid Valley City, Lingkaran Syed Putra; ⊘10am-10pm; 🚇Mid Valley), which also offers a good top-end hotel and serviced apartments. The KL Komuter Mid Valley station makes getting here a cinch. There are also Rapid KL buses to Chinatown and a free shuttle bus to Bangsar Light Rail Transit (LRT) station.

Eating & Drinking

There are food courts and a multitude of cafes and restaurants in both malls. Should the enclosed mall environment start getting to you, take a breather on the road separating the Megamall from Gardens Mall where there are several restaurants and cafes with outdoor seating including the **Library** (✆2282 6001; www.thelibrary.my; mains RM25-55; ⊘noon-midnight), which has live music in the evenings.

The Gardens' most classy restaurant and wine bar is **Sage** (✆2268 1328; www.sagekl.com; Level 6, Gardens Residences, Mid Valley, Jln Syed Putra; set lunch/dinner RM100/175; ⊘noon-2pm & 6-10.30pm Mon-Fri, 6-10.30pm only Sat), offering inventive cuisine using high-quality ingredients, along with a panoramic view across to Bangsar. More affordable is the Japanese restaurant **Yuzu** (✆2284 7663; 3rd fl, Gardens Mall; set meals from RM25; ⊘11am-10pm). The pictures in the menu do look better than what you get but portions are large and the prices are right.

Also in the Gardens is the top clubbing venue **Vertigo** (✆010-215 9701; www.facebook.com/VertigoClubKL; 6th fl, The Gardens, Mid Valley City; ⊘9pm-3am), which promotes itself as the epitome of chic and exclusivity and is popular with a monied youthful crowd.

Shopping

Mega is the only way to describe this complex, where you could easily lose yourself for a day or two: it's an ideal place to head if there's a tropical downpour or you just need to escape the heat for a few hours of air-con shopping, but do avoid it on the weekends and holidays if you're not into crowds.

Mid Valley Megamall alone has some 430 shops and restaurants as well as an 18-screen cinema, a bowling alley, a huge food court and even a colourful Hindu temple. One unusual emporium is the **World of Feng Shui** (www.wofs.com; 3rd fl, Mid Valley Megamall), specialising in goods to balance the positive energy in your life.

If the Megamall is proving too plebeian for your shopping tastes, luxury brands are in abundance in the connected Gardens Mall. There are even concierge-attended toilets (RM5 entry)! Anchored by Isetan and Robinsons department stores, here you'll also find many lovely fashion emporiums, including the funky unisex designs of local lad **Key Ng** (www.keyng.com.my; Gardens Mall), an art gallery, another multiplex and the spa and beauty floor.

Activities

Apart from going to the movies, there's a 38-lane bowling alley **Cosmic Bowl** (✆2287 8280; www.cosmicbowl.com.my; 3rd fl, Mid Valley Megamall; admission depending on time of day RM5-7; ⊘11am-1am Sun-Thu, to 2am Fri & Sat). **Megakidz** (✆2282 9300; www.megakidz.com.my; 3rd fl, Mid Valley Megamall; under 2/2-16yr Mon-Fri RM11/22, Sat & Sun RM14/28, crèche service for 2hr under/over 4yr RM30/35; ⊘10am-9.30pm) offers story-telling sessions, art activities, Mandarin lessons, an indoor adventure playground and a crèche service.

Dive Station Explorer (www.divestation.com.my; 3rd fl, Mid Valley Megamall) is an experienced operator and dive shop through which you can arrange three-day/two-night PADI open-water courses and other dive courses.

and tie-dye – all the elements of the flash Bollywood look are present in this boutique mainly for women but also with some fancy tops for men.

NU SENTRAL
MALL

Map p260 (www.nusentral.com; 1 Sentral Jln Travers; ⊙10am-10pm; ⊛KL Sentral) The city's newest mall is part of the ongoing development of KL Sentral. Here you'll find a branch of Parkson department store, MPH bookstore, a GSC multiplex and a food court.

BANGSAR SHOPPING CENTRE
MALL

Map p262 (BSC; www.bsc.com.my; 285 Jln Maarof; ⊙10am-10pm; ⊛Bangsar) BSC has carved a niche with KL's gourmets thanks to its fabulous food hall Jason's and collection of chic, happening restaurants, cafes and bars. Other retail reasons for heading here are to get a new outfit at British India, homewares at House & Co (www.houseand co.com.my), fancy footwear in Shoes Shoes Shoes, and traditional fashions at Terengganu Sonket and Balinese Lace.

There are also some very pukka tailors should you need a dress shirt or suit. Also look out for the monthly Seek & Keep artisan market showcasing local designers and products.

LONELY DREAM
FASHION

Map p262 (www.lonelydream.com; Lot 12, Telawi Sq, 39 & 41 Jln Telawi 3, Bangsar Baru; ⊙noon-8pm; ⊛Bangsar) Cookie and Sam are the stylish duo behind this cutting-edge boutique on the top floor of the new Telawi Square minimall. They stack their own label as well as clothes of other designers.

SHOES SHOES SHOES
SHOES

Map p262 (www.facebook.com/ShoesShoes Shoes3; 31A Jln Telawi 3, Bangsar; ⊙11am-9pm; ⊛Bangsar) Locals celebs and fashionistas love this home-grown brand of footwear as well as the bag line KLutched. There's a branch in Bangsar Shopping Centre up the road but this boutique, up a floor from the street, is the original.

EGG
FASHION

Map p262 (http://egg-fashion.com; 32 Jln Telawi 5, Bangsar Baru; ⊙10am-9pm; ⊛Bangsar) Colourful floral and geometric prints are used to effect on the fashions at this affordable local design business with clothes for men and women. There's also a branch in Mid Valley Megamall.

SILVERFISH BOOKS
BOOKS

Map p262 (☑2284 4837; www.silverfishbooks. com; 28-1 Jln Telawi, Bangsar Baru; ⊙10am-8pm Mon-Fri, to 6pm Sat; ⊛Bangsar) Good local bookshop and publisher of contemporary Malaysian literature and writings.

 # SPORTS & ACTIVITIES

MAJESTIC SPA
SPA

Map p260 (☑2785 8000; www.majestickl.com/ majestic_spa.html; Majestic Hotel, 5 Jln Sultan Hishamuddin; ⊛Kuala Lumpur) Charles Rennie Macintosh's Willow Tea Rooms in Glasgow are the inspiration for the Majestic's delightful spa where treatments are preceded by a refreshing tea or Pimms cocktail. After your pampering, outdoors and with a view of the colonial train station, there's a pool for a dip and sunbathe (bring earplugs to block out the traffic noise). A 90-minute massage will set you back about RM400.

HAMMAM
SPA

Map p262 (☑2282 2180; Lot 3F-7 & 8 Bangsar Village II, Jln Telawi 1; ⊙10am-7.30pm) The Moroccan steam bath comes to KL at this small but beautiful mosaic-tiled operation. A simple steam and scrub (called 'gommage') is RM150; throw in a massage or other treatment and you're looking at RM245 and up.

KIZSPORTS & GYM
HEALTH & FITNESS

Map p262 (☑2284 6313; www.kizsports.com. my; 3rd fl, Bangsar Village II, Jln Telawi 1; Mon-Fri RM24, Sat & Sun RM30; ⊙10am-8pm; ⊛Bangsar) Your little ones will be sure to have fun in their large soft play area and there's an extensive list of programs from belly dancing to taekwondo. Child-minding for children three years and over is RM35 per hour.

VIVEKANANDA ASHRAM
YOGA

Map p260 (☑4021 4657; www.sivananda.org.my; 220 Jln Tun Sambanthan, Brickfields; ⊛KL Sentral) This historic ashram, part of the global Ramakrishna movement, offers courses in kundalini yoga. Classes are usually on Tuesday at 6.30pm and are by donation. A statue of Swami Vivekananda stands in front of the handsome 1904 building.

Day Trips from Kuala Lumpur

Batu Caves p115
This dramatic limestone crag riddled with caverns is both a natural marvel and religious site with its holy Hindu shrines and colourful dioramas.

Forest Research Institute of Malaysia (FRIM) p117
Switch track from the drone of city traffic and air-conditioning to birdsong and all-encompassing greenery at this jungle park.

Fraser's Hill (Bukit Fraser) p118
Breathe easy at this classic, colonial-era, high-altitude resort on the Selangor–Pahang border that is also a top bird-spotting destination.

Klang Valley p120
Travel from city to coast, pausing at a range of fun attractions and sights including a giant water theme park, a mega-mosque and Klang's vibrant Little India.

Putrajaya p124
Malaysia's administrative hub is a showboat of daring contemporary and Islamic heritage architecture arranged around a pretty, artificial lake.

TOP SIGHT
BATU CAVES

One of Malaysia's national treasures, the venerable Hindu temples housed in and around these limestone caves have been a devotional sight for more than 120 years. It's always an atmospheric, colourful and fascinating place to visit but no more so than in late January or early February when a million pilgrims converge on the caves during the three-day Thaipusam.

History

The American naturalist William Hornaday is credited with 'discovering' the caves in 1878, but at least 15 years earlier Chinese settlers were collecting guano from here to fertilise their vegetable patches. Long before that indigenous peoples would also likely have used the caves for shelter.

Temple Cave

In 1891, K Thambusamy Pillai, founder of the Sri Mahamariamman Temple (p76) in KL, established a shrine in what is now known as the Temple Cave. During Thaipusam a statue of Murugan, also known as Lord Subramaniam, is transported in a silver chariot between the two temples.

A 42.5m golden statue of Murugan stands sentinel at the foot of a flight of 272 steps leading up to Temple Cave. Macaque monkeys scamper around the steps and shrines, which are dwarfed by the enormous cavern. A cable car to the cave entrance is planned for 2014.

Other Caves

At step 204, branch off to the **Dark Cave** (www.darkcavemalaysia.com; adult/child RM35/25; ☺10am-5pm Tue-Fri, 10.30am-5.30pm Sat & Sun, tours every 20 min) 🗗 to follow a 45-minute guided tour around 800m of the 2km of surveyed passageways with seven different chambers. Dramatic limestone formations, two species of bat and hundreds of other life forms,

DON'T MISS

➡ Temple Cave
➡ Dark Cave
➡ Ramayana Cave
➡ Zoo Negara

PRACTICALITIES

➡ ☎03-6189 6284
➡ www.batucaves muruga.org
➡ Temple Cave free, other caves admission charges apply
➡ ☺7am-9pm
➡ Ⓡ Batu Caves

EATING

There's a restaurant attached to the Cave Villa but the better place to eat is **Restoran Rani** (Batu Caves; meals RM8-12; ☉7am-10pm) to the right of the Temple Cave steps. It serves good-value vegetarian food including thali meals, roti and refreshing coconut juice straight from the nut.

The Batu Caves limestone outcrop is one of Malaysia's major rock-climbing locations. Read the web feature on Wild Asia (www.wildasia.org/main.cfm/library/Rock_Climbing_Batu_Caves) for a brief guide to the scene.

including the rare trapdoor spider, make this a fascinating excursion. See the website about organising a more challenging two- to three-hour tour, which involves crawling through the cave's narrow tunnels.

At the Batu Caves train-station end of the complex stands a 15m-tall statue of the monkey god Hanuman guarding the Sri Anjeneyar Temple. Behind this is a giant golden chariot pulled by 13 horses and the entrance to the newly restored art gallery of the **Ramayana Cave** (admission RM1; ☉9am-5pm) where scenes from this Hindu epic are depicted in vivid tableaux populated by acid-trip-coloured statues.

At the foot of the steps up to the Temple Cave is the **Cave Villa** (☑6154 2307; www.cavevilla.com.my; adult/child RM15/7; ☉9am-6.30pm; ⓡBatu Caves), fronted by a pond packed with koi carp. Psychedelically painted sculptures of Hindu gods arranged to tell parables from the Bhagavad Gita and other Hindu scriptures decorate the caves. There's also a 2000-sq-ft bird sanctuary, a reptile zoo and classical Indian dance shows on the hour.

Zoo Negara

A trip to Batu Caves can easily be combined with a visit to **Zoo Negara** (www.zoonegaramalaysia.my; adult/child RM50/25; ☉9am-5pm), 11km southeast. Laid out over 62 hectares around a central lake, the zoo is home to a wide variety of native wildlife, including tigers and orang-utans, as well as other animals, insects and aquatic life from Asia and Africa. Although some of the enclosures could definitely be bigger, it is one of Asia's better zoos: successful breeding programs include ones that have produced false gharials, African dwarf crocodiles and 200 of the highly endangered milky stork. You can buy bags of carrot chips and bunches of green bamboo to feed the elephants, camels, deer and giraffes yourself. It's also possible to spend a day as a volunteer here – see the website for details.

A taxi from central KL/Batu Caves will be around RM25/10. Metrobus 16 from Central Market and KL Rapid U23 (both RM3) from Titiwangsa monorail station also come here.

Orang Asli Museum

In the village of Gombak, 25km north of KL and 8.7km from Batu Caves, the **Orang Asli Museum** (☑6189 2113; ☉9am-5pm Sat-Thu) FREE is a fine introduction to the customs and culture of Malaysia's indigenous people. The fascinating exhibits include clothes made from the bark of *terap* and *ipoh* trees, personal adornments, musical instruments and hunting implements. Staff will play video documentaries on the Orang Asli, if you ask.

Bus U12 (RM3, 1½ hours) from Lebuh Ampang runs here. A taxi from Batu Caves costs around RM10.

TOP SIGHT
FOREST RESEARCH INSTITUTE OF MALAYSIA

Covering 600 hectares, and popular with locals who come to stroll in the shade of soaring trees, the Forest Research Institute of Malaysia (FRIM) was established in 1929 to conduct research into the sustainable management of Malaysia's rainforests. The junglelike park is planted with a wide variety of native flora including indigenous fruit trees, conifers and rare, old dipterocarps. Swinging through these trees are macaques and langurs (leaf monkeys).

Canopy Walkway

FRIM's highlight is its canopy walkway, hanging a vertigo-inducing 30m above the forest floor. It is reached by a steep trail from the information centre, where you should go first to register and to pick up maps of the other trails in the park. The 200m walkway will take you right into the canopy, offering great views of the rainforest, with the towers of KL rising in the distance behind.

Heading down from the walkway the trail picks its way through the jungle (follow the water pipe) to a shady picnic area where you can cool off in a series of shallow waterfalls. The return hike incorporating the walkway takes around two hours. Bring water with you.

Wooden Houses & Museum

Elsewhere in the park there's a couple of handsome traditional wooden houses, relocated from Melaka and Terengganu. Drop by the museum to learn a bit more about the work of FRIM and the make-up of Malaysian forest. Paths run through several arboreta highlighting different types of trees, and a wetland area. Next to the information centre is a pond containing a giant araipama, a South American freshwater fish.

It's best to bring a picnic but, if not, there's a canteen in the park.

Rimbun Dahan

For most of the year only the Hijjas family, their friends and a handful of talented writers and artists have access to **Rimbun Dahan** (6038-3690; www.rimbundahan.org/home.html), 18km and about a 20-minute taxi ride west of FRIM (or a 28km, 30-minute taxi ride from central KL). The artists' residency program, set up by architect Hijjas Kasturi (who designed the striking Tabung Haji and Menara Maybank buildings in KL) and his Australian wife Angela in 1994, culminates in a public show (usually held in March) in the subterranean gallery in their private estate.

The **Art for Nature** exhibition of visual arts, which helps raise funds for WWF Malaysia, is also held here, usually in late July or early August. These events are well worth attending, not only to see works by some of the brightest stars of Malaysia's art scene but also for the glimpse it allows into this serene compound that also has an indigenous herb and spice garden and two beautifully restored heritage buildings – a traditional Malay wooden house dating from 1901 that shows elements of Chinese design, and a handsome colonial bungalow transported from Penang.

DON'T MISS

➡ Canopy Walkway
➡ Traditional Wooden Houses
➡ Museum
➡ Rimbun Dahan

PRACTICALITIES

➡ FRIM
➡ ☑6279 7575
➡ www.frim.gov.my
➡ Selangor Darul Ehsan
➡ admission RM5, Canopy Walkway adult/child RM10/1
➡ ⊘information centre 8am-5pm Mon-Fri, 9am-4pm Sat & Sun, Canopy Walkway 9.30am-1.30pm Tue-Thu, Sat & Sun, museum 9am-4pm Tue-Sun
➡ ⊠KTM Komuter to Kepong, then taxi

Fraser's Hill (Bukit Fraser)

Explore

Of all the hill stations, Fraser's Hill (Bukit Fraser) retains the most colonial charm. Situated across seven densely forested hills at a cool altitude of 1524m, this quiet and relatively undeveloped place is best visited for gentle hikes and bird-watching.

Fraser's Hill is named after Louis James Fraser, an adventurous Scotsman who migrated to Malaysia in the 1890s and set up a mule-train operation to transport tin ore across the hills. He is also rumoured to have run gambling and opium dens, which had vanished (along with Fraser himself) by 1917, when Bishop Ferguson-Davie of Singapore came looking for the Scotsman. Recognising the area's potential as a hill station, the bishop wrote a report to the high commissioner on his return to Singapore. A couple of years later this 'little England' in the heart of the Malaysian jungle began to be developed.

The Best...

➡ **Activity** Bird-spotting
➡ **Place to Eat** Scott's Pub & Restaurant
➡ **Place to Stay** Ye Olde Smokehouse Fraser's Hill

Top Tip

If you plan to stay overnight, schedule your visit for midweek. Many places charge 20% to 40% more on weekends and public holidays.

Getting There & Away

➡ **Taxi** The route to Fraser's Hill is via Kuala Kubu Bharu (KKB) which is on the KTM Komuter train line (RM5.60). A taxi from KKB to Fraser's Hill is one-way/return RM80/200, or from KL's Pudu Sentral bus station RM200/350.

➡ **Car** If driving, note there's no petrol station in Fraser's Hill; the nearest ones are at Raub and KKB.

Need to Know

➡ **Area Code** 09
➡ **Location** On the Selangor–Pahang border, 100km north of KL.
➡ **Tourist Office** (FHDC; 362 2207; www.pkbf.org.my; Puncak Inn, Jln Genting; 8am-5pm Mon-Fri) Also see www.fraserhill.info.

 SIGHTS

BIRD INTERPRETATION CENTRE EXHIBITION

Fraser's Hill's main attraction is its abundant flora and fauna, in particular its birdlife. Some 265 species of birds have

---

SLEEPING IN FRASER'S HILL

There's plenty of accommodation but musty, damp rooms and cottages go with the territory. Rates typically include breakfast.

Ye Olde Smokehouse Fraser's Hill (362 2226; www.thesmokehouse.my; Jln Jeriau; d/ste from RM308/385) Exposed beams, log fires, four-poster beds and chintz – the Smokehouse goes for broke with its English-charm offensive.

Highland Resthouse Holdings Bungalows (in KL 09-362 2645; www.hrhbungalows.com;) Check the website of this company for details about the range of rooms and bungalows at Fraser's Hill, starting from RM180 per room at the eight-bedroom Pekan bungalow, a well-kept property overlooking the golf course, to RM2000 for full hire of the four-bedroom Jerantut bungalow.

Puncak Inn (09-3622 007; puncakinn1@yahoo.com; r with breakfast RM100, apt/bungalow RM120/300) Offers the best-value rooms in Fraser's in a handy central location. It also rents out studio, two- and three-bed apartments in the Fraser's Silverpark Resort, and four cottages that sleep between four and 15 people.

Shahzan Inn Fraser's Hill (362 3300; shahzan7@streamyx.com; Jln Lady Guillemard; r incl breakfast from RM150;) One of the most attractive places to stay. All rooms have balconies, a kettle and satellite TV; the ones overlooking the golf course are the nicest.

KUALA KUBU BHARU

Most travellers zip through Kuala Kubu Bharu, 72km north of KL, en-route to Fraser's Hill. However, the charming, stuck-in-time town known as KKB is the jumping off point for various adventurous outdoor activities such as rafting and kayaking on the Selangor Dam, Sungai Selangor and Sungai Chiling. A recommended outfitter is **Pierose Swiftwater** (www.raftmalaysia.com).

A popular jungle trek is to the 20m-tall Chiling Waterfall on Sungai Chiling. This is a 1½-hour walk from the so-called Rainbow Bridge on route 55 leading up to Fraser's Hill. The route is clearly marked, but it's a good idea to hire a guide, since you have to cross the river five times and it's important to be aware of flash flooding. **Happy Yen** (☑017-369 7831; www.happyyen.com; tour R250 per person) organises tours to the falls from KL.

KKB is connected to KL by the KTM Komuter train (RM5.60); you'll need to change at Rawang. From the station a taxi to the town centre costs around RM5. Accommodation is limited to basic hotels; better to use Fraser's Hill as a base, or the rough-luxe **Sekeping Serendah Retreat** (☑012-324 6552; www.serendah.com; cabins from RM500/650; ⊠), self-catering cabins in the rainforest near Serendah, 35km south of KKB and also on the train line.

been spotted here, including the Malaysian whistling thrush, the Kinabalu friendly warbler, the brilliantly coloured green magpie, and the long-tailed broadbill with its sky-blue chest. In June the hill station hosts its **International Bird Race**, in which teams of bird-watchers compete to record the highest number of species.

In the sports centre opposite the Puncak Inn, there's a Bird Interpretation Centre at the golf clubhouse; get the key from the staff at the Puncak Inn.

JERIAU WATERFALL   WATERFALL

Located about 4km northwest of the town centre, along Jln Air Terjun, is Jeriau Waterfall, where you can also swim. It's a 20-minute climb up from the road to reach the falls.

 EATING & DRINKING

There are a couple of small stores as you come into Fraser's Hill for self-catering supplies, as well as a hawker-stall complex beside the kids' playground. All the hotels have restaurants.

HILL VIEW   WESTERN, CHINESE $

(Hawker's Stalls, Pine Tree Rd; mains from RM10; ⊗9.30am-9pm) Simple dishes are cooked up by a family who have run this stall for a couple of generations.

SCOTT'S PUB & RESTAURANT   BRITISH $$

(www.thesmokehouse.my; Jln Genting; mains RM17-22; ⊗11am-10pm Thu-Tue) A slice of old England is re-created at this pub (run by the same firm as the Smokehouse), where you can sink a pint and indulge in all-day breakfasts, fish and chips, a steak or sandwiches. Live football screened from the English Premier League adds to the experience.

YE OLDE SMOKEHOUSE
FRASER'S HILL   BRITISH $$$

(www.thesmokehouse.my; Jln Jeriau; afternoon tea/meals RM20/80) You don't need to be a hotel guest to come and enjoy a meal or afternoon tea at the chintzy Smokehouse. The flaky pastry pies and roasts are recommended. If the weather's fine, it's possible to dine on the garden terrace.

 SPORTS & ACTIVITIES

PINE TREE TRAIL   HIKING

Pick up a leaflet from the Puncak Inn outlining various hikes, most of which are pretty straightforward and signposted. You'll need to arrange a guide for the 5km-long Pine Tree Trail, which takes around six hours and crosses three mountain peaks, including 1505m Pine Tree Hill; a recommended guide is **Mr Durai** (☑013-983 1633; durefh@hotmail.com), who charges around RM30 per hour.

GOLF COURSE
GOLF

(📞09-362 2129; Jln Genting; green fees weekday/weekend RM30/40, hire half/full set of clubs RM15/30) Opposite the Puncak Inn is the picturesque nine-hole golf course; guests at the Puncak and Shahzan Inns receive a 20% discount.

PADDOCK
HORSE RIDING

At the paddock to the east of the golf course, you can go horse riding (RM5 to RM8) or practise archery (RM8). Arrange via the tourist office.

ALLAN'S WATER
BOATING

You can hire a paddleboat through the tourist office (RM6 per 15 minutes) to explore this small lake next to the flower nursery. It was once used as a freshwater reservoir for the hill station and is named after the colonial engineer who designed it.

Klang Valley

Explore

Heading southwest of KL along the Klang Hwy, the Kota Darul Ehsan ceremonial arch marks the transition between the city and Selangor. Just over the boundary is the satellite city of Petaling Jaya (PJ), best visited for its shopping malls and great places to eat. Next along, Shah Alam, the staunchly Muslim state capital, blends into Klang, the old royal capital – pretty much all in one seamless stretch of housing estates and industrial parks.

Efficient public transport makes for easy day trips along the Klang Valley to see the scattered sights. For a complete escape from urbanised Malaysia, journey to the end of the rail line and hop on a ferry to Pulau Ketam, an island with a picturesque fishing village surrounded by mangroves.

The Best...

➡**Cool-Down Spot** Sunway Lagoon (p123)
➡**Island Escape** Pulau Ketam (p122)
➡**Secret Garden** 1 Utama (p123)

Top Tip

Check out PJ's contemporary-music pulse at **Merdekarya** (📞016-2020 529, 016-2071 553; www.merdekarya.com/; 352 Jalan 5/57, Petaling Garden) which hosts concerts, open-mic nights and sells local-interest books and CDs. It's on the 1st floor.

Getting There & Away

➡**Bus** From Pasar Seni in KL frequent buses fan out to PJ, Shah Alam and Klang.
➡**Train** The best way to get to Klang from KL (RM3.60, one hour, every 30 minutes), as the KTM Komuter station is closer to the sights. KTM Komuter trains terminate at Pelabuhan Klang next to the ferry terminal.

Need to Know

➡**Area Code** 📞03
➡**Location** PJ is 10km, Shah Alam 20km and Klang 32km southwest of KL
➡**Tourist Office** (www.tourismselangor.my)

◉ SIGHTS

◉ Shah Alam

MASJID SULTAN SALAHUDDIN ABDUL AZIZ SHAH
MOSQUE

(📞5159 9988; www.mssaas.gov.my; ⏰10am-noon & 2-4pm Sat-Thu) Called the Blue Mosque for its azure dome (larger than that of London's St Paul's Cathedral), this is one of Southeast Asia's biggest mosques. Covered in a rosette of verses from the Quran, the building accommodates up to 24,000 worshippers and is a sight to behold. Its four minarets, looking like giant rockets, are the tallest in the world (over 140m). You'll need to be appropriately dressed if you want to look inside.

CITY OF DIGITAL LIGHTS AT I-CITY
TECHNOLOGY PARK

(www.i-city.my; per car RM10; ⏰6pm-3am; 🚉Padang Jawa, then taxi) Some bright spark had the idea to jolly up a dull technology park with a million and one LED light displays. There are forests of multicoloured trees, giant peacocks and cacti, a massive screen showing free movies, **Snowalk** where the air-con is cranked up to keep the fairy-lit snowmen and penguins climatically happy, and outdoor amusement and water theme parks. Kids and collectors of supremely kitsch experiences will love it.

⊙ Klang

Once Selangor's royal capital, Klang is where the British installed their first Resident in 1874. Its few sights should take no more than a couple of hours to see, leaving you plenty of time to enjoy the real reason for heading here: satisfying your stomach in the restaurants of Klang's vibrant Little India.

Klang is small enough to see on foot. Heading south from the train station, along Jln Stesyn, you'll pass several attractive rows of Chinese shophouses (to the right).

LITTLE INDIA   NEIGHBOURHOOD

Running parallel to Jln Stesyn to the right is Jln Tengku Kelana, heart of Klang's colourful Little India. Especially frenetic around the Hindu festival of Deepavali, this Little India is more vibrant than those of KL, and includes several fortune tellers, who squat on the pavement and predict the future with the aid of green parrots trained to pick out auspicious cards.

GALERI DIRAJA SULTAN
ABDUL AZIZ   MUSEUM

(☏3373 6500; www.galeridiraja.com; Jln Stesen; ⊙10am-5pm Tue-Sun) FREE A grand white-washed 1909 colonial building houses the royal gallery, devoted to the history of the Selangor Sultanate (dating back to 1766); it contains a wide array of royal regalia, gifts and artifacts, including replicas of the crown jewels.

ISTANA ALAM SHAH   PALACE

(Jln Istana) Heading uphill along Jln Istana will bring you to the sultan's palace before the royal capital was moved to Shah Alam. The park opposite gives a pleasant view of the city.

MASJID DI RAJA
SULTAN SULEIMAN   MOSQUE

(Jln Kota Raja) East of the palace, along Jln Kota Raja, this former state mosque, opened in 1934, is a striking blend of art deco and Middle Eastern influences. Several sultans are buried here. Step inside to admire its stained-glass dome.

WORTH A DETOUR

GENTING HIGHLANDS

This hill station, 50km north of Kuala Lumpur on the Pahang border, is in stark contrast to the old English style of other Malaysian upland resorts, its raison d'être being **Resort World Genting** (☏03-2718 1888; www.rwgenting.com) – this glitzy casino is the only one in the country. In its slender favour is the cool weather; at 2000m above sea level there's no need for air-conditioning. Bird lovers should also note that this a prime location for **bird-watching**, with around 254 species seen here.

The 3.4km-long **Genting Skyway** (one-way RM6; ⊙7.30am-11pm Mon-Thu, to midnight Fri-Sun) is a gentle 11-minute cable-car glide above the dense rainforest. Kids will also enjoy the various theme-park attractions here including those at the **First World Indoor Theme Park** (adult/child RM32/30). The outdoor theme park is closed until 2016 to create a Twentieth Century Fox Theme Park.

Genting is an easy day trip from KL but, if you'd prefer to stay, the resort has a choice of five hotels (sleeping a total of 10,000 people). Rates vary enormously, the most expensive nights generally being Saturday and public holidays; check the website. There's no shortage of places to eat, including cheap fast-food outlets and noisy food courts.

Buses leave at hourly (and sometimes half-hourly) intervals from 7.30am to 8.30pm from KL's Pudu Sentral bus station (adult/child RM10.60/9.50, 1½ hours), and on the hour from 8am to 7pm from KL Sentral (RM10.30/9.20); the price includes the Skyway cable car. A taxi from KL will cost around RM70.

The **Go Genting Golden Package** (RM60) includes return transport from KL, the Skyway transfer and either an Indoor Theme Park ride pass or buffet lunch at the Coffee Terrace. Buy the pass from Genting's ticket office at KL Sentral or from its **main sales office** (☏2718 1118; www.rwgenting.com; 28 Jln Sultan Ismail, Wisma Genting; ⊙8.30am-6pm Mon-Fri, to 1pm Sat), where you can also book resort accommodation.

EATING

Petaling Jaya

KTZ FOOD DESSERTS **$**
(☎7877 2499; 66 & 68 Jln SS2/67; ☺4pm-1am)
Dessert such as delicious shaved ice sago *loh* and *tong sui* sweet bean, nut and fruit soups are enthusiastically slurped by an appreciative crowd at this standby of the SS2 restaurant area.

FRESH UNIQUE SEAFOOD 23 SEAFOOD **$$$**
(☎7960 2088; www.unique-seafood.com.my; Jln Kemajuan, SS13, Lot 9B; ☺noon-2.30pm & 6-10.30pm) Scotland clams, Boston lobsters, mantis prawns, Australian snow or Ireland roe crabs, even California geoduck – if it's got fins, scales or a shell there's a good chance that Unique will have it. A wall of tiered tanks hold a global bounty of flapping, squirming fish and crustaceans that form the backdrop to a dining hall packed with families digging in.

All the prices are clearly labelled – your choice is weighed first and the total given – if the price is too high it's OK to have them throw the fish back and choose something else. Once you've done the deal on the raw materials, the waiters will suggest how best it should be cooked, for which there will be an extra charge.

Bring a group and choose judiciously and you could average RM50 to RM80 per head –

a bargain for such fresh, expertly cooked food.

Klang

SENG HUAT BAK KUT TEH MALAY, CHINESE **$**
(☎012-309 8303; 9 Jln Besar; meals RM10; ☺7.30am-1pm & 5.30-8.30pm; ☑) Indian food is Klang's highlight, but it's not the only thing on offer: the town's Chinese community is also famous for inventing *bak kut the* (pork-rib soup with garlic and Chinese five spice). Sample the fragrant, flavoursome stew at this unpretentious eatery, steps away from the train station, just beneath the Klang Bridge – get here early though as it's popular and it runs out of meat towards the end of the opening sessions.

ASOKA INDIAN **$**
(105 Jln Tengku Kelana; meals RM5-10; ☺7am-11pm) Vividly orange-and-cream-painted parlour of Indian culinary goodness, including a great selection of sweets, juices and crispy *dosai* pancakes served with coconut chutney.

SRI BARATHAN MATHA VILAS INDIAN, CHINESE **$**
(34-36 Jln Tengku Kelana; meals RM5-10; ☺6.30am-10.30pm) It's hard to resist a bowl of this restaurant's signature dish of spicy mee goreng (fried noodles); the chef prepares them constantly in a giant wok beside the entrance.

> **WORTH A DETOUR**
>
> ### ISLAND ESCAPES
>
> The islands of **Pulau Ketam** and **Pulau Carey** – one reached by ferry, the other by road – are ideal antidotes to the Klang Valley's urban sprawl.
>
> Ketam means 'crab' and an abundance of these creatures is what first brought Chinese settlers to the so-named island, a 30-minute ferry trip (return RM14) through the mangroves from Pelabuhan Klang. On arrival you'll find a rickety yet charming fishing village built on stilts over the mudflats. Wander around the wooden buildings of the village then enjoy a Chinese seafood lunch at one of several restaurants. Ferries depart roughly every hour starting at 8.45am; the last ferry back from Pulau Ketam is at 5.30pm (6pm at weekends).
>
> If you don't have your own wheels, hire a taxi to get you out to Pulau Carey (from Klang one-way/return RM80/150), an island largely covered with palm-oil plantations. In tiny **Kampung Sungai Bumbon**, home to an Orang Asli tribe known as the Hma' Meri (also written as Mah Meri), you can see the woodcarvers who have put Hma' Meri art on the cultural map. There's also a **community centre** (☺9am-5pm) where you can pick up pretty woven baskets and other products made from dyed pandanus palm leaves as well as the interesting booklet in English about Hma' Meri culture.

★**MOHANA BISTRO**   INDIAN $$
([☎]3372 7659; 119 Jln Tengku Kelana; meals RM10-16; ⊙7am-10.30pm; ✍) Deservedly popular spot for banana-leaf curry spreads and spice-laden biryani rice. The waiters bring round trays of tempting veg and meat dishes to choose from.

SHOPPING

Klang Valley is stacked with malls, with Petaling Jaya particularly well served in this respect. The following ones are our pick of the crop.

 Petaling Jaya

SUNWAY PYRAMID   MALL
([☎]7494 3100; www.sunwaypyramid.com; skating rink admission incl skate hire Mon-Fri RM17, Sat & Sun RM22; ⊙skating rink 9am-8pm) Next to Sunway Lagoon and pretty much a tourist attraction in its own right. Distinguished by its giant lion gateway, faux Egyptian walls and crowning pyramid, this mall contains a skating rink as well as a bowling alley, a multiplex cinema and the usual plethora of shops and dining outlets.

CURVE   MALL
([☎]03-7710 6868; www.thecurve.com.my; ⊙10am-10pm) About 15km west of the centre of PJ, this sprawling shopping complex is worth a look for its various market events usually on the weekend and – a recent addition – the farmers and craft market on Friday (11am to 7pm). There's a free bus shuttle service here from the Royale Bintang Hotel (p131) in KL.

JAYA ONE   MALL
(www.jayaone.com.my/; 72A Jalan Universiti; ⊙10am-10pm) Home to the performing arts centre **PJ Live Arts** (www.pjlivearts.my) and a branch of hit bistro The Bee (which also hosts bands and other events). Every three months it also has a new-and-old goods stall event, **Markets@JayaOne** (www.markets.my). Take a taxi or bus from Asia Jaya Light Rail Transit (LRT) station.

1 UTAMA   MALL
(www.1utama.com.my; 1 Lebuh Bandar Utama, Bandar Utama; ⊙10am-10pm) The main reason for visiting this mall is for its 2790-sq-

metre Secret Garden – one of the largest roof gardens in the world with over 500 varieties of plants. There's also a mini rainforest in the mall's atrium and the climbing gym Camp5. There's a bus from Kelana Jaya LRT station.

AMCORP MALL   MALL
(http://amcorpmall.com; 8 Jln Persiaran Barat; ⊙10am-10pm) Don't overlook this dated but conveniently located mall next to Taman Jaya LRT station. Visit on the weekend when it hosts one of the Klang Valley's largest flea markets. Also come for the discount bookstore **BookXcess** (www.bookxcess.com).

 # SPORTS & ACTIVITIES

Petaling Jaya

SUNWAY LAGOON   THEME PARK
([☎]5639 0000; www.sunwaylagoon.com; 3 Jln PJS, 11/11 Bandar Sunway; adult/child RM120/90; ⊙10am-6pm) There are few more fun ways of cooling down on a sticky day than splashing around at this multizone theme park built on the site of a former tin mine and quarry. The highlights are the water slides, and the world's largest artificial surf beach. There's also a Wild West–themed section with all the regular thrill rides, an interactive wildlife zoo (ie you're allowed to stroke the giant tortoises and cuddle the hamsters) and an extreme park with all-terrain vehicles, a rock-climbing wall and paintball fights. Book online for discount tickets.

The easiest way here is take the LRT to Kelana Jaya (RM2.10), then bus T623 (RM1) or a taxi (RM15) to the Sunway Pyramid. Buses U63, U67 and U76 (RM3) run here from Pasir Seni in KL. A taxi from central KL will cost around RM25.

CAMP5   CLIMBING GYM
([☎]7726 0410; www.facebook.com/Camp5ClimbingGym; 5th fl, 1 Utama Shopping Centre, Bandar Utama Damansara; admission RM28, taster session/wall course RM48/100; ⊙2-11pm Mon-Fri, 10am-8pm Sat & Sun) The fifth floor of 1 Utama (p123) has been transformed into a state-of-the-art indoor climbing facility. One great advantage of climbing in this 24m-high space is that it's air-conditioned. To get here take the bus from Kelana Jaya LRT station.

Putrajaya

Explore

An eye-catching array of monumental architecture amid lush, manicured greenery is on display at Putrajaya, only in its second decade of existence. Covering 4932 hectares of former rubber and palm-oil plantations, the Federal Government's administrative hub was but a twinkle in the eye of its principal visionary – former prime minister Dr Mahathir – back in the early 1990s.

Billed as an 'intelligent garden city', Putrajaya is impressive, but like other planned cities it can also be a strange place to visit. Its heart is a 600-hectare artificial lake fringed by landscaped parks and an eclectic mix of buildings and bridges, best viewed when illuminated at night. However, it's still a long way off its envisioned population of over 300,000 and is practically devoid of streetlife.

The Best...

➡ **Lakeside Mosque** Putra Mosque
➡ **Botanical Garden** Taman Botani
➡ **Place to Eat** Selera Putra (p126)

Top Tip

Just over 97% of Putrajaya's population is Muslim – something to be aware of when choosing how to dress and behave while visiting the city's mosques.

Getting There & Away

➡ **Train** KLIA transit trains from KL Sentral and KLIA stop at the Putrajaya-Cyberjaya station (from KL Sentral it costs RM9.50 one way and takes 20 minutes).

➡ **Bus** Buses 100, 101 and 300 run from the train station to close to Dataran Putra (50 sen); a taxi there is RM13, while hiring one for an hour to tour the sights (the recommended option) is RM40.

➡ **Bicycle** Bicycles (RM4 per hour) can be hired from the tourist-information booth.

➡ **Tour** From the tourist-information booth and Putrajaya station, the two-hour **Best of Putrajaya bus tour** (☑03-8887 7690; RM1; ☺11.30am & 3pm Sat & Sun) runs on the weekends only.

Need to Know

➡ **Area Code** ☑03
➡ **Location** 25km south of KL and 20km north of KLIA
➡ **Tourist Office** (Dataran Putra; ☺8am-1pm & 2-5.30pm Sat-Thu, 8am-12.15pm & 2.45-5.30pm Fri)

SIGHTS

URBAN PUTRAJAYA   NEIGHBOURHOOD

Monumental buildings, each a different design, line the main boulevard Persiaran Perdana, which runs from the elevated spaceship-like **Putrajaya Convention Centre** (☑8887 6000; Presint 5), worth visiting for the views, to the circular **Dataran Putra** (Putra Sq). Look out for the Mughal-esque **Istana Kehakiman** (Palace of Justice), the modernist Islamic gateway fronting the **Kompleks Perdadanan Putrajaya** (Putrajaya Corporation Complex) and steel-clad **Tuanku Mizan Zainal Abidin Mosque**, also known as Masjid Besi (the Iron Mosque).

Framing Dataran Putra on two sides are **Perdana Putra**, housing the offices of the prime minister, and the handsome **Putra**

KUALA GANDAH ELEPHANT CONSERVATION CENTRE

Many tour operators in Kuala Lumpur offer day-trip packages (for around RM200) to the **Kuala Gandah Elephant Conservation Centre** (☑09-279 0391; www.wildlife. gov.my/webpagev4_en/bhg_ekogandah.html; Kuala Gandah, Lanchang; entry by donation; ⊙10am-4.45pm) about 150km east of KL.

This is the base for the Department of Wildlife and National Parks' Elephant Relocation Team, which helps capture and relocate rogue elephants from across Southeast Asia to other suitable habitats throughout the peninsula, such as at Taman Negara. Most of the elephants at the centre are work elephants from Myanmar, India and Thailand.

Visitors are first shown a video (viewings at 1pm, 1.30pm and 3.45pm daily, also 12.30pm Saturday and Sunday) about the elephants' plight, then can watch while the handlers wash down the big guys and feed them fruit (2pm Saturday to Thursday, 2.45pm Friday).

Mosque (⊙for non-Muslims 9am-1.30pm & 3-6pm Sat-Thu, 3-6pm Fri), which has space for 15,000 worshippers and an ornate pink-and-white-patterned dome, influenced by Safavid architecture from Iran.

There are nine bridges, all in different styles. The longest, at 435m, is the **Putra Bridge,** which mimics the Khaju Bridge in Esfahan, Iran. Also worthy of a photo is the futuristic sail-like **Wawasan Bridge** connecting Presint 2 and Presint 8.

PUTRAJAYA LAKE   LAKE

Putrajaya's bridges and buildings look their best when viewed from this 400-hectare, human-made lake. **Cruise Tasik Putrajaya** (☑8888 3769; www.cruisetasikputrajaya. com; ⊙10am-6pm Mon-Thu, to 8pm Fri & Sat, to 7pm Sun), located just beneath the Dataran Putra end of the Putra Bridge, offers two main options: the gondola-like Perahu Dondang Sayang boats (adult/child RM20/12), which depart any time for a 30-minute trip around the lake; and a 45-minute air-con cruise on the Belimbing boat (adult/child RM50/35), which leaves hourly.

TAMAN BOTANI   GARDENS

(☑8888 9090; Presint 1; ⊙9am-noon & 2-5pm Sat-Thu, 9am-11am & 3-5pm Fri) ⦿ FREE North of Perdana Putra, near the prime minister's official residence, this 93-hectare site features attractive tropical gardens, a visitors centre, a beautifully tiled Moroccan pavilion and lakeside restaurant. A tourist tram (RM4) trundles between the flower beds and trestles, and you can hire bicycles (RM2 per hour).

TAMAN WETLAND   PARK

(☑8887 7773; ⊙park 7am-7pm, nature interpretation centre 9am-6pm) ⦿ FREE Further north is this serene, contemplative space with peaceful nature trails, aquatic animals and water birds, fluttering butterflies and picnic tables overlooking the lake. Canoeing and boating trips can be arranged here.

SEPANG CIRCUIT   RACE TRACK

(☑03-8778 2222; www.sepangcircuit.com) The Sepang Circuit, located 30km south of Putrajaya and a 10-minute drive east of KLIA, is where Formula 1 holds the Malaysian Grand Prix every March or April. Tickets go for as little as RM100, which in 2009 included access to an after-race party that was headlined by top international music acts.

During the three days of the grand prix, plenty of special train and bus transport to the circuit is on offer, from around RM80 return from KL's city centre.

Other car and motorcycle races are held here throughout the year – check the website for details. On nonrace days call ahead to book a tour of the facilities, which includes entry to the **auto museum** (⊙9am-6pm) FREE; or take a spin on the go-karting track (RM40 for 10 minutes). Check the website for track days when the circuit is open to wannabe Michael Schumachers to rev up their own cars (RM200) or motorbikes (below 250cc RM70, over 250cc RM100).

DAY TRIPS FROM KUALA LUMPUR PUTRAJAYA

 EATING

ALAMANDA
MALL $

(www.alamanda.com.my; meals RM10; ⊙10am-10pm) Putrajaya's swish shopping mall is home to several restaurants as well as an excellent food court where you can join the local bureaucrats for a meal.

SELERA PUTRA
FOOD COURT $

(meals RM10; ⊙9am-7pm Mon-Fri, to 9pm Sat & Sun) At this food court beneath Dataran Putra take in the lakeside view while enjoying a wide range of inexpensive Malaysian dishes.

Sleeping

KLites' love of brands is reflected in the city's many international hotel chains. You can often grab great online deals for top-end accommodation, which compensates for a dearth of characterful midrange options. Budget sleeps are plentiful, too, but the best places fill up quickly, so book ahead – especially over public holidays.

Hostels & Guesthouses

Kuala Lumpur has plenty of inexpensive hostels and guesthouses. Most offer dorm beds (from as little as RM10) as well as basic rooms with shared or private bathrooms and a choice of fan or air-con.

If your budget is tight, there are grubby fleapits offering windowless boxy rooms, appealing only for their rock-bottom rates. For those who are more flush, however, there are also some very appealing 'flashpacker' hostels and guesthouses offering spacious, comfy dorms and private rooms with bells and whistles that are several steps up in quality than the norm as well as a preferable option to zero-personality budget business hotels.

Hotels

As a rule, the cheapest budget hotels offer poky box rooms, often with thin plywood partition walls and no windows; there may be a choice of private or shared bathrooms and fan or air-conditioning. In cheaper hotels, 'single' normally means one double bed, and 'double' means two double beds. To aid ventilation, the walls of cheaper rooms may not meet the ceiling, which is terrible for acoustics and privacy – bring earplugs.

At midrange hotels air-con is standard, and rooms typically come with TVs, phones, proper wardrobes and private bathrooms. Some midrange hotels also have restaurants, business centres and swimming pools.

With stiff competition at the top end of the market, KL's best hotels pull out all the stops. Rooms have every conceivable amenity, from in-room internet access (typically wi-fi), to safes, minibars, slippers and robes, and even prayer mats for Muslim guests. Look online for discount rates and also for news about several pending international openings including Four Seasons, Regent, Banyan Tree and the world's first Harrods Hotel, rising up next to the Pavilion KL mall.

Homestays

Staying with a Malaysian family in KL is possible, although few homestays will be centrally located. Contact local offices of **Tourism Malaysia** (www.tourismmalaysia.gov.my) for more information and also check sites such as iBilik and Cari Homestay.

Serviced Apartments & Longer-Term Rentals

Some of KL's best accommodation deals, particularly for longer stays, are offered by serviced apartments. Studios and suites tend to be far larger and better equipped than you'd get for a similar price at top-end hotels. There are also usually pools and gyms within the complexes, too. Complexes are scattered across the city, some attached to hotels and sharing their facilities. For short stays, breakfast is usually included.

Accommodation Websites

➡ **Agoda** (www.agoda.com)
➡ **iBilik** (www.ibilik.my)
➡ **Cari Homestay** (www.carihomestay.net)
➡ **Airbnb** (www.airbnb.com)
➡ **Lonely Planet** (hotels.lonelyplanet.com)

NEED TO KNOW

Price Ranges
$ under RM100
$$ RM100–RM400
$$$ over RM400

Discounts
Practically all midrange and top-end places offer promotions that substantially slash rack rates; booking online will almost always bring the price down. Room discounts will not apply during public holidays.

Taxes & Service Charges
At all budget places prices will be net, but at many others 10% service and 6% tax (expressed as ++) will be added to the bill.

Tipping
Not expected.

Wi-Fi
Often free but sometimes only in the hotel lobby. Top-end hotels can charge as much as RM40 per day for internet access.

Lonely Planet's Top Choices

BackHome (p132) Chic pit stop for flashpackers with a cool cafe and tree-studded courtyard.

Sekeping Tenggiri (p134) Rough luxe guesthouse plus top contemporary-art gallery.

Villa Samadhi (p131) Asian-chic style at a gorgeous villa in the embassy district.

Best by Budget

$
Classic Inn (p130) Good dorms and private rooms near all the delicious eats of Pudu.

Explorers Guesthouse (p130) Spacious, quality backpackers in great location.

Hotel Chinatown (2) (p133) Old standby with the market on the doorstep.

$$
Sekeping Tenggiri (p134) Rough luxe guesthouse with ace contemporary-art gallery thrown in.

Sarang Vacation Homes (p130) Friendly B&B operation in a variety of centrally located flats and houses.

Aloft Kuala Lumpur Sentral (p134) Playful, relaxed concept hotel steps from the KLIA Express.

$$$
E&O Residences Kuala Lumpur (p131) Live the life of a high-rolling expat at these gorgeous serviced apartments.

Majestic Hotel (p135) Reborn heritage hotel with modern tower wing and gorgeous spa.

Villa Samadhi (p131) Beautiful Asian-chic bolthole with gorgeous tree-shaded pool.

Best Heritage Hotels

Majestic Hotel (p135) Soak up the colonial style and take tea in the orchid room.

Carcosa Seri Negara (p135) Faded elegance amid the lush Lake Gardens.

Anggun Boutique Hotel (p130) Antique-style charmer with four-posters and patterned tile floors.

Best Designer Stays

Sekeping Sin Chew Kee (p131) Swoon-worthy pair of contemporary-art-decorated apartments.

YY38 Hotel (p130) Its duplex rooms have eye-popping individual themes.

Hotel Maya (p132) Holding its own as one of KL's design-darling digs.

Best Flashpacker Hostels

BackHome (p132) Stripped back concrete-chic dorms and rooms, plus a great cafe.

Reggae Mansion (p132) Chill out at this cool crashpad for the modern backpacker.

Grid 19 (p133) New contender with a hard-edged industrial look and bistro-bar.

Best Serviced Apartments

E&O Residences Kuala Lumpur (p131) Live the life of a high-rolling expat at these gorgeous serviced apartments.

Parkroyal Serviced Suites (p131) Sophisticated studios and suites in a convenient location.

Fraser Place Kuala Lumpur (p132) Functional, fashionable and facility-packed complex.

Where to Stay

Neighbourhood	For	Against
Golden Triangle & KLCC	Kuala Lumpur's top shopping, dining and nightlife is all within easy walking access. There's good public transport, too, with the many hotels nearby a monorail or Light Rail Transit (LRT) station.	Bring earplugs if you're staying in properties around Changkat Bukit Bintang as it gets very noisy at night.
Chinatown & Masjid Jamek	Best location for quality hostels and hanging out with other budget travellers. Good public transport and great food and local atmosphere on the doorstep.	The cheapest places to stay range from very basic to downright awful and/or brothels.
Masjid India & Kampung Baru	Worth looking online for homestay options in Kampung Baru. Reasonably good public transport links as well as excellent eating options.	Many budget and midrange hotels are scruffy and have little character. The nearby Chow Kit red-light district is seedy.
Lake Gardens, KL Sentral & Bangsar	Prime access to Kuala Lumpur International Airport (KLIA) and the rest of the city from KL Sentral. Interesting and lively Brickfields area a short walk away, as well as Lake Gardens.	Not as much street life as in Chinatown or Golden Triangle. Tons of construction ongoing in KL Sentral. Taxis to Bangsar and Mid-Valley can get snarled in traffic.

🛏 Golden Triangle: Bukit Bintang & Pudu

CLASSIC INN   HOSTEL $

Map p252 (📞2148 8648; www.classicinn.com.my; 52 Lg 1/77A, Changkat Thambi Dollah; dm RM45, s/d from 98/128; ❄ @ 🛜; monorail Imbi) Occupying a smartly renovated, yellow-painted shophouse on the southern edge of the Golden Triangle, this is a retro-charming choice with dorms and private rooms, a small grassy garden and welcoming staff. A second, more upmarket branch – Classic Inn Premium – opened along the street in late 2013.

RED PALM   HOSTEL $

Map p252 (📞2143 1279; www.redpalm-kl.com; 5 Tengkat Tong Shin; dm/s/d/tr incl breakfast RM30/55/75/105; @ 🛜; monorail Imbi) Cosy shophouse hostel offering small, thin-walled rooms with shared bathrooms. The communal areas are great and the owners charming.

★ THE YARD BOUTIQUE HOTEL   HOTEL $$

Map p252 (📞03-2141 1017; www.theyard.com.my; 623 (No 51D) Tengkat Tong Shin; d from R192; ❄ @ 🛜; monorail Bukit Bintang) A backstreet hostel been transformed into this calm, stylish oasis steps away from both the eats of Jln Alor and the bars of Changkat Bukit Bintang. Contemporary-design rooms are very comfy and great value for what they offer. Bring earplugs to block out the street noise.

SAHABAT GUEST HOUSE   GUESTHOUSE $$

Map p252 (📞2142 0689; www.sahabatguesthouse.com; 41 Jln Sahabat; d from RM109; ❄ @ 🛜; monorail Raja Chulan) This blue-painted eight-room guesthouse has eight tidy bedrooms, with tiny en suite bathrooms and a feature wall plastered in vivid patterned wallpaper. There's a small kitchen and a grassy front garden in which to relax. Rates are slightly higher from Friday to Sunday.

ANGGUN BOUTIQUE HOTEL   HOTEL $$

Map p252 (📞2145 8003; www.anggunkl.com; 7-9 Tengkat Tong Shin; d with breakfast from RM340; ❄ 🛜; monorail Imbi) Two 1920s shophouses have been combined to create this antique-style, boutique property that's a welcome addition to a busy strip. The rooftop restaurant and bar is a leafy oasis hung with twinkling lights. Avoid rooms facing the noisy street though – or bring earplugs.

SARANG VACATION HOMES   GUESTHOUSE $$

Map p248 (📞012-210 0218; www.sarangvacationhomes.com; 6 Jln Galloway; s/d from RM130/150; ❄ 🛜; monorail Imbi) Michael and Christina run this appealing bed-and-breakfast operation. They have houses, apartments and rooms for rent in five nearby locations. The furnishings are a bit worn, but the vibe is relaxed and welcoming and the location is excellent. It's a skip away from Jln Alor in a low-rise residential enclave.

★ YY38 HOTEL   HOTEL $$

Map p252 (📞2148 8838; www.yy38hotel.com.my; 38 Tengkat Tong Shin; s/d/loft r from RM100/120/360; ❄ 🛜; monorail Bukit Bintang) The bulk of the rooms here are fine but no-frills. However, the 7th floor offers 17 creatively designed duplexes, each sleeping three, with themes ranging from Marilyn Monroe to circus; it features a sawn-in-half classic mini as part of the decor!

RAINFOREST BED & BREAKFAST   HOSTEL $$

Map p252 (📞2145 3525; www.rainforestbnbhotel.com; 27 Jln Mesui; dm/d/tw incl breakfast RM39/115/140; ❄ @ 🛜; monorail Raja Chulan) The lush foliage sprouting around and tumbling off the tiered balconies of this high-quality guesthouse is eye-catching and apt for its name. Inside, bright-red walls and timber-lined rooms (some without windows) are visually distinctive, along with the collection of Chinese pottery figurines.

LODGE PARADIZE HOTEL   HOTEL $$

Map p250 (📞2143 1289; www.lodgeparadize.com; 2 Jln Tengah; d from RM132; ❄ @ 🛜; monorail Raja Chulan) Revamped from a 1940s apartment block, the Paradize offers good-value budget rooms at the back, which are more sheltered from traffic noise than the better-furnished rooms in the main building. Long-stay deals are also available. Sadly, swimming isn't permitted in the pool but the cafe beside it is famous for its Teochew rice porridge.

PICCOLO HOTEL   HOTEL $$

Map p252 (📞2146 5000; www.thepiccolohotel.com; 101 Jln Bukit Bintang; r from RM480; ❄ @ 🛜; monorail Bukit Bintang) Although its boutique look is somewhat cheaply thrown together, we do like the striking marine-life images decorating the walls at this hotel in the midst of the Bintang Walk shopping strip. Constant promotional rates via online bookings bring it down to the midrange category.

RADIUS INTERNATIONAL HOTEL   HOTEL $$
Map p252 (☑2715 3888; www.radius-internation-al.com; 51A Changkat Bukit Bintang; r from RM190; ✽ @ ☷; monorail Bukit Bintang) Looking worn and dated, this business hotel's big pluses are its location, decent-sized swimming pool and low online rates.

★ E&O RESIDENCES KUALA LUMPUR   APARTMENTS $$$
Map p250 (☑2023 2188; www.eoresidences.com; 1 Jln Tengah; 1-/2-bed apt RM490/790; ✽ @ ☎ ☷; monorail Raja Chulan) Chances are once you spend a night in these elegantly designed apartments with their clean-line furnishings and striking contemporary art you will not want to leave. There's a good gym and large outdoor pool in the landscaped court-yard garden. A buffet breakfast is served in the complex's Delicious Cafe.

★ SEKEPING SIN CHEW KEE   APARTMENTS $$$
Map p248 (www.sekeping.com; 3 Jln Sin Chew Kee; apt RM700; ✽ ☎; monorail Imbi) Architect Ng Seksan's pared-back, quirky style is in full evidence at his latest venture, tucked away on the edge of the Golden Triangle on a street of old houses. Raw yet beautiful, the two apartments here sleep up to six and have full kitchens and outdoor relaxation spaces, not to mention fab local art.

PARKROYAL SERVICED SUITES   APARTMENTS $$$
Map p252 (☑03-2084 1000; www.parkroyal-hotels.com; 1 Jln Nagansari; apt from RM424; ✽ @ ☎ ☷; monorail Raja Chulan) New property in a great location with designer studios and one- and two-bedroom suites. Good facilities include two outdoor pools (one on the roof).

PACIFIC REGENCY HOTEL SUITES   APARTMENTS $$$
Map p248 (☑2332 7777; www.pacific-regency.com; Jln Punchak, Menara Panglobal; apt from RM430; ✽ @ ☎ ☷; monorail Bukit Nanas) These upmarket self-catering studios and ser-viced apartments are good value compared with the rooms of a similar standard at KL's other five-star properties. Ask to see the newer rooms. Head to the roof to enjoy

the rooftop pool and Luna, one of the city's best bars.

WESTIN KUALA LUMPUR   HOTEL $$$
Map p252 (☑2731 8333; www.westin.com/kualalumpur; 199 Jln Bukit Bintang; d/apt from RM800/1300; ✽ @ ☎ ☷; monorail Bukit Bintang) The Westin's spacious rooms are modern and appealing and it's easy to see why long-term residents love its serviced apartments with their full kitchens and glassed-in bal-conies. It also has a good gym and stylish restaurants and bars.

HOTEL CAPITOL   HOTEL $$$
Map p252 (☑2143 7000; www.fhihotels.com; Jln Bulan; r from RM450; ✽ @ ☷; monorail Bukit Bintang) Bland but reliable and very central. The pricier loft-style and premium cor-ner rooms sport hip furnishings and good views. Guests have access to the nearby Federal Hotel's swimming pool.

ROYALE BINTANG KUALA LUMPUR   HOTEL $$$
Map p252 (☑03-2143 9898; www.royale-bintang-hotel.com.my; 17-21 Jln Bukit Bintang; r from RM534; ☷; monorail Imbi) A well run and pleasantly presented hotel; its outdoor pool is a plus.

🛏 KLCC & Jln Tun Razak

★ VILLA SAMADHI   HOTEL $$$
Map p250 (☑03-2143 2300; www.villasamadhi.com.my; 8 Jln Madge; r from RM500; ✽ @ ☎ ☷; ⛟ Ampang Park) It's hard to believe you're in the heart of KL while staying at this gor-geous boutique property that epitomises Asian chic. The black polished concrete, bamboo and reclaimed-timber rooms with luxurious light fixtures, idyllic central pool, lush foliage, rooftop bar (serving compli-mentary cocktails) and intimate modern Malay restaurant Mandi Mandi combine to conjure an antidote to urban stress.

G TOWER HOTEL   HOTEL $$$
Map p250 (☑2168 1919; www.gtowerhotel.com; 199 Jln Tun Razak; s/d from RM480/505; ✽ @ ☎ ☷; ⛟ Ampang Park) There's an exclu-sive atmosphere at this slickly designed property atop an office complex. Only hotel guests and tenants can access the gym, infinity pools and top-floor lounge, restau-rant and bar. Arty black-and-white prints set a sophisticated tone in the bedrooms.

Ask for one of the slightly bigger corner rooms, preferably with a view of Tabung Haji.

★FRASER PLACE KUALA LUMPUR
APARTMENTS **$$$**

Map p250 (☎2118 6288; http://kualalumpur.fras-ershospitality.com; 10 Jln Perak, Lot 163; apt from RM638; ✳@ 🛜🏊; monorail Bukit Nanas) Good workspaces and walk-in closets feature in these colourfully designed apartments. The facilities, including an outdoor infinity pool, gym, sauna and games room, are top notch.

IMPIANA
HOTEL **$$$**

Map p250 (☎2141 1111; www.impiana.com; 13 Jln Pinang; d incl breakfast from RM450; ✳@ 🛜🏊; monorail Raja Chulan) This chic property offers spacious rooms with parquet floors and lots of seductive amenities including a spa and infinity pool.

HOTEL MAYA
HOTEL **$$$**

Map p250 (☎2711 8866; www.hotelmaya.com.my; 138 Jln Ampang; r/ste with breakfast from RM700/1000; @ 🛜🏊; monorail Bukit Nanas) Still one of KL's most stylish hotels, even if there's wear and tear to some of its sleek timber-floored studios and suites. Rack rates include airport transfers, as well as a host of other goodies, while promotional rates – nearly half the official ones – include only breakfast and wi-fi. Its hydrotherapy pool is a plus.

GRAND HYATT KUALA LUMPUR
HOTEL **$$$**

Map p250 (☎2182 1234; www.kualalumpur.grand.hyatt.com; 12 Jln Pinang; r from RM510; ✳@ 🛜; monorail Raja Chulan) Elevators whisk you up to a panoramic entrance lobby that pits you eye to eye with the upper levels of the Petronas Towers. All the marble- and wood-clad rooms provide great city views and together with the top-class facilities are what you'd expect from this international brand.

TRADERS HOTEL KUALA LUMPUR
HOTEL **$$$**

Map p250 (☎2332 9888; www.tradershotels.com; KLCC, off Jln Kia Peng; d/ste from RM719/963; ✳@ 🛜🏊; 🚇KLCC) The views are good either way, but it's probably worth paying the small supplement for a room facing the Petronas Towers at this contemporary-design addition to KL's portfolio of luxe hotels. Its rooftop pool and bar is a famous KL hang-out.

MICASA ALL SUITE HOTEL
APARTMENTS **$$$**

Map p250 (☎2179 8000; www.micasahotel.com; 368B Jln Tun Razak; apt from RM420; ✳@ 🛜🏊; 🚇Ampang Park) A choice of one-, two- or three-bedroom suites – all reasonably priced, with wood floors and kitchens. Relax beside the large, palm-tree-fringed pool, or enjoy its small spa and the gourmet restaurant Cilantro.

MANDARIN ORIENTAL
HOTEL **$$$**

Map p250 (☎2380 8888; www.mandarinoriental.com/kualalumpur; Jln Pinang; r/ste from RM1080/3000; ✳@ 🛜🏊; 🚇KLCC) Backing onto the greenery of KLCC Park, the Mandarin is one for sybarites. Silks and batiks lend an Asian feel to the rooms, which have every conceivable amenity. The Oriental Club rooms are the ones to pick, allowing access to a lounge with a great view of the Petronas Towers. There's a spa and an infinity pool that seems to merge into the parkland beyond.

🛏 Chinatown & Masjid Jamek

★BACKHOME
HOSTEL **$**

Map p248 (☎2022 0788; www.backhome.com.my; 30 Jln Tun HS Lee; dm/d/tr incl breakfast from RM42/110/150; ✳@ 🛜; 🚇Masjid Jamek) This chic pit stop for flashpackers offers polished-concrete finishes, Zen simple decoration, fab rain showers and a blissful central courtyard sprouting spindly trees. It can be noisy on the street outside, but the hostel offers earplugs for light sleepers. Also check out its cool cafe, LOKL (p81).

★REGGAE MANSION
HOSTEL **$**

Map p248 (☎03-2072 6877; www.reggaehostels-malaysia.com/mansion; 49-59 Jln Tun HS Lee; dm/d from RM35/120; ✳@ 🛜; 🚇Masjid Jamek) Grooving to a beat that's superior to most backpacker places, including its own guest-houses in the heart of Chinatown, this is one cool operation. The decor is white-washed faux colonial with contemporary touches including a flash cafe-bar, rooftop bar, and mini cinema (RM7 including popcorn and a drink).

EXPLORERS GUESTHOUSE
HOSTEL **$**

Map p248 (☎03-2022 2928; www.theexplorersguesthouse.com; 128-130 Jln Tun HS Lee; dm/s/d from RM30/68/88; ✳@ 🛜; 🚇Pasar

Seni) Another of the new backpackers giving the Chinatown oldies a hiding. Explorers follows up a comfy, spacious lobby with clean, airy rooms, a roof terrace, colourfully painted walls as well as a few arty touches.

HOTEL CHINATOWN (2) — HOTEL $
Map p248 (☑2072 9933; www.hotelchinatown2.com; 70-72 Jln Petaling; s/d from RM69/90; ❄@🖥; ⛊Pasar Seni) The cheapest rooms have no windows but are away from the noisy main street. The lobby offers a comfy lounge area, water feature, book exchange and piano.

GRID 19 — HOSTEL $
Map p248 (☑9226 2629; www.grid9hotels.com; 9 Jln Maharajalela; dm/s/d from RM40/109/129; ❄@🖥; monorail Maharajalela) Steps from the monorail, this new flashpackers softens its concrete and steel industrial look with bold splashes of paint and equally colourful beanbags. Guests also get a free ticket to top club Zouk (p66).

YWCA — HOSTEL $
Map p248 (☑2070 1623; 12 Jln Hang Jebat; s/d/tr with shared bathroom RM30/50/70; monorail Hang Tuah, ⛊Hang Tuah) This quiet, simply decorated establishment tucked away east of Chinatown offers plain but very acceptable rooms with fan, desk and wardrobe. Only for women, couples and families.

WHEELERS GUEST HOUSE — HOSTEL $
Map p248 (☑2070 1386; www.backpackerskl.com/wheelers.htm; Level 2, 131-133 Jln Tun HS Lee; dm/r with shared bathroom from RM13/25,

r with private bathroom RM50; ❄@; ⛊Pasar Seni) Prison-like rooms, but this hostel does have a mini-aquarium, gay-friendly staff, a great rooftop terrace where free Friday-night dinners are hosted, and homemade yoghurt and muesli for breakfast.

HOTEL LOK ANN — HOTEL $
Map p248 (☑2078 9544; 113 Jln Petaling; dm/d/tr incl breakfast RM30/80/100; ❄🖥; ⛊Pasar Seni) Sadly, it's highly likely this classic Chinatown hotel will have to close during the construction of the new Mass Rapid Transit (MRT) line under Jln Sultan. If it's open you'll find sparklingly clean, spacious rooms with windows, TV, phone and large shower rooms. There's a kitchen and pleasant common area.

5 ELEMENTS HOTEL — HOTEL $$
Map p248 (☑2031 6888; www.the5elements hotel.com.my; Lot 243 Jln Sultan; s/tw/d incl breakfast from RM150/180/190; ❄@🖥; ⛊Pasar Seni) Offering a good range of rooms, some with views towards KL Tower, this hotel makes a credible stab at boutique stylings. We particularly liked the sensuous design motif snaking its way across the corridor and bedroom walls.

HOTEL 1915 — HOTEL $$
Map p248 (☑2026 0042; www.hotel1915kl.com.my; 49 Jln Leboh Ampang; r from RM118; ❄@🖥; ⛊Masjid Jamek) It's worth paying an extra RM10 at this appealing new hotel to get a room with a window. Each floor is named after a curry ingredient, but the decor is monochrome rather than spicy.

HOMESTAYS IN SUGAI PENCHALA

A jungle *kampong* (village) experience while not leaving Kuala Lumpur's city limits? Yes, it's possible by bedding down in Sungai Penchala, a 20-minute taxi ride (RM20) from Chinatown. Here are the options:

Bayan Indah (p101) This elegant rural escape, with four lovely ensuite rooms, balconies and lush gardens, was once the home of superfriendly food writer and cook Rohani Jelani, who serves delicious breakfasts and is a mine of local information. There's a minimum two-night stay and you get the run of the whole house which sleeps up to eight people, plus dinner and a cooking class for your party.

Nada Lama (☑016-308 0356, 017-616 4924; www.wix.com/nadalama/org; Jln Penchala Indah, Bukit Lanjan Damansara; r incl breakfast from RM180; 🖥) On the same property as the Balinese-style spa and restaurant, and surrounded by the forest, there are a couple of charming rustic cottages to stay in here. One of the cottages offers a sweeping view through the trees from the verandah of Petaling Jaya across the expressway and both have very modern bathrooms. A traditional Malay-style breakfast is served.

KLIA TRANSIT HOTELS

In case you fly in late or have an early flight from the airport, there are options close to Kuala Lumpur International Airport (KLIA).

The budget **Tune Hotel** (www.tunehotels.com; Lot PT 29, Jln KLIA S4; r from RM130), which rewards advance online bookings with the cheapest rates, has a branch near the old Low Cost Carrier Terminal, while the luxurious **Sama Sama** (☑8787 3333; www.samasamahotels.com; r from RM500; ※ @ ◌ ◌; ◌KLIA) is linked by a bridge to KLIA terminal 1.

If all you need to do is freshen up before or after your flight, and you don't need to go through immigration, there's also the **Airside Transit Hotel** (☑8787 4848; www.klairporthotel.com/airside-transit-hotel; Gate 5, Satellite Bldg, KLIA 1; d per 6hr RM185; ※ @). It has a fitness centre, business centre, spa and sauna, and all rooms come with attached bathroom and TV.

ANCASA HOTEL & SPA
KUALA LUMPUR   HOTEL $$
Map p248 (☑2026 6060; www.ancasa-hotel.com; Jln Tun Tan Cheng Lock; d from RM360; ※ @; ◌Plaza Rakyat) Promotions halve the rack rates at one of Chinatown's best midrange options, although there's a small surcharge for weekend stays. The comfortable rooms are well equipped. The hotel also has a Balinese-style spa and can arrange homestays around the peninsula. It also runs the business hotel **AnCasa Express** (Map p248; ☑03-2026 6060; www.ancasapudukualalumpur.com; 4th floor, Pudu Sentral, Jln Pudu; r from RM115; ※ @ ◌; LRT Plaza Rakyat) atop Pudu Sentral bus station.

OLYMPIC SPORT HOTEL   HOTEL $$
Map p248 (☑2078 7888; www.olympichotelkl.com.my; Jln Hang Jebat; d incl breakfast from RM158; ※ ◌; monorail Hang Tuah, ◌Hang Tuah) In a building belonging to Malaysia's National Olympic Committee (hence the name), this is a respectable performer for its price bracket. The location, close to Chinatown and both monorail and LRT terminals, is convenient yet quiet. The pleasantly decorated rooms are spacious.

Masjid India & Kampung Baru

TUNE HOTEL   HOTEL $
Map p256 (www.tunehotels.com; 316 Jln Tuanku Abdul Rahman; r from RM90; ※ @ ◌; monorail Medan Tuanku) Book online six months in advance and it's possible to snag a room with a bathroom for under RM50. The basic rate, however, just gets you the room – air-con, towel, toiletries and wi-fi access are extra.

FRENZ HOTEL   HOTEL $$
Map p256 (☑03-2693 7878; www.frenzhotel.com.my; 135 Jln TAR; s/d from RM210/260; ※ ◌; ◌Masjid Jamek) A step up from other midrange options in the area, with comfortable, clean rooms. Promotional rates are usually on offer, and breakfast (RM12) is served in Zam Zam restaurant next door.

⊟ Lake Gardens, KL Sentral & Bangsar

★SEKEPING TENGGIRI   GUESTHOUSE $$
(☑017-207 5977; www.tenggiri.com; 48 Jln Tenggiri; r from RM220; ※ ◌ ◌; ◌Bangsar) Even if it didn't provide access to architect Ng Seksan's superlative private collection of contemporary Malaysian art (displayed in the rooms of the adjoining house) this would be a lovely place to stay. The rough luxe mix of concrete, wood and wire decor (with cleverly recycled materials making up lamp fixtures) is softened by abundant garden greenery and a cooling plunge pool. There's a basic kitchen, a housekeeper and several great places to eat on nearby Lg Kurau.

The owners also run the similar **Sekeping Terasek** (Map p262; ☑017-207 5977; www.sekeping.com/terasek; 42A Jln Terasek, Bangsar; r/house RM200/1000; ※ ◌) ◌ nearby and Sekeping Sin Chew Kee (p131) in central KL.

★ALOFT KUALA
LUMPUR SENTRAL   HOTEL $$
Map p260 (☑2723 1188; www.starwoodhotels.com/alofthotels; 5 Jln Stesen Sentral; r from RM291; ※ @ ◌ ◌; ◌KL Sentral, monorail KL Sentral) Designed for the Google generation of young creatives, Aloft is industrial

chic meets plastic fantastic. Staff are super-friendly and you have to smile at the witty cartoon art in each of the spacious, well-designed rooms. Place a big tick against its infinity rooftop pool with one of the best views in KL.

YMCA HOTEL $$

Map p260 (✆2274 1439; www.ymcakl.com; 95 Jln Padang Belia; d & tw RM110, tr with shared bathroom RM130; ❄❋; ☒KL Sentral, monorail KL Sentral) Handy for KL Sentral, the Y has spick-and-span rooms with TVs, telephones and proper wardrobes (not just hangers on a wall hook). There are laundry facilities, a shop and cafe, as well as tennis courts for hire if you become a member (RM80 per year) which will also give you 10% off the hotel rates.

HILTON KUALA LUMPUR HOTEL $$$

Map p260 (✆2264 2264; www.hilton.com; 3 Jln Stesen Sentral; d/ste from RM650/1300; ❄@❋❒; ☒KL Sentral, monorail KL Sentral) Sharing a fabulous landscaped pool and spa with the Meridien next door, the Hilton is a design diva's dream. Sliding doors open to join the bathroom to the bedroom, picture windows present soaring city views and rooms are decked out from floor to ceiling in eye-catching materials.

MAJESTIC HOTEL HISTORIC HOTEL $$$

Map p260 (✆2785 8000; www.majestickl.com; 5 Jln Sultan Hishamuddin; r from RM500; ❄@❋; ☒Kuala Lumpur) Originally opened in 1932, and pre-WWII the KL equivalent of Raffles in Singapore, this long-shuttered hotel

reopened at the end of 2012. The heritage building has been impeccably refurbished, although the bulk of the rooms are in the newly built Tower wing. The Charles Rennie Mackintosh–inspired decor of the spa adds extra elegance while the Colonial Cafe and Tea Lounge play up to the heritage experience.

CARCOSA SERI NEGARA HOTEL $$$

Map p260 (✆2295 0888; www.carcosa.com.my; Taman Tasik Perdana Persiaran Mahameru; ste from RM1100; ❄@❋; ☒KL Sentral, monorail KL Sentral) Operating in reduced circumstances (the Carcosa mansion has long been shuttered for repairs) this heritage property – once the residence of British government representative Sir Frank Swettenham – rustles up colonial elegance. The Seri Negara mansion has five conservatively designed, spacious suites, perfect for non-rock-star VIPs. See how the other half live by splashing out on the hotel's excellent fulsome tea which you can enjoy overlooking a manicured lawn.

GARDENS HOTEL
& RESIDENCES HOTEL, APARTMENTS $$$

(✆2268 1111; www.stgiles-hotels.com/TheGardens; Gardens, Lingkaran Syed Putra; r/apt incl breakfast from RM448/694; ❄@❋❒; ☒Mid-Valley) Attached to the swanky Gardens Mall, this luxury hotel and serviced residences are very appealing. Wood panelling with lattice details and striking flower prints on the walls make the rooms' decor pop; the apartments are even better.

Melaka

Chinatown p143
Catch glimpses of old-time Melaka while wandering through this heritage district dotted with ornate temples and mosques.

Baba-Nonya Heritage Museum p143
Learn about Straits Chinese culture and history at this museum in a beautifully restored residence.

Fabulous Restaurants p146
Eat Chinese dim sum for breakfast, Nonya food for lunch and Pakistani tandoori for dinner.

Jonker's Walk Night Market p149
Peruse the trinket stands and graze on snacks while enjoying this lively weekend event.

Ride a Trishaw p138
Take your pick from the technicolour fake-flower-festooned trishaws for a fun trip around the city.

Explore

Back in the 15th century Melaka was one of the greatest trading ports in Southeast Asia. In the subsequent 600 years its fortunes have waxed and waned but now it's a massive tourist attraction thanks to its 2008 designation as a Unesco World Heritage Site.

You'll need at least two days to view the main historic sights including the Stadthuys, Porta de Santiago, St Paul's Church, the Sultanate Palace, Villa Sentosa and historic Chinatown, where you'll find the Baba-Nonya Heritage Museum. Escape the crowds at Bukit China graveyard, with sunset views of the city. Also don't miss the Jonker's Walk Night Market (Friday to Sunday) and the chance to sample the city's famed Malay-Chinese Nonya food – so delicious that it's reason enough to visit.

The Best...
→**Sight** Chinatown (p143)
→**Place to Eat** Nancy's Kitchen (p146)
→**Place to Drink** Cheng Ho Tea House (p148)

Top Tip
Avoid visiting on the weekends when there are so many photo-snapping tourists that the whole heritage district can feel like front row at a rock concert.

Getting There & Away
→**Air** Melaka International Airport, 20km north of Melaka in Batu Berendam, has connections to Kuala Lumpur and Penang.
→**Bus** Buses from KL (RM17.50 to RM27.50, every half hour, two hours) and Penang (RM50, twice daily, seven hours) arrive at Melaka Sentral bus station off Jln Tun Razak, in the north of town. A taxi into town should cost RM20, or you can take bus 17 (RM1.40).
→**Taxi** Taxis to KL (RM170) leave from Melaka Sentral.
→**Train** Tampin, 38km north of Melaka, is on the main north–south line from KL to Singapore. Taxis from Melaka cost around RM60 or take the Tai Lye bus (RM5, 1½ hours), which leaves every half-hour from Melaka Sentral.

Getting Around
→**Walking/Bicycle** Melaka is small enough to walk around or you can rent a bike for around RM3 per hour from guesthouses around Chinatown.
→**Bus** Bus 17 runs every 15 minutes from Melaka Sentral to the town centre, past the huge Mahkota Parade shopping complex, to Taman Melaka Raya and on to Medan Portugis.
→**Trishaw** Taking to Melaka's streets by trishaw is a must – by the hour they should cost about RM50, or RM20 for any one-way trip within the town, but you'll have to bargain hard.
→**Taxi** Charge around RM15 for a trip anywhere around town with a 50% surcharge between 1am and 6am.

Need to Know
→**Area Code** ✐06
→**Location** Melaka is 144km south of Kuala Lumpur.
→**Tourism Malaysia** (✐283 6220; Jln Mahkota; ☉9am-10pm) is located at the Menara Taming Sari tower; it has very knowledgable, helpful staff. The local **tourist office** (✐281 4803; www.melaka. gov.my; Jln Kota; ☉9am-1pm & 2-5.30pm) is diagonally across the square from Christ Church.

History
When Parameswara, a Hindu prince/pirate from Sumatra, arrived at a small Malay fishing village around 1401, he recognised its potential as a major port to attract merchants from all over the East. Not only was it located halfway between China and India, but it also had easy access to the spice islands of Indonesia. A solid foundation for this vision came about four years later with the arrival of the Chinese Muslim Admiral Cheng Ho in Melaka bearing gifts from the Ming emperor and the promise of protection from Siamese enemies.

Chinese settlers followed, who mixed with the local Malays to become known as the Baba and Nonya, the Peranakans or Straits Chinese. Indian traders also intermarried with Malays creating the Straits-born Indian community known as the Chitty. By the time of Parameswara's death in 1414, Melaka was a powerful

MELAKA

trading state. Its position was consolidated by the state's adoption of Islam in the mid-15th century.

In 1509 the Portuguese came seeking the wealth of the spice and in 1511 Alfonso de Albuquerque forcibly took the city. Under the Portuguese, the fortress of A'Famosa was constructed, and missionaries strove to implant Catholicism. While Portuguese cannons could easily conquer Melaka, they could not force Muslim merchants from Arabia and India to continue trading there, and other ports in the area, such as Islamic Demak on Java, grew to overshadow Melaka.

Suffering harrying attacks from neighbouring Johor and Negeri Sembilan, as well as from the Islamic power of Aceh in Sumatra, Melaka declined further. The city passed into Dutch hands after an eight-month siege in 1641. The Dutch ruled Melaka for about 150 years, during which time it again became the centre for peninsular trade, and built many fine buildings and churches which remain the most solid suggestion of European presence.

When the French occupied Holland in 1795, the British (as allies of the Dutch) temporarily assumed administration of the Dutch colonies. In 1824 Melaka was permanently ceded to the British.

Melaka, together with Penang and Singapore, formed the Straits settlements, the three British territories that were command posts for later expansion into the peninsula. However, under British rule Melaka was eclipsed by other Straits settlements and then superseded by the rapidly growing commercial importance of Singapore. Apart from a brief upturn in the early 20th century when rubber was an important crop, Melaka returned again to being a quiet backwater, patiently awaiting its renaissance as a tourist drawcard.

 SIGHTS

◉ Historic Town Centre

This area has a ridiculous number of museums clustered along Jln Kota. The **Islamic Museum** (admission RM1; ☺9am-5.30pm Wed-Sun), the **Architecture Museum** (admission RM2; ☺9.30am-5pm Tue-Sun), which focuses on local housing design, and the **Muzium Rakyat** (People's Museum; adult RM2; ☺9am-5.30pm Wed-Mon), which covers everything from *gasing uri* (top-spinning) to mutilation for beauty, are all worth visiting if you have time on your hands. Most of the others use a bland diorama format where visitors walk through a maze of wordy displays.

STADTHUYS HISTORIC BUILDING
(Town Sq; ☑282 6526; admission adult/child RM5/2; ☺9am-5.30pm Sat-Thu, 9am-12.15pm & 2.45-5.30pm Fri) Melaka's most unmistakable landmark and favourite trishaw pick-up spot is the Stadthuys, the imposing salmon-pink former town hall and governor's residence. It's believed to be the oldest Dutch building in the East, built shortly after Melaka was captured by the Dutch in 1641, and is a reproduction of the former Stadhuis (town hall) of the Frisian town of Hoorn in the Netherlands.

Housed inside the Stadthuys is the nicely presented **History & Ethnography Museum** (☺guided tours 10.30am & 2.30pm Sat & Sun), and also part of the complex is the mildly interesting **Literature Museum**, focusing on Malaysian writers. Admission to both museums (as well as the **Governor's House** and the **Democratic Government Museum**) is included in the admission price to Stadthuys.

TRICKED-OUT TRISHAWS

Nowhere else in Malaysia will you find such a wild and crazy collection of trishaws. Outrageously kitsch, the favourite decorations are plastic flowers, baby doll heads, religious paraphernalia, tinsel, Christmas lights and a sound system. While taking a ride in one of these things might be the most 'I'm a tourist' thing you do in Malaysia, it's good fun and supports an industry that is dying nearly everywhere else in the country. As a spectator, keep an eye out for Singaporean tourists hiring out trishaws en masse: the effect, with several '80s hits blaring at the same time, cameras snapping and all that glitzy decoration, turns the streets of Melaka into a circuslike parade.

KAMPUNG MORTEN & SUNGAI MELAKA

Dubbed a 'living museum', Kampung Morten is a picturesque village of 85 homes, including 52 in the traditional Malaccan style, filling a bend in the Melaka River. Very much a functioning *kampung* (village), it is named after JF Morten, the Commissioner of Lands in the 1920s. As long as you don't get there at the same time as a tour bus, a stroll around the village is a relaxing and interesting experience. You'll meet plenty of welcoming people and there are small home cafes and stalls at which to pause and grab refreshments.

The highlight is house museum **Villa Sentosa** (Peaceful Villa; ☑282 3988; Jln Kampung Morten; entry by donation; ⊙flexible but around 9am-6pm). A member of the family living here will show you around their 1920s traditional wooden home and its collection of objects, including Ming-dynasty ceramics and a 100-year-old copy of the Quran.

A pleasant way to reach Kampung Morten from Chinatown is to walk alongside the **Sungai Melaka**. Some effort has been made by the local authorities to create a pleasant walkway, along which you'll see many colourful murals painted on the backs of the buildings; images include those of Parameswara, Melaka's founder; Admiral Zheng He; and Princess Hang Li Po of the Ming Dyansty, who married Sultan Mansur Shah. You'll also pass mangroves and the wooden stilt houses of **Kampung Jawa**, a still functioning fishing village.

Sadly, construction of The Shore, an utterly out-of-scale development of apartments and commercial buildings on the bend before Kampung Mortem, means you must detour briefly away from the river. Alternatively, if you take the Melaka River Cruise (p151), you can ask to be dropped off near Kampung Mortem.

PORTA DE SANTIAGO   RUIN

(A'Famosa; Jln Bandar Hilir) A quick photo stop at this fort, built by the Portuguese in 1511, is a must. The Dutch were busy destroying the bulk of the fort when Sir Stamford Raffles came by in 1810 and saved what remains today.

In 2006 work on the Menara Taming Sari revolving tower uncovered another part of the famous wall. The revolving tower was relocated further inland, the remains of the fortress walls were reconstructed and they are now home to the 13-metre high **Melaka Malay Sultanate Water Wheel** replica. The original wheel would have been used to channel the river waters for the large number of traders swarming Melaka during the 15th and 16th centuries.

ST PAUL'S CHURCH   RUIN

(Jln Kota) St Paul's Church is a breezy sanctuary reached after a steep flight of stairs. Originally built by a Portuguese captain in 1521, the church offers views over Melaka from the summit of Bukit St Paul. The church was regularly visited by St Francis Xavier, and following his death in China the saint's body was temporarily interred here for nine months before being transferred to Goa, where it remains today. Visitors can look into his ancient tomb (surrounded by a wire fence) in the centre of the church, and a marble statue of the saint gazes wistfully over the city.

When the Dutch completed their own Christ Church in 1590 at the base of the hill, St Paul's fell into disuse. Under the British a lighthouse was built and the church eventually ended up as a storehouse for gunpowder. The church has been in ruins for more than 150 years.

SULTANATE PALACE   MUSEUM

(Jln Kota; admission RM3; ⊙9am-6pm) Housing a cultural museum, this wooden replica of the palace of Mansur Shah, the famous sultan who ruled Melaka from 1456 to 1477, is based on descriptions of the original palace from *Sejarah Melayu* (Malay Annals; a chronicle of the establishment of the Malay sultanate and 600 years of Malay history), and is built entirely without nails.

MARITIME MUSEUM
& NAVAL MUSEUM   MUSEUM

(Jln Quayside; admission RM5; ⊙9am-5.30pm Sun-Thu, to 9pm Fri & Sat) Housed in a huge recreation of the *Flor de la Mar*, a Portuguese ship that sank off the coast of Melaka, the

Melaka City

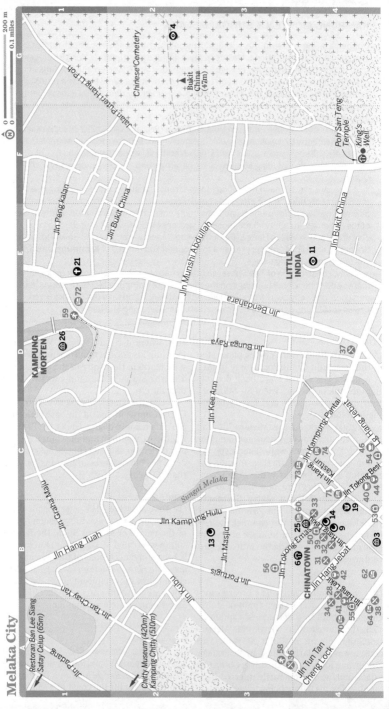

Restoran Ban Lee Siang Satay Celup (65m)

Chitty Museum (420m); Kampung Chitty (510m)

Jln Padang

Jln Tan Chay Yan

Jln Hang Tuah

Jln Graha Maju

Jln Kubu

Jln Portugis

Jln Masjid

Jln Kampung Hulu

Sungai Melaka

Jln Kee Ann

Jln Bunga Raya

Jln Munshi Abdullah

Jln Pengkalan

Jln Bukit China

Jln Puteri Hang Li Poh

Chinese Cemetery

Bukit China (47m)

KAMPUNG MORTEN

26

59

21

72

Jln Bendahara

LITTLE INDIA

11

Jln Bukit China

Poh San Teng Temple

King's Well

4

37

13

CHINATOWN

56

25 60 33

6

31 39

32 42

50

34 28

41

55

70

64

38

58

36

Jln Tokong Emas

Jln Hang Jebat

Jln Hang Lekiu

Jln Hang Lekir

Jln Tun Tan Cheng Lock

14

9

19

3

62

53

44

40

46

54

73

71

74

Jln Hang Kasturi

Jln Kampung Pantai

Lg Hang Jebat

Jln Hang Lekir

Jln Tokong Besi

0   200 m
0   0.1 miles

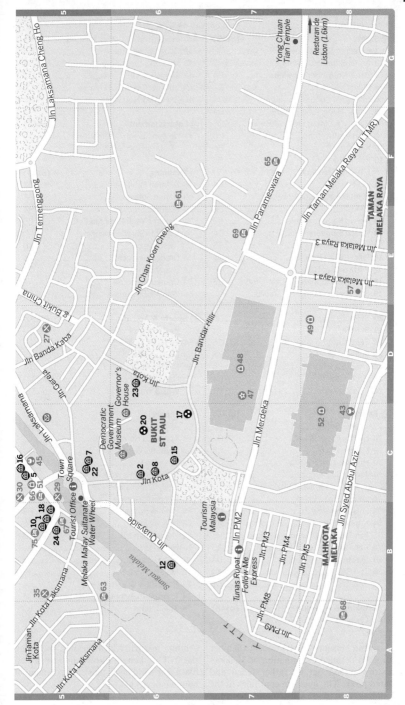

Melaka City

Maritime Museum merits a visit. Clamber up for a detailed examination of Melaka's history, picked out by rather faded and dated props. The museum continues in the building next door with more absorbing exhibits featuring local vessels, including the striking *Kepala Burung* (a boat carved like a feathered bird), plus an assortment of nautical devices.

⊙ Chinatown

Chinatown is the heart of Melaka and is by far the most interesting area to wander around. Stroll along **Jln Tun Tan Cheng Lock**, formerly called Heeren St, which was the preferred address for wealthy Baba (Straits-born Chinese) traders who were most active during the short-lived rubber boom of the early 20th century. The centre street of Chinatown is **Jln Hang Jebat**, formerly known as Jonker St (or Junk St Melaka), which was once famed for its antique shops but is now more of a collection of clothing and crafts outlets and restaurants. On Friday, Saturday and Sunday night, the street is transformed into the Jonker's Walk Night Market (p149). Finally, the northern section of **Jln Tokong Emas** (also known as Harmony St) houses a mosque, Chinese temple and a handful of authentic Chinese shops.

BABA-NONYA HERITAGE MUSEUM MUSEUM

(☑283 1273; 48-50 Jln Tun Tan Cheng Lock; adult/child RM15/7; ⊙10am-12.30pm & 2-4.30pm Wed-Mon) Touring this traditional Peranakan townhouse takes you back to a time when women hid behind elaborate partitions when guests dropped by, and every social situation had its specific location within the house. The captivating museum is arranged to look like a typical 19th-century Baba-Nonya residence. The highlight is the tour guides, who tell tales of the past with a distinctly Peranakan sense of humour.

8 HEEREN STREET HISTORIC BUILDING

(8 Jln Tun Tan Cheng Lock; ⊙11am-4pm Tue-Sat) **FREE** This 18th-century Dutch-period residential house was restored as a model conservation project. The project was partially chronicled in the beautifully designed coffee-table book *Voices from the Street,* which is for sale at the house along with other titles. You can also pick up an *Endangered Trades: A Walking Tour of Malacca's Living Heritage* (RM5) booklet and map for an excellent self-guided tour of the city centre.

CHENG HOON TENG TEMPLE CHINESE TEMPLE

(Qing Yun Ting or Green Clouds Temple; 25 Jln Tokong Emas; ⊙7am-7pm) Malaysia's oldest traditional Chinese temple (dating from 1646) remains a central place of worship for the Buddhist community in Melaka. Notable for its carved woodwork, the temple is dedicated to Kuan Yin, the goddess of mercy. Across the street from the main temple is a **traditional opera theatre**.

MASJID KAMPUNG HULU MOSQUE

(cnr Jln Masjid & Jln Kampung Hulu) This is the oldest functioning mosque in Malaysia and was, surprisingly, commissioned by the Dutch in 1728. The mosque is made up of predominantly Javanese architecture with a multitiered roof in place of the

MELAKA SIGHTS

WORTH A DETOUR

AYER KEROH

About 15km northeast of Melaka, Ayer Keroh (also spelled Air Keroh) has several contrived tourist attractions that are largely deserted on weekdays.

The main attraction is the **Taman Mini Malaysia/Asean** (adult/child RM4/2; ⊙9am-6pm), a large theme park that has examples of traditional houses from all 13 Malaysian states, as well as neighbouring Association of South-East Asian Nations (Asean) countries. Also here is **Hutan Rekreasi Air Keroh** (Air Keroh Recreational Forest) **FREE**, part secondary jungle and part landscaped park with paved trails, a 250m canopy walk, picnic areas and a forestry museum.

A new attraction is the **Melaka Bird Park** (☑233 0333; www.facebook.com/pages/Melaka-Bird-Park/218550151603144; Taman Botanikal, Lebuh Ayer Keroh; adult/child RM20/12; ⊙9am-6pm), Malaysia's largest aviary at 5.2 hectares. You can view over 700 local and international species and get a bird's-eye view from along a canopy walkway.

Kids will like the lushly landscaped **Melaka Zoo** (adult/child RM7/4, night zoo RM10/5; ⊙9am-6pm daily, night zoo 8-11pm Fri & Sat), the second-largest zoo in the country (with 200 different species). The animals here are in good condition compared with many zoos in Asia.

Ayer Keroh can be reached on bus 19 from Melaka (RM2, 30 minutes), or a taxi will cost around RM45.

standard dome; at the time of construction, domes and minarets had not yet come into fashion.

KAMPUNG KLING MOSQUE
MOSQUE

(Jln Tokong Emas) This hoary mosque has a multitiered *meru* roof (a stacked form similar to that seen in Balinese Hindu architecture), which owes its inspiration to Hindu temples, and a Moorish watchtower minaret typical of early mosques in Sumatra.

SRI POYATHA VENAYAGAR
MOORTHI TEMPLE
HINDU TEMPLE

(Jln Tokong Emas) Built in 781, this was one of the first Hindu temples built in the country. It is dedicated to the Hindu deity Venayagar.

CHENG HO CULTURAL MUSEUM
MUSEUM

(☑283 1135; 51 Lg Hang Jebat; adult/child RM20/10; ☉9am-6pm Mon-Thu, to 7pm Fri-Sun) A lengthy paean to Ming Admiral Cheng Ho (Zheng He), this museum charts the tremendous voyages of the intrepid Chinese Muslim seafarer. It's your classic Malaysian museum with lots of dioramas and re-created scenes with dummies, but the subject is very interesting so you could spend a few hours in here.

👁 Around the City Centre

BUKIT CHINA
CEMETERY

(Jln Puteri Hang Li Poh) More than 12,500 graves, including about 20 Muslim tombs, cover the 25 grassy hectares of this serene hill. Since the times of British rule there have been several attempts to acquire Bukit China for road widening, land reclamation or development purposes. Fortunately, Cheng Hoon Teng Temple, with strong community support, has thwarted these attempts.

In the middle of the 15th century the sultan of Melaka imported the Ming emperor's daughter from China as his bride, in a move to seal relations between the two countries. She brought with her a vast retinue, including 500 handmaidens, to Bukit China and it has been a Chinese area ever since. **Poh San Teng Temple** sits at the base of the hill and was built in 1795. To the right of the temple is the **King's Well**, a 15th-century well built by Sultan Mansur Shah.

🚶 Neighbourhood Walk
Melaka's Heritage Zone

START TOWN SQUARE
END SUNGAI MELAKA
LENGTH 2.5KM; THREE HOURS

Start from the ❶ **Town Square**, with its fountain emblazoned with four bas-relief images of Queen Victoria and affixed with a plaque. The picturesque backdrop is the Dutch-era ❷ **Stadthuys** (p138).

Take the bridge over Sungai Melaka, turn left and stroll along Jln Tun Tan Cheng Lock. Formerly called Heeren St, this narrow road has typical Peranakan houses that fuse Chinese, Dutch and British influences in a style that has been described as Chinese Palladian and Chinese baroque. A finely restored example of this style can be found at ❸ **8 Heeren St** (p143).

An intriguing insight into the local vernacular can be gleaned from the ❹ **Baba-Nonya Heritage Museum** (p143). Opposite the Hotel Puri, the classical-style building set back from the street is the ❺ **Chee Mansion**, a Chinese family shrine not open to the public.

Opposite the ❻ **Eng Choon (Yong Chun) Association** is a well-kept Chinese guildhall containing a small shrine to two Taoist deities. Chinese characters written on the building mean 'peace to the country and the people'. Backtrack along Jln Tun Tan Cheng Lock and walk north up Jln Hang Lekir along which is ❼ **Leong San Thong (Dragon Hill Hall)**, built in 1928. At the junction, turn left onto Jln Hang Jebat, formerly known as Jonker St, once famed for its antique and craft shops and still a great street to peruse.

Continuing northwest, you'll approach the all-white ❽ **Hang Kasturi's Tomb** on your right; there is no historical evidence that the tomb is the final resting place of the great warrior. Further along on your left is the small, modern and pink ❾ **Guanyin Temple (Guanyin Tang)**, dedicated to the Buddhist goddess of compassion. Seated in the second hall is the Taoist Jade Emperor, flanked by two attendants.

Turn right here and head up Jln Tokong Emas (Temple St) and past the ❿ **Wah Teck Kiong Temple** and the

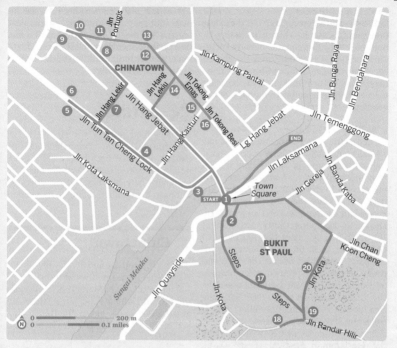

11 Guangfu Temple (Guangfu Gong), before arriving at the elaborate and celebrated **12 Cheng Hoon Teng Temple** (p143). Opposite is the more recently constructed **13 Xianglin (Fragrant Forest) Temple**, which endeavours to follow the layout of a traditional Chinese Buddhist temple. Adding splashes of colour to Jln Tokong Emas are the Chinese shops selling red and gold lanterns, paper money and funerary preparations.

Further along Jln Tokong Emas you'll pass the recently restored **14 Kampung Kling Mosque** and **15 Sri Poyatha Venayagar Moorthi Temple**. Slightly further ahead is the **16 Sanduo Temple (Sanduo Miao)**, another Chinese shrine encapsulating effigies of Da Bo Gong, Jin Hua Niang Niang (whom women entreat for children) and Kuan Yin.

Backtrack and turn left along the exterior wall of the mosque back along Jln Hang Lekiu (Fourth Cross St) to Jln Hang Jebat. Stroll back to Lg Hang Jebat (First Cross St) and the bridge, noting the decorative touches along the way – mosaics, tiling, inlaid coloured stones, carvings, Western-style balustrades, balconies, shutters and ornamentation.

Cross back to the Town Square and clamber up the steps leading to the top of Bukit St Paul, topped by the fabulous ruins of **17 St Paul's Church** (p139). There are steps down the hill from the church to **18 Porta de Santiago** (p139), once the main gate of the Portuguese fortress A'Famosa, originally constructed by Alfonso de Albuquerque in 1512.

To the northeast, at the base of Bukit St Paul, is the **19 Sultanate Palace** (p139). Across the way, in a British villa dating from 1911, is the **20 Proclamation of Independence Memorial**, a museum charting the history of Malaysia's progression to independence. There's too much to read and perhaps not enough to look at (although the Japanese officer's sword from occupation days is noteworthy). Ironically, this grand building topped by Mogul-inspired domes was once the Malacca Club, a bastion of colonialism.

Follow Jln Kota around the base of Bukit St Paul and head back to the Town Square. Conclude your walk by ambling along the short brick promenade on the eastern bank of Sungai Melaka (parallel with Jln Laksmana), and take in riverine views, bars, the occasional barber and walls of distinctive Dutch bricks.

ST PETER'S CHURCH — CHURCH

(Jln Bendahara) St Peter's Church is the oldest functioning Catholic church in Malaysia, built in 1710 by descendants of early Portuguese settlers. On Good Friday the church comes alive when Melakan Christians flock here, many of them making it the occasion for a trip home from far-flung parts of the country.

KAMPUNG CHITTY — NEIGHBOURHOOD

As well as the Baba-Nonya, Melaka also has a small community of Chitty – Straits-born Indians, offspring of the Indian traders who intermarried with Malay women. Having arrived in the 1400s, the Chitties are regarded as older than the Chinese-Malay Peranakan community. Their area of town, known as Kampung Chitty, lies west of Jln Gajah Berang, about 1km northwest of Chinatown; look for the archway with elephant sculptures beside the Mutamariman Temple. It's a pretty district in which to wander and see Malay-style houses. The tiny **Chitty Museum** (281 1289; 9.30am-5pm Tue-Sun) is a community effort with a collection of colourful artefacts.

The best time to visit is in May, during the **Mariamman Festival** (Pesta Datuk Charchar), a Hindu celebration during which you might also be fortunate enough to witness a traditional Indian wedding ceremony.

LITTLE INDIA — NEIGHBOURHOOD

Heading east from Kampung Chitty, past Chinatown and across the river, is Melaka's surprisingly plain Little India. While it's not nearly as charming as the historic centre or Chinatown, this busy area along Jln Bendahara and Jln Temenggong is a worthwhile place for soaking up some Indian influence and grabbing an excellent banana-leaf meal. During Deepavali a section of Jln Temenggong closes to traffic to make way for Indian cultural performances and street-food vendors.

EATING

Melaka's food mirrors the city's eclectic, multicultural DNA. Peranakan cuisine (Nonya; prepared here with a salty Indonesian influence) is the most famous type of cooking here, but there's also Portuguese Eurasian food, Indian, Chinese, Indonesian and more.

Chinatown

On Friday, Saturday and Sunday nights, Jln Hang Jebat turns into the not-to-be-missed Jonker's Walk Night Market (p149). Besides the official Hainan Food Street, there are also hawker stalls along Jln Hang Jebat and on Jln Tokong Emas where it meets Jln Portugis.

★ NANCY'S KITCHEN — NONYA $

(15 Jln Hang Lekir; meals RM10; 11am-5.30pm, closed Tue) In a town already known for its graciousness, this home-cooking Nonya restaurant is our favourite for friendly service. If you want an intimate meal, head elsewhere. The server is as chatty and full of suggestions as they come, and will have you making conversation with the other handful of customers in no time. It's like a happy dinner (or lunch) party with particularly good food. Try the house special-

---

DON'T LEAVE MELAKA WITHOUT TRYING...

laksa – regional version distinguished by its coconut milk and lemongrass flavours

popiah – uber–spring roll stuffed with shredded carrots, prawns, chilli, garlic, palm sugar and much, much more

cendol – shaved-ice monstrosity of jellies, syrup and coconut milk

Nonya pineapple tarts – buttery pastries with a chewy pineapple jam filling

chicken rice ball – Hokkien-style chicken and balled-up rice dumplings

asam fish heads – spicy tamarind fish-head stew

satay celup – like fondue but better; you dunk tofu, prawns and more into bubbling soup and cook it to your liking

devil curry – fiery Eurasian chicken curry

WORTH A DETOUR

MEDAN PORTUGIS

There's really not much reason to head out to this nondescript neighbourhood other than to eat. On Friday and Saturday evenings, head to **Restoran de Lisbon** (Medan Portugis), where you can sample Malay-Portuguese dishes at outdoor tables. Try the delicious local specialities of chilli crabs (RM20) or the distinctly Eurasian devil curry (RM10). Any other time of the week, Medan Portugis has food stalls serving similar dishes to those found at restaurants at seaside tables.

ity, chicken with candlenut (a large white nut used to make a mild, creamy sauce). Still hungry? Nancy also offers cooking courses.

HAINAN FOOD STREET HAWKER $

(Jln Hang Lekir; dishes from RM3; ⏱6pm-midnight Fri, Sat & Sun) About a dozen very good food stalls serving everything from Hainan chicken pie, Nonya laksa and Japanese BBQ open with the Jonker's Walk Night Market on weekends.

LOW YONG MOW CHINESE $

(☎282 1235; Jln Tokong Emas; dim sum RM1-8; ⏱5am-noon, closed Tue) Famous Malaysia-wide for large and delectably well-stuffed *pao* (steamed pork buns), this place is Chinatown's biggest breakfast treat. With high ceilings, plenty of fans running and a view of Masjid Kampung Kling, the atmosphere oozes all the charms of Chinatown. It's great for early-bus-departure breakfasts and is usually packed with talkative, newspaper-reading locals by around 7am.

POH PIAH LWEE NONYA $

(Jln Kibu; dishes from RM3; ⏱9am-5pm) An authentic and lively hole in the wall with one specialist cook preparing delicious Hokkein-style *popiah* (lettuce, bean sprouts, egg and chilli paste in a soft sleeve; RM2), another making near-perfect *rojak* (fruit and vegetable salad in a dressing made from shrimp paste, lime juice, sugar and peanuts, RM3) while the third whips up a fantastic laksa (RM3).

JONKER 88 HERITAGE DESSERTS $

(88 Jln Hang Jebat; ⏱11am-10pm Tue-Thu, to 11pm Fri & Sat, to 9pm Sun) Many locals say this is Melaka's best *cendol* (a pandan-leaf-flavoured desert served with shaved ice, red beans, jaggery syrup and coconut milk, from RM3). There are several variations on the theme, including a durian version, and the laksa here rocks as well. There's always a line on weekends.

VEGETARIAN RESTAURANT VEGETARIAN $

(43 Jln Hang Lekiu; mains around RM3; ⏱7.30am-2.30pm Mon-Sat; 🍴) Every Chinatown needs its basic vegetarian cafe and this is Melaka's. All the local specialities from laksa and wonton mee to 'fish balls' are here but, although they taste as good as the real thing, are completely meat-free.

LIMAU-LIMAU CAFE WESTERN $

(9 Jln Hang Lekiu; fruit juice from RM6, mains from RM7; ⏱9.30am-6.30pm Sun-Fri, to 9.30pm Sat; 🍴🖥) Decorated with dark-coloured ceramics and an arty twist, this long-running quiet cafe serves the same predictably good salads, sandwiches, fruit juices and milk shakes. It's also a mellow stop for internet and wi-fi.

★PAK PUTRA RESTAURANT PAKISTANI $$

(56 Jln Taman Kota Laksmana; tandoori from RM8; ⏱dinner, closed every other Mon) This fabulous Pakistani place cooks up a variety of meats and seafood in clay tandoori ovens perched on the footpath. Apart from the tandoori try the *taw* prawns (cooked with onion, yoghurt and coriander, RM11) or mutton rogan josh (in onion gravy with spices and chilli oil, RM9). Everything is so good that dinner conversation is often reduced to oohs and ahs of gustatory delight.

HOE KEE CHICKEN RICE MELAKAN $$

(4 Jln Hang Jebat; meals around RM20; ⏱8.30am-3pm, closed last Wed of month) Come here to try the local specialities, chicken rice ball and *asam* fish heads (fish heads in a spicy tamarind gravy). You'll need to arrive here off-hours or expect to wait, especially on weekends. The restaurant's setting, with wood floors and ceiling fans, is lovely; the food can be hit or miss.

HARPER'S CAFE FUSION $$

(2 & 4 Lg Hang Jebat; meals RM40; ⏱4pm-1am Mon & Wed-Sat, 11am-1am Sun) Perched elegantly over Sungai Melaka, breezy

Harper's serves excellent (though small) Malay-European fusion dishes in a rather stark decor. It's worth visiting for the food, though the service can be slow.

THE BABOON HOUSE   BURGERS $$

(89 Jln Tun Tan Cheng Hok; burgers around RM14; ☺10am-5pm Mon, Wed & Thu, to 7pm Fri-Sun; ☎) This arty cafe, housed in a long Peranakan-style building with a couple of light, plant-filled courtyards, specialises in burgers on homemade buns. The food is OK but really it's best as a place to chill over a drink and snack.

✗ Little India to Bukit China

There's a whole string of local-style Chinese cafes around Jln Bunga Raya (ever-full of chattering locals) that serve chicken or duck rice as well as rice, noodle and soup dishes at very low prices.

★CAPITOL SATAY   MELAKAN $

(☑283 5508; 41 Lg Bukit China; meals around RM8) Famous for its *satay celup* (a Melakan adaptation of satay steamboat), this place is usually packed and is one of the cheapest outfits in town. Stainless-steel tables have bubbling vats of soup in the middle where you dunk skewers of okra stuffed with tofu, sausages, chicken, prawns and bok choy. Side dishes include pickled eggs and ginger.

★SELVAM   INDIAN $

(☑281 9223; 3 Jln Temenggong; meals around RM8; ✗) ✔ This is a classic banana-leaf restaurant always busy with its loyal band of local patrons ordering tasty and cheap curries, roti and tandoori chicken sets. Even devout carnivores will second-guess their food preferences after trying the Friday-afternoon vegetarian special with 10 varieties of veg.

RESTORAN BAN LEE
SIANG SATAY CELUP   MELAKAN $

(☑284 1935; 45E Jln Om Kim Wee; meals around RM8; ☺5pm-midnight) This place is a little out of the way but locals claim the ingredients are the freshest. Go pick out your skewers from the fridge then cook them in the boiling vats of delectable satay sauce.

DRINKING & NIGHTLIFE

Unlike much of Malaysia, Melaka is studded with watering holes. The Friday-, Saturday- and Sunday-night Jonker's Walk Night Market in Chinatown closes down Jln Heng Lekir to traffic and the handful of bars along the lane become a mini street party with tables oozing beyond the pavements and live music.

★CHENG HO TEA HOUSE   TEAHOUSE

(Jln Tokong Besi; ☺10am-5pm) In an exquisite setting that resembles a Chinese temple garden courtyard, relax over a pot of fine Chinese tea (from RM15) or take a tea-appreciation course with owner and tea connoisseur, Pak.

GEOGRAPHÉR CAFE   BAR

(☑281 6813; www.geographer.com.my; 83 Jln Hang Jebat; ☺10am-1am Wed-Sun) This ventilated, breezy bar with outside seating and late hours, in a prewar corner shophouse, is a godsend. Seat yourself with a beer amid the throng and applaud long-time resident artist and musician Mr Burns as he eases through gnarled classics. A tasty choice of local and Western dishes and laid-back but professional service rounds it all off.

SHANTARAM   BAR

(9 Jln Tokong Emas; ☺9pm-2am) 'Give piss a chance' is the mantra of this relaxed bar run by famed Melaka hippy artist Soon. If you like Soon's trademark cut-out collage art you can find more of his crazy creations at the used bookshop he runs at 45 Jln Kampung Pantai.

ZHENG HO TEA HOUSE   TEAHOUSE

(☑016-764 0588; 3 Jln Kuli; tea ceremony for 4 people RM20) The best place in town for tea ceremony, this place is humble but the family are simply lovely and it just feels good to be here. There are also a few rooms for rent upstairs (from RM130 including one home cooked meal).

VOYAGER TRAVELLERS LOUNGE   CAFE, BAR

(☑281 5216; 40 Lg Hang Jebat; ☎) Ease back into a wicker chair and order a cold beer (and/or an all-day Western-style breakfast) from the glowing bar built out of recycled bottles. There are often night-time activities on, from movies to mellow live music, and Yaksa, the young owner, can help arrange activities throughout Melaka.

MIXX
CLUB

(2nd fl, Mahkota Arcade, Jln Syed Abdul Aziz; RM10; ☺10pm-late Tue-Sat) Melaka's hottest club has two parts: Paradox, a laser-lit warehouse-style venue where international DJs spin techno and electronic beats; and Arris, which has a garden area and live bands. It ain't KL but for Melaka this place is very hip. Cover is charged on Friday and Saturday nights only (when the place gets *very* crowded) and includes one drink.

ELEVEN
CLUB

(11 Jln Hang Lekir) This is *the* place to go if you want to get your groove on in Chinatown. Yes, there's hip heritage lounge-style seating and Eurasian food, but head here after around 11pm (weekends in particular) and resident DJs spin their best and the dance floor fills. It has been dubbed Melaka's only gay bar but it's a very relaxed scene and you'll find all sorts hanging out.

☆ ENTERTAINMENT

WILDLIFE THEATRE
WILDLIFE SHOWS

(www.wildlifetheatre.com.my; Pulau Melaka; weekdays adult/child RM15/10, weekends RM20/15; ☺shows at 3pm & 6pm) This won't rival marine-mammal shows in Europe or the Americas but the sea lions here do a good job of entertaining kids. There are also birds, snakes and cultural shows from the Iban of Sarawak. While animal shows are always dubious in the treatment of their flock, this place is less depressing than you'd expect.

GOLDEN SCREEN CINEMA
DATARAN PAHLAWAN
CINEMA

(☎281 0018; www.gsc.com.my; 3rd fl, Dataran Pahlawan; tickets RM9) These silver screens show everything from Western blockbusters to Bollywood flicks.

SHOPPING

Taking time to browse Chinatown's eclectic mix of shops is an activity in itself. Melakan favourites include Nonya beaded shoes, Nonya 'clogs' (with a wooden base and a single plastic-strip upper), antiques (know your stuff and haggle aggressively), Southeast Asian and Indian clothing, handmade tiles, charms, crystals and more. Peek into the growing array of silent artists studios, where you might see a painter busy at work in a back room.

★JONKER'S WALK
NIGHT MARKET
MARKET

(Jln Hang Jebat; ☺6-11pm Fri-Sun) Melaka's weekly shopping extravaganza keeps the

---

MELAKA'S ART GALLERIES

Almost hidden between the gaudy trinket shops and humble local businesses are an array of eclectic art galleries that make for a lovely day of browsing. Opening hours are erratic but many try to be open from 10am to 6pm and most close on Wednesday. The following are some of our favourites listed by location so you could incorporate them into a walking tour:

Paku Pakis Collection (21 Jln Tukang Besi) Go here for Leong Hock Khoon's Baba-Nonya–inspired art that ranges from realism to modern and stylised.

Shih Wen Naphaporn Artist Studio (14 Jln Tuna Tan Cheng Lock) A husband and wife duo. Chiang Shiwen is Melaka born and creates Cubo-futuristic works while Thai Naphapone Phanwiset uses fish, fruit and the female form as her muse in marvelous neutral-toned pieces.

Tham Siew Inn Artist Gallery (49 Jln Tun Tan Teng Lock) Than Siew works mostly with water colours while his son makes traditional stone Chinese stamps to order (from RM60).

Kim Hai Gallery (42 Jln Tun Tan Cheng Lock) Paints apples to create mosaics of colour.

Titi Art Gallery (4 Jln Tokong) Titi Kawok paints village and fishing landscapes as modern images.

ℹ COCONUT KUNG FU

While enjoying the Jonker's Walk Night Market, don't miss the performance by kung fu master Dr Ho Eng Hui at the southern end of Jln Hang Jebat. He eats fire and throws knives, but the real reason to stick around is to see him pummel his finger into a coconut. Yes, he really appears to do this (his knarled finger adds evidence) and he's been entertaining folks with the trick for over 35 years. Dr Ho Eng Hui is in fact a doctor, and the purpose of his performance is to sell a 'miracle oil' (RM10) that cures aches and pains.

shops along Jln Hang Jebat open late while trinket sellers, food hawkers and the occasional fortune teller close the street to traffic. It has become far more commercial, attracting scores of Singaporean tourists over the years, but it is an undeniably colourful way to spend an evening shopping and grazing.

⭐**ORANGUTAN HOUSE**   CLOTHING
(www.charlescham.com; 59 Lg Hang Jebat; ⊙10am-6pm Thu-Tue) All shirts are the work of local artist Charles Cham and have themes ranging from Chinese astrology animals to rather edgy topics (at least for Malaysia) such as 'Use Malaysian Rubber' above a sketch of a condom. Other branches are at **96 Jln Tun Tan Cheng Lok** (⊙closed Tue) and **12 Jln Hang Jebat** (⊙closed Thu).

WAH AIK SHOEMAKER   SHOES
(56 Jln Tokong Emas) Raymond Yeo continues the tradition begun by his grandfather in the same little shoemaker's shop that has been in his family for generations. The beaded Nonya shoes here are considered Melaka's finest and begin at a steep but merited RM300. Tiny silk bound-feet shoes (from RM90) are also available.

HUEMAN STUDIO   ART
(9 Jln Tokong Emas; ⊙11am-3pm) Kooi Hin's colourful woodblock prints take up traditional Chinese themes such as astrology and calligraphy. His shop is packed with other attractive souvenir gifts.

DATARAN PAHLAWAN   MALL
(Jln Merdeka) Melaka's largest mall, with a collection of upscale designer shops and restaurants in the western half and an odd, nearly underground-feeling craft-and-souvenir market in the eastern portion.

MAHKOTA PARADE SHOPPING COMPLEX   MALL
(☏282 6151; Lot B02, Jln Merdeka) For practical needs such as books, cameras, pharmaceuticals or electronics, head to this shopping complex.

HATTEN SQUARE   MALL
(Jln Merdeka) This fashion-heavy mall – with Hatten Hotel on top – is linked by pedestrian bridge to Dataran Pahlawan and Mahkota Parade Malls; you could theoretically spend days in these three massive complexes without ever going outside.

 # SPORTS & ACTIVITIES

Reflexology centres appear to be on every corner in central Melaka. If you have specific ailments – anything from migraines to water retention – many will create a special treatment for you. There are also ear candles, fire cupping, body scrubs and more. A one-hour massage at these types of places is usually RM60 while a half-hour foot massage costs RM30.

Historic walking tours are offered through several hotels. Particularly recommended are the ones organised by the Majestic Malacca hotel (RM150 per person, free to hotel guests).

Head to the fourth to sixth floors of the Dataran Pahlawan mall for a fun centre with ever-changing activities including carnival-style games, billiards and karaoke. The best at the time of research was **Super Roller** (6th floor, Dataran Pahlawan mall; incl skate rental RM25; ⊙11am-11pm Mon-Thu, to midnight Fri & Sat), a black-lit, neon-painted roller disco dubbed the 'biggest in Malaysia', although it's actually about the size of a lap pool.

NANCY'S KITCHEN   COOKING COURSE
(☏283 6099; 15 Jln Hang Lekir; per person RM100) Nancy of this near-legendary Nonya restaurant teaches recommended cookery classes on request. Reserve well in advance.

WOK & WALK   COOKING COURSE
(☏Hotel Equatorial 282 8333; Hotel Equatorial, Jln Parameswara; 2-day packages per person from

RM340) Nonya cooking workshops include six signature dishes. Packages can include a stay at Hotel Equatorial and meals at the hotel restaurant.

PERANAKAN CULINARY JOURNEY
COOKING COURSE

(⚑289 8000; www.majesticmalacca.com; Majestic Malacca Hotel, 188 Jln Bunga Raya; per person RM285) Learn about each ingredient and the history of a couple of Nonya dishes with a master Peranaken chef at the Majestic Malacca Hotel; eat the results after.

BIOSSENTIALS PURI SPA
SPA

(⚑282 5588; www.hotelpuri.com; Hotel Puri, 118 Jln Tun Tan Cheng Lock; spa services from RM80; ⊙Thu-Mon) This international-calibre spa in a sensual garden has a delicious menu of treatments including steams, body wraps, scrubs, facials and a variety of massages.

MASSA SŪTRA
MASSAGE

(⚑016-662 503; www.massasutra.com; 20 Jln Kubu; 1hr massage RM60) We can say with conviction that Chris Loh is a master masseur (using Thai or Zen techniques).

MELAKA RIVER CRUISE
CRUISE

(⚑281 4322, 286 5468; www.melakarivercruise. com; adult/child RM15/7; ⊙9am-11.30pm) Forty-minute riverboat cruises along Sungai Melaka (Melaka River) leave from two locations: one from the 'Spice Garden' on the corner of Jln Tun Mutahii and Jln Tun Sri Lanang in the north of town, and one at the quay near the Maritime Museum. Cruises go 9km upriver past Kampung Morten and old *godown* (river warehouses) with a recorded narration explaining the riverfront's history.

ECO BIKE TOUR
BIKE TOUR

(⚑019-652 5029; www.melakaonbike.com; 117 Jln Tiang Dua; RM100 per person, min 2 people) Explore the fascinating landscape around Melaka with Alias on his three-hour bike tour through 20km of oil-palm and rubber-tree plantations and delightful *kampung* (village) communities surrounding town.

🛏 SLEEPING

So many new places are opening up in Melaka that accommodation options are particularly vulnerable to change. The good news is that quality is improving, but the bad news is that there's simply not enough tourism (except on weekends when everything books fast) to keep all these places open. Rooms have private showers and dorms have shared bathrooms, unless otherwise stated.

🛏 Chinatown

If you have the option of staying in Chinatown, do it. This is the vibrant historic centre of the city although it can get both busy and noisy.

★RIVER VIEW GUESTHOUSE
GUESTHOUSE $

(⚑012-327 7746; riverviewguesthouse@yahoo. com; 94 & 96 Jln Kampung Pantai; dm RM20, r RM45-70; ✳✦) Bordering the ambient riverfront promenade, this immaculate guesthouse is housed in a large heritage building. There's a big shared kitchen and common area and the hosts begin your stay with a handy map of town and directions to all their favourite sights and restaurants.

Homemade cake is often on offer and you can choose to get through town via the serene riverside promenade at the back door rather than the busy streets of Chinatown at the front. The owner's overflow property, **Rooftop Guesthouse** (⚑327 7746; 39 Jln Kampong Pantai) is almost as nice but doesn't offer the riverfront perk.

CAFE 1511 GUESTHOUSE
GUESTHOUSE $

(⚑286 0150; www.cafe1511.com; 52 Jln Tun Tan Cheng Lock; s/d incl breakfast RM60/90; @✦) Set in a beautiful Peranakan mansion, the small, simple, spotless rooms here are jazzed up by tasteful international art on the walls. The place has an old-style feeling, set to the music of a water fountain in the light well that extends from the restaurant below.

Note that the guesthouse doesn't take guests under 30 years old. Because of demand the guesthouse recently opened an overflow property, Dlaksmana Guesthouse, which isn't as heritage-y but is in a more quiet location a block out of Chinatown.

JALAN JALAN GUESTHOUSE
GUESTHOUSE $

(⚑283 3937; www.jalanjalanguesthouse.com; 8 Jln Tukang Emas; dm/s/d RM15/30/50; @✦) A lovely hostel in a restored old shophouse painted periwinkle blue. Fan-cooled rooms with one shared bathroom are spread out over a tranquil inner garden-courtyard. As with some other older places, though, noise from your neighbours might keep you awake at night. The hosts get great reviews and there's bike rental available.

★ **HOTEL PURI**   HOTEL $$

(☎282 5588; www.hotelpuri.com; 118 Jln Tun Tan Cheng Lock; r incl breakfast RM164-564; ✳️🛜📶) One of Chinatown's gems, Hotel Puri is an elegant creation in a superb old renovated Peranakan mansion. Its elaborate lobby, decked out with beautiful old cane and inlaid furniture, opens to a gorgeous courtyard garden. Standard rooms have butter-yellow walls, crisp sheets, satellite TV, wi-fi and shuttered windows. There's an on-site spa (Biossentials Puri Spa), and breakfast is taken in the courtyard or air-conditioned dining area.

HEEREN HOUSE   GUESTHOUSE $$

(☎281 4241; www.melaka.net/heerenhouse; 1 Jln Tun Tan Cheng Lock; incl breakfast s RM119-139, d RM129-149, f RM259; ✳️) Lodging here positions you right in the heart of Chinatown, on the waterfront and within range of top local restaurants and sights. The airy, clean and lovely rooms (six in all) in this former warehouse largely overlook the river, and have polished floorboards, traditional furniture (some with four-poster beds) and clean showers.

COURTYARD@HEEREN   HOTEL $$

(☎281 0088; www.courtyardatheeren.com; 91 Jln Tun Tan Cheng Lock; d RM200-250, f RM 250-300, ste RM300-800; ✳️🛜) Modern rooms here are each decorated uniquely with light and bright decor paired with antique wood furniture. Some have minimalist arty stained-glass details, modern takes on Chinese latticework or drapey canopies. Not many rooms have windows but there's plenty of light pouring in from the open central courtyard. It's very professionally run with great service.

HANGOUT@JONKER   HOTEL $$

(☎282 8318; www.hangouthotels.com; 19 & 21 Jln Hang Jebat; r incl light breakfast from RM147; ✳️@🛜) Opened as a second site by a popular hostel in Singapore, this location shares the same high standards of cleanliness and amenities (hang-out lounges, free movies and internet) but the spare modern style of concrete and tile is a little out of place in

Melaka. Prices go up 20% on weekends and holidays.

★ **45 LEKIU**   HISTORIC GUESTHOUSE $$$

(☎012-623 4459; www.45lekiu.com; 45 Jln Hang Lekiu; weekdays/weekends RM999/1099; ✳️🛜📶) At this gorgeous restoration project, and its sister property The Stables, the whole house is yours and both have basic cooking facilities. 45 Lekiu is the more upscale with big old beams, exposed original brickwork and clean, modern decor; it sleeps up to four people. A bougainvillea-filled courtyard has an elongated dipping pool and the upper terrace overlooks Melaka's ancient rooftops.

Work on another restoration project opposite 45 Leiku was well advanced on our last visit; it promises to be as desirable a residence as its stablemates

THE STABLES   HISTORIC GUESTHOUSE

(☎012-623 4459; http://thestablemalacca.com; No D Jln Hang Kasturi; weekdays/weekends RM300/360; ✳️🛜) Sister property to 45 Leiku, this former stables sleeps two and has louvered, heritage-style doors, wood floors, period tiles and timber beams. The furnishings and finishing touches are artistically modern.

CASA DEL RIO   HOTEL $$$

(☎6289 6888; www.casadelrio-melaka.com; 88 Jln Kota Laksmana; r RM778-1008, ste RM1928-3858; ✳️🛜📶) The biggest hotel in the Chinatown heritage area with a fabulous location right on the river. The palatial architecture blends Portuguese/Mediterranean with Malaysian for a result that's uniquely airy and grand. Rooms are massive with bathrooms fit for a Portuguese princess and river-view rooms capture the feel of Asia and Venice combined. There's a rooftop infinity pool that overlooks the river and common areas are strewn with loungable couches and tons of cushions.

🛏 Jalan Taman Melaka Raya & Around

This area is in the heart of Melaka's mall shopping zone and is only a short walk to the historic centre and Chinatown.

EMILY TRAVELLERS HOME   GUESTHOUSE $

(☎012-301 8574; 71 Jln Parameswara; dm/s RM16/24, d RM32-48; 🛜) Enter the humble entrance off the busy road and step into another dimension filled with plants, koi ponds, a bunny hopping around (Mr Playboy) and happy, mingling people. Every room is different, from funky cottages with semi-outdoor 'jungle showers' to simple wooden rooms in the house. Note that this place is rustic and it's not for you if you need hot water or air-con.

HOLIDAY INN HOTEL **$$**
(☎255 9000; www.melaka.holidayinn.com; Jln Sayed Abdul Aziz; r RM240-575; ❄@📶🏊) Boldly facing historic Melaka like a gleaming white, middle finger, rooms here are comfy, new and carpeted, yet bland. Ask for a top-storey room for fantastic views over the Strait of Melaka.

HOTEL EQUATORIAL HOTEL **$$$**
(☎282 8333; www.equatorial.com; Jln Parameswara; r RM300-1000; ❄📶🏊) While it's a bit frayed around the edges, somehow this adds to the old charm of this centrally located hotel. Good discounts online can cut prices nearly in half for excellent value. Service is well mannered and the overall presentation is crisp. There's a swimming pool, ladies-only pool, a quality fitness centre, tennis court and wi-fi access. It's worth upgrading to one of the deluxe rooms (RM500), which have either balconies or heaps of extra room space. Special packages are available through the hotel, which include tours and specials such as cookery courses.

Little India to Bukit China

This is a varied area that will let you see a less touristed side of the city while still remaining close to the sights.

★**APA KABA HOME & STAY** GUESTHOUSE **$**
(☎283 8196; www.apakaba.hostel.com; 28 Kg Banda Kaba; r incl breakfast RM40-90; ❄📶) Nestled in a quiet and authentic Malay *kampung* that seems to magically float in a bubble in the heart of town, this homestay-style guesthouse is in a simple yet beautiful old Malay house complete with creaky wood floors, louvred shutters and bright paint.

You can chill out in the enormous garden (look for ripe mangoes) or take a stroll out the back gate through tiny lanes that meander into Chinatown.

★**MAJESTIC MALACCA** HOTEL **$$$**
(☎289 8000; www.majesticmalacca.com; 188 Jln Bunga Raya; r RM410-2000; ❄@📶🏊) Melaka's most elegant hotel is an interesting mix: the lobby is in a 1920s colonial Chinese mansion while the bulk of the hotel is in a tasteful modern building behind. Rooms continue with this old and new theme with hardwood floors, sheer ivory-coloured drapes and heritage-style wood furnishings – yet all are very modern in their level of comfort. Of course the place is stacked with amenities including a small swimming pool, gym, a top-notch spa and stellar service.

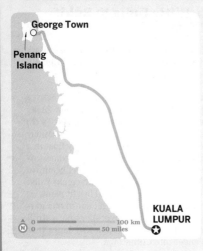

George Town

Penang Island

KUALA LUMPUR

0   100 km
0   50 miles

Penang

George Town's Heritage Zone p157

Learn about the city's architectural heritage and its cultural life on a walking tour of the Unesco zone.

Cheong Fatt Tze Mansion p161

Get a virtual crash course in feng shui at this faithfully restored mansion that once belonged to a Chinese business magnate.

Hawker Food p166

Gorge on George Town's seemingly never-ending spread of edible delights at multiple street stalls and cafes.

Penang National Park p175

Hike through jungles to deserted beaches where monkeys scamper.

Penang Hill p178

Enjoy the cool breezes and fantastic views from atop the island's highest peak.

Explore

The island of Penang, 'Pearl of the Orient', is one of Malaysia's most tolerant, cosmopolitan and exciting destinations. Its historic capital George Town is a dynamic and atmospheric place that requires at least two days to explore. Here you'll find trishaws pedalling past watermarked Chinese shophouses, blue joss smoke curling around ornate temples; gold-embroidered saris displayed in shop windows; mosques sending a call to the midday prayer; and delicious cuisine practically every other step.

There's more, however, to this 293-sq-km island, than just George Town. Hike through lush jungle to deserted beaches at Penang National Park, take a cooking course at the Tropical Spice Garden, or stand beneath the awesome goddess of mercy at the Kek Lok Si Temple – it's all part of the Penang experience.

The Best...

→ **Giant Temple** Kek Lok Si Temple (p178)
→ **Deserted Beach** Pantai Kerachut in Penang National Park (p175)
→ **Off the Beaten Track** Kampung Pulau Betong (p180)

Top Tip

Penang is best visited during major festivals and events such as Chinese New Year and the George Town Festival, but book accommodation well in advance.

Getting There & Away

→ **Air Bayan Lepas International Airport** (☏643 4411) Eighteen kilometres south of George Town.

→ **Boat** Apart from the ferry to Butterworth, there are two daily services to Langkawi (adult/child one way RM60/45, return RM115/85; 1¾ to 2½ hours) offered by **Langkawi Ferry Service** (LFS; ☏264 3088; www.langkawi-ferry.com; PPC Bldg, Pesara King Edward; ☺7am-5.30pm Mon-Sat, to 3pm Sun) and other operators.

→ **Bus** Long-distance buses to George Town arrive at the **Sungei Nibong Bus Station** (www.rapidpg.com.my; Jln Sungai Dua, Gelugor), just to the south of Penang Bridge; services to Kuala Lumpur (KL; RM35, five hours) run every 30 minutes from 7am to 1am and there are also frequent

① GETTING TO & FROM BUTTERWORTH

Butterworth, the city on the mainland bit of Penang state (known as Sebarang Perai), is home to Penang's main train station and is the departure point for ferries to Penang island. Unless you're taking the train or your bus has pulled into Butterworth's busy bus station from elsewhere, you'll probably not need to spend any time here.

The cheapest way to get between Butterworth and George Town is via the **ferry** (per adult/car RM1.20/7.70; ☺5.30am-1am). The terminal is linked by walkway to Butterworth's bus and train stations. Ferries take passengers and cars every 10 minutes from 5.30am to 9.30pm, every 20 minutes until 11.15pm, and hourly after that until 1am. The journey takes 10 minutes and fares are charged only for the journey from Butterworth to Penang; returning to the mainland is free.

If you choose to take a taxi to/from Butterworth (approximately RM50), you'll cross the 13.5km Penang Bridge, one of the longest bridges in the world. There's a RM7 toll payable at the toll plaza on the mainland, but no charge to return.

PENANG

services to Melaka (RM45, seven hours). A taxi from Sungei Nibong to George Town costs RM25. Buses to destinations in Malaysia can be boarded at Sungai Nibong and more conveniently, the **Komtar Bus Station** (www.rapidpg.com.my; Jln Penang, Georgetown); international destinations only at the latter.

→ **Train** Penang's train station is next to the ferry terminal, bus and taxi station in Butterworth. There are three daily trains to KL (six hours, RM34 to RM67) and one to Hat Yai in Thailand (four hours, RM26 to RM108); check with www.ktmb.com.my for fares and schedules.

Getting Around

→**To/From the Airport** The fixed taxi fare to most places in central George Town is RM44.70. Taxis take about 30 minutes from the centre of town to the airport, while the bus takes at least an hour. Bus

401 runs to and from the airport (RM3) every half-hour between 6am and 11pm daily and stops at Komtar Bus Station and **Weld Quay Bus Terminal** (19-24 Pengkalan Weld, George Town).

➡️**Bus** Buses around Penang are run by the government-owned **Rapid Penang** (www.rapidpg.com.my). Fares are between RM1.40 and RM4. Most routes originate at Weld Quay Bus Terminal on Pengkalan Weld and most do also stop at Komtar Bus Station and along Lebuh Chulia.

DESTINATION	ROUTE NO	PICK-UP
Batu Ferringhi	101	Pengkalan Weld, Lebuh Chulia, Komtar
Bayan Lepas International Airport, Teluk Kumbar	401	Pengkalan Weld, Lebuh Chulia
Penang Hill	204	Pengkalan Weld, Lebuh Chulia, Komtar, Air Itam
Persiaran Gurney	103	Pengkalan Weld, Air Itam, Komtar
Sungei Nibong Bus Station	401	Pengkalan Weld, Lebuh Chulia, Komtar
Teluk Bahang	101, 102	Pengkalan Weld, Botanical Gardens, Bayan Lepas International Airport

➡️**Car** You can rent cars at **La Belle** (📞262 7717; www.labelle.net.my; 48 Lebuh Leith) in George Town. At Bayan Lepas International Airport you'll find **New Bob Rent-A-Car** (📞644 1111; www.bobcar.com.my; ⊗8am-10pm Mon-Fri, to 8pm Sat & Sun), **Avis** (📞643 9633; www.avis.com; ⊗8am-9pm Mon-Fri, to 5pm Sat & Sun), **Kasina** (📞644 7893; www.kasina.com.my; ⊗7.30am-10pm Mon-Sat, 8.30am-5pm Sun) and **Pacific Rent-A-Car** (PRAC; 📞643 8891; www.iprac.com; ⊗7.30am-10pm Mon-Sat, 8am-6pm Sun).

➡️**Motorcycle** You can hire motorcycles from many places, including guesthouses and shops along Lebuh Chulia or out at Batu Ferringhi. Manual bikes start at about RM20 and automatic ones about RM30, for 24 hours.

➡️**Taxi** Penang's taxis have meters, which drivers refuse to use, so negotiate the fare before you set off. Typical fares to places outside of the city centre start at around RM12. Taxis can be found on Jln Penang, near the Cititel Hotel, at the Weld Quay Bus Terminal and near Komtar Bus Station.

➡️**Trishaw** A touristy, fun way to negotiate George Town's backstreets. Around RM40 per hour, but agree on the fare before departure.

Need to Know

➡️ **Area Code** 📞04

➡️ **Location** Penang is 370km northwest of Kuala Lumpur.

➡️ **www.visitpenang.gov.my** Official website of state tourism entity; great for details on festivals and events. Also helpful are **Penang Tourist Guide Association** (📞261 4461; www.ptga.my; 7 Lebuh Cannon, George Town) and **Tourism Malaysia** (📞262 0066; www.tourism.gov.my; 10 Jln Tun Syed Sheh Barakbah; ⊗8am-5pm Mon-Fri).

History

Little is known of Penang's early history. Chinese seafarers were aware of the island, which they called Betelnut Island, as far back as the 15th century, but it appears to have been uninhabited. It wasn't until the early 1700s that colonists arrived from Sumatra and established settlements at Batu Uban and the area now covered by southern George Town. The island came under the control of the sultan of Kedah, but in 1771 the sultan signed the first agreement with the British East India Company, handing them trading rights in exchange for military assistance against Siam.

Fifteen years later Captain Francis Light, on behalf of the East India Company, took possession of Penang, which was formally signed over in 1791. Light renamed it Prince of Wales Island, as the acquisition date fell on the prince's birthday. Light permitted new arrivals to claim as much land as they could clear and this, together with a duty-free port and an atmosphere of liberal tolerance, quickly attracted settlers from all over Asia. By the turn of the 18th century, Penang was home to more than 10,000 people.

Penang briefly became the capital of the Straits Settlements (which included Melaka and Singapore) in 1826, until it was superseded by the more thriving Singapore. By the middle of the 19th century, Penang had become a major player in the Chinese opium

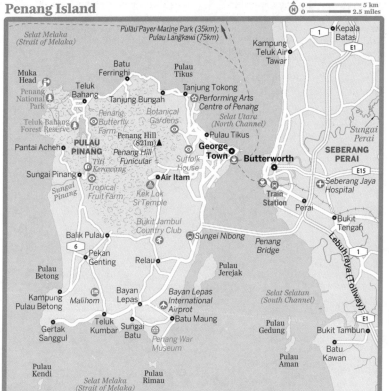

trade, which provided more than half of the colony's revenue. It was a dangerous, rough-edged place, notorious for its brothels and gambling dens, all run by Chinese secret societies.

There was little action in Penang during WWI but WWII was a different story. When it became evident that the Japanese would attack, Penang's Europeans were immediately evacuated, leaving behind a largely defenceless population. Japan took over the island on 19 December 1941, only 12 days after the attack on Pearl Harbour in the US. The following three and a half years were the darkest of Penang's history.

Things were not the same after the war. The local impression of the invincibility of the British had been irrevocably tainted and the end of British imperialism seemed imminent. The Straits Settlements were dissolved in 1946; Penang became a state of the Federation of Malaya in 1948 and one of independent Malaysia's 13 states in 1963.

With its free-port status withdrawn in 1969, Penang went through several years of decline and high unemployment. Over the next 20 years, the island was able to build itself up as one of the largest electronics manufacturing centres of Asia and is now sometimes dubbed the 'Silicon Valley of the East'. Today, Penang is the only state in Malaysia that has elected an ethnic Chinese chief minister since independence.

George Town

Explore

It's full of car exhaust fumes and has a marked lack of footpaths, but George Town is able to woo even the most acute city-phobe with its explosive cultural mishmash

George Town

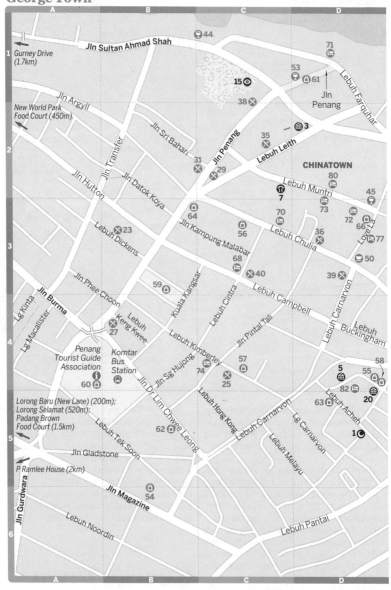

in a scene fit for a movie set. The city's historic centre, a Unesco World Heritage Site, is best explored on foot (or in a trishaw) over several unhurried days, with stops to graze on delicious Indian curries, spicy Malay specialities or local Chinese noodle creations – this is the food capital of Malaysia.

Though each of the city's districts is distinct, they do overlap; you'll find Chinese temples in Little India and mosques in Chinatown. Outside the historic core there are other sights easily accessed on day trips, such as Penang Hill, Kek Lok Si Temple and the beaches of Batu Ferringhi and Teluk Bahang.

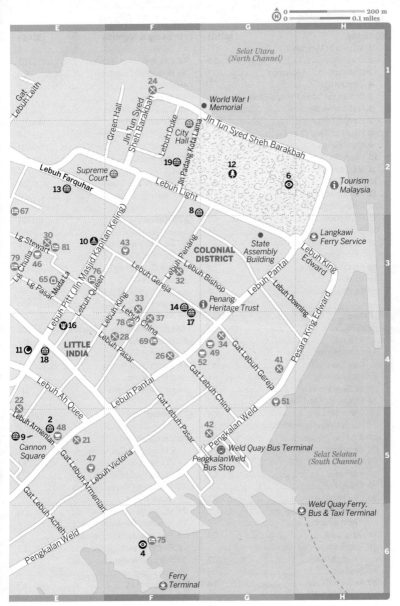

The Best...

➡ **Sight** Khoo Kongsi (p161)

➡ **Place to Eat** Hawker Stalls (p166)

➡ **Place to Drink** Canteen (p169)

Top Tip

An excellent guide to the city's buildings that also covers many of the main sights is the *George Town World Heritage Site Architectural Walkabout*, available at the **Penang Heritage Trust** (PHT; ☎264 2631;

George Town

www.pht.org.my; 26 Lebuh Pantai; ⊙9am-5pm Mon-Fri, to 1pm Sat).

⊙ SIGHTS

⊙ Chinatown

KHOO KONGSI — HISTORIC BUILDING
(www.khookongsi.com.my; 18 Cannon Sq; adult/child RM10/1; ⊙9am-6pm) The *kongsi* (clanhouse) is a major node of overseas Chinese communities, and the Khoo Kongsi is the most impressive one in Penang.

The Khoo, who trace their lineage back 25 generations, are a successful clan, and they're letting the world know. Stone carvings dance across the entrance hall and pavilions, many of which symbolise or are meant to attract good luck and wealth. Note the Sikh guardian watchman at the entrance. The interior is dominated by incredible murals depicting birthdays, weddings and, most impressively, the 36 celestial guardians (divided into two panels of 18 guardians each). The fiery overhead lighting comes courtesy of enormous paper lamps. Gorgeous ceramic sculptures of immortals, carp, dragons, and carp becoming dragons (a traditional Chinese motif symbolising success) dance across the roof ridges. As impressive as all of this is, Khoo Kongsi was once more ostentatious; the structure caught fire on the night it was completed in 1901, an event put down to divine jealousy. The present *kongsi* dates from 1906. At research time, a hotel was being built on the premises.

CHEONG FATT TZE MANSION — HISTORIC BUILDING
(www.cheongfatttzemansion.com; 14 Lebuh Leith; admission RM12; ⊙tours 11am, 1.30pm & 3pm Mon-Sat) Built in the 1880s, the magnificent 38-room, 220-window Cheong Fatt Tze Mansion was commissioned by Cheong Fatt Tze, a Hakka merchant-trader who left China as a penniless teenager and eventually established a vast financial empire throughout east Asia, earning himself the dual sobriquets 'Rockefeller of the East' and the 'Last Mandarin'.

The mansion, rescued from ruin in the 1990s, blends Eastern and Western designs, with louvred windows, art nouveau stained glass and beautiful floor tiles, and is a rare surviving example of the eclectic architectural style preferred by wealthy Straits Chinese of the time. The best way to experience the house, now a boutique hotel, is to stay here; otherwise hour-long guided tours give you a glimpse of the beautiful interior.

KUAN YIN TENG — BUDDHIST TEMPLE
(Temple of the Goddess of Mercy; Lebuh Pitt; ⊙24hr) This temple is dedicated to Kuan Yin – the goddess of mercy, good fortune, peace and fertility. The temple, which was built in the early 19th century by the first Hokkien and Cantonese settlers in Penang, is not so impressive architecturally, but it's very central and popular with the Chinese community. It seems to be forever swathed in smoke from the outside furnaces where worshippers burn paper money, and from the incense sticks waved around inside. It's a very active place, and Chinese theatre shows take place on the

GEORGE TOWN STREET NAMES

Finding your way around George Town can be slightly complicated since many roads have both a Malay and an English name. While many street signs list both, it can still be confusing. We use primarily the Malay name. Here are the two names of some of the main roads:

MALAY	ENGLISH
Lebuh Gereja	Church St
Jln Masjid Kapitan Keling	Pitt St
Jln Tun Syed Sheh Barakbah	The Esplanade
Lebuh Pantai	Beach St
Lebuh Pasar	Market St

To make matters worse, Jln Penang may also be referred to as Jln Pinang or as Penang Rd – but there's also a Penang St, which may also be called Lebuh Pinang! Similarly, Chulia St is Lebuh Chulia but there's also a Lg Chulia, and this confuses even the taxi drivers.

LOCAL KNOWLEDGE

CLANHOUSES

Between the mid-1800s and the mid-1900s, Penang welcomed a huge influx of Chinese immigrants, primarily from China's Fujian province. To help introduce uncles, aunties, cousins, 10th cousins, old neighbourhood buddies and so on to their new home, the Chinese formed clan associations and built clanhouses to create a sense of community, provide lodging and help find employment for newcomers. In addition to functioning as 'embassies' of sorts, clanhouses also served as a deeper social, even spiritual, link between an extended clan, its ancestors and its social obligations.

As time went on, many clan associations became extremely prosperous and their buildings became more ornate. Clans – called 'secret societies' by the British – began to compete with each other over the decadence and number of their temples. Thanks to this rivalry, today's Penang has one of the densest concentrations of clan architecture found outside China. Arguably George Town's most impressive clanhouse is the Khoo Kongsi (p161), while other notable clanhouses include the following:

Cheah Kongsi (8 Lebuh Armenian; ⊘9am-5pm) **FREE** Besides serving as a temple and assembly hall, this building has also been the registered headquarters of several secret societies. Each society occupied a different portion of the temple, which became a focal point during the 1867 riots. The fighting became so intense that a secret passage existed between here and Khoo Kongsi for a quick escape.

Teochew Temple (Han Jiang Ancestral Temple; Lebuh Chulia; ⊘9am-5pm) **FREE** This 1870 clanhouse was renovated in 2005 by Chinese artisans and features informative displays on the immigration of the eponymous Chinese group.

Yap Kongsi (71 Lebuh Armenian; ⊘9am-5pm) **FREE** The main structure here, today painted a distinct shade of light green and originally built in 1924 in 'Straits Eclectic' style, is not always open to the public; instead, stop in at the adjacent temple, Choo Chay Keong.

goddess's birthday, celebrated on the 19th day of the second, sixth and ninth lunar months.

The temple was being renovated when we were in town, and there's talk of adding a visitor centre.

DR SUN YAT SEN'S PENANG BASE   MUSEUM

(120 Lebuh Armenian; admission RM3; ⊘10am-5pm Mon-Sat) Dr Sun Yat Sen was the leader of the 1911 Chinese revolution, which overturned the Ching dynasty and established China as the first republic in Asia. He lived in George Town with his family for about six months in 1910. This house was not his residence but was the central meeting place for his political party. It was here the 1910 Canton uprising was planned – although unsuccessful, the uprising was a turning point for the revolution's success. Today the structure serves as a museum documenting Dr Sun Yat Sen's time in Penang, and even if you're not interested in history, it is worth a visit simply for a peek inside a stunningly restored antique shophouse.

ACHEEN ST MOSQUE   MOSQUE

(Lebuh Acheh; ⊘7am-7pm) Built in 1808 by a wealthy Arab trader, the Acheen St Mosque was the focal point for the Malay and Arab traders in this quarter – the oldest Malay *kampung* (village) in George Town. It's unusual for its Egyptian-style minaret – most Malay mosques have Moorish minarets.

HAINAN TEMPLE   CHINESE TEMPLE

(Lebuh Muntri; ⊘9am-6pm) Dedicated to Mar Chor Poh, the patron saint of seafarers, this temple was founded in 1870 but not completed until 1895. A thorough remodelling for its centenary in 1995 refreshed its distinctive swirling dragon pillars and brightened up the ornate carvings.

⊙ Colonial District & Little India

PINANG PERANAKAN MANSION   MUSEUM

(www.pinangperanakanmansion.com.my; 29 Lebuh Gereja; adult/child RM10/5; ⊘9.30am-5.30pm Mon-Sat) This building rivals the Cheong Fatt Tze Mansion as the most stunning restored residence in the city. Every door, wall and archway is carved and often painted in gold leaf; the grand rooms are furnished with majestic wood furniture with intricate mother-of-pearl inlay; and bright-coloured paintings and fascinating B&W photos of the family in regal Chinese dress grace the walls. The house belonged to Chung Keng Quee, a 19th-century merchant, secret-society leader and community pillar – he was also one of the wealthiest Baba-Nonyas of that era.

In a separate building running through to Lebuh China is the new **Straits Chinese Jewelry Museum** (29 Lebuh Gereja; admission RM20; ☺9.30am-5.30pm) which houses a dazzling collection of vintage bling and glittery ornamentation. Guides will explain the significance and cultural relevance of the various pieces and provide some insight into the craftsmanship behind them.

After visiting the house, be sure to also check out **Chung Keng Kwi Temple**, the adjacent ancestral hall, which by comparison feels decidedly less flashy.

PENANG MUSEUM   MUSEUM
(www.penangmuseum.gov.my; Lebuh Farquhar; admission RM1; ☺9am-5pm Sat-Thu) This is one of the best-presented state museums in Malaysia. There are engaging exhibits on the customs and traditions of Penang's various ethnic groups, with photos, documents, costumes, furniture and other well-labelled displays. Upstairs, the history gallery has a collection of early-19th-century watercolours by Captain Robert Smith, an engineer with the East India Company, and prints showing landscapes of old Penang. You can also play videos of Penang's many cultural festivals.

HOUSE OF YEAP CHOR EE   MUSEUM
(www.houseeyce.com; 4 Lebuh Penang; adult/child RM8/free; ☺10am-6pm Tue-Sun) This museum, housed in an exquisitely restored three-storey shophouse mansion, is dedicated to a former resident, itinerant barber-turned-banker Yeap Chor Ee. In addition to family photos and mementos, the museum has interesting exhibits on Chinese immigration to Penang. An audio tour is available for RM10, and admission is free if you dine at Sire, the attached restaurant.

CLAN JETTIES   HISTORIC NEIGHBOURHOOD
(Pengkalan Weld) FREE During the late 18th and early 19th centuries, Pengkalan Weld was the centre of one of the world's most thriving ports and provided plentiful work for the never-ending influx of immigrants. Soon a community of Chinese grew up around the quay, with floating and stilt houses built along rickety docks; these docking and home areas became known as the clan jetties.

PENANG GEORGE TOWN

GEORGE TOWN'S STREET ART

Officially sponsored street art is not common in Malaysia, but in George Town it has been embraced by the community and provides a quirky counterpoint to the city's urban beauty. Many sides of buildings in the heritage zone are adorned with cartoon steel art pieces created by the **Sculpture At Work studio** (http://sculptureatwork.com). These artworks detail local customs and heritage with humour.

For the 2012 George Town Festival imaginative murals were commissioned from the young Lithuanian artist Ernest Zacharevic, who combines objects such as a bicycle (on Lebuh Armenian) and a chair (on Lebuh Pitt) with his figurative paintings. The street art has been a smash hit with visitors constantly lining up to be photographed beside the Lebuh Armenian piece in particular – when it was vandalised in August 2012, locals quickly cleaned it up again.

Street art is, of course, not designed to last. So for the 2013 George Town Festival many other pieces of street art and installations were created including the series **101 Lost Kittens** (www.facebook.com/101lostkittens) and the **Secret Gardens of Earthly Delights**, a series of pop-up landscaping projects. This evolution of George Town's streets into an ever-changing gallery of free art and creativity is one of the most exciting developments in the city.

Pick up a free map pinpointing the various art sites from George Town Festival's office at 90 Lebuh Armenian and look at www.penang-traveltips.com (scroll down and click on George Town Street Art) for up-to-date details of the various public artworks around town.

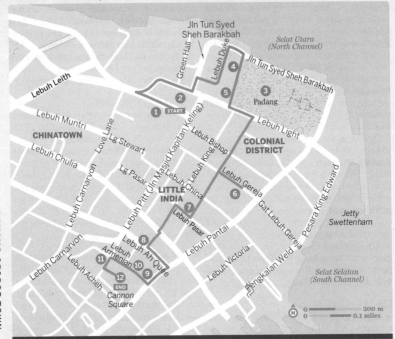

Neighbourhood Walk
Five Cultures on Two Feet

START PENANG MUSEUM
END KHOO KONGSI
LENGTH 2.25KM, THREE TO FOUR HOURS

This walk will give you a glimpse of George Town's cultural grab bag: English, Indian, Malay, Baba-Nonya and Chinese.

Starting at ① **Penang Museum** (p163), head west and then north towards the waterfront, passing the ② **Supreme Court**. Note the statue of James Richardson Logan, advocate for nonwhites during the colonial era. Walk up Lebuh Duke to the waterfront, then right and right again down Jln Padang Kota Lama past the green ③ **padang** and grandiose architecture of the ④ **City Hall** and ⑤ **Town Hall**. Proceed left along Lebuh Light, then right on Lebuh Penang. A short detour finds the impressive ⑥ **Pinang Peranakan Mansion** (p162), the old digs of one of George Town's great Baba-Nonya merchant barons.

Continue down Lebuh Penang into ⑦ **Little India** and take a deep breath of all that spice; if it's around lunchtime, refuel with a curry. At Lebuh Pasar, head right past shops selling milky Bengali sweets, then left at Lebuh King to the ⑧ **intersection of Lebuh King and Lebuh Ah Quee**, a literal example of Penang's cultural crossroads: to your south is a Chinese assembly hall and rows of fading Chinese shopfronts; to your north is a small Indian mosque; and across the street is a large Malaysian cafeteria.

Left onto Lebuh Ah Quee, right on Jln Pantai, then right on ⑨ **Lebuh Armenian** (if you want to go off-map to explore side lanes and alleyways, this is the time to do it). The street became a centre for Chinese secret societies and was one of the main fighting stages of the 1867 riots. Stroll past the street art of the two boys on a real bike near the entrance of ⑩ **Cheah Kongsi** (p162), home to the oldest Straits Chinese clan association in Penang.

At the corner of Lebuh Pitt is the small 1924 Hokkien clanhouse ⑪ **Yap Kongsi** (p162), its outer altar decorated in symbols from the *Tao Teh Ching*. Left and left onto Cannon Sq brings you to ⑫ **Khoo Kongsi** (p161), the most impressive *kongsi* in the city.

Today the clan jetties are low-income areas with a jumble of dilapidated floating houses and planks, and are becoming popular tour-bus stops. If you get here sans tour bus, it's a fun place to wander around, with docked fishing boats, folks cooking in their homes and kids running around. There is also a homestay (p174) option here.

FORT CORNWALLIS HISTORIC SITE

(Lebuh Light; adult/child RM2/1; ⊙9am-7pm) For all its size, this fort isn't particularly impressive; only the outer walls stand, enclosing a rather aged and spare park within. The fort is named for Charles Cornwallis, perhaps best known for surrendering at the Battle of Yorktown to George Washington, effectively ending the American Revolution. It was at the site of the fort that Captain Light first set foot on the virtually uninhabited island in 1786 and established the free port where trade would, he hoped, be lured from Britain's Dutch rivals. Between 1808 and 1810 convict labour replaced the then-wooden building materials with stone. The star-profile shape of the walls allowed for overlapping fields of fire against enemies

PROTESTANT CEMETERY CEMETERY

(Jln Sultan Ahmad Shah; ⊙24hr) Here you'll find the graves of Captain Francis Light and many others, including governors, merchants, sailors and Chinese Christians, who fled the Boxer Rebellion in China (a movement opposing Western imperialism and evangelism) only to die of fever in Penang, all under a canopy of magnolia trees. Also here is the tomb of Thomas Leonowens, the young officer who married Anna – the schoolmistress to the King of Siam made famous by *The King and I*.

SRI MARIAMMAN TEMPLE HINDU TEMPLE

(Lebuh Pitt; ⊙7am-7pm) For local Tamils, this temple fulfils the purpose of a Chinese clanhouse; it's a reminder of the motherland and the community bonds forged within the diaspora. Sri Mariamman was built in 1883 and is George Town's oldest Hindu house of worship. It is a typically South Indian temple, dominated by the *gopuram* (entrance tower).

Penang's Thaipusam procession begins here, and in October a wooden chariot takes the temple's deity for a spin around the neighbourhood during Vijayadasami festivities.

MASJID KAPITAN KELING MOSQUE

(cnr Lebuh Buckingham & Lebuh Pitt; ⊙7am-7pm) Penang's first Indian Muslim settlers (East India Company troops) built Masjid Kapitan Keling in 1801. The mosque's domes are yellow, in a typically Indian-influenced Islamic style, and it has a single minaret. It looks sublime at sunset. Mosque officials can grant permission to enter.

EATING

People come to George Town just to eat. Even if you thought you came here for another reason, your priorities might change dramatically once you start digging into the Indian, Chinese, Malay and various hybrid treats available. Days revolve around where and what to eat, and three meals a day starts to sounds depressingly scant. And it's the same for locals, for whom eating out is a daily event.

Chinatown

SUP HAMEED MALAY $

(48 Jln Penang; mains from RM3; ⊙24hr) On the surface, this is very much your typical *nasi campur* (buffet of curried meats) shop found all over Malaysia, and we don't recommend eating here during the day. But come night, Hameed sets out tables on the street and serves his incredibly rich soups (try *sup kambing* – goat soup), served with slices of white bread.

THO YUEN RESTAURANT CHINESE $

(92 Lebuh Campbell; dim sum RM1-5; ⊙6am-3pm Wed-Mon) Our favourite place for dim sum. It's packed with newspaper-reading loners and chattering groups of locals all morning long, but you can usually squeeze in somewhere – as long as you arrive early. Servers speak minimal English but do their best to explain the contents of their carts.

SKY HOTEL CHINESE $

(Lebuh Chulia; mains from RM6; ⊙10am-3pm) It's incredible that this gem sits in the middle of the greatest concentration of travellers in George Town, yet is somehow almost exclusively patronised (in enthusiastic numbers) by locals. It is incumbent on you to try the *char siew* (barbequed pork), *siew bak* (pork

PENANG GEORGE TOWN

HAWKER-STALL HEAVEN

George Town's reputation as a must-see destination hinges greatly on its food, and the best the city has to offer is served at hawker stalls and food courts. Not eating at a stall in George Town is like missing the Louvre in Paris – you simply have to do it.

Hawker-stall vendors run flexible schedules, so don't be surprised if one isn't there during your visit. Most importantly, avoid Mondays and Thursdays when many vendors tend to stay at home. Dishes generally fall between RM3 and RM10.

Lorong Baru (New Lane, cnr Jln Macalister & Lg Baru; ⏰dinner) If you ask locals where their favourite hawker stalls are, after listing a few far-flung places, they'll always mention this night-time street extravaganza, not for a particular stall but because all the food is reliably good. There's an emphasis on Chinese-style noodle dishes, and we particularly liked the *char koay kak* stall, which in addition to spicy fried rice cakes with seafood, also does great *otak otak* (a steamed fish curry). Lg Baru intersects with Jln Macalister about 250m northwest of the intersection with Jln Penang.

Gurney Drive (Persiaran Gurney; ⏰dinner) Penang's most famous food area sits amid modern high-rises bordered by the sea. It's posh for a hawker area so the food is a bit pricier than elsewhere, but you'll find absolutely everything from Malay to Western. It's particularly known for its laksa stalls (try stall 11). For the best *rojak* (fruit-and-vegetable salad dressed with chilli sauce and black shrimp paste with peanuts) head to the famous Ah Chye. Gurney Dr is located about 3km west of George Town near Gurney Plaza mall; a taxi here will set you back RM15.

Esplanade Food Centre (Jln Tun Syed Sheh Barakbah; ⏰dinner) You can't beat the seaside setting of this food centre, which is nestled right in the heart of George Town's Colonial District. One side is called 'Islam' and serves halal Malay food, and the other is called 'Cina' and serves Chinese and Malay specialities, including the absolutely delicious *rojak* at Rojak Ho Wei Jeng. Esplanade is often very quiet on Monday and Wednesday.

Padang Brown Food Court (Jln Pantai; ⏰lunch & dinner Fri-Wed) Everyone in town knows that this is the spot for delectable *popiah* (spring rolls), although the *won ton mee* (egg noodles served with pork dumplings or sliced roast pork) and *bubur caca* (dessert porridge made with coconut milk and banana) are other good reasons to try the food in this area. In the afternoons try the *yong tau foo* (clear Chinese soup with fish balls, lettuce, crab sticks, cuttlefish and more). Padang Brown is about 1.5km west of the centre of George Town, off Jln Dato Keramat; a taxi here will cost about RM15.

Lorong Selamat (cnr Jl Macalister & Lg Selamat; ⏰dinner Sat-Thu) The south end of Lg Selamat is the place to go for the city's most famous *char kway teow* (broad noodles, clams and eggs fried in chilli and black bean sauce), but you'll also find lip-smacking *won ton mee* and other Chinese Penang favourites. Lg Baru intersects with Jln Macalister about 500m northwest of Jln Penang.

New World Park Food Court (Lg Swatow; ⏰11am-7pm) Every stall serves something different at this ultramodern, covered food court with mist-blowing fans and shiny industrial decor. The *ais kacang* (shaved-ice dessert with syrup, jellies, beans and sometimes even corn on top) here gets particularly good reviews. There are also a number of fast-food-feeling restaurants in this complex including Nonya and Indian. New World is off Jln Hutton, about 400m northwest of Jln Transfer.

Red Garden Food Paradise & Night Market (Lebuh Leith; ⏰lunch & dinner) This place has a convenient location in the heart of Chinatown and offers a wide selection of food, including most local specialities. It's a good choice for families looking for something easy and has lots of options for fussy eaters.

belly), *siew cheong* (honey-sweetened pork) and roast duck.

JOO HOOI   HAWKER $
(cnr Jln Penang & Lebuh Keng Kwee; mains from RM3; ⊙11am-6pm) The hawker centre equivalent of one-stop shopping, this cafe-style joint has all of Penang's best dishes in one location: laksa, *rojak, char kway teow* (broad noodles, clams and eggs fried in chilli and black bean sauce), *lor bak* (deep-fried meats served with dipping sauces), *cendol* (shaved ice with palm sugar, coconut milk and jellies) and fresh fruit juices.

KHENG PIN   HAWKER $
(80 Jln Penang; mains from RM4; ⊙7am-3pm Tue-Sun) Locals swear by the specialities at this aged hawker joint, most famously *lor bak* (deep-fried meats dipped in sauce) and Hainan chicken rice (steamed chicken with broth and rice), one of the great fast foods of east Asia.

EE BENG
VEGETARIAN FOOD   CHINESE, VEGETARIAN $
(20 Lebuh Dickens; meals around RM5; ⊙7am-9pm; ☑) Popular self-service place for cheap, mostly vegetarian food of the tofu and green vegetables variety.

★**TEKSEN**   CHINESE $$
(18 Lebuh Carnavon; mains from RM10; ⊙noon-2.30pm & 6-9pm Wed-Mon) A recent 'branding and uplifting enterprise' has elevated this longstanding restaurant a couple of steps up from Penang's typically gritty shophouse restaurants. There's a lengthy menu translated into English but we suggest you do as the locals do and ask the staff for the daily specials – this strategy rewarded us with some great soups, a tasty Malaysian-style stir-fry of morning glory and sambal, and a delicious dish of stir-fried roast pork. Highly recommended.

KASHMIR   INDIAN $$
(Oriental Hotel, 105 Jln Penang; mains RM6.90-54.90; ⊙11am-10pm) Don't be fooled by this hotel-basement restaurant's cheesy 1970s denlike interior; Kashmir serves some super-delicious tandoori. Attentive service, an assertive Indian soundtrack and yes, cocktails, complete the package.

GOH HUAT SENG   CHINESE $$
(59A Lebuh Kimberley; hotpot RM40-80; ⊙5-9.30pm) With five decades under its belt, Goh Huat Seng continues to serve Teo Chew–style hotpot the old way: in charcoal-fired steamboats. Get some friends together and enjoy some communal dipping or, if you've got the language skills, order classic Teo Chew dishes from the restaurant's Chinese-language menu on the wall.

EDELWEISS   SWISS $$
(38 Lebuh Armenian; mains RM18-39.50; ⊙11am-10pm Tue-Sun) Items such as currywurst and bratwurst carry a distinct German accent, while fondue and rösti (Swiss-style potato pancakes) give Edelweiss its Swiss twang. The antique-filled dining room is a delight, and there's a small selection of pricey imported beers.

★**CHINA HOUSE**   INTERNATIONAL $$$
(☑263 7299; www.chinahouse.com.my; 153 & 155 Lebuh Pantai; ⊙9am-midnight) Where do we start? This new complex of three conjoined heritage buildings features two dining outlets; a cafe-bakery, Kopi C (p169); two galleries; and a bar, Canteen.

BTB (mains RM38-68; ⊙6.30-10.30pm), the flagship dining venue, does a short but appetising menu of Middle Eastern– and Mediterranean-influenced dishes; think seared sea bass with Ras-el-Hanout spices, cauliflower puree and roasted pumpkin, pine-nut and pomegranate dressing.

Courtyard Cafe (mains RM12-30; ⊙5pm-midnight) does a more casual burger and tapas menu. Whew.

★**KEBAYA**   NONYA $$$
(☑264 2333; www.seventerraces.com; Seven Terraces, Lg Stewart; 4-course menu RM100; ⊙7-10pm Tue-Sun) The restaurant attached to this splendid new hotel, both decorated with a gorgeous collection of antiques, offers an inspired contemporary spin on Nonya cuisine. The confit duck with five spice, plums and oranges is delectable – and don't miss the pandan-infused crème brûlée.

✗ Colonial District & Little India

MADRAS NEW
WOODLANDS RESTAURANT   INDIAN $
(60 Lebuh Penang; mains from RM1.50, set lunch RM5.25; ⊙8.30am-10pm; ☑) It draws you in with its display of Indian sweets outside

(try the *halwa*), but once you experience the food you might not have room for dessert. Tasty banana-leaf meals and north Indian specialities are the mainstays, as well as the thickest mango lassi in town. The daily set lunch for RM5.25 might be Penang's greatest food bargain.

QUAY CAFÉ
ASIAN, VEGETARIAN $

(2 Gat Lebuh Gereja; mains RM5-15; ☺10am-3pm Mon-Sat; 🖉) Slick cafeteria serving Asian-style meat-free dishes. Expect set meals, an emphasis on noodle dishes, and fresh juices and herbal teas.

SRI ANANDA BAHWAN
INDIAN $

(55 Lebuh Penang; mains from RM3; ☺7am-10pm; 🖉) Busy and tidy *nasi campur*–type restaurant, seemingly forever full of chatting locals, which serves up tandoori chicken, *roti canai* (flaky, flat bread) and *murtabak* (*roti canai* filled with meat or vegetables). There's also an air-con dining hall.

KARAI KUDI
INDIAN $

(20 Lebuh Pasar; set meals from RM6.50, mains RM4-20; ☺11am-11pm; 🖉) This outrageously tasty air-con place specialises in South Indian Tamil Chettinad cuisine but also serves tandoori at dinner. Banana-leaf meals are huge and some sets include ice cream for dessert.

HUI SIN VEGETARIAN RESTAURANT
CHINESE, VEGETARIAN $

(11 Lebuh China; meals around RM4; ☺8am-4pm Mon-Sat; 🖉) This excellent-value buffet restaurant is the place to go for a filling meat-free lunch. Take what you want from the selection of vegetables, curries and bean curds on offer, and you'll be charged accordingly.

LEAF HEALTHY HOUSE
CHINESE, VEGETARIAN $$

(🖉262 7007; www.facebook.com/TheLeaf-HealthyHouse; 5 Lebuh Penang; mains from RM9; ☺11.30am-3pm & 5.30-9pm Mon-Sat; 🖉) Fresh salads, juices, healthy rice and noodle dishes are served at this this appealing veggie cafe which grows its own herbs out front and also rents out bicycles.

VIA PRE
ITALIAN $$

(www.via-pre.com; 5 Pengkalan Weld; mains RM6.90-54.90; ☺10am-10.30pm) This KL-based Italian staple has imported a previously unknown level of sophistication to sleepy George Town. Expect traditional Italian dishes, tasty pizzas and superb desserts in a beautifully refurbished warehouse overlooking the mainland.

WELD QUAY SEAFOOD RESTAURANT
CHINESE $$

(Tree Shade Seafood Restaurant; Pengkalan Weld; mains RM10-50; ☺lunch & dinner Thu-Tue) Named for its location under a giant tree, this is where locals head for cheap and tasty seafood. Pick your aquatic protein from the trays out front, and the staff will fry, steam, soup or grill it up for you. Located directly across from the Weld Quay Bus Terminal.

🍴 Persiaran Gurney, Jalan Burma & Around

⭐SEA PEARL LAGOON CAFE
CHINESE $$

(🖉899 0375; off Jln Tanjong Tokong; dishes from RM8; ☺11am-10pm Thu-Tue) On the surface, this somewhat gritty open-air place isn't much different than many of George Town's hawker cafes. But the view looking out over the North Channel and the food – salt roasted prawns, *ikan bakar* (fish grilled with sambal) and excellent satay – combine to make it one of our favourite places to eat outside the city centre.

Sea Pearl Lagoon is located 7km northwest of George Town, in Tanjong Toking next to Thai Pak Koong Temple; a taxi here from central George Town will set you back about RM25.

NYONYA BREEZE
NONYA $$

(50 Lg Abu Siti; mains RM8.60-22; ☺11am-10pm Wed-Mon) Considered by many local Peranakans to serve the best Nonya food, this cafeteria-like place makes you feel at home while you sample exquisite specialities such as *kari kapitan* (chicken curry with coconut milk and kaffir lime) and *sambal goreng* (prawns, eggplant and cashews in chilli sauce). There are a lot of daily specials and weekday lunchtime set meals (RM13.90).

Lg Abu Siti intersects with Jln Burma, about 500m northwest of Jln Transfer.

ISARIBI TEI
JAPANESE $$

(cnr Jln Burma & Jln Chow Thye; set menu RM22-40; ☺11am-10pm) Fresh, expertly prepared sushi is served in a vine-covered hardwood setting that looks more like the heart of the jungle than the middle of the city. Beyond sushi, Japanese-style grilled-fish set menus are the speciality with salmon, cod, trout and much more on offer.

Isaribi Tei is 1.5km northwest of Jln Transfer; a taxi here will set you back about RM15.

CHOCK DEE THAI **$$**

(231D Jln Burma; mains RM13-50; ⊙11am-10pm Sun-Tue) Chock Dee has garnered an impressive reputation among local eaters. Menu highlights include squid in lemon sauce and *hor mok,* Thai-style *otak otak* (steamed curry).

Chock Dee is on Jln Burma about 750m northwest of Jln Transfer; a taxi here will cost around RM12.

🍷 DRINKING & NIGHTLIFE

Between the largely hotel-based bars and some rather commercial-feeling pubs and clubs, George Town doesn't have much of a sophisticated bar scene. That said, there are a few fun places for a night out.

★CANTEEN BAR

(www.chinahouse.com.my; China House, 183B Lebuh Victoria; ⊙5pm-midnight) This is about as close as George Town comes to a hipster bar – minus the pretension. Canteen has an inviting artsy-warehouse vibe, there's live music from Thursday to Sunday, and great bar snacks available every night. Canteen is also accessible via China House's entrance on Lebuh Pantai.

HI, TEA!

Penang's English, Chinese and Indian legacies have left an appreciation for tea that remains strong today. More recent immigrants to George Town have imported an enviable Western-style cafe culture.

Suffolk House (www.suffolkhouse.com.my; 250 Jln Ayer Itam; high tea for 2 RM68; ⊙2.30-6pm) For the ultimate English tea experience, head out of town to this 200-year-old Georgian-style mansion, where high tea, featuring scones and cucumber sandwiches, can be taken inside or in the garden. Suffolk House is located about 6.5km west of George Town; a taxi here will cost around RM15.

Ten Yee Tea Trading (33 Lebuh Pantai; ⊙9.30am-6.30pm Mon-Sat) Fine teas are on sale here but the fun part is deciding which to buy. For RM20 you choose a tea (which you can share with up to five people), then a specialist shows you how to prepare it the proper Chinese way. A full explanation of all the different brews is given alongside the tea drinking.

Jing-Si Books & Cafe (31 Lebuh Pantai; ⊙noon-8pm) A stylish oasis of spiritual calm, this outlet for a Taiwanese Buddhist group's teachings is a wonderful place to revive in hushed surroundings over a pot of interesting teas or coffees – all of which go for the reasonable price of RM5.

Kopi C (www.chinahouse.com.my; China House, 153 & 155 Lebuh Pantai; mains from RM10; ⊙9am-midnight) Located in the rambling China House complex, this cafe-bakery does good coffee and some of the best pastries and ice creams (on a good day 16 of the latter – we like the salted caramel) we've encountered in Southeast Asia.

1885 (☎261 8333; Eastern & Oriental Hotel, 10 Lebuh Farquahar; English afternoon tea RM52; ⊙2-5pm) The E&O Hotel's main restaurant offers a daily English afternoon tea with scones, smoked salmon and, of course, cucumber sandwiches.

Café 55 (www.coffeeatelier.com; Coffee Atelier, 47-55 Lg Stewart; coffee from RM8; ⊙8.30am-5pm Tue-Sun) In what was formerly a coffee roaster (ask to see the former roasting oven out back), this sophisticated cafe, with attached gallery, does both new-school and old-school coffee drinks.

David Brown's (www.penanghillco.com.my; Penang Hill; afternoon tea RM34-78; ⊙9am-6pm) Outside George Town, at the top of Penang Hill, this is yet another atmospheric destination for colonial-style high tea.

★ B@92 — BAR

(92 Lebuh Gereja; ⊘noon-late) Need a drinking buddy while in town? Resident Serbian Aleksandar is more than happy to oblige. Food, an eclectic music selection and friendly regulars make B@92 the kind of bar you wish you could throw in your backpack and carry with you across Southeast Asia. Ask about the origin of Aleks' skull ring, and you might just get a discount.

COZY IN THE ROCKET — CAFE

(262-264 Lebuh Pantai; mains RM25; ⊘10am-5pm Tue-Sun; 🛜) Named after the owners Hong and Yen's favourite song, this arty, airy place offers a winning combo of a courtyard garden, good coffee, refreshing drinks and tasty pasta dishes. It can get very busy at lunch, so don't come then if you're in a hurry.

MUGSHOT CAFE — CAFE

(302 Lebuh Chulia; ⊘8am-9pm; 🛜) Chalk up your misdemeanor and make like one of the 'Usual Suspects' at this superpopular new cafe serving a variety of sandwiches. The homemade fruity yoghurts in glass jars are also luscious. Plans are in the works for a guesthouse here.

THAT LITTLE WINE BAR — BAR

(www.thatlittlewinebar.com; 54 Jln Chow Thye; ⊘5pm-midnight Mon-Sat) A cosy yet chic bar and lounge run by a German chef and his wife. Enjoy a selection of wine – glasses start at RM20 – and champagne cocktails. Accompany your drink with tapas (RM18 to RM60) and slightly heavier mains (RM28 to RM65). Jln Chow Thye is located off Jln Burma, about 1.5km northwest of Jln Transfer; a taxi here will set you back about RM15.

BEACH BLANKET BABYLON — BAR

(32 Jln Sultan Ahmad Shah; ⊘11am-1am Mon-Fri, to 2am Sat & Sun) The open-air setting and relaxed vibe contrast with the rather formal restaurant with which this bar is linked. Saturday night is men's night at this gay-friendly spot, with half price on standard pours and a discount on beer for males.

FARQUHAR'S BAR — BAR

(Eastern & Oriental Hotel, 10 Lebuh Farquhar; ⊘11am-1am) Colonial British-style bar inside the E&O Hotel, serving beer, traditional pub food and cocktails; try its signature drink, the Eastern & Oriental sling (RM38), brought to you by a white-coated barman.

There's live music Thursday to Saturday, and Happy Hour between 5pm and 8pm.

BEHIND 50 LOVE LANE — BAR

(Lebuh Muntri; ⊘6pm-1am Wed-Mon) Pocket-sized, retro-themed bar that draws a largely local following, despite being close to the backpacker strip. There's a classic-rock soundtrack and a short menu of Western-style comfort dishes (RM14.90 to RM18.90).

UPPER JLN PENANG BARS — BAR

(Jln Penang; ⊘8pm-2am) This strip of road at the far northern end of Jln Penang is George Town's rather commercial-feeling entertainment strip. There's a row of about 10 open-air and air-con bars, but most flock to the megaclubs: Slippery Senoritas offers live-music shows that are as corny as the bar's name suggests, although it's popular and all in good fun; while Voodoo offers much of the same in a slightly more sophisticated package.

QEII — BAR, CLUB

(8 Pengkalan Weld; ⊘6pm-1am Mon-Tue, 1pm-2am Wed-Sat, 3pm-2am Sun) QEII, with 360-degree views of the Strait of Melaka, serves passable pizza and better ambience; on Friday and Saturday nights, it transforms into a dance club.

🛍 SHOPPING

UNIQUE PENANG — ARTS & CRAFTS

(www.uniquepenang.com; 62 Love Lane; ⊘5pm-midnight Sun-Fri, 9pm-midnight Sat) This shophouse gallery features the work of the friendly young owners, Clovis and Joey, as well as the colourful paintings of the latter's young art students. As the couple point out, paintings are notoriously hard to squeeze in a backpack, so nearly all of the gallery's art is available in postcard size.

ROZANAS BATIK — HANDICRAFTS

(81B Lebuh Aceh; ⊘11.30am-6.30pm) Tiny shop featuring the owner's beautiful handmade batik items. If you want to learn more, take a walk-in two-hour class in the adjacent studio (RM50 to RM75).

SPRINGSFIELD — ARTS & CRAFTS

(8 Muda Lane; ⊘9am-6pm) Pick up some hand-painted Peranakan tiles (made in Vietnam) at this boutique in a restored shophouse. There are a few other interesting local-style

knick-knacks available, and the profits go to help stray animals.

CHINA JOE'S
ARTS & CRAFTS

(95 Lebuh Armenian; ☺9am-7pm) Sells colourful fabrics – both new and antique – boxes, stationery, bags and other classy Asian bric-a-brac. There's a gallery upstairs and an adjacent tea salon.

88 ARMENIAN STREET
ARTS & CRAFTS

(88 Lebuh Armenian; ☺10am-6pm Mon-Sat) This address houses three floors of art: the ground floor showcases the exquisite fused-glass creations of Penang artist Wong Keng Fuan, the 1st floor is the showroom for Jonathan Yun's sculptural jewellery, and the 2nd floor houses Howard Tan's Penang-centric photos.

GALLERY 29
ARTS & CRAFTS

(www.rebeccaduckett.com; 29 Lebuh China; ☺9am-6pm) Rebecca Duckett's gallery shows off her modern yet traditionally inspired art in colourful splashes. There is also a good selection of books on local topics, and vintage items and crafts on offer.

STRAITS QUAY
MALL

(www.straitsquay.com; Jln Seri Tanjung Pinang, Tanjung Tokong; ☺10.30am-10pm) Built on reclaimed land just outside the city centre, this flashy mall includes a few stand-out stores: **Séntuhan** (www.sentuhan.com; ☺10.30am-10pm) sells a unique selection of crafts and homewares made by disadvantaged Malaysian women; and the **Royal Selangor Visitor Centre** (www.visitorcentre.royalselangor.com; 3A-G-1, Straits Quay, Jln Seri Tanjung Pinang; ☺10.30am-10pm) offers a course in making pewter sculptures daily at 11am, 2.30pm and 4.30pm (per person RM60).

If you're not into shopping, it's also home to the **Performing Arts Centre of Penang** (www.penangpac.org) and there are a couple of decent restaurants and bars strategically positioned to soak up the sea breezes.

Straits Quay is located about 7km northwest of George Town; buses 101 and 104 pass the mall (RM4), and a taxi here will cost about RM20. Enquire about a shuttle boat from the Eastern & Oriental Hotel to the mall.

BAN HIN
ANTIQUES

(Lebuh Chulia; ☺9am-7pm) This old shophouse is literally stuffed full of old adverts, packages, tins, ceramics, toys and other quasi-

antiques. Located roughly across from Banana Boutique Hotel.

BEE CHIN HEONG
ANTIQUES

(58 Lebuh Kimberley; ☺10am-8.30pm) This interesting outlet sells a colourful, bewildering assortment of religious statues, furniture and temple supplies; if you're after a huge Chinese couch, a household shrine or have RM55,000 to spend on a 2m-tall carved-wood Buddha, this is the place to come. Even if you're not buying, it's still worth a look around.

GURNEY PLAZA
MALL

(Persiaran Gurney; ☺10am-10pm) Penang's classiest mall, with international chain stores such as the Body Shop and Esprit. Mac users will find an Apple store here, and there's a massive music shop, bookshop and several electronics outlets. There's also a mini theme park, fitness centre and a health spa. Gurney Plaza is located about 3km west of George Town; a taxi here will set you back RM15.

CHOWRASTER BAZAAR
MARKET

(Jln Penang; ☺8am-6pm) This sweaty old market hall is where to go for a frenetic, souk-like experience. It's full of food stalls and vendors selling headscarves, batik shirts, fabrics and *kebaya* (blouses worn over a sarong).

KOMTAR
MALL

(Jln Penang; ☺10am-10pm) Penang's oldest mall is housed in a 64-storey landmark tower (at one time the tallest building in Malaysia). There are hundreds of shops in a place with the feel of an ageing bazaar. Here you'll find everything from clothes, shoes and electronics to everyday goods, and you can take an elevator ride (RM5) from the ground floor to the 58th floor where there's a lookout area with views over the island.

Adjacent **Prangin Mall** (www.prangin-mall.com; 33 Jln Dr Lim Chwee Leong; ⊙10am-10pm) has a cinema showing the odd Western blockbuster; **1st Avenue** (www.1st-avenue-mall.com.my; 182 Jln Magazine, George Town; ⊙10am-10pm) is another mall with similarly international shops.

SAM'S BATIK HOUSE CLOTHING

(159 Jln Penang; ⊙8am-7pm) Nicknamed 'Ali Baba's Cave', this deep shop of silky and cottony goodness is the best place in town to buy sarongs, batik shirts and Indian fashions. Girls can go nuts over hand-embroidered dresses while the guys try on Bollywood shirts.

PENANG GEORGE TOWN

🛏 SLEEPING

George Town has all the accommodation possibilities you would expect in a big, bustling tourist city, from the grungiest hostels to the swankiest hotels, although it's worth noting that there's not a whole lot to choose from in the midrange. Cacophonic Lebuh Chulia and quieter Love Lane make up the heart of Penang's backpacker land, crammed with cheap hostels and hotels – it pays to check a few out before parting with your cash.

Be warned that during holidays, most notably Chinese New Year (January or February), hotels tend to fill up very quickly and prices can become ridiculously inflated; if you intend to stay at this time, book well in advance.

🛏 Chinatown

ROOMMATES HOSTEL $

(☏261 1567; www.roommatespenang.com; 178 Lg Chulia; dm incl breakfast RM28-30; ❄@🛜) This new hostel – allegedly the island's smallest – boasts a young, communal, chummy vibe. There are 16 podlike dorm beds and a living room–like communal area, but the real highlight is Yen, the friendly owner, who leads guests on free pub-crawls, eating tours and other activities.

RYOKAN HOSTEL $

(☏250 0287; www.myryokan.com; 62 Lebuh Muntri; dm incl breakfast RM35-38, r RM136; ❄@🛜) As the name suggests, this new flashpackers has a minimalist – if not particularly

Japanese – feel. The dorms, which range from four to six beds, are almost entirely white (except for the pink women's dorms, which also include a large mirror), and the bunk-style beds include a private light and power point. 'Chillax', TV and reading rooms are also stylish and inviting, and come equipped with iPads. The similarly white private rooms with en suite bathrooms are comfortable yet overpriced, and lack windows.

REGGAE PENANG HOSTEL $

(☏262 6772; www.reggaehostelsmalaysia.com; 57 Love Lane; dm incl breakfast RM28-30; ❄@🛜) Another brick in Malaysia's Reggae empire, this expansive heritage building has several four- to 12-bed dorm rooms. Beds are double-decker pod style, and have individual lights, power point and free wi-fi. The lobby, outfitted with pool table and coffee shop, feels more like a bar than a hostel. Perfect for the social traveller.

★NEW ASIA HERITAGE HOTEL HOTEL $$

(☏262 6171; www.newasiahotel.com; 71 Lebuh Kimberley; r RM88-158; ❄🛜) As we were told by the gruff-but-friendly manager here, 'The most important thing about this hotel is that everything is the same in every room.' And he's right; the 24 rooms in this clean, well-run, comfortable midranger are similarly equipped with TV, air-con, and relatively attractive and functional furniture, although some rooms are slightly larger and have huge balconies. If you favour value rather than style, this would be your best option in George Town.

MOON TREE 47 HOTEL $$

(☏264 4021; 47 Lebuh Muntri; r RM80-120; ❄🛜) The main structure of this antique shophouse holds three rooms, all sharing a bathroom, while out back are three two-level suites (three additional family rooms were being built at research time). The place has a funky, retro vibe and friendly service, making it perfect for young couples or solo travellers; however, some people might be put off by some of the hotel's rather rustic amenities and features.

MUNTRI MEWS HISTORIC HOTEL $$

(☏263 5125; www.muntrimews.com; 77 Lebuh Muntri; r RM300-360; ❄@🛜) This building's original owners would no doubt be shocked to learn that their former stablehouse (mews) is today an attractive boutique hotel.

The nine rooms have an elegant minimalist vibe, with each room boasting an inviting lounge area and a retro black-and-white tiled bathroom, but conspicuously at this price range, no wardrobe, minibar or safe.

CHULIA HERITAGE BOUTIQUE HOTEL $$

(✆263 3380; www.chuliaheritagehotel.com; 380 Lebuh Chulia; r RM90-280; ✲🛜) The White House would probably be a more apt name for this recently opened hotel. It's housed in an all-white former mansion, with smallish rooms also decked out in virginal white, with, of course, white furnishings and amenities. It's all very pure and clean-looking, if somewhat lacking in atmosphere (and colour). The cheapest rooms lack windows and share bathrooms.

CAMPBELL HOUSE HISTORIC HOTEL $$

(✆261 8290; www.campbellhousepenang.com; 106 Lebuh Campbell; r incl breakfast RM270-550; ✲@🛜) This former hotel, dating back to 1903, is seeing a new life as a thoughtful, sumptuous boutique. The European owners have employed their extensive experience in the luxury world to include amenities such as locally sourced, organic toiletries, beautiful Peranakan tiles in the bathrooms, Nespresso machines and high-quality mattresses.

★23 LOVE LANE HISTORIC HOTEL $$$

(✆262 1323; www.23lovelane.com; 23 Love Lane; r incl breakfast 800-1200; ✲@🛜) The 10 rooms here, which are found both in the main structure (a former mansion) or the surrounding buildings (former kitchen and stables), tastefully combine antique furniture and fixtures with modern design touches and artsy accents. There are lots of open spaces and high ceilings to catch the breezes, inviting communal areas, a peaceful aura, and service that complements the casual, homey vibe.

STRAITS COLLECTION APARTMENTS $$$

(✆262 7299; www.straitscollection.com; 89-95 Lebuh Armenia; ste from RM450; ✲@🛜) If you've dreamed of living in a retro-chic restored Chinese shophouse, head here. Each residence is essentially a house (but no cooking facilities), artfully decorated with regional antiques, bright-coloured cushions and high-design rugs. Each is different but all have some sort of unforgettable detail such as light-well courtyards, wooden Japanese bathtubs or ancient sliding doors.

EASTERN & ORIENTAL HOTEL LUXURY HOTEL $$$

(E&O; ✆222 2000; www.eohotels.com; 10 Lebuh Farquhar; ste incl breakfast RM350-2480; ✲@🛜🏊) One of the rare hotels in the world where historic opulence has gracefully moved into the present day. Originally established by the Sarkies brothers in 1885, today the hotel comprises the Heritage Wing, which includes the original domed lobby, and additional new wings including the tower extension that opened in 2013. The suites seamlessly blend European comfort with Malaysian style. Rooms with a sea view are worth the extra outlay.

SEVEN TERRACES LUXURY HOTEL $$$

(✆264 2333; www.7terraces.com; Lg Stewart; ste incl breakfast RM550-2200; ✲@🛜🏊) Crafted from a row of seven shophouses, this is one of the more luxurious places to stay in central George Town. The 18 two-storey suites (including three even larger multiroom 'apartments') have been decorated with an eclectic mix of original antiques, reproductions and contemporary pieces, and surround a central courtyard. A restaurant and bar (open to the public) face the main street.

CHEONG FATT TZE MANSION HISTORIC HOTEL

(✆262 5289; www.cheongfatttzemansion.com; 14 Lebuh Leith; r incl breakfast RM420-800; ✲@🛜) Stay in the Blue Mansion, an 'heirloom with rooms', for the ultimate Eastern colonial experience. The house is arranged around a plant-filled central courtyard from which the greatest *chi* energy emanates. Each room is uniquely themed and has a dreamy name like 'fragrant poem' or 'jolie', and represents a moment of Cheong Fatt Tze's life. A delicious courtyard breakfast is included in the price. Some guests say they have trouble sleeping here despite the wonderful energy, peace and quiet; old folks say it's the ghosts. The mansion is also a tourist attraction and is gay-friendly.

🛏 Colonial District & Little India

RED INN COURT HOSTEL $

(✆261 1144; www.redinncourt.com; 35B & 35C Lebuh Pitt; incl breakfast dm RM28-35, r RM88-108; ✲@🛜) A low-key, newish backpackers with lots of services and communal amenities. Service here is friendly and personal, although the lobby has a some-what commercial 'Tourist Information' office feel.

★ REN I TANG
HISTORIC HOTEL $$

(📞250 8383; www.renitang.com; 82A Lebuh Penang; r from RM180; 🌐🛜) A wonderful restoration job has been done on this early-19th-century building in the heart of Little India that once housed Southeast Asia's old-est Chinese medical hall wholesaler. There's a good range of rooms which are simply but comfortably decorated in a heritage style. Reminders of the building's former status abound.

A small museum about the medical hall is in the works and there's also a cafe, Tang's Bistro.

PG CHEW JETTY HOMESTAY
HOMESTAY $$

(📞019-554 4909; pgcjhomestay@gmail.com; Chew Jetty; r with shared bathroom RM80-120; 🌐🛜) For the epitome of a local experience, book one of the basic rooms in this pier-bound home at the edge of George Town's biggest clan jetty. As the name implies, you'll be crashing with a local family. The noise from grandma's TV is free, although breakfast will set you back an extra RM5.

★ CHINA TIGER
HOMESTAY $$$

(📞264 3580, 012-501 5360; www.chinatiger.info; 25 & 29 Lebuh China; apt RM500, all-inclusive homestay RM950; 🌐@🛜) You have your choice of experiences here: be completely independent in either of two open-concept self-catering apartments above an art gal-lery, or live in Chinese heritage elegance in one of the two homestay-style apartments attached to the owner's restored shophouse home. If you can't decide, keep in mind that the latter option involves being pampered and taken around town by your hosts.

🛏 Persiaran Gurney, Jalan Burma & Around

PALANQUINN
BOUTIQUE HOTEL $$

(📞227 1088; www.palanquinn.com; 39 Lg Bang-kok; r RM200-350; 🌐@🛜) Palanquinn com-prises three houses dating back to 1927; its six rooms feel spacious and homey. We par-ticularly liked the huge bathrooms – some with retractable roof – in most units. And you'd be hard-pressed to find a friendlier and more courteous host than Kelvyn.

Lg Bangkok is located just off Jln Burma, about 2.5km north of Jln Transfer, a RM15 taxi ride from central George Town.

MANGO TREE PLACE
BOUTIQUE HOTEL $$$

(📞246 2132; www.mangotreeplace.com; 29 Jln Phuah Hin Leong; r incl breakfast RM380-600; 🌐@🛜) You have to step inside one of the three rather standard-looking shophouses dating back to 1934 to grasp the young, fun vibe of this hotel. Open spaces, pri-mary colours, attractive subtle furniture and natural light establish the feel here. Ground-floor rooms have a garden terrace while the upper-floor rooms have two bed-rooms; all share an expansive communal area equipped with a computer.

Jln Phuah Hin Leong is off Jln Burma, about 1km north of Jln Transfer; a long walk or a RM15 taxi ride from central George Town.

G HOTEL
HOTEL $$$

(📞238 0000; www.ghotel.com.my; 168 Persiaran Gurney; r incl breakfast RM450-1248; 🌐@🛜🖥) The 303 rooms here are studies in minimal-ist, cubist cool – collections of geometric form set off by swatches of blocky colour. There's a good crowd of creative and simply successful professionals blowing through the doors, giving the G a vibe that's as Man-hattan as it is Malaysia. The hotel is about 3.5km northwest of central George Town; a taxi here will cost RM15.

Batu Ferringhi, Teluk Bahang & Around

Explore

Batu Ferringhi is the best easy-access beach stop on Penang, and it does make a pleasant break from the city. However, the beach doesn't count among Malaysia's fin-est; the water isn't as clear as you might expect, swimming often means battling jellyfish, and the beach itself can be dirty. The vast majority of the area's accommoda-tion and restaurants are located along Jln

Batu Ferringhi, the main strip, a short walk from the beach.

Teluk Bahang is the quiet (sometimes deathly so) beach a few kilometres past Batu Ferringhi. The best reason for heading out this way is to spend time in Penang National Park which also has deserted beaches to which you can hike. Other attractions include the Tropical Spice Garden where you can take cooking lessons and a new theme park.

The Best...
→ **Sight** Penang National Park
→ **Place to Eat** Tree Monkey (p176)
→ **Activity** Cooking course at Tropical Spice Garden (p176)

Top Tip
Avoid visiting Batu Ferringhi on weekends when you'll have to share the beach with hoards of day trippers.

Getting There & Away
→ **Bus** Bus 101 runs from Weld Quay Bus Terminal and from Komtar Bus Station, in George Town, and takes around 30 minutes to reach Batu Ferringhi, and 40 minutes to Teluk Bahang (both RM4). Bus 501 from Teluk Bahang (RM2) will get you to the Tropical Fruit Farm, Butterfly Farm and Escape theme park.
→ **Taxi** To Batu Ferringhi/Teluk Bahang from George Town expect to pay at least RM35/40.

◉ SIGHTS

(Taman Negara Pulau Pinang; admission free, canopy walkway adult/child RM7/5; ⊙canopy walkway 10am-1pm & 2-4pm Sat-Thu) At just 2300 hectares, Penang National Park is the smallest in Malaysia; it's also one of the newest, attaining national-park status in 2003. It has some interesting and challenging trails through the jungle, as well as some of Penang's finest and quietest beaches.

The **office** (☎881 3500; ⊙8am-6pm) at the park entrance has a few maps and leaflets and can help you plan your day. Just across from the main park office is the **Penang Nature Tourist Guide Association** (PNTGA;

☎881 4788; www.pntga.org; ⊙8am-6pm) office, which offers guide services with a slew of options, such as trekking (four hours for RM100) and many where you can hike one way then get a ride back in a boat (four hours including boat transport for two people RM200), and also specialist tours such as bird-watching, seasonal visits to a turtle hatchery and mangrove tours. It's best to reserve longer tours in advance with agencies around George Town or at your hotel.

The park entrance is a short walk from Teluk Bahang's main bus stop. From here it's an easy 20-minute walk to the 250m-long **canopy walkway**, suspended 15m up in the trees from where you can hear water flowing from the mountain and get a view over the broccoli-headed park. The walkway was being renovated when we stopped by, and closes if it's raining. From here, you have the choice of heading towards Teluk Tukun and Muka Head or to Pantai Kerachut. The easiest walk is the 20-minute stroll to **Teluk Tukun** beach where Sungai Tukun flows into the ocean. There are some little pools to swim in here. Following this trail along the coast about 25 minutes more brings you to the private University of Malaysia Marine Research Station, where there is a supply jetty, as well as **Tanjung Aling**, a nice beach to stop at for a rest. From here it's another 45 minutes or so down the beach to **Teluk Duyung**, also called Monkey Beach, after the numerous primates who scamper about here on the beach on **Muka Head**, the isolated rocky promontory at the extreme northwestern corner of the island. On the peak of the head, another 15 minutes along, is an off-limits 1883 lighthouse and an Achenese-style graveyard. The views of the surrounding islands from up here are worth the sweaty uphill jaunt.

A longer and more difficult trail heads left from the suspension bridge towards **Pantai Kerachut**, a beautiful white-sand beach that is a popular spot for picnics and is a green turtle nesting ground. Count on about two hours to walk to the beach on the well-used trail. On your way is the unusual meromictic lake, a rare natural feature composed of two separate layers of unmixed freshwater on top and seawater below, supporting a unique mini-ecosystem. From Pantai Kerachut beach you can walk about two hours onward to further-flung and isolated **Teluk Kampi**, which is the longest beach in the park; look for trenches along the coast that are remnants of the Japanese occupation in WWII.

TROPICAL SPICE GARDEN
GARDENS

(☎881 1797; www.tropicalspicegarden.com; Jln Teluk Bahang; adult/child RM14/10, incl tour RM22/15; ⊕9am-6pm) Along the road from Teluk Bahang to Batu Ferringhi is this oasis of tropical, fragrant fecundity of more than 500 species of flora, with an emphasis on spices. Ferns, bamboo, ginger and heliconias are among the lush vegetation and you might spot a giant monitor lizard or two. The restaurant here, Tree Monkey, is also excellent and the garden also offers **cooking courses** (RM200; ⊕lessons 9am-1pm Mon-Sat). To get here, take bus 101 towards Teluk Bahang and ask to get off at the Spice Garden (RM2). There's a beautiful roadside white-sand beach just across from the gardens.

ESCAPE
AMUSEMENT PARK

(☎881 1106; www.escape.my; 282 Jln Teluk Bahang; adult/child RM60/45; ⊕9am-6pm) Come prepared! Adults report being more challenged than their kids by the adventurous games and attractions, some of which involve climbing and jumbing, at this new eco-themed play park near the Penang Butterfly Farm.

TROPICAL FRUIT FARM
FARM

(www.tropicalfruits.com.my; tour adult/child RM35/28; ⊕9am-5pm) About 2km south of Teluk Bahang is this 10-hectare hillside farm, which cultivates more than 250 types of tropical and subtropical fruit trees, native and hybrid. Its one-hour tours include fruit tastings and a glass of fresh juice.

PENANG BUTTERFLY FARM
GARDENS

(www.butterfly-insect.com; 830 Jln Teluk Bahang; adult/child RM27/15; ⊕9am-5pm) Several thousand live butterflies representing more than 150 species flap around here like buttery pastel clouds. There are also some fascinating beetles, lizards and spiders crawling about.

✖ EATING & DRINKING

In Batu Ferringhi you can get a beer at most non-Halal places, but toes-in-the-sand-type beach bars are few – **Bora Bora** (Jln Batu Ferringhi; ⊕noon-1am Sun-Thu, to 3am Fri & Sat) is an exception.

In Teluk Bahang the main shopping area along the road heading east to Batu Ferringhi has a few coffee shops where you'll find cheaper Chinese dishes and seafood, as well as a couple of South Indian places that sell *murtabak* (flat, flaky bread filled with pieces of mutton, chicken or vegetables) and *dosa* (savoury Indian pancakes).

★ TREE MONKEY
THAI $$

(Tropical Spice Garden, Jln Teluk Bahang; mains RM12.80-48.80; ⊕9am-11pm) A Thai owner oversees a huge variety of tasty Southeast Asian and Thai dishes, including several 'tapas' sets (RM30 to RM98). This is alfresco at its best, under a thatched roof and surrounded by gorgeous gardens with a view of the sea. It's also an excellent place for a sunset cocktail.

LONG BEACH
MALAY $

(Jln Batu Ferringhi; mains from RM4; ⊕6.30-11.30pm) This buzzy, centrally located hawker centre has the usual selection of Chinese noodle dishes, Indian breads and meat curries, and Malay seafood dishes.

BUNGALOW
INTERNATIONAL $$

(☎886 8686; www.lonepinehotel.com; Lone Pine Hotel, 97 Jln Batu Ferringhi; mains RM16-48) The eponymous bungalow dates back to the 1940s, and is where the Lone Pine hotel sprang from. Today, the restaurant maintains the historical link with dishes such as Chicken chop and Macaroni pie – remnants of the era when Hainanese chefs, former colonial-era domestic servants, dominated restaurant kitchens. Other Malaysian and international dishes are available.

FERRINGHI GARDEN
INTERNATIONAL $$

(Jln Batu Ferringhi; mains RM20.80-95.80; ⊕dinner) Everyone falls in love with the outdoor setting here of terracotta tiles and hardwoods surrounded by bamboo, tall potted plants, hanging mosses and cut orchids in elegant vases. Unfortunately the menu, which emphasises steaks and prawns, isn't as inspiring. During the daytime hours, an adjacent cafe serves breakfast and real coffee – a relative rarity in Batu Ferringhi.

Ferringhi Garden is located a block or so west of the Holiday Inn.

TARBUSH
MIDDLE EASTERN $$$

(www.tarbush.com.my; Jln Batu Ferringhi; mains RM12-55; ⊕10am-1am) Middle Eastern tourists and residents have brought their food to

Batu Ferringhi, and Lebanese restaurants line the town's main strip. The best of the lot is most likely this branch of a KL restaurant empire. There's lots to choose from, but we like the two 'mezze platters', which bring together everything from tabouli (a bulgur salad) to *kibbeh* (meatballs with bulgur).

 ## ACTIVITIES

You'll find plenty of watersports rental outfits along the beach; they tend to rent wave runners (per 30 minutes RM120), as well as offer waterskiing (per 15 minutes RM60) and parasailing (per ride RM80) trips.

After these activities you might need a relaxing massage. All sorts of foot masseuses will offer you their services; expect to pay around RM40 for a 30-minute deep-tissue massage.

SLEEPING

Batu Ferringhi has lots of somewhat overpriced, chain-style resorts catering to families, and quite a few extremely overpriced, homestay-type budget places, but very little in between. Teluk Bahang is only 4km from Batu Ferringhi so if the few sleeping options here don't suit you, there are plenty more over there.

LAZY BOYS
GUESTHOUSE $
(☎881 2486; www.lazyboystravelodge.net; off Jln Batu Ferringhi; dm RM18, r RM35-150; ✳) This is the type of budget place some travellers live for and others flee from. Think of your university dorm if it was run by a laid-back Malaysian rocker, and you begin to get the idea. Dorms and rooms are clean enough, and there are amenities ranging from a kitchen to free laundry, but the music room (complete with drum kit) and spotty service are bad signs for those who cherish convenience and/or quiet. Lazy Boys is just off the main strip, approximately across from Tarbush restaurant.

BABA GUEST HOUSE
GUESTHOUSE $
(☎881 1686; babaguesthouse2000@yahoo.com; 52 Batu Ferringhi; r RM50-95; ✳) This is a wonderfully ramshackle, blue-painted house that shows off the heart and soul of its resident (and very active) Chinese family. Rooms are large and spotless – although

bare – and most have shared bathrooms, while the dearer air-con rooms come with a fridge and shower.

CHALET SPORTFISHING
HOTEL $$
(☎881 9190; Jln Teluk Bahang; r RM80-130; ✳🛜) Probably Teluk Bahang's most comfortable place to stay, the two floors of plain rooms are at the edge of the beach and look over the fishing pier. The more expensive rooms have up to five beds. The Malay owner doesn't speak a great deal of English.

★LONE PINE HOTEL
RESORT $$$
(☎886 8686; www.lonepinehotel.com; 97 Jln Batu Ferringhi; incl breakfast r RM680-840, ste RM950-2940; ✳@🛜▨) Dating back to the 1940s, the Lone Pine is one of Batu Ferringhi's oldest resorts. A 2010 remodel and expansion has given the hotel a new lease on life, while still preserving many of its classier original aspects. The 90 rooms all have some kind of perk, personal plunge pools, for example, or private gardens. They also feel quite large, and are decorated with splashes of colour and attractive furniture. The grounds have a stately, national-park-like feel, with hammocks suspended between the pines (actually casuarina trees), and a huge saltwater pool as a centrepiece.

RASA SAYANG RESORT
RESORT $$$
(☎881 1966; www.shangri-la.com; Jln Batu Ferringhi; incl breakfast r RM1080-2130, ste RM1710-10,000; ✳@🛜▨) Part of the Shangri-La chain, this is a vast and luxurious establishment – the island's only five-star resort – that feels like something out of a South Sea dream. Rooms are large and decorated with fine hardwood furniture, and cloud-like white duvets float on the beds; all have balconies and many have sea views. There's a yoga studio, tennis courts, a putting green and several restaurants. The hotel's Chi Spa is among the poshest on Penang.

HARD ROCK HOTEL
RESORT $$$
(☎881 1711; www.penang.hardrockhotels.net; Jln Batu Ferringhi; incl breakfast r RM700-1300, ste RM1350-4000; ✳@🛜▨) If you can stomach the corny hypercorporate vibe (and the unrelenting gaze of Beatles memorabilia), this resort – at research time, Batu Ferringhi's youngest – can be a fun place to stay. There's a particular emphasis on family friendliness, with child-friendly pools, kid-friendly suites and teen-themed play areas (complete with pool table and video games).

The Rest of the Island

Explore

Travelling around Penang, you'll find the same cultural mix as in George Town but in smaller doses and with a more paradisical backdrop. There are hilltop views, quaint fishing villages, quirkly temples and smaller satellite islands to discover.

If travelling by motorcycle or car, plan to spend a minimum of five hours, including plenty of sightseeing and refreshment stops, to make the 70km circuit of the island. Note there is no round-island bus. If you are really fit, you could try cycling but you'll need to allow all day or – better still – consider scheduling a stop in Teluk Bahang for the night to rest the thighs. The north-coast road runs beside the beaches.

The Best...

⇒ **Sight** Kek Lok Si Temple
⇒ **Island** Pulau Jerejak
⇒ **Beach** Pantai Pasir Panjang (p180)

Top Tip

Hai Boey Seafood (☎013-488 1114; 29 MK9 Pasir Belanda, Teluk Kumbar; mains RM8-50; ☺11am-10pm) in Teluk Kumbar is one of Penang's most famous destinations for seafood; call ahead to reserve a table on weekends or holidays. Buses 401 and 401E pass Teluk Kumbar (RM4); a taxi here will cost about RM60.

◉ SIGHTS

◉ Penang Hill

PENANG HILL   HILL
(www.penanghill.gov.my; funicular adult/child RM30/15, museum admission free; ☺6.30am-7pm Mon-Fri, to 9pm Sat & Sun, funicular every 30min during opening hours) The top of Penang Hill, 821m above George Town, is generally about 5°C cooler than at sea level, and provides a cool retreat from the sticky heat below. From the summit there's a spectacular view over the island and across to the mainland. There are some gardens, a simple food court, an exuberantly decorated Hindu temple and a mosque as well as David Brown's (p169), a colonial-style British restaurant serving everything from beef Wellington to high tea.

On weekends and public holidays lines for the funicular can be horrendously long, with waits of up to 30 minutes, but on weekdays queues are minimal. From the trail near the upper funicular station you can walk the 5.5km to the Botanical Gardens (Moon Gate) in about three hours. The easier 5.1km tarred jeep track from the top also leads to the gardens, just beyond the Moon Gate. From Weld Quay Bus Terminal, Komtar Bus Station or Lebuh Chulia, you can catch the frequent bus 204 (RM2). A taxi here from the centre of George Town will set you back about RM25.

BOTANICAL GARDENS   GARDENS
(www.penangbotanicgardens.gov.my; Waterfall Rd; ☺5am-8pm) FREE Don't join the throngs of Penang visitors who miss these 30-hectare gardens, which are also known as the Waterfall Gardens after the stream that cascades through from Penang Hill, or the Monkey Gardens for the many long-tailed macaques that scamper around. Don't be tempted to feed them: monkeys do bite, and there's a RM500 fine if you're caught. You'll also see dusky leaf monkeys, black giant squirrels and myriad giant bugs and velvety butterflies, which are all considerably more docile.

Once a granite quarry, the gardens were founded in 1884 by Charles Curtis, a tireless British plant lover who collected the original specimens and became the first curator. Today Penangites love their garden and you'll find groups practising t'ai chi, jogging, picnicking and even line dancing here.

The Botanical Gardens are located about 8km outside of George Town. To get there, take bus 102 (RM2) from Komtar Bus Station or Weld Quay Bus Terminal; a taxi will cost at least RM25.

◉ Air Itam & Jelutong

KEK LOK SI TEMPLE   BUDDHIST TEMPLE
(cable car one way/return RM4/2; ☺9am-6pm, cable car 8.30am-5.30pm) The 'Temple of Supreme Bliss' is also the largest Buddhist temple in Malaysia and one of the most recognisable buildings in the country. Built by

ESCAPING THE WORLD

Every now and then a Lonely Planet writer comes across a place so special it makes all the days of tirelessly slogging through sweaty cheap hotels worth it. **Malihom** (✆226 4466; www.malihom.com; all-inclusive RM570-700; ❄ @ 🤖 🛋) is one of those places. Nine 100-year-old rice barns were imported from Thailand and brought up to this 518m peak where they have been restored to a cramped but comfortable state in a Balinese style. But you won't want to stay inside; walk around the small complex to gawk at the 360-degree view over hills of jungle, the sea and several villages. The most serene infinity pool on the island is guarded by white Buddhas; the grounds are a perfect balance of shade, flowers and koi ponds; there's a conference room and yoga studio; and indoor hang-out areas perfect for sipping espresso or a glass of wine from the cellar, reading a book or watching movies. Basically you come here to completely relax because, aside from a few walks, mountain biking or fruit picking, there's blissfully little to do.

The retreat is located off winding Rte 6 between Balik Pulau and Kampung Sungai Batu, and you'll need to be shuttled in its 4WD up the steep hill that leads to Malihom.

an immigrant Chinese Buddhist in 1890, Kek Lok Si is a cornerstone of the Malay-Chinese community, who provided the funding for its two-decade-long building (and ongoing additions).

To reach the entrance, walk through a maze of souvenir stalls, past a tightly packed turtle pond and murky fish ponds, until you reach **Ban Po Thar** (Ten Thousand Buddhas Pagoda; admission RM2) a seven-tier, 30m-high tower. The design is said to be Burmese at the top, Chinese at the bottom and Thai in between. A **cable car** whisks you to the highest level, which is presided over by an awesome 36.5m-high bronze statue of Kuan Yin, goddess of mercy.

There are several other temples in this complex, as well as shops and a **vegetarian restaurant** (mains from RM5; ⊙10am-7pm Tue-Sun).

A taxi here from the centre of George Town starts at about RM25, or you can hop on bus 204 to Air Itam (RM2).

P RAMLEE HOUSE   MUSEUM

(4A Jln P Ramlee; ⊙10am-5.30pm Tue-Thu, Sat & Sun, 10am-noon & 3-5.30pm Fri) **FREE** This centre consists of three sections dedicated to Malaysia's biggest megastar, P Ramlee. Ramlee was particularly known for his singing; he also acted in and directed 66 films in his lifetime. Opposite the large building that functions as a performing-arts centre, a small museum contains artefacts and photos about P Ramlee's life. Adjacent to the museum is Ramlee's birthplace, a humble, thoroughly restored *kampung* house built in 1926.

P Ramlee's music plays as a constant soundtrack throughout the grounds. Although visitors may not be familiar with his work, the old photos and the house are interesting, and there are a few kitschy souvenirs in the museum's gift shop.

P Ramlee House is about 5km west of George Town; heading south on Jln Perak from Jln Dato Keramat, turn right on Jln P Ramlee – the house is about 300m down this road. A taxi here will cost RM15.

SUFFOLK HOUSE   HISTORIC BUILDING

(www.suffolkhouse.com.my; 250 Jln Ayer Itam; tour/self-guided RM15/10; ⊙10am-6pm) This impressive Georgian-style mansion is built on the site of the original residence of Francis Light, founder of the colony and native of Suffolk, England. Situated on the banks of the Air Itam river, 6.5km west of George Town's centre, it's a grand square building with sweeping verandahs, a massive ballroom and a breezy colonial plantation feel.

The renovation of the grounds and exterior were completed in 2007, but the interior has relatively little to see, and a visit is probably best combined with high tea at the attached restaurant (p169). A taxi here will cost around RM15.

⊙ Pulau Jerejak

Lying 1.5 nautical miles off Penang's southeast coast, thickly forested Pulau Jerejak has been home to a leper colony and a prison in its time, and is today occupied by the **Jerejak Rainforest Resort** (✆658 7111; www.jerejakresort.com; r RM210-420; ❄ @ 🤖 🛋).

Packages available through its website, which usually include transport, breakfast and a massage, make staying here good value. Camping (RM80 to RM100) is also an option.

The resort has its own jetty, with boats leaving roughly every two hours (adult/child RM6/3). **Day-trip package tours** (adult RM50-60, child RM30-35) allow access to the pool and other activities including rock climbing.

No buses run past the jetty; a taxi from George Town will cost around RM50.

⊙ Batu Maung

At the end of the Bayan Lepas Expressway you'll reach the turn-off to the Chinese fishing village of Batu Maung. Once home to a biodiverse mangrove swamp, encroaching development from the Bayan Lepas Industrial Zone has resulted in extensive clearing. Development here is expected to skyrocket with the building of the new bridge linking Penang to the mainland. It's Penang's deep-sea fishing port so there are plenty of dilapidated, brightly painted boats along the coast.

The renovated seaside temple here, **Sam Poh Temple** `FREE` has a shrine dedicated to the legendary Admiral Cheng Ho, who was also known as Sam Poh. The temple sanctifies a huge 'footprint' on the rock that's reputed to belong to the famous navigator.

Perched on top of the steep Bukit Batu Maung is the **Penang War Museum** (✆626 5142; Bukit Batu Maung; adult/child RM35/17; ⊙9am-6pm & 7-11pm) This former British fort, built in the 1930s, was used as a prison and torture camp by the Japanese during WWII. Today, the crumbling buildings have been restored as a memorial to those dark days. Barracks, ammunition stores, cookhouses, gun emplacements and other structures can be explored here, which also offers 'suspense and eerie' night visits and paintball (from RM75).

Also in town is the **Penang Aquarium** (Pekan Batu Maung; adult/child RM5/2; ⊙10am-5pm Thu-Tue), which houses 25 tanks filled with colourful fish; there is a tactile tank with a young green turtle, and visitors can also feed koi.

Bus 307 leaves for Batu Maung every half-hour from Weld Quay Bus Terminal and Komtar Bus Station (RM4); a taxi here will cost about RM50.

⊙ Kampung Pulau Betong

This is a fishing village utterly off the beaten track with delightful *kampung* houses, flowers and colourful docked boats. At around 5.30pm the fishing boats come in and sell their fish at the little market near the dock. Bus 403 runs from Balik Pulau as far as the market (RM1.40), but if you walk another 1.5km you'll come to **Pantai Pasir Panjang**, an empty, pristine beach with white sand the texture of raw sugar – one of the prettier spots on the island for the few who make the effort to get here. The beach is backed by a National Service Training Centre for young graduates entering the army. Be vigilant if you go into the water – there's a heavy undertow.

Understand Kuala Lumpur

Kuala Lumpur Today

The general election of 2013 saw the BN coalition retain control of the country as well as KL, where the city council is centrally appointed. The opposition PK coalition remains in the driver's seat for Selangor. Now it's full speed ahead on major infrastructure developments for the capital, including a new mass rapid transit (MRT) line and the River of Life urban regeneration project.

Best in Print

Urban Odysseys (ed Janet Tay & Eric Forbes) Short stories that capture KL's multifaceted cultural flavour.

KL Noir Three volumes of short stories zoning in on the city's sinister and spooky underbelly.

My Life as a Fake (Peter Carey) Reworking of Frankenstein evokes the sultry side of KL.

Found in Malaysia (The Nut Graph) Compilation of 50 interviews with notable Malaysians from the news and analysis website (www.thenut graph.com).

The Consumption of Kuala Lumpur (Zaiddin Sardar) How the once-sleepy capital has evolved into a modern economic marvel.

Best on Film

Entrapment (1999) The climax of this Sean Connery and Catherine Zeta-Jones thriller takes place at KL's Petronas Towers.

Septet (2004) Chinese boy falls for Malay girl in Yasmin Ahmad's romantic comedy.

GE13 & After

In the months leading up to the 5 May 2013 general election (GE13), opposition parties, political commentators and the public had been calling attention to irregularities and unfairness in Malaysia's electoral system. Unbalanced constituency sizes, lack of access to the media for campaigning, and possibility of gerrymandering were the main concerns. Major rallies in KL saw tens if not hundreds of thousands marching for fair and free elections.

Once votes had been cast and counted, BN had lost seven seats in the national parliament but emerged as the majority winner, thus again able to form a government with Najib Razak back as prime minister. The opposition parties in PK won a majority of votes overall, but this counted for little given Malaysia's first past the post election system. PK did, however, hold onto government in Selangor, the state surrounding the federal territory of KL, which it had first captured in the 2008 election.

On 8 May it was reported that 120,000 people, many clad in black, showed up at a stadium just outside the city limits to protest the election results. However a 'Malaysian Spring' was not in the offing. With racially divisive rhetoric in the air (Najib had referred to a 'Chinese tsunami' of voters as being responsible for the coalition's losses) people from all sides called for community harmony and the need to double down on the objectives of the 1Malaysia policy.

Improving Public Transport

If one thing unites all KLites, it's their frustration with public transport. Squashed into a monorail or train carriage at rush hour, or stuck in a highway traffic jam, it's easy to share their pain. To address the problem the government is upgrading and integrating the

Mass Rapid Transit (MRT) system with the addition of three new lines, including a circular one that will span the KL–Klang Valley conurbation. The first new line – a link between Sungai Buloh and Kajang, 9.5km of which will be underground – is planned to be operational by 2016 when it will serve 400,000 passengers daily.

In the meantime, the MRT's construction is causing even more traffic congestion in KL as underground stations are dug in central areas such as Bukit Bintang and Chinatown. It's also controversial because of opposition to the compulsory acquisition of land, in particular along Jln Sultan. Businesses such as Hotel Lok Ann, a *kopitiam* and hotel that has occupied a prominent corner of Jln Sultan since 1938, have been forced to close; the owners are taking their case against the compulsory acquisition of their land to the High Court. The Gospel Hall (dating to 1939) on Jln Hang Jebat could also be in danger, if the tunnelling damages its foundations.

KL's Controversial Tower

Groups such as Rakan KL and the Preservation of Jalan Sultan have been campaigning against the destruction of heritage buildings in Chinatown and the old Merdeka Park, location of the planned 118-storey Warisan Merdeka – Malaysia's tallest building – that will rise next to Stadium Merdeka and Stadium Negara by 2017.

The estimated cost of the tower, slated to be the new headquarters of PNB (Malaysia's largest fund management company and a key instrument in the government's pro-Malay affirmative action policies) is RM5 billion. 'This project is not a waste. We want a building that will become a symbol of a modern, developed country', said Prime Minister Najib, going on to remind critics that past costly construction projects, such as the Penang Bridge and the Petronas Towers, were initially greeted with antipathy.

River of Life

The MRT project is one of the mega-spend projects that are part of the government's Economic Transformation Programme to make Malaysia a high income nation by 2020. Another is the River of Life plan which will restore the Klang River from a polluted sinkhole into a clean and liveable waterfront with parks and other beautification efforts. One of the first small components on this project has been the pedestrianisation of Medan Pasar and the efforts to highlight the built heritage of the part of the city where KL was first established.

if Kuala Lumpur were 100 people

45 would be Malay
43 would be Chinese
10 would be Indian
2 would be Other

belief systems
(% of population)

46 Islam
36 Buddhism
9 Hinduism
6 Christianity
2 Other
1 Taoism

population per sq km

KUALA LUMPUR   MALAYSIA

≈ 125 people

History

By the end of the 19th century, in less than 50 years, Kuala Lumpur had grown from a jungle-bound mining settlement to the grand colonial capital of the Malay peninsula. It was here that British rule on the peninsula ended in 1957 and that the modern nation, Malaysia, was born in 1963. Though many government departments moved to Putrajaya in the 1990s, KL continues to function as the heart of Malaysia's economic, political and social life.

Compared with Indian Muslim traders, the Portuguese contributed little to Malay culture; attempts to introduce Christianity and the Portuguese language were never a big success, though a dialect of Portuguese, Kristang, is still spoken in Melaka and this is also where you'll find Malaysia's oldest functioning church.

The Melaka Empire

To understand how Kuala Lumpur came to be founded it's important to first go back four-and-a-half centuries to when the seat of Malay power was Melaka. Legend has it that this great trading port was founded by Parameswara, a renegade Hindu prince-cum-pirate from a little kingdom in southern Sumatra, who washed up around 1401 on the Malay coast. As a seafarer, Parameswara recognised a good port when he saw one and immediately lobbied the Ming emperor of China for protection from the Thais in exchange for generous trade deals. Thus the Chinese came to Malaysia.

Equidistant between India and China, Melaka became a major stop for freighters from India loaded with pepper and cloth, and junks from China loaded with porcelain and silks, which were traded for local metal and spices. Business boomed as regional ships and *perahu* (Malay-style sampans) arrived to take advantage of trading opportunities. The Melaka sultans soon ruled over the greatest empire in Malaysia's history, their territory including what is today Kuala Lumpur and the surrounding state of Selangor.

The Portuguese & Dutch Eras

In 1509, the death knell of the Melaka Sultanate was sounded by the arrival of the Portuguese. They laid siege to Melaka in 1511, capturing the city and driving the sultan and his forces back to Johor. Portuguese

TIMELINE	1400	1509	1641
	Hindu prince and pirate Parameswara flees his home on the island of Temasek (Singapore) following an invasion. Sailing up the peninsula, he founds what will become the trading port of Melaka.	Portuguese traders sail into Melaka. Although at first greeted warmly, the sultan later acts on the advice of his Indian Muslim councillors and attacks the Portuguese ships, taking 19 prisoners.	After a siege lasting several months, the Dutch, with the help of the Johor sultanate, wrest Melaka from the Portuguese; this marks the start of Melaka's decline as a major trading port.

domination lasted 130 years, though the entire period was marked by skirmishes with local sultans.

Vying with the Portuguese for control of the spice trade, the Dutch formed an alliance with the sultans of Johor. A joint force of Dutch and Johor soldiers and sailors besieged Melaka in 1641 and wrested the city from the Portuguese.

Despite maintaining control of Melaka for about 150 years, the Dutch never fully realised the potential of the city. High taxes forced merchants to seek out other ports and the Dutch focused their main attention on Batavia (now Jakarta) as their regional headquarters.

It was the Dutch who brought in Muslim Bugis mercenaries from Sulawesi to establish the present hereditary sultanate in Selangor in 1740.

East India Company

British interest in the region began with the need for a halfway base for East India Company (EIC) ships plying the India–China maritime route. The first base was established on the island of Penang in 1786.

Meanwhile, events in Europe were conspiring to consolidate British interests on the Malay Peninsula. When Napoleon overran the Netherlands in 1795, the British, fearing French influence in the region, took over Dutch Java and Melaka. When Napoleon was defeated in 1818, the British handed the Dutch colonies back.

The British lieutenant-governor of Java, Stamford Raffles – yes, *that* Stamford Raffles – soon persuaded the EIC that a settlement south of the Malay Peninsula was crucial to the India–China maritime route. In 1819, he landed in Singapore and negotiated a trade deal that saw the island ceded to Britain in perpetuity, in exchange for a significant cash tribute. In 1824, Britain and the Netherlands signed the Anglo-Dutch Treaty dividing the region into two distinct spheres of influence. The Dutch controlled what is now Indonesia, and the British controlled Penang, Melaka, Dinding and Singapore, which were soon combined to create the 'Straits Settlements'.

The Lure of Tin

Tin ore deposits had been mined in the interior of Selangor, certainly for decades and possibly for more than a century, before two nephews of the Sultan of Selangor sponsored an expedition of 87 Chinese miners up the Klang River in 1857. Within a month all but 18 of the group were dead from malaria. However, sufficient tin was found around Ampang to encourage further parties of miners to follow. The jungle trading post where these prospectors alighted, at the meeting point of the Klang and Gombak rivers, was named Kuala Lumpur, meaning 'muddy confluence'.

It's thought that the word Malay (or Melayu) is based on the ancient Tamil word *malia*, meaning 'hill'. Other Malay words like *bahasa* (language), *raja* (ruler) and *jaya* (success) are Sanskrit terms imported to the area by Indian visitors as early as the 2nd century AD.

1795	1826	1857	1859
The British take over Melaka and Dutch Java; after the defeat of Napoleon in 1818 both are returned to the Dutch but Melaka's fortress A'Famosa is left in ruins.	Having swapped Bencoolen on Sumatra for the Dutch-controlled Melaka, the British East India Company combines this with Penang and Singapore to create the Straits Settlements.	Raja Abdullah and Raja Juma'at, nephews of Abdul Samad, fourth Sultan of Selangor, sponsor an expedition of 87 Chinese miners up the Klang River to search for more tin.	Chinese trader Hiu Siew is appointed the first Kapitan Cina (meaning Chinese Captain) of the growing jungle settlement that had become known as Kuala Lumpur.

In 1859, traders Hiu Siew and Ah Sze set up shop in KL close to where the Central Market stands today. As more prospectors came to seek their fortunes, the backwater settlement was quickly becoming a brawling, noisy, violent boomtown, ruled over by so-called 'secret societies', Chinese criminal gangs, and later *kongsi* (clan associations). In 1861 Hiu Siew, having proved himself adept in this fast evolving world, was appointed by Raja Abdullah as the first Kapitan Cina or head of the Chinese community. Despite this precedent, it is Yap Ah Loy, the third of KL's six Kapitan Cinas, who is generally credited as the city's founder.

British Malaya

In Peninsular Malaya, Britain's policy of 'trade, not territory' was challenged when trade was disrupted by civil wars within the Malay sultanates of Negeri Sembilan, Selangor, Pahang and Perak. These wars were partly fought over the rights to collect export duties on the tin at Klang. In 1874 the British started to take political control by appointing British Residents in Perak and Selangor. The following year the same political expediency occurred in Negeri Sembilan and Pahang.

The civil war laid waste to Kuala Lumpur but thanks to Yap Ah Loy it soon bounced back: he reopened the shutdown tin mines and recruited thousands of miners to work them. By the end of the 1870s KL was back in business and booming to such an extent that the British were no longer content to leave its administration to the Kapitan Cina. In 1880, the British Resident Bloomfield Douglas moved the state capital from

YAP AH LOY

He was only 17 when he left his village in southern China in search of work in Malaya. Fifteen years later, in 1868, Yap Ah Loy had shown sufficient political nous, organisational ability and street smarts to secure the role of KL's third Kapitan Cina. He took on the task with such ruthless relish that he's now credited as the founder of KL.

Yap's big break was being the friend of KL's second Kapitan Cina, Liu Ngim Kong. When Liu died in 1869, Yap took over and managed within a few years to gather enough power and respect to be considered the leader of the city's previously fractured Chinese community. According to legend, Yap was able to keep the peace with just six policemen, such was the respect for his authority.

Yap amassed great wealth through his control of the tin trade as well as more nefarious activities, such as opium trading and prostitution, which thrived in the mining boomtown. He founded the city's first school in 1884 and, by the time he died a year later, was the richest man in KL. A short street in Chinatown is named after him and he is worshiped as a saint at the Sze Ya Temple, which he founded.

1867	1868	1880	1882
A war over the tax spoils of tin starts between Raja Abdullah, administrator of Klang, and Raja Mahadi. The war ends in 1874.	Yap Ah Loy, commonly considered the founder of Kuala Lumpur, becomes third Kapitan Cina. When he dies in 1885 he owns a quarter of the city's buildings.	Following the tin boom of 1879 and a swelling KL population, the British Resident in Selangor, Bloomfield Douglas, moves the state capital from Klang to Kuala Lumpur.	Frank Swettenham becomes new British Resident in KL and sets about rebuilding the city in brick following devastating fires and floods in 1881.

Klang to Kuala Lumpur and took up residence on the Bluff, the high ground west of the Klang River that flanked what was then a vegetable garden for the Chinese and which would later become the Padang, a sports field for the British.

Colonial KL

When Frank Swettenham, the third British Resident of Selangor, arrived to take up his post in 1882, KL was yet again in ruins following a major fire and a flood the previous year. He ruled that KL be rebuilt in brick, creating the Brickfields area in the process where the building blocks of the reborn colonial city were crafted. Swettenham also commissioned the country's first railway linking the tin mines of KL with the port at Klang, later renamed Port Swettenham in his honour.

By 1886, scrappy, disease-ridden KL had morphed into one of the 'neatest and prettiest Chinese and Malay towns in the Colony or the States', according to Sir Frederick Weld, Governor of the Straits Settlements. The city's most prestigious building – the Sultan Abdul Samad Building housing the government offices – was completed in 1897, a year after KL had become the capital of the newly formed Federated Malay States of Negeri Sembilan, Pahang, Perak and Selangor.

The early 20th century was the dawn of the age of the motorcar and the subsequent global demand for rubber for tyres further improved KL's fortunes. Rubber plantations spread around the city and across the peninsula. City life improved, with amenities such as piped water and electricity coming online. Local Chinese millionaires such as Chua Cheng Bok and Loke Yew built grand mansions; the biggest would eventually become the old Istana Negara (National Palace) after WWII.

WWII

A few hours before the bombing of Pearl Harbor in December 1941, Japanese forces landed on the northeast coast of Malaya. Within a few months they had taken over the entire peninsula and Singapore.

Although Britain quickly ceded Malaya and Singapore, this was more through poor strategy than neglect. Many British soldiers were captured or killed and others stayed on and fought with the Malayan People's Anti-Japanese Army (MPAJA) in a jungle-based guerrilla war maintained throughout the occupation.

The Japanese achieved very little in Malaya. The British had destroyed most of the tin-mining equipment before their retreat, and the rubber plantations were neglected. However, Chinese Malaysians faced brutal persecution – the atrocities of the occupation were horrific even by the standards of WWII.

F Spencer Chapman's memoir *The Jungle is Neutral* relates the author's experience with a British guerrilla force based in the Malaysian jungles during the Japanese occupation of Malaya and Singapore.

HISTORY COLONIAL KL

A History of Malaya by Barbara and Leonard Andaya brilliantly explores the evolution of 'Malayness' in Malaysia's history and the challenges of building a multiracial, post-independence nation.

1888	1896	1904	1935
Alfred Venning, State Treasurer, starts to lay out a botanical garden in the valley where a small stream is dammed to create a lake. Within a decade KL has its Lake Gardens.	Perak, Selangor, Negeri Sembilan and Pahang join as Federated Malay States, with Kuala Lumpur as the capital. The sultans lose political power to British Residents.	The rail link between KL and Port Swettenham (now Pelabuhan Klang) is completed. Lines are later extended to Ipoh, Penang and Singapore, making KL the region's rail hub.	The British scrap the position of Resident General of the Federated States, decentralising its powers to the individual states, to discourage the creation of a united, self-governing country.

CREATING A MULTICULTURAL NATION

British rule radically altered the ethnic composition of Malaya. Chinese and Indian immigrant workers were brought into the country as they shared a similar economic agenda and had less nationalist grievance against the colonial administration than the native Malays, who were pushed from the cities to the countryside. The Chinese were encouraged to work the mines, the Tamil Indians to tap the rubber trees and build the railways, the Ceylonese to be clerks in the civil service, and Sikhs to man the police force.

Even though 'better-bred' Malays were encouraged to join a separate arm of the civil service, there was growing resentment among the vast majority of Malays who felt they were being marginalised in their own country. A 1931 census revealed that the Chinese numbered 1.7 million and the Malays 1.6 million. Malaya's economy was revolutionised, but the impact of this liberal immigration policy continues to reverberate today.

The Japanese surrendered to the British in Singapore in 1945. Despite the eventual Allied victory, Britain had been humiliated by the easy loss of Malaya and Singapore to the Japanese, and it was clear that its days of controlling the region were numbered.

Federation of Malaya

Revolusi '48 (http://revolusi48.blogspot.com, in Bahasa Malaysia), the sequel to Fahmi Reza's doco *10 Tahun Sebelum Merdeka* (10 Years Before Merdeka), chronicles the largely forgotten armed revolution for national liberation launched against British colonial rule in Malaya in 1948.

In 1946 the British persuaded the sultans to agree to the Malayan Union, which amalgamated all the peninsular Malayan states into a central authority and came with the offer of citizenship to all residents regardless of race. In the process, the sultans were reduced to the level of paid advisers, the system of special privileges for Malays was abandoned and ultimate sovereignty passed to the king of England.

The normally acquiescent Malay population were less enthusiastic about the venture than the sultans. Rowdy protest meetings were held throughout the country, and the first Malay political party, the United Malays National Organisation (UMNO; www.umno-online.com) was formed. This led to the dissolution of the Malayan Union and the creation of the Federation of Malaya in 1948, which reinstated the sovereignty of the sultans and the special privileges of the Malays.

The Emergency

While the creation of the Federation of Malaya appeased Malays, the Chinese felt betrayed, particularly after their massive contribution to the war effort. Many joined the Malayan Communist Party (MCP),

1941	1946	1948	1951
Within a month of invading, the Japanese take KL and occupy the peninsula. The Chinese residents are badly treated and the city's economy stagnates for nearly four years.	After public opposition to the proposed Malay Union, the United Malays National Organisation (UMNO) forms, signalling a rising desire for political independence from Britain.	Start of the Emergency, when the Malayan Communist Party (MCP) take to the jungles and begin fighting a guerrilla war against the British that would last for 12 years.	Sir Henry Gurney, British high commissioner to Malaya, is assassinated by MCP rebels, a terrorist act that alienates many moderate Chinese from the party.

which promised an equitable and just society. In 1948 the MCP took to the jungles and embarked on a 12-year guerrilla war against the British. Even though the insurrection was on par with the Malay civil wars of the 19th century, it was classified as an 'emergency' for insurance purposes.

The effects of the Emergency were felt most strongly in the countryside, where villages and plantation owners were repeatedly targeted by rebels. In 1951 the British high commissioner was assassinated on the road to Fraser's Hill. His successor, General Sir Gerald Templer, set out to 'win the hearts and minds of the people'. Almost 500,000 rural Chinese were resettled into protected 'new villages', restrictions were lifted on guerrilla-free areas and the jungle-dwelling Orang Asli were brought into the fight to help the police track down the insurgents.

In 1960 the Emergency was declared over, although sporadic fighting continued and the formal surrender was signed only in 1989.

Merdeka & Malaysia

Malaysia's march to independence from British rule was led by UMNO, which formed a strategic alliance with the Malayan Chinese Association (MCA; www.mca.org.my) and the Malayan Indian Congress (MIC; www.mic.org.my). The new Alliance Party led by Tunku Abdul Rahman won a landslide victory in the 1955 election. At midnight on 31 August 1957 *merdeka* (independence) was declared in a highly symbolic ceremony held at the Padang in KL; the Union flag was lowered and the Malayan flag hoisted.

In 1961 Tunku Abdul Rahman proposed a merger of Singapore, Malaya, Sabah and Sarawak. But when modern Malaysia was born in July 1963 it immediately faced a diplomatic crisis. The Philippines broke off relations, claiming that Sabah was part of its territory (a claim upheld to this day), while Indonesia laid claim to the whole of Borneo, invading parts of Sabah and Sarawak before finally giving up its claim in 1966.

The marriage between Singapore and Malaya was also doomed from the start. Ethnic Chinese outnumbered Malays in both Malaysia and Singapore and the new ruler of the island-state, Lee Kuan Yew, refused to extend constitutional privileges to the Malays in Singapore. Riots broke out in Singapore in 1964 and in August 1965 Tunku Abdul Rahman was forced to boot Singapore out of the federation.

13 May 1969

As the 1960s progressed, impoverished Malays became increasingly resentful of the economic success of Chinese Malaysians, while the Chinese grew resentful of the political privileges granted to Malays. The

Noel Barber's *War of the Running Dogs* is a classic account of the 12-year Malayan Emergency. The title refers to what the communist fighters called the opposition who were loyal to the British.

HISTORY MERDEKA & MALAYSIA

1957–2007 Chronicle of Malaysia edited by Philip Matthews is a beautifully designed book showcasing 50 years of the country's history in news stories and pictures.

1953	1954	1957	1963
Formation of Parti Perikatan (Alliance Party) between UMNO, the MCA and MIC. Two years later it wins 80% of the vote in Malaya's first national elections.	The Department of Aboriginal Affairs Malaysia is set up to protect the Orang Asli from modern encroachments and exploitation.	On 31 August *merdeka* (independence) is declared in Malaya; Tunku Abdul Rahman becomes the first prime minister and the nine sultans agree to take turns as king.	Malaysia comes into being in 1963 with the addition of Singapore and the British Borneo territories of Sabah and Sarawak; Brunei pulls out at the 11th hour, and Singapore is booted out in 1965.

POLITICS

situation reached breaking point when the Malay-dominated government attempted to suppress all languages except Malay and introduced a national policy of education that ignored Chinese and Indian history, language and culture.

In the 1969 general elections, the Alliance Party lost its two-thirds majority in national parliament and had tied for control of Selangor State with the opposition made up of the Democratic Action Party (DAP; http://dapmalaysia.org/newenglish) and Gerakan (the People's Movement; www.gerakan.org.my). On 13 May, a black day etched in the city's collective memory, at an UMNO-organised post-election meeting in Kuala Lumpur, Chinese onlookers were said to have taunted those in attendance. The Malays retaliated, the situation quickly flaring into a full-scale riot, which Malay gangs used as a pretext to loot Chinese businesses, killing hundreds of Chinese in the process.

A curfew was immediately imposed on KL and a state of emergency announced with parliament suspended for two years. Stunned by the savagery of the riots, the government decided that if there was ever going to be harmony between the races, the Malay community needed to achieve economic parity. To this end the New Economic Policy (NEP), a socio-economic affirmative action plan, was introduced.

The Alliance Party also invited opposition parties to join them and work from within. The expanded coalition was renamed the Barisan Nasional (BN; National Front), which continues to rule Malaysia to this day.

Amir Muhammad's *Malaysian Politicians Say the Darndest Things Vols 1 & 2* (see www.kinibooks.com) gathers together jaw-dropping statements uttered by the local pollies over the last three decades – including 'If you come across a snake and a man from a certain ethnic community, you should hit the man first'.

Enter Mahathir

In 1981 former UMNO member Mahathir Mohamad became prime minister. Under his watch Malaysia's economy went into overdrive, growing from one based on commodities such as rubber to one firmly rooted in industry and manufacturing. Government monopolies were privatised, and heavy industries such as steel manufacturing (a failure) and the Malaysian car (successful but heavily protected) were encouraged. Multinationals were successfully wooed to set up in Malaysia, and manufactured exports began to dominate the trade figures.

During Mahathir's premiership the main media outlets became little more than government mouthpieces. The sultans lost their right to give final assent on legislation, and the once proudly independent judiciary appeared to become subservient to government wishes, the most notorious case being that of Anwar Ibrahim. Mahathir also permitted widespread use of the Internal Security Act (ISA) to silence opposition leaders and social activists, most famously in 1987's Operation Lalang when 106 people were arrested and the publishing licences of several newspapers were revoked.

1969	1971	1974	1976
Following the general election, on 13 March a race riot erupts in KL, killing hundreds. A national emergency is declared and parliament suspended as KL is put under curfew.	Parliament convenes and the New Economic Policy (NEP) is introduced with the aim of putting 30% of Malaysia's corporate wealth in the hands of Malays within 20 years.	After the Sultan of Selangor cedes Kuala Lumpur to the state, making it a Federal Territory, KL citizens lose representation in the Selangor State Legislative Assembly.	Hussein Onn becomes Malaysia's third prime minister following the death of Abdul Razak. His period of office is marked by efforts to foster unity between Malaysia's disparate communities.

BUMIPUTRA PRIVILEGES

When introduced in 1971 the aim of the New Economic Policy (NEP) was that 30% of Malaysia's corporate wealth be in the hands of indigenous Malays, or *bumiputra* ('princes of the land'), within 20 years. A massive campaign of positive discrimination began which handed majority control over the army, police, civil service and government to Malays. The rules extended to education, scholarships, share deals, corporate management and even the right to import a car.

By 1990 *bumiputra* corporate wealth had risen to 19%, but was still 11% short of the original target. Poverty in general fell dramatically, a new Malay middle class emerged and nationalist violence by Malay extremists receded. However, cronyism and discrimination against Indians and Chinese increased, while Malays still account for three in four of the poorest people in the country.

Affirmative action in favour of *bumiputra* continues today but there is a growing recognition that it is hampering rather than helping Malaysia. Former law minister Zaid Ibrahim was reported in the *New York Times* as saying that Malaysia had 'sacrificed democracy for the supremacy of one race' because of the economic privileges given to *bumiputra*. In September 2010 Prime Minister Najib advocated a fundamental reform of the pro-Malay policies, but fell short of calling for the outright scrapping of the system.

In the opposite corner are those such as former PM Mahathir who believes that *bumiputra* would suffer the most if the administration were to implement a 100% meritocracy-based system. A July 2010 poll by the independent Merdeka Centre shows that Malays in general are split on the matter: 45% believing the policies only benefit the rich and well-connected; 48% thinking they are good for the general public.

Economic & Political Crisis

In 1997, after a decade of near constant 10% growth, Malaysia was hit by the regional currency crisis. Characteristically, Mahathir blamed it all on unscrupulous Western speculators deliberately undermining the economies of the developing world for their personal gain. He pegged the Malaysian ringgit to the US dollar, bailed out what were seen as crony companies, forced banks to merge and made it difficult for foreign investors to remove their money from Malaysia's stock exchange. Malaysia's subsequent recovery from the economic crisis, which was more rapid than that of many other Southeast Asian nations, further bolstered Mahathir's prestige.

At odds with Mahathir over how to deal with the economic crisis had been his deputy prime minister and heir apparent, Anwar Ibrahim (www.anwaribrahim.com). Their falling out was so severe that in September 1998 Anwar was not only sacked but also charged with

Dr Mahathir Mohamad's first book, *The Malay Dilemma,* in which he postulated that Malay backwardness was due to hereditary and cultural factors, was banned in 1970.

1981	1987	1995	1998
Dr Mahathir Mohamad becomes prime minister and introduces policies of 'Buy British Last' and 'Look East', in which the country strives to emulate Japan, South Korea and Taiwan.	The police launch Operation Lalang (Operation Weeding), arresting 106 activists and opposition leaders under the Internal Security Act (ISA).	Mahathir announces the construction of a new administrative capital, Putrajaya, as part of a Multimedia Super Corridor stretching from KL to the new international airport at Sepang.	After six years of planning and construction, the Petronas Towers officially open. The twin towers hold the title of tallest building in the world until 2004.

corruption and sodomy. Many Malaysians, feeling that Anwar had been falsely arrested, took to the streets chanting Anwar's call for '*reformasi*'. The demonstrations were harshly quelled and in trials that were widely criticised as unfair, Anwar was sentenced to a total of 15 years' imprisonment. The international community rallied around Anwar with Amnesty International proclaiming him a prisoner of conscience.

Amir Muhammad's 2009 documentary *Malaysian Gods* commemorates the decade since the Reformasi movement began in 1998 with the sacking of Anwar Ibrahim as deputy PM.

BN felt the impact in the following year's general elections when it suffered huge losses, particularly in the rural Malay areas. The gainers were the fundamentalist Islamic party, PAS (standing for Parti Islam Se-Malaysia; www.pas.org.my), which had vociferously supported Anwar, and a new political party, Keadilan (People's Justice Party; www.keadilanrakyat.org), headed by Anwar's wife, Wan Azizah.

Abdullah vs Mahathir

Prime Minister Mahathir's successor, Abdullah Badawi, was sworn into office in 2003 and went on to lead BN to a landslide victory in the following year's election. In stark contrast to his feisty predecessor, the pious and mild-mannered Abdullah impressed voters by taking a non-confrontational, consensus-seeking approach. He set up a royal commission to investigate corruption in the police force (its recommendations have yet to be implemented) and called time on several of the massively expensive mega projects that had been the hallmark of the Mahathir era, including a new bridge across the Strait of Johor to Singapore.

MALAYSIA'S GOVERNMENT

Malaysia is made up of 13 states and three federal territories (Kuala Lumpur, Pulau Labuan and Putrajaya). Each state has an assembly and government headed by a *menteri besar* (chief minister). Nine states have hereditary rulers (sultans), while the remaining four have government-appointed governors, as do the federal territories. In a pre-established order, every five years one of the sultans takes his turn in the ceremonial position of Yang di-Pertuan Agong (king).

Malaysia's current prime minister is Najib Tun Razak, who heads up the Barisan Nasional (BN) coalition of the United Malays National Organisation (UMNO) and 13 other parties. The official opposition, Pakatan Rakyat (PR), is a coalition between Parti Keadilan Rakyat (PKR), the Democratic Action Party (DAP) and Parti Islam Se-Malaysia (PAS), the leader being Anwar Ibrahim. All sit in a two-house parliament: a 70-member Senate (*Dewan Negara;* 26 members elected by the 13 state assemblies, 44 appointed by the king on the prime minister's recommendation) and a 222-member House of Representatives (*Dewan Rakyat;* elected from single-member districts). National and state elections are held every five years.

2003	2004	2007	2008
Having announced his resignation the previous year, Dr Mahathir steps down as prime minister in favour of Abdullah Badawi. He remains very outspoken on national policies.	A month after the election in which BN takes 199 of 219 seats in the lower house of parliament, Anwar Ibrahim sees his sodomy conviction overturned and is released from prison.	As the country celebrates 50 years since independence it is also shaken by two anti-government rallies in November in which tens of thousands of protestors take to the streets of KL.	In the March election BN retains power but suffers defeats to the opposition coalition Pakatan Rakyat (PR) in August, Anwar Ibrahim becomes PR leader following his re-election to parliament.

This decision was the straw that broke the doctor's back, causing the former PM to publicly lambast his successor – an outburst that was largely ignored by the mainstream media. Mahathir turned to the internet to get his views across and raged against press censorship – which many found pretty rich given his own autocratic record while in power.

BN on the Ropes

Released from jail in 2004, Anwar returned to national politics in August 2008 upon winning the by-election for the seat vacated by his wife. This was despite sodomy charges again being laid against the politician in June and his subsequent arrest in July.

In the March 2008 election, UMNO and its coalition partners in Barisan Nasional (BN) saw their parliamentary dominance slashed to less than the customary two-thirds majority. Pakatan Rakyat (PR), the opposition People's Alliance, led by Anwar Ibrahim, not only bagged 82 of parliament's 222 seats but also took control of four out of Malaysia's 13 states, including the key economic bases of Selangor and Penang. PR subsequently lost Perak following a complex powerplay between various defecting MPs.

Abdullah Badawi resigned in favour of his urbane deputy, Mohd Najib bin Tun Abdul Razak (typically referred to as Najib Razak), in April 2008. Son of Abdul Razak, Malaysia's second prime minister after independence, and nephew of Razak's successor, Hussein Onn, Najib has been groomed for this role ever since he first entered national politics at the age of 23 in 1976.

Since December 2011 Malaysia's king, who is also is the head of state and leader of the Islamic faith, has been the Sultan Abdul Halim of Kedah. This is the second time the octogenarian has held the position, the first being from 1970 to 1975.

2009	**2011**	**2012**	**2013**
In April, Najib Tun Razak succeeds Abdullah Badawi as prime minister; the 1Malaysia policy is introduced to build respect and trust between the country's different races.	The first of the rallies organised by the civil rights organisation Bersih brings tens of thousands of people onto the streets of central KL in support of free and fair elections.	In January a second set of sodomy charges against opposition leader Anwar Ibrahim are thrown out of court. In April, another Bersih rally in KL is violently broken up by police.	General elections in May see BN hold on to power at the national level but fail to recapture Selangor from governance by the opposition coalition PR.

Life in Kuala Lumpur

The following provides an insight into how KLites go about their daily lives at work, home and play, in a city the *New York Times* has termed an 'experiment in urban living'. Routines will differ slightly according to ethnicity and adherence to traditional cultural values, but these very differences – and the general acceptance of them – is what makes KL such an appealing and cosmopolitan metropolis.

A City of Immigrants

Many of the people you'll encounter in KL don't actually live here: of the Greater KL/Klang Valley population of around 6 million, only 1.6 million live within the city boundaries; the rest are residents of satellite cities such as Petaling Jaya (PJ).

The very birth of KL coincided with an influx of Chinese immigrants, mainly Hakka and Hokien. They were followed by Cantonese, Swatow, Hainanese and, from India and the subcontinent, Tamils, Punjabis, Bengalis, Sikhs, Sinhalese and more, each bringing with them their own dialects and customs. What they all shared was a desire to build a new and more prosperous life.

That process is ongoing. KL continues to be a magnet for economic migrants from Malaysia and across the region (in particular Pakistan, Bangladesh, Indonesia, Nepal and Myanmar). Wander around Chinatown on a Sunday or Bukit Bintang on any night of the week and it's almost as if you've touched down in a convention of the United Nations.

For all the city's seeming harmony, underlying ethnic and religious tensions are a fact of life: many KLites openly acknowledge the lack of integration between the principal Malay, Chinese and Indian communities. There are also worries that Malaysia's tolerant brand of Islam is becoming more conservative, impacting the lives of KLites across the board.

Daily Routine

Performance of religious rites – lighting incense sticks or a ghee candle for an altar, or kneeling in the direction of Mecca to pray – may be the individual response to the dawn of the day. Such differences aside, there are similarities that can be observed in the daily routines of all KLites.

Expat Resources

Angloinfo (http://kuala lumpur.angloinfo. com)

Expat Go (www.expatgo malaysia.com)

Expatriate Lifestyle (www.expatriate lifestyle.com)

Our average Mr or Ms KL, engaged in an office job, may leave their home (most likely in PJ or elsewhere in the Klang Valley) early – say around 7am – to avoid the worst of the morning rush hour of traffic into the city. Until public transport improves, they are wedded to their car as their primary means of transport.

Having reached the city, they will drop by a street stall to pick up a triangular packet of *nasi lemak* rice for breakfast along with a plastic bag filled with *teh tarik*, the milky, sweet tea of choice. This can be consumed in the office but, should they prefer not to have crumbs on their desk, there's always a nearby *kopitiam* serving a zingy *kopi-o* and *kaya* toast as a breakfast alternative or mid-morning snack.

While they may well flick through a daily newspaper such as the *Star*, most KLites approach the old-school, government-linked media with scepticism, preferring to get their news from trusted online sources such as Malaysiakini (www.malaysiakini.com). They love their blogs, too – both reading and writing them – so don't be surprised to find your neighbour at the *kopitiam* Instagramming their meal and adding a review for the online community.

If you're beginning to get the idea that eating drives the daily routine, then you'd be absolutely right. Every snacking opportunity is taken right up to late-night supper with your mates at the local *mamak* (Indian Muslim food stall). And, if your average KLite is savvy, they'll hang on in the city until well after rush hour before attempting the commute home – especially if the heavens have opened, bringing traffic on the federal highways to a frustratingly slow crawl.

Work

The most important change in the social structure of Malaysia (and by extension KL) has been the rise of the Malay community since independence. Following the riots of 1969, the New Economic Policy (NEP) was introduced. This programme of positive discrimination was designed to bring marginalised Malays and Orang Asli – known collectively as *bumiputra* – into the political and economic mainstream. Although not wholly successful, 40 years on, the end result in KL is a city where the vast majority of government and government-affiliated jobs are held by Malays. They make up most of the police force, army, civil service and parliament.

With ambitious and talented Chinese and Indian Malaysians shut out of the best public sector roles, these communities have tended to

'The Chinese do the work, the Malays take the credit, and the Indians get the blame.' A line from Huzir Sulaiman's satirical play *Atomic Jaya* sums up a commonly held belief among KLites.

TALKING THE TALK

As a federation of former British colonies, Malaysia is a fantastic country to visit for English speakers, but linguists will be pleased to tackle the region's multitude of other languages. Malaysia's national language is Bahasa Malaysia. This is often a cause of confusion for travellers, who logically give a literal translation to the two words and call it the 'Malaysian language'. In fact you cannot speak 'Malaysian'; the language is Malay.

Other languages commonly spoken in the region include Tamil, Hokkien, Cantonese and Mandarin, but there are also Chinese dialects, various other Indian and Orang Asli languages and even, in Melaka, a form of 16th-century Portuguese known as Kristang. All Malaysians speak Malay, and many are fluent in at least two other languages.

Even if you stick to English, you'll have to get used to the local patois – Manglish – which includes plenty of Mandarin, Cantonese and Tamil words and phrases. Many words are used solely to add emphasis and have no formal meaning, which can make things a little confusing. Used incorrectly, Manglish can come across as quite rude, so listen carefully and take local advice before trying it out in polite company. To get you started here are a few of the most common Manglish words and expressions:

Ah Suffix used for questions, eg 'Why late, ah?'

Got Used for all tenses of the verb 'to have' or in place of 'there is/are' eg 'Got money, ah?' and 'Got noodles in the soup.'

Lah Very common suffix used to affirm statements, eg 'Don't be stupid lah!'

Le Used to soften orders, eg 'Give le.'

Liao Used similarly to 'already', eg 'Finished liao.'

Lor Used for explanations, eg 'Just is lor.'

Meh An expression of skepticism, eg 'Really meh.'

One Adds emphasis to end of a sentence, eg 'That car so fast one.'

Ready Another form of 'already', eg 'No thanks, eat ready.'

thrive in the private sector, in particular retail and property development. As the nation's capital, there's almost every other type of economic activity in KL, barring major heavy industry (which can still be found nearby in the Klang Valley). Finance, banking – KL is a major hub for Islamic Financing – and the oil and gas business are all key alongside tourism, education and healthcare.

The city's unemployment rate is low at 2.7% and likely to remain so as KL shows every sign of continuing to have a robust economy. The city is increasingly courting multinational companies to set up shop by emphasising its liberal business environment, track record in innovation, and highly educated workforce. This has led to a growing expat population.

One of the aims of the federal government's Economic Transformation Programme is to have KL rank among the top 20 cities in the world in terms of economic growth and livability by 2020.

Home Life

One of the most remarkable aspects of KL as a city is the diversity of living areas that are crammed into its 243 sq km. The old heart of the city around Chinatown and Masjid Jamek is compact and relatively low rise compared to the condominium tower blocks springing up across Bukit Bintang and around the KLCC. Further out of the centre are the affluent residential areas of Ampang, Bangsar, Damansara Heights, Mont Kiara and Sri Hartamas. Less-wealthy KLites might live in outlying areas such as Cheras or Setapak. There's even typical Malay *kampung* within the city limits, such as Sungai Penchala.

KL has the country's most expensive housing, with average house prices of close to RM500,000. The cost of renting a one-bedroom apartment in central KL is around RM2000 a month. With average monthly salaries around RM3000 it's easy to see why many young people have little choice but to remain living at home with their parents or spend long hours commuting from more affordable areas in the Klang Valley. The city government (known as DBKL, short for Dewan Bandaraya Kuala Lumpur) recognise the problem and in July 2013 announced plans to increase the number of affordable housing units it provides from 4800 to 10,000, all within reach of public transport.

The online community magazine Poskod (http://poskod.my) has interesting features on KL's cultural and social life. They also promote grassroots campaigns and have their own project BetterKL to improve urban living.

Play

Eating out is *the* much-loved local pastime. Bar culture certainly exists, but Islam also means that an average KLite's night out on the town is as likely to be spent in a cafe nursing a bubble tea or cappuccino as quaffing beers and cocktails.

KL malls are popular one-stop destinations not just for their dining and shopping possibilities but also for leisure activities such as bowling, cinema going, browsing art exhibitions, ice skating and even practising rock climbing.

For a weekend break, locals are likely to hop in their cars for a trip to the family *kampong,* Melaka or Ipoh for the food, or Port Dickson on the coast of Negeri Sembilan for the beach. Cheap flights on the likes of AirAsia and other budget carriers mean a quick trip to Penang or Singapore – other major foodie destinations – could also be on the agenda.

Multiculturalism, Religion & Culture

Since the interracial riots of 1969, when distrust between the Malays and Chinese peaked, Malaysia has forged a more tolerant multicultural society. Though ethnic loyalties remain strong, the emergence of a single 'Malaysian' identity is now a much-discussed and lauded concept, even if it is far from being actually realised. Religious and ethnic tensions remain a fact of life, particularly in KL where the different communities coexist rather than mingle. Intermarriage is rare and education remains largely split along ethnic lines.

The Ethnic Mix

There are distinct cultural differences between Malaysia's three main ethnic communities – Malays, Chinese and Indians. There's also the Peranakan (Straits Chinese) and other mixed-race communities to take into account, alongside older aboriginal nations – the Orang Asli of Peninsular Malaysia – comprising scores of different tribal groups and speaking well over 100 languages and dialects.

Kuala Lumpur continues, as it always has been, to be a city of immigrants: there are communities of Indonesians and Thais (many of whom live in the Kampung Baru) as well as Pakistanis, Bangladeshis, Nepalis and citizens of Myanmar (Burma), some of whom are refugees. People from the Middle East have also settled here. The Western expat population is relatively small in comparison.

The Malays

All Malays, Muslims by birth, are supposed to follow Islam, but many also adhere to older spiritual beliefs and *adat*. With its roots in the Hindu period, *adat* places great emphasis on collective responsibility and maintaining harmony within the community – almost certainly a factor in the general goodwill between the different ethnic groups in Malaysia.

The enduring appeal of the communal *kampung* (village) spirit shouldn't be underestimated – many an urban Malay hankers after it, despite the affluent Western-style living conditions they enjoy at home. In principle, villagers are of equal status, though a headman is appointed on the basis of his wealth, greater experience or spiritual knowledge. Traditionally the founder of the village was appointed village leader *(penghulu* or *ketua kampung)* and often members of the same family would also become leaders. A *penghulu* is usually a haji, one who has made the pilgrimage to Mecca.

The Muslim religious leader, the imam, holds a position of great importance in the community as the keeper of Islamic knowledge and the leader of prayer, but even educated urban Malaysians periodically turn to *pawang* (shamans who possess a supernatural knowledge of harvests and nature) or *bomoh* (spiritual healers with knowledge of curative plants and

Government economic policies since the early 1970s have favoured Malays, thus helping defuse this community's fears and resentment of Chinese economic dominance. The cost has been Chinese and Indian Malaysians becoming second-class citizens in a country where they also have roots stretching back generations.

the ability to harness the power of the spirit world) for advice before making any life-changing decisions.

The Chinese

The Malay surname is the child's father's first name. This is why Malaysians will use your given name after the Mr or Ms; to use your surname would be to address your father.

Religious customs govern much of the Chinese community's home life, from the moment of birth, which is carefully recorded for astrological consultations later in life, to funerals which also have many rites and rituals. It is common to see Malaysian Chinese wafting sticks of incense outside their homes and businesses. There's also a strong attachment to the original area of China from where a family originated, seen in the attachment of families to specific temples or clanhouses *(kongsi)*.

The Chinese, who started arriving in the region in early 15th century, came mostly from the southern Chinese province of Fujian and eventually formed one-half of the group known as Peranakans. They developed their own distinct hybrid culture, whereas later settlers, from Guangdong and Hainan provinces, stuck more closely to the culture of their homelands, including keeping their dialects.

If there's one cultural aspect that all Malaysian Chinese agree on it's the importance of education. It has been a very sensitive subject among the Malaysian Chinese community since the attempt in the 1960s to phase out secondary schools where Chinese was the medium of teaching, and the introduction of government policies that favour Malays in the early 1970s. The constraining of educational opportunities within Malaysia for the ethnic Chinese has resulted in many families working doubly hard to afford the tuition fees needed to send their offspring to private schools within the country and to overseas institutions.

The Indians

Like the Chinese settler, Indians in Malaysia hail from many parts of the subcontinent and have different cultures depending on their religions – mainly Hinduism, Islam, Sikhism and Christianity. Most are Tamils, originally coming from the area now known as Tamil Nadu in southern India where Hindu traditions are strong. Later, Muslim Indians from northern India followed along with Sikhs. These religious affiliations dictate many of the home life customs and practices of Malaysian Indians, although one celebration that all Hindus and much of Malaysia takes part in is Deepavali.

A small, English-educated Indian elite has always played a prominent role in Malaysian society, and a significant merchant class exists. However, a large percentage of Indians – imported as indentured labourers by the British – remain a poor working class.

Orang Asli Sights
....
Orang Asli Museum, Gombak
....
National Museum, Kuala Lumpur
....
Kampung Sungai Bumbon, Pulau Carey

The Orang Asli

The indigenous people of Malaysia – known collectively as Orang Asli – played an important role in early trade, teaching the colonialists about forest products and guiding prospectors to outcrops of tin and precious metals. They also acted as scouts and guides for anti-insurgent forces during the Emergency in the 1950s.

Despite this, the Orang Asli remain marginalised in Malaysia. According to the most recent government data published in December 2004, Peninsular Malaysia had just under 150,000 Orang Asli (Original People); 80% live below the poverty line, compared with an 8.5% national average. The tribes are generally classified into three groups: the Negrito; the Senoi; and the Proto-Malays, who are subdivided into 18 tribes, the smallest being the Orang Kanak with just 87 members.

THE PERANAKANS

Peranakan means 'half-caste' in Malay, which is exactly what the Peranakans are: descendants of Chinese immigrants who from the 16th century onwards settled principally in Singapore, Melaka and Penang and married Malay women.

The culture and language of the Peranakans is a fascinating melange of Chinese and Malay traditions. The Peranakans took the name and religion of their Chinese fathers, but the customs, language and dress of their Malay mothers. They also used the terms Straits-born or Straits Chinese to distinguish themselves from later arrivals from China.

Another name you may hear for these people is Baba-Nonyas, after the Peranakan words for men *(baba)* and women *(nonya)*. The Peranakans were often wealthy traders who could afford to indulge their passions for sumptuous furnishings, jewellery and brocades. Their terrace houses were brightly painted, with patterned tiles embedded in the walls for extra decoration. When it came to the interior, Peranakan tastes favoured heavily carved and inlaid furniture.

Peranakan dress was similarly ornate. Women wore fabulously embroidered *kasot manek* (beaded slippers) and *kebaya* (blouses worn over a sarong), tied with beautiful *kerasong* (brooches), usually of fine filigree gold or silver. Men – who assumed Western dress in the 19th century, reflecting their wealth and contacts with the British – saved their finery for important occasions such as the wedding ceremony, a highly stylised and intricate ritual dictated by *adat* (Malay customary law).

The Peranakan patois is a Malay dialect but one containing many Hokkien words – so much so that it is largely unintelligible to a Malay speaker. The Peranakans also included words and expressions of English and French, and occasionally practised a form of backward Malay by reversing the syllables.

There are dozens of different tribal languages and most Orang Asli follow animist beliefs, though there are vigorous attempts to convert them to Islam.

Since 1939 Orang Asli concerns have been represented and managed by a succession of government departments, the latest iteration being JAKOA (www.jakoa.gov.my), an acronym for Jabatan Kemajuan Orang Asli (Orang Asli Development Department) which came into being in 2011. JAKOA's primary goal is 'to protect the Orang Asli and their way of life from the rapid development and exploitation of external parties as well as provide facilities and assistance in education, health and socioeconomic development'.

In the past, Orang Asli land rights have often not been recognised, and when logging, agricultural or infrastructure projects require their land, their claims are generally regarded as illegal, so it remains to be seen how the new government department changes this.

Religion

Peninsular Malaysia was Buddhist and Hindu for a thousand years before the local rulers adopted Islam. Today Islam is the state religion of Malaysia, and freedom of religion is guaranteed by the nation's constitution. The various Chinese religions are also strongly entrenched. Christianity has a presence, but it's never been strong in Peninsular Malaysia. About the only major religion you won't come across is Judaism.

Islam

The religion is believed to have spread through contact with Indian Muslim traders and gained such respect that by the mid-15th century the third ruler of Melaka, Maharaja Mohammed Shah (r 1424–44), had

ISLAM & POLITICS

Islam has always played a key role in Malaysian politics. The fundamentalist Islamic party PAS (Parti Islam se-Malaysia) has a policy aim to install an Islamic government in Malaysia. However, since it has teamed up with the PKR and DAP in the PR opposition alliance it has toned down this message and made a greater effort to reach out to non-Malays.

In an effort to outflank PAS's religious credentials, UMNO has from its dominant position with the BN been inching Malaysia closer to becoming a more conservative Islamic state. Some local authorities have tried to ban or restrict dog ownership (conservative Muslims see dogs as unclean) and prosecute couples for holding hands or kissing in public. There was a move for policewomen, regardless of their religion, to wear the *tudong* (headscarf) at official parades. There have also been several high-profile demolitions of non-Muslim religious buildings (including a couple of 19th-century Hindu temples) for allegedly not having proper planning permission.

converted. His son Mudzaffar Shah took the title of sultan and made Islam the state religion. With its global trade links, Melaka became a hub for the dissemination of Islam and the Malay language across the region.

The Malay strain of Islam is not like Arabia's more orthodox Islamic traditions. It absorbed rather than conquered existing beliefs, and was adopted peacefully by Malaysia's coastal trading ports. Islamic sultanates replaced Hindu kingdoms – though the Hindu concept of kings remained – and the Hindu traditions of *adat* continued despite Islamic law dominating. Malay ceremonies and beliefs still exhibit pre-Islamic traditions, but most Malays are ardent Muslims – to suggest otherwise would cause great offence.

With the rise of Islamic fundamentalism, the calls to introduce Islamic law and purify the practices of Islam have increased; yet, while the federal government of Malaysia is keen to espouse Muslim ideals, it is wary of religious extremism.

Islam in Malaysia: Perceptions & Facts by Dr Mohd Asri Zainul Abidin, the former Mufti of Perlis, is a collection of articles on aspects of the faith as practised in Malaysia.

Islamic Festivals

➡ **Ramadan** The highpoint of the Islamic festival calendar, Ramadan is when Muslims fast from sunrise to sunset. It always occurs in the ninth month of the Muslim calendar and lasts between 29 and 30 days, based on sightings of the moon. Fifteen days before the start of Ramadan, on Nisfu Night, it is believed the souls of the dead visit their homes. On Laylatul Qadr (Night of Grandeur), during Ramadan, Muslims celebrate the arrival of the Quran on earth, before its revelation by the Prophet Mohammed.

➡ **Hari Raya Puasa** (also known as Hari Raya Aidilfitri) marks the end of the month-long fast, with two days of joyful celebration and feasting – this is *the* major holiday of the Muslim calendar. The start of Ramadan moves forward 11 days every year in line with the Muslim lunar calendar.

➡ **Mawlid al-Nabi** Usually in March and celebrating the birth of the Prophet Mohammed.

➡ **Hari Raya Haji** A two-day festival usually in November marking the successful completion of the hajj – the pilgrimage to Mecca – and commemorating the willingness of the Prophet Ibrahim (the biblical Abraham) to sacrifice his son. Many shops, offices and tourist attractions close and locals consume large amounts of cakes and sweets.

➡ **Awal Muharram** The Muslim New Year which falls in November or December.

Key Beliefs & Practices

Most Malaysian Muslims are Sunnis, but all Muslims share a common belief in the Five Pillars of Islam:

➡ **Shahadah (the declaration of faith)** 'There is no God but Allah; Mohammed is his Prophet.'

➡ **Salat (prayer)** Ideally five times a day, in which the muezzin (prayer leader) calls the faithful to prayer from the minarets of every mosque.

➡ **Zakat (tax)** Usually taking the form of a charitable donation.

➡ **Sawm (fasting)** Includes observing the fasting month of Ramadan.

➡ **Hajj (pilgrimage to Mecca)** Every Muslim aspires to do the hajj at least once in their lifetime.

Muslim dietary laws forbid alcohol, pork and all pork-based products. Restaurants where it's OK for Muslims to dine will be clearly labelled 'halal'; this is a stricter definition than places that label themselves simply 'pork-free'.

A radical Islamic movement has not taken serious root in Malaysia but religious conservatism has grown over recent years. For foreign visitors, the most obvious sign of this is the national obsession with propriety, which extends to newspaper polemics on female modesty and raids by the police on 'immoral' public establishments, which can include clubs and bars where Muslims may be drinking.

More Muslim women wear the hijab (a head covering also known regionally as the *tudong*) today than, say, 20 years ago. In 2011, a young Muslim filmmaker Norhayati Kaprawi made the documentary *Siapa Aku?* (Who Am I?), which examines some of the reasons behind this, interviewing a spectrum of Malaysian women from across the country. Shamsul Amri Bahruddin, director of the Institute of Ethnic Studies at the National University of Malaysia, is quoted within the film as saying that 'conformity is the most dominating factor on why women in Malaysia wear a *tudong*.'

On the other hand, the *New York Times* in 2011 reported that Malaysia was leading the way in the Islamic world with regard to embracing women as preachers and teachers of the Muslim faith, an area traditionally dominated by men, citing Zaleha Kamaruddin, the first female rector appointed to head the country's International Islamic University. However, women preachers still are not allowed to lead prayers at mosques.

Chinese Religions

The Chinese communities in Malaysia usually follow a mix of Buddhism, Confucianism and Taoism. Buddhism takes care of the afterlife, Confucianism looks after the political and moral aspects of life, and Taoism contributes animistic beliefs to teach people to maintain harmony with the universe.

But to say that the Chinese have three religions is too simplistic a view of their traditional religious life. At the first level Chinese religion is animistic, with a belief in the innate vital energy in rocks, trees, rivers and springs. At the second level people from the distant past, both real and mythological, are worshipped as gods. Overlaid on this are popular Taoist, Mahayana Buddhist and Confucian beliefs.

On a day-to-day level most Chinese are much less concerned with the high-minded philosophies and asceticism of the Buddha, Confucius or Lao Zi than they are with the pursuit of worldly success, the appeasement of the dead and the spirits, and seeking knowledge about the future. Chinese religion incorporates elements of what Westerners

The most popular Chinese gods and local deities, or *shen*, are Kuan Yin, the goddess of mercy; Kuan Ti, the god of war and wealth; and Toh Peh Kong, a local deity representing the spirit of the pioneers and found only outside China.

MULTICULTURALISM, RELIGION & CULTURE RELIGION

might call 'superstition' – if you want your fortune told, for instance, you go to a temple. The other thing to remember is that Chinese religion is polytheistic. Apart from the Buddha, Lao Zi and Confucius, there are many divinities, such as house gods, and gods and goddesses for particular professions.

Hinduism

Hinduism in the region dates back at least 1500 years and there are Hindu influences in cultural traditions, such as *wayang kulit* (shadow-puppet theatre) and the wedding ceremony. However, it is only in the last 100 years or so, following the influx of Indian contract labourers and settlers, that it has again become widely practised. Hinduism has three basic practices: *puja* (worship), the cremation of the dead, and the rules and regulations of the caste system. Although still very strong in India, the caste system was never significant in Malaysia, mainly because the labourers brought here from India were mostly from the lower classes.

Adat, with its roots in the region's Hindu period and earlier, is customary law that places great emphasis on collective rather than individual responsibility and on maintaining harmony.

Hinduism has a vast pantheon of deities, although the one omnipresent god usually has three physical representations: Brahma, the creator; Vishnu, the preserver; and Shiva, the destroyer or reproducer. All three gods are usually shown with four arms, but Brahma has the added advantage of four heads to represent his all-seeing presence.

Animism

The animist religions of Malaysia's indigenous peoples are as diverse as the peoples themselves. While animism does not have a rigid system of tenets or codified beliefs, it can be said that animists perceive natural phenomena to be animated by various spirits or deities, and a complex system of practices is used to propitiate these spirits.

Ancestor worship is also a common feature of animist societies; departed souls are considered to be intermediaries between this world and the next.

THAIPUSAM

The most spectacular Hindu festival in Malaysia is Thaipusam, a wild parade of confrontingly invasive body piercings. The festival, which originated in Tamil Nadu (but is now banned in India), happens every year in the Hindu month of Thai (January/February) and is celebrated with the most gusto at the Batu Caves, just outside Kuala Lumpur.

The greatest spectacle is the devotees who subject themselves to seemingly masochistic acts as fulfilment for answered prayers. Many carry offerings of milk in *paal kudam* (milk pots), often connected to the skin by hooks. Even more striking are the *vel kavadi* – great cages of spikes that pierce the skin of the carrier and are decorated with peacock feathers, pictures of deities and flowers. Some penitents go as far as piercing their tongues and cheeks with hooks, skewers and tridents.

The festival is the culmination of around a month of prayer, a vegetarian diet and other ritual preparations, such as abstinence from sex or sleeping on a hard floor. While it looks excruciating, a trance-like state stops participants from feeling pain; later the wounds are treated with lemon juice and holy ash to prevent scarring. As with the practice of firewalking, only the truly faithful should attempt the ritual. It is said that insufficiently prepared devotees keep doctors especially busy over the Thaipusam festival period with skin lacerations, or by collapsing after the strenuous activities.

Thaipusam is also celebrated in Penang at the Nattukotai Chettiar Temple and the Waterfall Hilltop Temple.

Religious Issues

Freedom of Religon?

Islam is Malaysia's state religion, which has an impact on the cultural and social life of the country at several levels. Government institutions and banks, for example, are closed for two hours at lunchtime on Friday to allow Muslims to attend Friday prayers.

Government censors, with Islamic sensitivities in mind, dictate what can be performed on public stages or screened in cinemas. This has led to Beyoncé cancelling her shows when asked to adhere to strict guidelines on dress and performance style, and to the banning of movies such as *Schindler's List* and *Babe* – the themes of Jews being saved from the Holocaust and a cute pig star are not to Muslim tastes. In 2008, Malaysia's leading Islamic council issued an edict against yoga, fearing the exercises could corrupt Muslims.

Syariah (Islamic law) is the preserve of state governments, as is the establishment of Muslim courts of law, which since 1988 cannot be overruled by secular courts. This has had a negative impact on Muslims wishing to change their religion and divorced parents who cannot agree on a religion by which to raise their children. The end result is that Malaysian Muslims who change their religion or practice no faith at all hardly ever make their choice public.

Those that do, such as Lina Joy, a Malay convert to Christianity, face insurmountable difficulties. After battling for nine years through the legal system, Ms Joy failed in 2007 to be allowed to have her choice of religion recognised on her identity card. Malaysia's high court ruled that she first needed permission from the *syariah* court – an institution that would treat her action as apostasy to be punished.

It's believed only one woman – 88-year-old Wong Ah Kui (legally known as Nyonya Tahir) – has ever been officially allowed to leave Islam in Malaysia, and then only after she had died in 2006 and her family wanted to have a Buddhist funeral.

Anti-Semitism

Penang once had a Jewish community large enough to support a synagogue (closed in 1976) and there's been a Jewish cemetery in George Town since 1805. Elsewhere in Malaysia, Jewish life is practically unknown.

Sadly, anti-Semitism, ostensibly tied to criticism of Israel, is a feature of Malaysia. In KL's bookshops it's not difficult to find anti-Semitic publications like *The Protocols of the Elders of Zion*. Former prime minister Mahathir is the most infamously outspoken Malaysian anti-Semite: in 2003 he made a speech to an Islamic leadership conference claiming the USA is a tool of Jewish overlords, and he once cancelled a planned tour of Malaysia by the New York Philharmonic because the programme included work by a Jewish composer.

More recently, after the July 2011 Bersih rally in KL to demand greater transparency in electoral law, the UMNO-owned Malay newspaper *Utusan Malaysia* claimed such demonstrations would make the country vulnerable to interference by Jews and Israel. The Malaysian government later distanced itself from the newspaper's comments.

Israeli passport holders are not permitted to enter Malaysia without clearance from the Ministry of Home Affairs, and very few local Muslims differentiate between Israelis and Jews generally – something worth noting if you're Jewish and travelling in the region.

MULTICULTURALISM, RELIGION & CULTURE RELIGION

BOMOH

Malaysian politicians have been known to call in a *bomoh* – a traditional spiritual healer and spirit medium – during election campaigns to assist in their strategy and provide some foresight.

Women in Malaysia

Malaysian women take part in all aspects of society, from politics and big business to academia and the judicial system; in 2010 Malaysia appointed its first two female Islamic-court judges. However, women in all communities, particularly those with conservative religious values, face restrictions on their behaviour despite the general openness of Malaysian society. Arranged marriage is common among Muslim and Hindu families, and the concept of 'honour' is still a powerful force in internal family politics.

Although the wearing of the *tudong* (headscarf) is encouraged, Muslim women are permitted to work, drive and go out unchaperoned, though the religious authorities frequently crack down on *khalwat* (close proximity, ie couples who get too intimate in public), which is considered immoral. Full *purdah* (the practice of screening women from men or strangers by means of all-enveloping clothes) is rare – if you do see this it's likely to be worn by women visiting from the Persian Gulf.

Recent changes to Islamic family law have made it easier for men to marry and divorce multiple wives and claim a share of their property. Muslim parties are also campaigning to remove the crime of marital rape from the statute books and bring in new laws requiring four male witnesses before a rape case can come to trial. In response to these moves, Marina Mahathir, the daughter of the former prime minister, compared the lot of Malaysia's Muslim women to that of blacks under apartheid in South Africa.

Sisters in Islam (www.sistersin islam.org.my) is a website run by and for Malaysian Muslim women who refuse to be bullied by patriarchal interpretations of Islam.

Arts & Architecture

The belief driving the inaugural Cooler Lumpur Festival in 2013 was that the creativity of KLites in the arts and culture was not just 'cool' but 'cooler'. Take a close look at the city's contemporary arts scenes and it's difficult not to agree. Mirroring the eclectic range of artistic pursuits is the city's built environment which segues from elegant, traditional *kampong* houses to soaring, post-modern edifices endowed with Islamic flourishes.

Literature

A 1911 scandal, involving the wife of a headmaster at a KL school who was convicted in a murder trial after shooting dead a male friend, was the basis for Somerset Maugham's short story and play *The Letter*. Anthony Burgess picked up the thread of the dying days of British colonial rule in the region in *The Malayan Trilogy*, written in the 1950s when he was a school teacher in the country: it was Burgess who coined the phrase 'cooler lumpur'. *The Malayan Life of Ferdach O Haney* is a fictionalised account of the author Frederick Lees' experiences in 1950s Malaya; Lees was uniquely placed to observe mid-20th-century life in KL in his role as a top-ranking civil servant.

The literary baton has long since been passed to locally born writers such as Tash Aw (www.tash-aw.com), whose debut novel, *The Harmony Silk Factory*, won the 2005 Whitbread First Novel Award; the Man Booker Prize–nominated author Tan Twan Eng (www.tantwaneng.com), whose literature fuses a fascination with Malaysia's past and the impact of Japanese culture; and Preeta Samarasan (http://preetasamarasan.com), whose novel *Evening is the Whole Day* shines a light on the experiences of an Indian immigrant family in the early 1980s.

Samarasan is one of the writers whose work features in *Urban Odysseys*, edited by Janet Tay and Eric Forbes, a mixed bag of short stories set in KL. Another excellent collection of locally penned short stories about different aspects of sexuality is *Body 2 Body*, edited by Jerome Kugan and Pang Khee Teik. This anthology has a story by Brian Gomez, whose comedy-thriller *Devil's Place* is fun to read and very evocative of its KL setting. Kam Raslan's *Confessions of an Old Boy* is another comic tale, this time following the adventures both at home and abroad of politico Dato' Hamid.

Leading promoters of the KL lit scene are Sharon Bakar (http://the-bookaholic.blogspot.co.uk) and Bernice Chauly (http://bernicechauly.com). They host two monthly literary events around town: Readings@ Seksan and Ceritaku@No Black Tie. Pieces read out at the Readings events have been published in two volumes of *Readings from Readings*.

A snappy read is Amir Muhammad's *Rojak: Bite-Sized Stories*, in which the multitalented artist and writer gathers a selection of the 350-word vignettes, many of them comic, that he penned as part of the British Council–sponsored creative writing project City of Shared Stories (http://cityofshared storieskuala lumpur.com).

Dance

There are several tourist-oriented dance shows in KL at which you can see traditional Malay dances from the peninsula; the main one is at the Malaysian Tourism Centre.

WAYANG

During important festivals for the Chinese community, such as Chinese New Year, there are street performances of *wayang* (Chinese opera) in KL. Shows feature dramatic music, high-pitched romantic songs and outrageous dances in spectacular costumes. Performances can go for an entire evening, but typically you don't have to understand Chinese to follow the simple plots.

Traditional Indian dance is taught and performed at the Temple of Fine Arts in Brickfields. Malaysian dance legend Ramli Ibrahim founded Sutra Dance Theatre in 1983, a troupe that also takes Indian classical dance as the basis for its choreography. They have their own small dance theatre in Titiwangsa and also put on shows at Kuala Lumpur Performing Arts Centre (KLPAC). This is the venue you're most likely to catch other contemporary dance performances by local troupes such as Nyoba Kan (www.nyobakan.blogspot.com), who specialise in the Japanese dance form *buto*.

There are various dance festivals held in KL throughout the year including My Dance Festival (www.mydancefestival.net), which includes dance films and masterclasses as well as live performances.

Although traditional dramatic forms, such as *wayang kulit* (shadow-puppet theatre) remain popular in Malaysia, it's rare for such shows to be performed in KL.

Drama

Local playwrights have to tread carefully when dealing with controversial topics such as race and religion but you'd be surprised by how much they can get away with compared with what's acceptable in the cinema, on TV and for popular music performances.

Musicals, particularly those about national heroes – from the sultanate-era warrior Hang Tuah to former PM Mahathir – are very popular; you'll likely find them staged at the Istana Budaya and KLPAC. There is also a strong interest in English-language theatre, as well as in Malay, Indian and Chinese languages.

The most interesting productions are generally staged at KLPAC, the Actors Studio (www.theactorsstudio.com.my) and the Five Arts Centre (www.fiveartscentre.org), the latter two both based in Taman Tun Dr Ismail on the outskirts of KL. The Black Box at Publika is another venue that's popular for alternative and cutting-edge performances.

Online Arts Resources

Arts.com.my (www.arts.com.my)

Malaysia Design Archive (www.malaysiadesignarchive.org)

MyDance Alliance (www.mydancealliance.org)

KL Dance Watch (http://kldancewatch.wordpress.com)

Music

Traditional & Classical

Traditional Malay music is based largely on *gendang* (drums) but other percussion instruments include the gong and various tribal instruments made from seashells, coconut shells and bamboo. The Indonesian-style *gamelan* (a traditional orchestra of drums, gongs and wooden xylophones) also crops up on ceremonial occasions. The Malay *nobat* uses a mixture of percussion and wind instruments to create formal court music.

For Western-style classical music, attend a performance by the Malaysian Philharmonic Orchestra at Dewan Filharmonik Petronas at the base of the Petronas Towers.

Chinese and Islamic influences are felt in the music of *dondang sayang* (Chinese-influenced romantic songs) and *hadrah* (Islamic chants, sometimes accompanied by dance and music). The KL-based Dama Orchestra (www.damaorchestra.com) combines modern and traditional Chinese instruments and plays songs that conjure up 1920s and '30s Malaysia.

Popular Music

Snapping at the high heels of demure Malaysian pop songstress Siti Nurhaliza (http://sitizone.com) are Zee Avi (www.zeeavi.com), who was signed by the US label Bushfire Records for her eponymous debut album; and the sultry Yuna (www.yunamusic.com), who has also cut a US record deal.

Winner of three AIM awards (the Malaysian equivalent of the Grammys) in 2004 for his debut album, *Monumental,* is singer-songwriter Reshmonu (www.reshmonu.com); his 2009 release, *Harapan* (Hope), blends local rhythms and instruments into R'n'B and Latin grooves such as samba and bossa nova. Famous for his distinctive look of braided hair with flowing extensions, the multitalented 32-year-old has opened concerts for the likes of Alicia Keys and the Prodigy, and featured on Lonely Planet's TV program *Six Degrees: Kuala Lumpur.*

Generally, though, KL's indie music scene is erratic, with artists not always being able to go the distance for local let alone international recognition. That said, some consistent talents to keep eyes and ears open for include the following:

➡ Azmyl Yunor, a singer-songwriter who's been cutting discs and making music since 1997; his 2012 album, *Wilayah,* was made with his touring band the Sigarettes.

➡ Isaac Entry, a singer-songwriter in a similar vein to Zee Avi, who released his first CD in 2010 on a label created by jazz venue No Black Tie.

➡ The Impatient Sisters, three actual sisters from Kuantan, penning and playing quirky soul and folksy pop songs.

➡ OJ Law (http://ojlaw.co), whose rock/soul mash-up *Yesterday Is A Distant Dream* was one of *Time Out KL*'s albums of the year for 2012.

➡ Citizen's of Ice Cream, one of the artists on the indie Malaysian record label Soundscape Records (www.soundscape-records.com).

The Wknd (the-wknd.com) is the go-to site for the KL music scene, with details of up-and-coming artists, gig listings, online tracks, videos and more.

Cinema

Although Malaysia's film industry dates back to the 1930s, its heyday was the 1950s, when P Ramlee took to the silver screen. This Malaysian icon acted in 66 films, recorded 300 songs, and even became a successful film director – his directorial debut, *Penarik Becha* (The Trishaw Man; 1955), is a classic of Malay cinema.

On the international art house scene, a well-known Malaysian director is Taiwan resident Tsai Ming Liang. His starkly beautiful but glacially

---

YASMIN AHAMAD

The multi-award-winning Yasmin Ahamad was only 51 when she died after suffering a stroke in July 2009. Starting her career in advertising, Ahamad made just six movies for the cinema and one for TV but established such a reputation that she was feted both at home and abroad and is considered the most culturally important Malaysian film-maker since P Ramlee.

It was Ahamad's 2004 film *Sepet* that first shook up contemporary Malaysian cinema. About a Chinese boy and Malay girl falling in love, the movie cut across the country's race and language barriers and in turn upset many devout Malays, as did her follow up, *Gubra* (2006), which dared to take a sympathetic approach to prostitutes. Causing less of stir were *Mukshin* (2007), a romantic tale about Malay village life; and what would be her final movie, *Talentime* (2009), about the run-up to an inter-school performing arts contest.

Find out more about her work from Amir Muhammad's tribute book, *Yasmin Ahamad's Films* (www.matabaribooks.com), written just a month after her funeral.

slow interracial romance, *I Don't Want to Sleep Alone,* was filmed entirely on location in KL. It was banned and later released with massive cuts for presenting an allegedly 'negative depiction of Malaysia'.

Amir Muhammad's work also pushes the boundaries on issues that the government prefers not be discussed in the public arena. His movie *Lelaki Komunis Terakhir* (The Last Communist Man; 2006) was banned, along with his follow-up movie *Apa Khabar Orang Kampung* (Village People Radio Show; 2007) – find out more about them at www. redfilms.com.my. Look out for Muhammad's book *120 Malay Movies.*

Muhammad's producer and a pioneer of the Malaysian new wave of directors is James Lee, whose best-known pictures are *Room To Let* (2002) and *Beautiful Washing Machine* (2004). You can find out about and purchase some of these films and those of other local indie directors at www.dahuangpictures.com.

Dain Said's 2012 action drama *Bunohan* (www. bunohan.com) swept the board at various local film festivals and awards and has also attracted good press internationally.

Visual Arts

Malaysia has a damned impressive contemporary art scene and KL is the best place to access it both at public galleries and several private collections that are open to visitors by appointment.

Among the most interesting and internationally successful contemporary Malaysian artists are Jalaini Abu Hassan ('Jai'), Wong Hoy Cheong, landscape painter Wong Perng Fey, and Australian-trained multimedia artist Yee I-Lann. Amron Omar has focused for nearly 30 years on *silat* (a Malay martial art) as a source of inspiration for his paintings, a couple of which hang in the National Art Gallery in KL.

Latiff Mohidin, who is also a poet, is a Penang-based artist whose work spans several decades and has featured in a retrospective at the National Visual Arts Gallery; he's considered a national treasure. One of his stainless steel sculptures, *Kinetic 1,* is in the lobby of the Petronas Towers.

Abdul Multhalib Musa's sculptures have won awards and he created several pieces in Beijing for the 2008 Olympics. One of Musa's rippling steel tube creations is in the garden at Rimbun Dahan, while another can be spotted outside Wisma Selangor Dredging, 142C Jln Ampang, in KL.

Architecture

Traditional Malay

In the grounds of Badan Warisan Malaysia, the National Museum and FRIM, ornate examples of traditional wooden architecture have been transported from other parts of the country, reconstructed and opened for public inspection.

Vividly painted and handsomely proportioned, traditional wooden Malay houses are also perfectly adapted to the hot, humid conditions of the region. Built on stilts, with high, peaked roofs, they take advantage of even the slightest cooling breeze. Further ventilation is achieved by full-length windows, no internal partitions, and lattice-like grilles in the walls. The layout of a traditional Malay house reflects Muslim sensibilities. There are separate areas for men and women, as well as distinct areas where guests of either sex may be entertained.

The best examples of this type of architecture in KL are found scattered across Kampung Baru, the most Malay part of the city.

Shophouses & Colonial

Thanks to fires and civil war, not to mention their own fragile nature, none of the wood and *attap* (thatch) huts of the original settlers of KL have survived. However, from the 1880s onwards the city was built in brick with tiled roofs and stucco facades. Grand civic buildings such as those around Merdeka Square signalled the British desire to stamp their colonial mark on the city. It's also from this era that KL's first brick shophouses started appearing, some of which can still be found along Jln Tun HS Lee.

THE TWO ARTHURS

Arthur Bennison Hubback (1871–1948) and Arthur Charles Norman (1858–1944) are the two colonial-era architects whose fanciful Indo-Saracenic style of buildings have leant distinction to Kuala Lumpur's cityscape since the late 19th century. Hubback is most famous for designing Masjid Jamek, the graceful mosque with its Mogul domes and scalloped horseshoe arches; the spectacular Kuala Lumpur Railway Station; and the matching Malayan Railways Administration Building. Norman was responsible for the collection of buildings around Merdeka Square, most notably the Sultan Abdul Samad Building; and Carcosa Seri Negara, home of the British Resident Sir Frank Swettenham and now a luxury hotel.

Shophouses are exactly what they sound like – a shop at the front with living quarters above and to the rear. Constructed in terraces, each unit is long and narrow, approximately 6m by 24m. An open courtyard in the middle of the building provides light and ventilation. Walkways sheltered by verandahs at the front provide protection from both the rain and harsh sunlight. They are know as *kaki lima* ('five foot ways') because they were supposed to be five feet wide – not all are.

As KL became more prosperous so did the style of shophouse architecture. Look around Chinatown and the Masjid Jamek and Masjid India areas and you'll see shophouses with Grecian pediments and columns and fancy window frames, the Neoclassical style of the 1910s; Dutch-inspired gables, a style known as Dutch Patrician from the 1920s; and the geometric art deco style of the 1930s. The wealthiest constructed palladian-style villas such as Loke Mansion and the former Istana Negara. Jln Ampang, the road leading out to the former tin mines of Ampang, used to be lined with these mansions – only a handful remain including the ones used for the Malaysian Tourism Centre and the Pakistan High Commission.

Postcolonial

Following independence there was a conscious effort to break with the florid styles of architecture of the past, particularly when it came to public building works. This resulted in the elegant lines of the Masjid Negara (National Mosque), Stadium Merdeka (built for the declaration of independence in 1957) and neighbouring Stadium Negara.

Elaborate murals, with the Malaysian nation as their theme, were sometimes incorporated into these buildings: find them in Stadium Negara, the facades of the National Museum and Dewan Bahasa dan Pustaka (Institute of Language and Literature) on the corner of Jln Wisma Putra.

Some projects, such as the National Parliament (built in 1963 and designed by William Ivor Shipley), the National Museum, Menara Maybank and Istana Budaya incorporate distinctive motifs from traditional Malay architecture and art. Others, such as the beautiful Dayabumi Complex, and – later – the Petronas Towers, take their design references from Islam.

Among Malaysia's postcolonial architects of note is Hijjas Kasturi, who designed the Tabung Haji and Menara Maybank buildings; the giant shark fin of Menara Telekom, on the border between KL and Petaling Jaya and adorned with 22 outdoor 'sky gardens', one on every third floor; and the Bank Negara Malaysia Museum and Art Gallery. It's possible at certain times of the year to visit Kasturi's home, Rimbun Dahan, also a centre for developing traditional and contemporary art forms.

TY Lee is the architect responsible for designing KL's art deco Central Market (1936) and Chin Woo Stadium (1953), an example of early modern style with stripped back art deco elements.

Contemporary & Future Developments

Since the announcement of its planned construction in 2010, controversy has surrounded Warisan Merdeka, a 118-storey tower slated to rise between Chinatown and Stadium Merdeka. Various protests have been held and pressure groups, such as Rakan KL (www.rakankl.com), continue to push against the construction of what will be the tallest building in Malaysia. Still, the RM5 billion project looks set to go ahead, part of a general construction boom across the city that has seen many new skyscrapers sprout from the ground and tunnels being dug for the new MRT line.

Next to Pudu Sentral, Plaza Rakyat is a development that has been on hold since 1998 because of the Asian financial crisis at that time. This central KL eyesore, covering 15.3 acres, has been given a possible reprieve by soaring property prices. The land alone is estimated to be worth between RM670 and RM800 million. Nearby, the former Pudu jail site also awaits development.

It's the RM1 billion River of Life project that has the most potential to transform the way residents and visitors see the city's architecture. With its focus on the rejuvenation and revitalisation of the Klang River, the project also includes establishing heritage routes through the most historic parts of KL including Chinatown, where the Medan Pasar has recently been pedestrianised and surrounding buildings cleaned up.

Kuala Lumpur: A Sketchbook showcases lovely watercolour paintings by Chin Kon Yit and text by Chen Voon Fee that together vividly capture the capital's rich architectural heritage.

Environment & Wildlife

Even though, these days, it's very far from a city in the jungle (more like a city surrounded by palm oil plantations!) there are pockets of old growth forest to discover in and around KL that are havens for wildlife and sanctuaries for soaring tropical trees and plants. Easily accessible from KL are major national parks, such as Taman Negara, home to much of the amazing flora and fauna that once blanketed Peninsular Malaysia.

Wildlife

Apes & Monkeys

The monkeys you're most likely to encounter living wild around KL are macaques, the stocky, aggressive monkeys that solicit snacks from tourists at nature reserves and rural temples such as those at Batu Caves. If you are carrying food, watch out for daring raids and be wary of bites as rabies is a potential hazard.

Leaf-eating langurs, such as the slivered leaf monkey whose fur is frosted with grey tips, are also quite common – spot them at the Forest Research Institute of Malaysia (FRIM) swinging high through the trees.

To see Malaysia's signature animal, the orang-utan, you'll have to drop by Zoo Negara; in Malaysia, these charismatic apes are found living wild only in the jungles of Sabah and Sarawak.

The Encyclopedia of Malaysia: The Environment by Professor Sham Sani Dato, one volume of an excellent series of illustrated encyclopedias, covers everything you need to know about Malaysia's environment.

Dogs, Cats & Civets

The animals you're most likely to see in KL are domesticated dogs and cats. However, local Muslims consider dogs unclean, hence many have negative attitudes towards them. In 2009 villagers from Pulau Ketam in Selangor rounded up over 300 strays and dumped them on two uninhabited islands. According to reports from animal welfare agency SPCA Selangor, the starving dogs turned to cannibalism to survive.

Cats hardly fare any better, with many local species of wild cats facing extinction because of hunting and the trade in body parts for traditional medicines. The Malayan tiger is now extremely rare on the peninsula, as are leopards and black panthers (actually black leopards). Smaller bay cats, leopard cats and marbled cats fare slightly better, in part because they need less territory and eat smaller prey (birds and small mammals). You may also spot various species of civet, a separate family of predators with vaguely catlike features but longer snouts and shaggier coats.

Bats & Birds

Malaysia has more than 100 species of bat, most of which are tiny, insectivorous species that live in caves and under eaves and bark. Fruit bats (flying foxes) are only distantly related; they have well-developed eyes and do not navigate by echolocation. They are often seen taking wing at dusk.

More than 650 species of birds live on Peninsular Malaysia. You can spot exotic species in many urban parks or aviaries such as KL Bird Park, but for rarer birds you'll have to head to the jungle and the hillsides. The Malaysian Nature Society is helping to promote Genting Highlands as a prime birding location and Fraser Hill (Bukit Fraser) is already an established bird-spotting location.

If you see parts of or products made from endangered species for sale, call the 24-hour Wildlife Crime Hotline (☏019-356 4194).

Reptiles

Some 250 species of reptile have been recorded in Malaysia, including 140 species of snake. Cobras and vipers pose a potential risk to trekkers, although the chances of encountering them are low. Large pythons are sometimes seen in national parks and you may also encounter 'flying' snakes, lizards and frogs (all these species glide using wide flaps of skin). Even in city parks, you stand a good chance of running into a monitor lizard, a primitive-looking carrion feeder notorious for consuming domestic cats.

Plants

The wet, tropical climate of this region produces an amazing range of trees, plants and flowers, including such signature species as the carnivorous pitcher plant, numerous orchids and the parasitic rafflesia (or 'corpse flower'), which produces the world's largest flower – a whopping 1m across when fully open. However, vast tracts of rainforest have been cleared to make way for plantations of cash crops such as rubber and palm oil. Just look out of the window on the flight into Kuala Lumpur International Airport and you'll see endless rows of oil palms.

Ian Buchanan spent eight years creating the exquisite illustrations and text for *Fatimah's Kampung*, a parable about how Malaysia is in the process of sacrificing nature and traditional values for economic development.

Palm-Oil Plantations

The oil palm, a native of West Africa that was introduced into Malaysia in the 1870s, is probably now the most common tree in Malaysia. The country's first palm-oil plantation was established in 1917; today, according to the Malaysian Palm Oil Council (www.mpoc.org.my), Malaysia is the world's leading producer of palm oil, accounting for over 40% of global production. The oil is extracted from the orange-coloured fruit, which grows in bunches just below the fronds. It is used

---

IMPROVING WILDLIFE CONSERVATION

At the end of 2010 Malaysia started to enforce its new Wildlife Conservation Act, which includes fines of up to RM100,000 and long prison sentences for poaching, smuggling of animals and other wildlife-related crimes. This first revision of such laws in more than 30 years has been welcomed by local pressure groups including Traffic Southeast Asia (www.traffic.org/southeast-asia) and the Malaysian Nature Society.

Smuggling of live animals and animal parts is a particular problem in the region. Pangolins, also known as scaly anteaters, are the most traded species even though they are protected under Malaysian law; their scales, believed to have medicinal properties, can fetch up to RM800 per kg. In July 2010 police looking for stolen cars also uncovered an illegal 'mini zoo' in a KL warehouse containing 20 species of protected wildlife including a pair of rare birds of paradise worth RM1 million.

A month later, the notorious animal smuggler Alvin Wong was nabbed at Kuala Lumpur International Airport after his bag burst open revealing 95 boa constrictors, two rhinoceros vipers and a mata mata turtle. In November, Wong – described as 'the Pablo Escobar of wildlife trafficking' in *The Lizard King* by Bryan Christy (http://thelizardkingbook.com), a fascinating account of international animal and reptile smuggling – was sentenced to five years in jail.

primarily for cooking, although it can also be refined into biodiesel – an alternative to fossil fuels.

For all the crop's benefits, there have been huge environmental consequences to the creation of vast plantations that have replaced the native jungle and previously logged forests; in 2003 Friends of the Earth reported that palm-oil production was responsible for 87% of deforestation in Malaysia. The use of polluting pesticides and fertilisers in palm-oil production also undermines the crop's eco credentials. Palm-oil plantations convert land into permanent monoculture, reducing the number of plant species by up to 90%. Oil palms require large quantities of herbicides and pesticides that can seep into rivers; drainage may lower water tables, drying out nearby peat forests (and releasing huge quantities of greenhouse gases in the process). Plantations also fragment the natural habitats that are especially important to large mammals.

The Palm Oil Action Group (www.palmoilaction.org.au) is an Australian pressure group raising awareness about palm oil and the need to use alternatives. Roundtable on Sustainable Palm Oil tries to look at the issue from all sides while seeking to develop and implement global standards. Proforest (www.proforest.net) has also been working with Wild Asia (www.wildasia.org) on the Stepwise Support Programme, designed to promote sustainability within the palm-oil industry.

> Malaysia's jungles support a staggering amount of life: around 14,500 species of flowering plant and tree, 210 species of mammal, 600 species of bird, 150 species of frog, 80 species of lizard and thousands of types of insect.

National Parks & Other Protected Areas

Malaysia's jungles contain some of the world's oldest undisturbed areas of rainforest. It's estimated they've existed for about 100 million years, as they were largely unaffected by the far-reaching climatic changes brought on elsewhere by the Ice Age.

Fortunately, quite large areas of some of the best and most spectacular of these rainforests have been made into national parks, in which all commercial activity is banned. The British established the first national park in Malaysia in 1938 and it is now included in Taman Negara, the crowning glory of Malaysia's network of national parks, which crosses the borders of Terengganu, Kelantan and Pahang; tour companies in KL run trips here.

In addition to this and the 27 other national and state parks across the country (23 of them located in Malaysian Borneo), there are various government-protected reserves and sanctuaries for forests, birds, mammals and marine life. Right in the heart of the KL you can visit the KL Forest Eco Park.

Environmental Issues

Malaysia's federal government maintains that it is doing its best to balance the benefits of economic development with environmental protection and conservation. Others, including a long list of wildlife and environment protection agencies and pressure groups, beg to differ, pointing out how big business continues to have the ear of government when decision time rolls around.

A positive development was the reelection in 2013 of state governments for Penang and Selangor, both of which are controlled by opposition parties to the national ruling BN coalition. Penang intends to become Malaysia's first 'green state' and Selangor has also introduced a raft of pro-environmental policies including introducing a 'no plastic bag' policy at shops at the weekends.

> **Conservation Organisations**
> ....
> Malaysian Nature Society (www.mns.org.my)
> ....
> Orangutan Foundation (www.orangutan.org.uk)
> ....
> Sahabat Alam Malaysia (SAM; www.foe-malaysia.org)
> ....
> WWF-Malaysia (www.wwf.org.my)

Deforestation

Malaysia's logging and oil palm businesses provide hundreds of thousands of jobs, yet they also wreak untold ecological damage and have caused the displacement and consequent cultural erosion of many tribal peoples.

There's a disparity between government figures and those of environmental groups, but it's probable that more than 60% of Peninsular Malaysia's rainforests have been logged, with similar figures applying to Malaysian Borneo. Government initiatives such as the National Forestry Policy have led to deforestation being cut to 900 sq km a year, a third slower than previously. The aim is to reduce the timber harvest by 10% each year, but even this isn't sufficient to calm many critics who remain alarmed at the rate at which Malaysia's primary forests are disappearing.

Close to KL, the Forest Research Institute of Malaysia (FRIM) is pioneering new ways of preserving and regenerating Malaysia's rainforests. For more information on government forestry projects visit the website of the Forestry Department (www.forestry.gov.my).

Environmental groups such as TrEES (www.trees.org.my) have also been campaigning for the protection of the rainforests and water catchment area along the eastern flank of Selangor. In 2010, 93,000 hectares of these uplands were gazetted as the Selangor State Park, making it the peninsula's third-largest protected area of forest after Taman Negara and Royal Belum State Park. Find out more about it at http://selangor-statepark.blogspot.com.

Sign up to be a voluntary forest monitor at Forest Watch (www.timalaysia-forestwatch.org.my), a project by Transparency International Malaysia.

River of Life

Following successes in Melaka and Penang on cleaning up polluted rivers, the focus has now turned to KL and the Klang Valley. The literal translation of Kuala Lumpur is 'muddy estuary' and anyone gazing on any of the milky-coffee-coloured waterways that flow through the city would still find that name appropriate. Following moves in 2010 by the Selangor state government to clean up a 21km stretch of Sungai Klang around Klang, the federal government has stepped in to offer to coordinate the project. This makes sense as the 120km-long heavily polluted river flows through the capital on its way to the coast.

KL's RM4 billion River of Life project includes a plan to clean up a 110km stretch along the Klang River basin, shifting the water quality from its current Class III–Class V status (not suitable for body-contact) to Class IIb (suitable for body-contact recreational usage) by year 2020. Also part of the project are beautification proposals for the riverbanks including new parks and walkways.

HAZE

The region's environment faces an ongoing threat from the so-called 'haze' – smoke from fires set by Indonesian farmers and plantation companies to clear land for agricultural purposes. The haze is at its worst around March and September/October, just before the rainy season.

Cutting Carbon Emissions

At the 2009 climate change conference in Copenhagen, Prime Minister Najib pledged to slash Malaysia's carbon emissions by 40% by 2020. According to the International Energy Agency, the country emitted 6.68 tonnes of carbon dioxide per capita in 2007, more than twice the world's average, and the fourth-highest amount in the region after Brunei, Taipei and Singapore. Compared to these three countries, Malaysia's emission per capita percentage change between 1990 and 2007 was the highest, growing by 143%.

In order to reach its stated goal the federal government has added green technology to the portfolio of the Ministry of Energy and Water and announced the launch of a national green technology policy. The details remain sketchy, however, and the overall aim sits awkwardly with the continuing expansion of local budget airlines such as AirAsia.

Survival Guide

Transport

ARRIVING IN KL

Most likely you'll arrive at Kuala Lumpur International Airport (KLIA), although a handful of flights land at Sky-Park Subang Terminal. Coming overland from Singapore or Thailand, possible arrival points include KL Sentral for trains and Pudu Sentral for buses. There are several other bus terminals around the capital with long-distance connections to Malaysian destinations.

Ferries from Sumatra, Indonesia, dock at Pelabuhan Klang, which is connected by rail with KL Sentral.

Flights, cars and tours can be booked at lonelyplanet.com.

KLIA

Kuala Lumpur International Airport (KLIA; ☏8777 8888; www.klia.com.my), which comprises two terminals, is 75km south of the city centre at Sepang.

Bus

The **Airport Coach** (www. airportcoach.com.my; one way/ return RM10/18) takes an hour to KL Sentral; for RM18 it will take you to any central KL hotel from KLIA and pick you up for the return journey for RM25. The bus stand is clearly signposted inside the terminal.

Taxi

Taxis from KLIA operate both on a fixed-fare coupon system and the meter. Buy your taxi coupon before you exit the arrivals hall; standard taxis cost RM75 (up to three people), premier taxis for four people RM103 and family-sized minivans seating up to eight RM200. The journey will take around one hour.

Given the extra charges on the metered taxis for tolls and pick up at the airport (RM2), plus the unknown traffic factor, the fixed-fare coupon is the way to go. Going to the airport by taxi, make sure that the agreed fare includes tolls; expect to pay RM65 from Chinatown or Jln Bukit Bintang.

Train

The fastest way to the city is on the comfortable **KLIA Ekspres** (www.kliaekspres.com; adult/child one way RM35/15, return RM70/30), taking 28 minutes, with departures every 15 to 20 minutes from 5am to 1am. From KL Sentral you can transfer to your final destination by monorail, LRT, KTM Komuter train or by taxi.

The **KL Transit train** (adult/child one way RM35/15) also connects KLIA with KL Sentral (35 minutes), stopping at three other stations en route (Salak Tinggi, Putrajaya and Cyberjaya, and Bandar Tasik Selatan).

If flying from KL on Malaysia Airlines, Cathay Pacific, Royal Brunei or Emirates you can check your baggage in at KL Sentral before making your way to KLIA.

CLIMATE CHANGE & TRAVEL

Every form of transport that relies on carbon-based fuel generates CO_2, the main cause of human-induced climate change. Modern travel is dependent on aeroplanes, which might use less fuel per kilometre per person than most cars but travel much greater distances. The altitude at which aircraft emit gases (including CO_2) and particles also contributes to their climate change impact. Many websites offer 'carbon calculators' that allow people to estimate the carbon emissions generated by their journey and, for those who wish to do so, to offset the impact of the greenhouse gases emitted with contributions to portfolios of climate-friendly initiatives throughout the world. Lonely Planet offsets the carbon footprint of all staff and author travel.

SkyPark Subang Airport

Firefly and Berjaya Air flights land at **SkyPark Subang Airport** (Sultan Abdul Aziz Shah Airport; ☑7845 1717; www.subangskypark.com), around 20km west of the city centre.

Taxi

Taxis charge around RM40 into the city, depending on traffic which can be heavy during rush hour.

KL Sentral Train Station

All long-distance trains depart from KL Sentral, hub of the **KTM** (Keretapi Tanah Melayu Berhad; ☑1300 88 5862; www.ktmb.com.my; ⏰info office 9am-9pm, ticket office 7am-10pm) national railway system. The information office in the main hall can advise on schedules and check seat availability.

There are daily connections with Butterworth, Wakaf Baharu (for Kota Bharu and Jerantut), Johor Bahru, Thailand and Singapore; fares are cheap, especially if you opt for a seat rather than a berth (for which there are extra charges), but journey times are slow.

The opulent **Eastern & Oriental Express** (www.orient-express.com) also stops in KL Sentral, connecting with Singapore, Butterworth (for Penang) and Bangkok.

Light Rail Transit (LRT)

The Kelana Jaya–Terminal Putra line passes through KL Sentral.

KTM Komuter Trains

KTM Komuter (☑1300 88 5862; http://ktmkomuter.com. my; ⏰6am-11.45pm) trains connect KL with the Klang

KL'S NEW MRT

To give it its full title, the **Klang Valley Mass Rapid Transit (KVMRT) project** (www.mymrt.com.my) involves the construction of a rail-based public transport network which, together with the existing light rail transit (LRT), monorail, KTM Komuter, KLIA Ekspres and KLIA Transit systems, aims to ease the road traffic congestion that plagues the Greater Kuala Lumpur/ Klang Valley region. The ambitious target is to make half of all journeys in the Klang Valley area ones by public transport.

Launched in 2011, the project aims to create three new commuter rail lines, the first of which is the 51km Sungai Buloh–Kajang line; 9.5km of this link will run underground and drilling for the tunnels is causing disruption currently in parts of KL city centre. Phase one, from Sungai Buloh to Semantan, will be operational by 2016. The remaining part of the line to Kajang will be finished the following year.

Valley and Seremban every 15 to 20 minutes.

Monorail

The **monorail** (www.klmonorail.com.my; RM1.20-2.50; ⏰6am-midnight) terminates at KL Sentral; it's a handy way to reach central locations.

Taxi

KL Sentral runs a coupon system for taxis – look for the counters near the exits from the KLIA Expres/Transit lines and main KTM/KTM Komuter lines. The fare to Chinatown/Golden Triangle/ KLCC is RM12.

Pudu Sentral Bus Station

Steps from Chinatown and also close to the Golden Triangle, this crowded **bus station** (Map p248; left luggage per day per bag RM3; ⏰6am-midnight) serves destinations around the peninsula as well as Singapore and Thailand. It's the kind of place you want to get in and out of quickly. The crowds provide plenty of cover for pickpockets and bag snatchers, and agents for various

bus companies will pounce on you as soon as you enter. Close to the main entrance is an information counter. Located at the rear is a left-luggage counter and tourist police.

Plaza Rakyat is the nearest LRT station.

Terminal Bersepadu Selatan

Connected to the Bandar Tasik Selatan train station hub, about 15 minutes south of KL Sentral, is **Terminal Bersepadu Selatan** (☑03-9051 2000; www.tbsbts.com. my; Bandar Tasik Selatan) serving destinations south of KL including Melaka, Muar, Johor Bahru and Singapore.

Putra Bus Station

A number of mainly east-coast Malaysia services arrive at this station opposite PWTC (Putra World Trade Centre) station (easily reached by taking the LRT to PWTC, or a KTM Komuter train to Putra station).

Pekeliling Bus Station

Buses arrive here from central peninsula locations including Kuala Lipis, Raub and Jerantut. It's next to Titiwangsa LRT and monorail stations, just off Jln Tun Razak.

Pelabuhan Klang Port

Ferries from Tanjung Balai (Asahan) and Dumai in Sumatra arrive here. The KTM station is opposite the ferry terminal; trains to KL Sentral take just over an hour.

GETTING AROUND

KL Sentral is the hub of a rail-based urban network consisting of the KTM Komuter, KLIA Ekspres, KLIA Transit, LRT and Monorail systems. Unfortunately the systems – all built separately – are poorly integrated. There is no combination ticket covering all services, and at stations where there's an interchange between the services they're rarely conveniently connected. That said, you can happily get around much of central KL

on a combination of rail and monorail services.

Bus

Most buses are provided by either **Rapid KL** (☎7885 2585; www.rapidkl.com.my) or **Metrobus** (☎5635 3070). There's an **information booth** (◷7am-9pm) at the Jln Sultan Mohammed bus stop in Chinatown. Rapid KL buses are divided into four classes, and tickets are valid all day on the same class of bus:

Bas Bandar (routes starting with B, RM2) services run around the city centre.

Bas Utama (routes starting with U, RM2) services run from the centre to the suburbs.

Bas Tempatan (routes starting with T, RM1) services run around the suburbs.

Bas Ekspres (routes starting with E, RM4) are express buses to distant suburbs.

You can also buy an all-day ticket covering all nonexpress buses (RM4) and a ticket covering all Rapid KL buses and trains (RM7).

Local buses leave from half a dozen small bus stands around the city – useful stops in Chinatown include Jln Sultan Mohamed (by

Pasar Seni), Bangkok Bank (on Lebuh Pudu) and Medan Pasar (on Lebuh Ampang).

Car

KL is the best place to hire a car for touring the peninsula, though driving out of KL is complicated by a confusing one-way system and contradictory road signs that can throw off your sense of direction. All the major rental companies have offices at KLIA. City offices – generally open from 9am to 5.30pm weekdays and 9am to 1pm Saturday – include the following:

Avis (☎03-2162 2144; www.avis.com.my; Rennaissance Hotel, Jln Ampang)

Hertz (☎03-2026 2497; www5.hertz.com; Ground Floor, Wisma MPL, Jln Raja Chulan)

Orix (☎2142 3009; www.orixauto.com.my; Ground fl, Federal Hotel, 35 Jln Bukit Bintang)

KL Monorail

The air-conditioned **monorail** (www.klmonorail.com.my; RM1.20-2.50; ◷6am-midnight) zips from KL Sentral to Titiwangsa, linking up many of the city's sightseeing areas.

KTM Komuter Trains

KTM Komuter (☎1300 88 5862; http://ktmkomuter.com.my; ◷6am-11.45pm) train services run every 15 to 20 minutes from 6am to 11.45pm and use KL Sentral as a hub. There are two lines: Tanjung Malim–Sungai Gadut and Batu Caves–Pelabuhan Klang.

Light Rail Transit

As well as buses, Rapid KL runs the **Light Rail Transit** (LRT; RM1-2.80; ◷6am-11.45pm)

MYRAPID & TOUCH 'N GO CARDS

If you're staying for an extended period in KL or Malaysia, consider the prepaid **MyRapid** (www.myrapid.com.my) card, valid on Rapid KL buses, the monorail and the Ampang and Kelana Jaya LRT lines. It costs RM10 (including RM8 in credit) and can be bought at monorail and LRT stations. Just tap at the ticket gates or when you get on the bus and the correct fare will be deducted. Rapid KL also offers the **Rapidpass Flexi Touch 'n Go**, valid from one to 30 days (RM10 to RM150).

The **Touch 'n Go card** (www.touchngo.com.my) can be used on all public transport in the Klang Valley, at highway toll booths across Malaysia and at selected parking sites. The cards, which cost RM10 and can be reloaded with values from RM20 to RM500, can be purchased at KL Sentral and the central LRT stations KLCC, Masjid Jamek and Dang Wangi.

system, running every six to 10 minutes. There are three lines: Ampang–Sentul Timur, Sri Petaling–Sentul Timur and Kelana Jaya–Terminal Putra. The network is poorly integrated because the lines were constructed by different companies. As a result, you may have to follow a series of walkways, stairs and elevators, or walk several blocks down the street.

Buy single journey tokens or MyRapid cards from the cashier or electronic ticket machines. An electronic control system checks tickets/tokens as you enter and exit via turnstiles (you tap the token on the way in and insert it in the gate on the way out). You can buy an all-day pass for RM7, which also covers you for Rapid KL buses.

Taxi

KL has plenty of air-conditioned taxis, which queue up at designated taxi stops across the city. You can also flag down moving taxis, but drivers will stop only if there is a convenient place to pull over. Fares start at RM3 for the first two minutes, with an additional 20 sen for each 45 seconds. From midnight to 6am there's a surcharge of 50% on the metered fare, and extra passengers (more than two) adds 20 sen each to the starting fare. Luggage placed in the boot is an extra RM1 and there's a RM12 surcharge for taxis to KLIA.

Unfortunately, some drivers have limited geographical knowledge of the city. Some also refuse to use the meter, even though this is a legal requirement. Taxi drivers lingering outside luxury hotels or tourist hot spots such as KL Bird Park are especially guilty of this behaviour. Note that KL Sentral and some large malls such as BB Plaza and Pavilion have a coupon system for taxis where you pay in advance at a slightly higher fee than the meter.

If a driver demands a fixed fare, bargain hard, or walk away and find another taxi. As a guide, you can get right across the centre of town for RM10 on the meter even in moderate traffic. Always ask for a receipt and check to see that they haven't included spurious extra charges, such as for baggage you don't have.

TOURS

If you need a guide or assistance getting around, many local agencies offer various tours of the city and attractions around KL.

KL Hop-On Hop-Off

(☑2166 6162; www.myhoponhopoff.com; adult/child 24hr RM38/17, 48hr RM65/29; ☺8.30am-8.30pm) This double-decker, wi-fi-enabled, air-con tourist bus makes a circuit of the main tourist sites half-hourly throughout the day. Stops include KLCC, Jln Bukit Bintang, Menara KL, Chinatown, Merdeka Square and the attractions of Lake Gardens. Tickets, which can be bought on the bus, last all day and you can get on and off as often as you like.

Going Places Tours (Map p248; ☑2078 4008; goingplaces-kl.com; Original Backpackers Inn, 60a Jln Sultan, Chinatown) Offers tours tailored to the backpacker market, including more adventurous options such as rafting, caving and rock-climbing adventures.

Tour 51 Malaysia (Map p250; ☑2161 8830) Runs a decent selection of half-day city tours (RM60) and day trips to places such as Putrajaya, Kuala Selangor and Pulau Ketam (RM150 to RM190). Can be booked via **Malaysian Travel Business** (Map p250, ☑2163 0162; MTC, 109 Jln Ampang), an agency with desks at the Malaysian Tourist Centre.

Travel Han (Map p248; ☑2031 0899; www.han-travel. com; Kompleks Selangor, Jln Sultan) One of the many agents offering tours to Taman Negara National Park in the north of Peninsular Malaysia, which is a 4343-sq-km reserve protecting one of the world's oldest tropical rainforests. Three-day, two-night packages from KL start from RM160 per person.

Directory A–Z

Customs Regulations

The following can be brought into Malaysia duty free:

➡ 1L of alcohol

➡ 225g of tobacco (200 cigarettes or 50 cigars)

➡ souvenirs and gifts not exceeding RM200 (RM500 when coming from Labuan or Langkawi)

Cameras, portable radios, perfume, cosmetics and watches do not incur duty. Prohibited items include weapons (including imitations), fireworks, 'obscene and prejudicial articles' (pornography, for example, and items that may be considered inflammatory or religiously offensive) and drugs. Drug smuggling carries the death penalty in Malaysia. Visitors can carry only RM1000 in and out of Malaysia; there's no limit on foreign currency.

Electricity

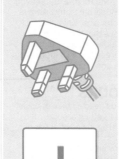

240V/50Hz

Emergency

Ambulance & Fire (☑994)
Police (☑999)
Tourist Police (☑2166 8322)

Gay & Lesbian Travellers

Malaysia is a predominantly Muslim country and the level of tolerance for homosexuality is vastly different from its neighbours. Sex between men is illegal at any age and *syariah* Islamic laws (which apply only to Muslims) forbid sodomy and cross-dressing. Fortunately, outright persecution of gays and lesbians is rare.

Nonetheless, gay and lesbian travellers should avoid behaviour that attracts unwanted attention. Malaysians are quite conservative about displays of public affection. Although same-sex handhold-

---

PRACTICALITIES

➡ Connect to the reliable electricity supply (220V to 240V, 50 cycles) with a UK-type three-square-pin plug.

➡ Read English-language newspapers the *New Straits Times,* the *Star* and the *Malay Mail*.

➡ Listen to Traxx FM (www.traxxfm.net; 90.3 FM), HITZ FM (www.hitz.fm; 92.9 FM) and MIX FM (www.mix.fm; 94.5 FM) for pop music and BFM (www.bfm.my; 89.9FM) and Fly FM (www.flyfm.com.my; 95.8 FM) for news.

➡ Watch the two government TV channels, TV1 and TV2, and four commercial stations, TV3, NTV7, 8TV and TV9, as well as a host of satellite channels.

➡ Use the metric system for weights and measures.

ing is quite common for men and women, this is rarely an indication of sexuality; an overtly gay couple doing the same would attract attention, though there is little risk of vocal or aggressive homophobia.

There's actually a fairly active gay scene in KL. The lesbian scene is more discreet, but it exists for those willing to seek it out. Start looking for information on www.utopia-asia.com or www.fridae.com, both of which provide good coverage of gay and lesbian events and activities across Asia.

The **PT Foundation** (www.ptfmalaysia.org) is a voluntary nonprofit organisation providing education on HIV/AIDS and sexuality, and care and support programs for marginalised communities in Malaysia.

Health
Before You Go

➡ Take out health insurance.

➡ Pack medications in their original, clearly labelled containers.

➡ Carry a signed and dated letter from your physician describing your medical conditions and medications, including their generic names.

➡ If you have a heart condition bring a copy of your ECG (taken just prior to travelling).

➡ Bring a double supply of any regular medication in case of loss or theft.

RECOMMENDED VACCINATIONS

Proof of yellow-fever vaccination will be required if you have visited a country in the yellow-fever zone (Africa or South America) within the six days prior to entering Malaysia. The World Health Organization (WHO) recommends the following vaccinations for travellers to Malaysia:

Adult diphtheria and tetanus Single booster recommended if none in the previous 10 years.

Hepatitis A Provides almost 100% protection for up to a year. A booster after 12 months provides at least another 20 years' protection.

Hepatitis B Now considered routine for most travellers. Given as three shots over six months. A rapid schedule is also available, as is a combined vaccination with hepatitis A.

Measles, mumps and rubella (MMR) Two doses of MMR are required unless you have had the diseases. Many young adults require a booster.

Polio There have been no reported cases of polio in Malaysia in recent years. Only one booster is required as an adult for lifetime protection.

Typhoid Recommended unless your trip is less than a week and only to developed cities. The vaccine offers around 70% protection, lasts for two to three years and is given as a single shot. Tablets are also available, however the injection is usually recommended as it has fewer side effects.

Varicella If you haven't had chickenpox, discuss this vaccination with your doctor.

RESOURCES

Lonely Planet's *Asia & India: Healthy Travel* guide is packed with useful information. Other recommended references include *Travellers' Health* by Dr Richard Dawood and *Travelling Well* by Dr Deborah Mills.

Online resources:

Centers for Disease Control and Prevention (CDC; www.cdc.gov)

MD Travel Health (www.mdtravelhealth.com)

World Health Organization (www.who.int/ith)

In Malaysia
AIR POLLUTION

If troubled by the air pollution, leave KL for a few days to get some fresh air.

AVAILABILITY OF HEALTH CARE

There are good clinics and international-standard hospitals in Kuala Lumpur, Melaka and Penang. Over-the-counter medicines and prescription drugs are widely available from reputable pharmacies across Malaysia.

HEAT

It can take up to two weeks to adapt to Malaysia's hot climate. Swelling of the feet and ankles is common, as are muscle cramps caused by excessive sweating. Prevent cramps by avoiding dehydration and excessive activity in the heat.

Dehydration is the main contributor to heat exhaustion. Symptoms include feeling weak, headache, irritability, nausea or vomiting, sweaty skin, a fast weak pulse and a normal or slightly elevated body temperature. Treat by getting out of the heat, applying cool wet cloths to the skin, laying flat with legs raised and rehydrating with water containing a quarter of a teaspoon of salt per litre.

Heat stroke is a serious medical emergency. Symptoms come on suddenly and include weakness, nausea, a hot dry body with a body temperature of over 41°C, dizziness, confusion, loss of coordination, fits and eventually collapse and loss of consciousness. Seek medical help and commence cooling by getting the person out of the heat, removing their clothes and applying cool wet cloths or ice to their body, especially to the groin and armpits.

Prickly heat – an itchy rash of tiny lumps – is caused by sweat being trapped under the skin. Treat by moving out of the heat and into an air-conditioned area for a few hours and by having cool showers. Creams and ointments clog the skin so they should be avoided.

INFECTIOUS DISEASES
The following are the most common for travellers:

Dengue Fever Becoming increasingly common in cities. The mosquito that carries dengue bites day and night, so use insect avoidance measures at all times. Symptoms can include high fever, severe headache, body ache, a rash and diarrhoea. There is no specific treatment, just rest and paracetamol – do not take aspirin as it increases the likelihood of haemorrhaging.

Giardiasis Relatively common and transmitted through personal contact and contaminated food and water. Symptoms include nausea, bloating, excess gas, fatigue and diarrhoea. The treatment of choice is Tinidazole, with Metronidazole being a second option.

Hepatitis A This food- and water-borne virus infects the liver, causing jaundice (yellow skin and eyes), nausea and lethargy. All travellers to Malaysia should be vaccinated against it.

Hepatitis B The only sexually transmitted disease (STD) that can be prevented by vaccination, hepatitis B is spread by body fluids.

Hepatitis E Transmitted through contaminated food and water and has similar symptoms to hepatitis A, but is far less common. It is a severe problem in pregnant women and can result in the death of both mother and baby. There is currently no vaccine, and prevention is by following safe eating and drinking guidelines.

HIV Unprotected sex is the main method of transmission.

Influenza Can be very severe in people over the age of 65 or in those with underlying medical conditions such as heart disease or diabetes; vaccination is recommended for these individuals. There is no specific treatment, just rest and paracetamol.

Malaria Uncommon in Peninsular Malaysia and antimalarial drugs are rarely recommended for travellers. However, there may be a small risk in rural areas. Remember that malaria can be fatal. Before you travel, seek medical advice on the right medication and dosage for you.

Rabies A potential risk, and invariably fatal if untreated, rabies is spread by the bite or lick of an infected animal – most commonly a dog or monkey. Pretravel vaccination means the postbite treatment is greatly simplified. If an animal bites you, gently wash

---

DON'T LET THE BEDBUGS BITE

Bedbugs live in the cracks of furniture and walls and migrate to the bed at night to feed on you. They are more likely to strike in high-turnover accommodation, especially hostels, though they can be found anywhere. An appearance of cleanliness is no guarantee there are no bedbugs. Protect yourself with the following strategies:

➡ Ask the hotel or hostel what it does to avoid bedbugs. It's a common problem and reputable establishments should have a pest-control procedure in place.

➡ Keep your luggage elevated off the floor to avoid having the critters latch on – this is one of the common ways bedbugs are spread from place to place.

➡ Check the room carefully for signs of bugs – you may find their translucent light-brown skins or poppy-seed-like excrement.

If you do get bitten try the following:

➡ Treat the itch with antihistamine.

➡ Thoroughly clean your luggage and launder all your clothes, sealing them afterwards in plastic bags to further protect them.

➡ Be sure to tell the management – if staff seem unconcerned or refuse to do anything about it complain to the local tourist office and write to us.

the wound with soap and water, and apply iodine-based antiseptic. If you are not prevaccinated you will need to receive rabies immunoglobulin as soon as possible.

Typhoid This serious bacterial infection is spread via food and water. Symptoms include high and slowly progressive fever, headache, a dry cough and stomach pain. Vaccination, recommended for all travellers spending more than a week in Malaysia, is not 100% effective so you must still be careful with what you eat and drink.

INSECT BITES & STINGS

Lice Most commonly inhabit your head and pubic area. Transmission is via close contact with an infected person. Treat with numerous applications of an antilice shampoo such as Permethrin.

Ticks Contracted after walking in rural areas. If you are bitten and experience symptoms such as a rash at the site of the bite or elsewhere, fever, or muscle aches, see a doctor. Doxycycline prevents tick-borne diseases.

Leeches Found in humid rainforest areas. Don't transmit disease but their bites can be itchy for weeks afterwards and can easily become infected. Apply an iodine-based antiseptic to any leech bite to prevent infection.

Bees or wasps If allergic to their stings, carry an injection of adrenaline (eg an Epipen) for emergency treatment.

Jellyfish In Malaysian waters most are not dangerous. If stung, pour vinegar onto the affected area to neutralise the poison. Take painkillers, and seek medical advice if your condition worsens.

SKIN PROBLEMS

Fungal rashes can occur in moist areas that get less air such as the groin, arm-

---

DRINKING WATER

⇒ Never drink tap water.

⇒ Check bottled water seals are intact at purchase.

⇒ Avoid ice in places that look dubious.

⇒ Avoid fresh juices if they have not been freshly squeezed or you suspect they may have been watered down.

⇒ Boiling water is the most efficient method of purifying it.

⇒ Iodine, the best chemical purifier, should not be used by pregnant women or those who suffer thyroid problems.

⇒ Ensure your water filter has a chemical barrier such as iodine and a pore size of less than four microns.

---

pits and between the toes. Treatment involves keeping the skin dry, avoiding chafing and using an antifungal cream such as Clotrimazole or Lamisil. The fungus *tinea versicolor* causes small, light-coloured patches, most commonly on the back, chest and shoulders. Consult a doctor.

Immediately wash all wounds in clean water and apply antiseptic. If you develop signs of infection (increasing pain and redness) see a doctor. Divers should be particularly careful with coral cuts as they become easily infected.

SUNBURN

Always use a strong sunscreen (at least SPF 30), and always wear a wide-brimmed hat and sunglasses outdoors. If you become sunburnt, one percent hydrocortisone cream applied twice daily to the burn is helpful.

TRAVELLERS DIARRHOEA

By far the most common problem affecting travellers, travellers diarrhoea is commonly caused by a bacterium. Treatment consists of staying well hydrated; use a solution such as Gastrolyte. Antibiotics such as Norfloxacin, Ciprofloxacin or Azithromycin will kill the bacteria quickly.

Loperamide is a 'stopper' only (it will slow the frequency of stools/bowel movements), but it can be helpful in certain situations, eg if you have to go on a long bus ride. Seek medical attention quickly if you do not respond to an appropriate antibiotic.

WOMEN'S HEALTH

Sanitary products are readily available in Malaysia. Heat, humidity and antibiotics can contribute to thrush. Treat with antifungal creams and pessaries such as Clotrimazole. A practical alternative is a tablet of fluconazole (Diflucan).

Internet Access

Internet cafes are everywhere; the going rate per hour is RM3. If you're travelling with a wi-fi–enabled device, you can get online at hundreds of cafes, restaurants, bars and many hotels for free.

Legal Matters

In any dealings with the local police forces it will pay to be deferential. You're most likely to come into contact with them either through reporting a crime (some of the big cities in Malaysia have tourist police stations for this purpose) or while driving. Minor misdemeanours may be overlooked, but don't count on it.

Drug trafficking carries a mandatory death penalty. A number of foreigners have been executed in Malaysia, some for possession of very small quantities of heroin. Even possession of small amounts of marijuana can bring down a lengthy jail sentence and a beating with the *rotan* (cane).

Medical Services

KL is an increasingly popular destination for health tourism, from cosmetic surgery to dental veneers. Medical centres and dentists are found in all the big malls and a private consultation will cost around RM35. Pharmacies are all over town; the most common is Guardian, in most malls.

Dentists

Dental Pro (☑2287 3333; www.dentalpro.org; 8 Lengkok Abdullah, Bangsar Utama; ◷10am-6pm Mon-Sat)

Pristine Dental Centre (☑2287 3782; 2nd fl, Mid Valley Megamall, Mid Valley City, Lingkaran Syed Putra; ◷10am-6pm)

Health Centres

Klinik Medicare (☑2287 7180; 2nd fl, Mid Valley Megamall, Mid Valley City, Lingkaran Syed Putra; ◷10am-10pm)

Twin Towers Medical Centre KLCC (☑2382 3500; www.ttmcklcc.com.my; Level 4, Suria KLCC, Jln Ampang; ◷8.30am-6pm Mon-Sat)

Hospitals

Hospital Kuala Lumpur (☑2615 5555; www.hkl.gov. my; Jln Pahang) North of the centre.

Tung Shin Hospital (☑2072 1655; http://tungshin. com.my; 102 Jln Pudu)

Pharmacies

Kien Fatt Medical Store (☑2072 1648; 59 Jln Petaling; ◷8.30am-5.30pm Mon-Sat; ⛽Pasar Seni) In business since 1943, this traditional pharmacy sells both Chinese and Western medicines. A qualified English-speaking doctor is available for consultations (RM13).

Money

Most banks and shopping malls provide international ATMs (typically on the ground floor or basement level). Moneychangers offer better rates than banks for changing cash and (at times) travellers cheques; they're usually open later and at weekends and are found in shopping malls.

ATMs & Credit Cards

MasterCard and Visa are the most widely accepted brands. Banks will accept credit cards for over-the-counter cash advances, or you can make ATM withdrawals if you have your PIN. Many banks are also linked to international banking networks such as Cirrus (the most common), Maestro and Plus, allowing withdrawals from overseas savings accounts.

Maybank (www.maybank2u.com.my), Malaysia's biggest bank with branches everywhere, accepts both Visa and MasterCard. Hongkong Bank accepts Visa, and the Standard Chartered Bank accepts MasterCard. If you have any questions about whether your cards will be accepted in Malaysia, ask your home bank about its reciprocal relationships with Malaysian banks.

Contact details for credit card companies in Malaysia:

American Express (☑2050 0000; www.americanexpress.com/malaysia)

Diners Card (☑2161 1055; www.diners.com.my)

MasterCard (☑1800 804 594; www.mastercard.com/sea)

Visa (☑1800 802 997; www.visa-asia.com)

Currency

The ringgit (RM) is made up of 100 sen. Coins in use are 1 sen, 5 sen, 10 sen, 20 sen and 50 sen; notes are RM1, RM5, RM10, RM50 and RM100.

Taxes & Refunds

There is no general sales tax but there is a government tax of 6% at some midrange and all top-end hotels and many larger restaurants, in addition to the 10% service fee. This is often expressed as '++' next to the price.

Travellers Cheques & Cash

Malaysian banks are efficient and there are plenty of moneychangers. Banks usually charge a commission for cash and cheques (around RM10 per transaction, with a possible extra fee for each cheque), whereas moneychangers have no charges but their rates are more variable.

All major brands of travellers cheques are accepted. Cash in major currencies is also readily exchanged, though the US dollar has a slight edge.

Opening Hours

Banks 10am to 3pm Monday to Friday, 9.30am to 11.30am Saturday

Restaurants noon to 2.30pm and 6pm to 10.30pm

Shops 9.30am to 7pm, malls 10am to 10pm

Post

Pos Malaysia Berhad runs a fast and efficient postal system. Post offices are open from 8am to 5pm from Monday to Saturday, but closed on the first Saturday of the month and on public holidays.

Aerograms and postcards cost 50 sen to send to any destination. Letters weighing 20g or less cost 90 sen to Asia, RM1.40 to Australia or New Zealand, RM1.50 to the UK and Europe, and RM1.80 to North America. A 1kg parcel to most destinations will cost around RM35 by sea and RM70 by air. Registered mail costs an extra RM3.90 (letters and parcels up to 2kg only). Main post offices sell packaging materials and stationery.

For international postal services, go to the main **Pos Malaysia office** (www.pos.com.my; Jln Raja Laut; ◷8.30am-6pm Mon-Sat, closed 1st Sat of month), across the river from Central Market. Branch post offices are found all over KL, including:

Pos Malaysia (Map p262; 48 Jln Telawi, Bangsar Baru)

Pos Malaysia (Jln TAR, near the crossing with Jln Sultan Ismail, Little India)

Pos Malaysia (3rd fl, Jln Sultan Ismail, Sungei Wang Plaza)

Pos Malaysia (Basement level, Suria KLCC, Jln Ampang)

DHL (www.dhl.com.my) Bangsar Baru (www.dhl.com.my; 60 Jln Telawi, Bangsar Baru; ◷9am-9pm Mon-Fri, 10am-6pm Sat, 11am-5pm Sun); Central Market (Map p262; www.dhl.com.my; Ground fl, Central Market, Jln Hang Kasturi; ◷10am-9.30pm).

Public Holidays

As well as fixed secular holidays, various religious festivals (which change dates annually) are national holidays. These include Chinese New Year (in January/February), the Hindu festival of Deepavali (in October/November), the Buddhist festival of Wesak (April/May) and the Muslim festivals of Hari Raya Haji, Hari Raya Puasa, Mawlid al-Nabi and Awal Muharram (Muslim New Year).

Fixed annual holidays include the following:

New Year's Day 1 January

Federal Territory Day 1 February (Kuala Lumpur and Putrajaya only)

Sultan of Selangor's Birthday Second Saturday in March (Selangor only)

Labour Day 1 May

Yang di-Pertuan Agong's (King's) Birthday First Saturday in June

Governor of Penang's Birthday Second Saturday in July (Penang only)

National Day (Hari Kebangsaan) 31 August

Christmas Day 25 December

School Holidays

Schools break for holidays five times a year. The actual dates vary from state to state but are generally in January (one week), March (two weeks), May (three weeks), August (one week) and October (four weeks).

Safe Travel

KL is generally very safe, but watch for pickpockets on crowded public transport. One ongoing irritation is the state of the pavements. The covers thrown over drains can give way suddenly, dumping you in the drink or worse, so walk around them. Flooding can also be a problem – carry an umbrella and be prepared to roll up your trousers to wade through giant puddles.

Animal Hazards

Rabies occurs in Malaysia, so any bite from an animal should be treated very seriously. Be cautious around monkeys, dogs and cats. On jungle treks look out for centipedes, scorpions, spiders and snakes. Mosquitoes are likely to be the biggest menace. The risk of malaria is low and antimalarial tablets are rarely recommended but dengue fever is a growing problem, so take precautions to avoid mosquito bites by covering up exposed skin or wearing a strong repellent containing DEET.

Scams

The most common scams involve seemingly friendly locals who invite you to join rigged card games, or shops who trick travellers into buying large amounts of gold jewellery or gems at elevated prices. Anyone who accosts you in the street asking 'where you come from' or claiming to have a 'relative studying abroad' may be setting you up for a scam – the best option is not to reply at all.

At the Malaysia–Thailand border, don't believe anyone who claims that you are legally required to change sums of money into ringgit or baht before crossing the border – no such regulation exists.

Theft & Violence

Malaysia is not particularly prone to theft or violence. However, muggings and bag snatches do happen, particularly after hours and in the poorer, rundown areas of cities. Be wary of demonstrations, particularly over religious or ethnic issues, as these can turn violent.

Use credit cards only at established businesses and guard your credit-card numbers closely.

Carry a small, sturdy padlock you can use for cheap hotel-room doors and hostel

AREA & TELEPHONE CODES

Country code for Malaysia ☎60

Directory enquiries ☎103

International access code from Malaysia ☎00

International operator ☎108

Kuala Lumpur ☎03

Melaka ☎06

Penang ☎04

Singapore ☎02

lockers, and to keep prying fingers out of your bags in left-luggage rooms.

Telephone

Landline services are provided by the national monopoly **Telekom Malaysia** (TM; www.tm.com.my).

Fax

Fax facilities are available at Telekom offices in the cities and at some main post offices. If you can't find one of these try a travel agency or large hotel.

International Calls

The easiest and cheapest way to make international calls is to buy a local SIM card for your mobile phone. Only certain payphones permit international calls. You can make operator-assisted international calls from local Telekom offices. To save money on landline calls, buy a prepaid international calling card (available from convenience stores).

Local Calls

Local calls cost 10 sen for three minutes. Payphones take coins or prepaid cards, which are available from Telekom offices and convenience stores. Some also take international credit cards. You'll also find a range of discount calling cards at convenience stores and mobile-phone counters.

Mobile Phones

If you have arranged global-roaming with your home provider, your GSM digital phone will automatically tune in to one of the region's digital networks. If not, buy a prepaid SIM card for one of the local networks on arrival. The rate for a local call is around 40 sen per minute. There are three mobile phone companies, all with similar call rates and prepaid packages:

Celcom (☎013 or 019 numbers; www.celcom.com.my)

DiGi (☎016 numbers; www.digi.com.my)

Maxis (☎012 or 017 numbers; www.maxis.com.my)

Time

Peninsular Malaysia is eight hours ahead of GMT/UTC (London). Noon in KL is

➡ 8pm in Los Angeles

➡ 11pm in New York

➡ 4am in London

➡ 2pm in Sydney and Melbourne

Toilets

Western-style sit-down loos are becoming the norm, but there are some places with Asian squat toilets. Toilet paper is not usually provided; instead, you will find a hose or a spout on the toilet seat, which you are supposed to use as a bidet, or

a bucket of water and a tap. If you're not comfortable with the 'hand-and-water' technique, carry packets of tissues or toilet paper wherever you go.

Public toilets in malls usually charge an entry fee, which often includes toilet paper.

Tourist Information

Tourism Malaysia (www.tourismmalaysia.gov.my) Has a network of domestic offices that are good for brochures and free maps but rather weak on hard factual information. Its overseas offices are useful for predeparture planning. There are regional offices in Kuala Lumpur, Melaka and Penang.

Visit KL (Map p248; ☎2698 0332; www.visitkl.gov.my; KL City Gallery, Merdeka Square; 🚇Masjid Jamek) Official city tourist office.

KL Tourist Association (Map p260; ☎2287 1831; www.klta.org.my; National Museum, Jln Damansara; ⏰9am-5pm Mon-Fri, to 1pm Sat) Good for brochures and general information on the city.

Malaysian Tourism Centre (MaTiC) (Map p250; ☎9235 4900; http://matic.gov.my; 109 Jln Ampang; ⏰8am-10pm; monorail Bukit Nanas) Housed in a mansion built in 1935 for rubber and tin tycoon Eu Tong Seng, this is KL's most useful tourist office. Also hosts good cultural performances.

Travellers with Disabilities

For the mobility impaired, KL, Melaka and Penang can be a nightmare. There are often no footpaths, kerbs can be very high, construction sites are everywhere, and crossings are few and far between. On the upside, taxis are cheap and both Malaysia Airlines and KTM (the national rail service) offer 50% discounts for travellers with disabilities.

Before setting off get in touch with your national support organisation (preferably with the travel officer, if there is one). Also try the following:

Accessible Journeys (☎800-846 4537; www.disabilitytravel.com) In the US.

Mobility International USA (☎541-343 1284; www.miusa.org) In the US.

Nican (☎02-6241 1220; www.nican.com.au) In Australia.

Tourism For All (☎0845 124 9971; www.tourismforall.org.uk) In the UK.

Visas

Visitors must have a passport valid for at least six months beyond the date of entry. You may also be asked to provide proof of a ticket for onward travel and sufficient funds to cover your stay. The following gives a brief overview of the visa requirements – full details are available on the website www.kln.gov.my.

Citizens of Israel cannot enter Malaysia. Nationals of most other countries are given a 30- or 60-day visa on arrival, depending on the expected length of stay. As a general rule, if you arrive by air you will be given 60 days automatically, though coming overland you may be given 30 days unless you specifically ask for a 60-day permit.

Visa Extensions

Depending on your nationality, it may be possible to extend your visa at an immigration office in KL, Melaka or Penang for an additional one or two months. Extensions tend to be granted only for genuine emergencies. It's normally easier to hop across the border to Thailand, Singapore or Indonesia and re-enter the country – this counts as a new visit, even if you re-enter the same day.

Women Travellers

The key to travelling with minimum hassle in Malaysia is to blend in with the locals, which means dressing modestly and being respectful, especially in areas of stronger Muslim religious sensibilities. Regardless of what local non-Muslim women wear, it's better to be safe than

sorry – we've had reports of attacks on women ranging from minor verbal aggravation to physical assault. Hard as it is to say, the truth is that women are much more likely to have problems in Malay-dominated areas, where attitudes are more conservative.

In Malay-dominated areas you can halve your hassles just by tying a bandanna over your hair (a minimal concession to the headscarf worn by most Muslim women). When visiting mosques, cover your head and limbs with a headscarf and sarong (many mosques lend these at the entrance). At the beach, most Malaysian women swim fully clothed in T-shirts and shorts, so don't even think about going topless.

Be proactive about your own safety. Treat overly friendly strangers, both male and female, with a good deal of caution. In cheap hotels check for small peepholes in the walls and doors; when you have a choice, stay in a Chinese-operated hotel. On island resorts, stick to crowded beaches, and choose a chalet close to reception and other travellers. After dark, take taxis and avoid walking alone in quiet or seedy parts of town.

Language

The official language of Kuala Lumpur, Melaka and Penang is Malay, or Bahasa Malaysia, as it's called by its speakers. It belongs to the Western Austronesian language family and is very similar to Indonesian.

There are several Indian and Chinese languages spoken in the region as well, such as Hokkien, Cantonese, Tamil and Malayalam. English is also widely understood.

Malay pronunciation is easy to master. Each letter always represents the same sound and most letters are pronounced the same as their English counterparts, with c pronounced as the 'ch' in 'chat' and sy as the 'sh' in 'ship'. Note also that kh is a guttural sound (like the 'ch' in the Scottish loch), and that gh is a throaty 'g' sound.

Syllables generally carry equal emphasis – the main exception is the unstressed e in words such as besar (big) – but the rule of thumb is to stress the second-last syllable.

BASICS

In Malaysia, kamu is an egalitarian second-person pronoun, equivalent to 'you' in English. The polite pronoun for the equivalent of English 'I/we' is kami. In polite speech, you wouldn't normally use first-person pronouns, but would refer to yourself by name or form of address, eg Makcik nak pergi ke pasar (Auntie wants to go to the market).

When addressing a man or a woman old enough to be your parent, use pakcik (uncle) or makcik (aunt). For someone only slightly older than yourself, use abang or bang (older brother) and kakak or kak (older sister). For people old enough to be your grandparents, datuk and nenek (grandfather and grandmother) are used. For a man or a woman you meet on the street you can also use encik or cik respectively.

Hello.	Helo.
Goodbye.	
(by person leaving)	Selamat tinggal.
(by person staying)	Selamat jalan.
Yes.	Ya.
No.	Tidak.
Please.	
(to ask for something)	Tolong.
(to offer something)	Silakan.
Thank you.	Terima kasih.
You're welcome.	Sama-sama.
Excuse me.	Maaf.
Sorry.	Minta maaf.
How are you?	Apa khabar?
Fine, thanks.	Khabar baik.
What's your name?	Siapa nama kamu?
My name is ...	Nama saya ...
Do you speak English?	Bolehkah anda berbicara Bahasa Inggeris?
I don't understand.	Saya tidak faham.

WANT MORE?

For in-depth language information and handy phrases, check out Lonely Planet's Malay Phrasebook. You'll find it at shop.lonelyplanet.com, or you can buy Lonely Planet's iPhone phrasebooks at the Apple App Store.

ACCOMMODATION

Do you have any rooms available?	Ada bilik kosong?
How much is it per night/person?	Berapa harga satu malam/orang?
Is breakfast included?	Makan pagi termasukkah?

air-con	pendingin udara
bathroom	bilik air
campsite	kawasan perkhemahan
double room	bilik untuk dua orang
guesthouse	rumah tetamu
hotel	hotel
mosquito coil	ubat nyamuk
single room	bilik untuk seorang
window	tingkap
youth hostel	asrama belia

DIRECTIONS

Where is ...?	Di mana ...?
What's the address?	Apakah alamatnya?
Can you write the address, please?	Tolong tuliskan alamat itu?
Can you show me (on the map)?	Tolong tunjukkan (di peta)?
Go straight ahead.	Jalan terus.
Turn left.	Belok kiri.
Turn right.	Belok kanan.

at the corner	di simpang
at the traffic lights	di tempat lampu isyarat
behind	di belakang
in front of	di hadapan
near	dekat
next to	di samping/di sebelah
opposite	berhadapan dengan

EATING & DRINKING

We'd like a table for (five), please.	Tolong bagi meja untuk (lima) orang.
Can I see the menu?	Minta senarai makanan?
What's in this dish?	Ini termasuk apa?
I'd like ...	Saya mahu...
I'm a vegetarian.	Saya makan sayur-sayuran sahaja.
Not too spicy, please.	Kurang pedas.
Please add extra chilli.	Tolong letak cili lebih.
Thank you, that was delicious.	Sedap sekali, terima kasih.
Please bring the bill.	Tolong bawa bil.

Key Words

| bottle | botol |
| breakfast | makan pagi |

children's menu	menu kanak-kanak
cold	sejuk
cup	cawan
dinner	makan malam
drink	minuman
food	makanan
food stall	gerai
fork	garfu
glass	gelas
grocery store	kedai makanan
highchair	kerusi tinggi
hot (warm)	panas
knife	pisau
lunch	makan tengahari
market	pasar
menu	menu
plate	pinggan
restaurant	restoran
spicy	pedas
spoon	sudu
vegetarian (food)	sayuran saja
with	dengan
without	tanpa

Meat & Fish

(dried) anchovies	ikan bilis
beef	daging lembu
brains	otak
catfish	ikan keli
chicken	ayam
cockles	kerang
crab	ketam
duck	itik
fish	ikan
freshwater fish	ikan air tawar
goat	kambing
lamb	anak biri-biri
liver	hati
lobster	udang karang
mussels	kepah
mutton	biri-biri
oysters	tiram
pig	babi
rabbit	arnab
salted dried fish	ikan kering
saltwater fish	ikan air masin
shrimp	udang
squid	sotong
tripe	perut

Fruit & Vegetables

apple	epal
banana	pisang
beans	kacang
cabbage	kubis
carrot	lobak
cauliflower	kubis bunga
coconut	kelapa
corn	jagung
cucumber	timun
eggplant	terung
guava	jambu
jackfruit	nangka
mango	mangga
mangosteen	manggis
mushrooms	kulat
onion	bawang
orange	oren
papaya	betik
peanuts	kacang
pineapple	nenas
potato	kentang
pumpkin	labu
soursop	durian belanda
starfruit	belimbing
watermelon	tembikai

Other

bread	roti
cake	kueh
chilli sauce	sambal
noodles	mee
oil	minyak
(black) pepper	lada hitam
rice (cooked)	nasi
rice (uncooked)	beras
salt	garam
soy sauce	kicap
sugar	gula
sweets	manisan
tofu	tahu
vinegar	cuka

Drinks

beer	bir
boiled water	air masak
citrus juice	air limau
coconut milk	air kelapa muda
coffee	kopi
cordial	pekatan
frothed tea	teh tarik
milk	susu
palm tree spirits	todi
rice wine	tuak
tea	teh
water	air
(grape) wine	wain

EMERGENCIES

Help!	Tolong!
Go away!	Pergi!
I'm lost.	Saya sesat.
There's been an accident.	Ada kemalangan.
Call a doctor!	Panggil doktor!
Call the police!	Panggil polis!
I'm ill.	Saya sakit.
It hurts here.	Sini sakit.
I'm allergic to (antibiotics).	Saya alergik kepada (antibiotik).

SHOPPING & SERVICES

I'd like to buy ...	Saya nak beli ...
I'm just looking.	Saya nak tengok saja.
Can I look at it?	Boleh saya lihat barang itu?
I don't like it.	Saya tak suka ini.
How much is it?	Berapa harganya?
It's too expensive.	Mahalnya.
Can you lower the price?	Boleh kurang sedikit?
There's a mistake in the bill.	Bil ini salah.

Signs

Masuk	Entrance
Keluar	Exit
Buka	Open
Tutup	Closed
Pertanyaan	Information
Dilarang	Prohibited
Tandas	Toilets
Lelaki	Men
Perempuan	Women

credit card	*kad kredit*
mobile phone	*telefon bimbit*
phonecard	*kad telefon*
post office	*pejabat pos*
signature	*tanda tangan*
tourist office	*pejabat pelancong*

TIME & DATES

What time is it?	*Pukul berapa?*
It's (seven) o'clock.	*Pukul (tujuh).*
Half past (one).	*Pukul (satu) setengah.*
in the morning	*pagi*
in the afternoon	*tengahari*
in the evening	*petang*
yesterday	*semalam*
today	*hari ini*
tomorrow	*esok*
Monday	*hari Isnin*
Tuesday	*hari Selasa*
Wednesday	*hari Rabu*
Thursday	*hari Khamis*
Friday	*hari Jumaat*
Saturday	*hari Sabtu*
Sunday	*hari Minggu*
January	*Januari*
February	*Februari*
March	*Mac*
April	*April*
May	*Mei*
June	*Jun*
July	*Julai*
August	*Ogos*
September	*September*
October	*Oktober*
November	*November*
December	*Disember*

Question Words

What?	*Apa?*
When?	*Bila?*
Where?	*Di mana?*
Which?	*Yang mana?*
Who?	*Siapa?*
Why?	*Kenapa?*

TRANSPORT

Public Transport

bicycle-rickshaw	*beca*
boat	*bot*
bus	*bas*
plane	*kapal terbang*
ship	*kapal*
taxi	*teksi*
train	*keretapi*

I want to go to ...	*Saya nak ke ...*
What time does the (bus) leave?	*(Bas) bertolak pukul berapa?*
What time does the (train) arrive?	*(Keretapi) tiba pukul berapa?*
Does the bus stop at the (restaurant)?	*Bas ini berhenti di (restoran)?*
Can you tell me when we get to ...?	*Tolong beritahu saya bila kita sudah sampai di ...?*
I want to get off at ...	*Saya nak turun di ...*
The (bus) has been delayed.	*(Bas) itu telah terlambat.*
The (train) has been cancelled.	*(Keretapi) itu telah dibatalkan.*

first class	*kelas pertama*
one-way ticket	*tiket sehala*
return ticket	*tiket pergi-balik*
second class	*kelas kedua bisnis*

first	*pertama*
last	*terakhir*
next	*berikutnya*

airport	*lapangan terbang*
bus stop	*perhentian bas*
ticket office	*pejabat tiket*
timetable	*jadual*
train station	*stesen keretapi*

Driving & Cycling

I'd like to hire a ...	*Saya nak menyewa ...*
bicycle	*basikal*
car	*kereta*
jeep	*jip*
motorcycle	*motosikal*

LANGUAGE GLOSSARY

child seat	*tempat duduk bayi*
diesel	*disel*
helmet	*topi keledar*
mechanic	*mekanik*
petrol/gas	*minyak*
pump	*pam*
service station	*stesen minyak*
unleaded petrol	*petrol tanpa plumbum*
Is this the road to ...?	*Inikah jalan ke ...?*
How many kilometres?	*Berapa kilometer?*
Can I park here?	*Boleh saya letak kereta di sini?*
How long can I park here?	*Beberapa lama boleh saya letak kereta di sini?*
The (car) has broken down at ...	*(Kereta) saya telah rosak di ...*
The (motorbike) won't start.	*(Motosikal) saya tidak dapat dihidupkan.*
I have a flat tyre.	*Tayarnya kempis.*
I've run out of petrol.	*Minyak sudah habis.*
I've had an accident.	*Saya terlibat dalam kemalangan.*

Numbers

1	*satu*
2	*dua*
3	*tiga*
4	*empat*
5	*lima*
6	*enam*
7	*tujuh*
8	*lapan*
9	*sembilan*
10	*sepuluh*
20	*dua puluh*
30	*tiga puluh*
40	*empat puluh*
50	*lima puluh*
60	*enam puluh*
70	*tujuh puluh*
80	*lapan puluh*
90	*sembilan puluh*
100	*seratus*
1000	*seribu*

GLOSSARY

adat – Malay customary law

alor – groove; furrow; main channel of a river

ampang – dam

Baba-Nonya – descendants of Chinese immigrants to Melaka and Penang who intermarried with Malays and adopted many Malay customs; also known as Peranakan, or Straits Chinese; sometimes spelt Nyonya

Bahasa Malaysia – Malay language; also known as Bahasa Melayu

bandar – seaport; town

baru – new; common in placenames

batik – technique of imprinting cloth with dye to produce multicoloured patterns

batu – stone; rock; milepost

bendahara – chief minister

bomoh – spiritual healer

bukit – hill

bumiputra – literally, sons of the soil; indigenous Malays

bunga raya – hibiscus flower (national flower of Malaysia)

genting – mountain pass

gopuram – Hindu temple tower

istana – palace

jalan – road

kampung – village; also spelt kampong

kedai kopi – coffee shop

kongsi – Chinese clan organisations, also known as ritual brotherhoods, heavenman-earth societies, triads or secret societies; meeting house for Chinese of the same clan

kopitiam – traditional coffee shop

kota – fort; city

kris – traditional Malay wavy-bladed dagger

KTM – Keretapi Tanah Melayu; Malaysian Railways System

kuala – river mouth; place where a tributary joins a larger river

laut – sea

lebuh – street

lorong – narrow street; alley

LRT – Light Rail Transit (Kuala Lumpur)

mamak – Indian Muslim

masjid – mosque

merdeka – independence

muezzin – mosque official who calls the faithful to prayer

negara – country

negeri – state

nonya – see Baba-Nonya

Orang Asli – literally, Original People; Malaysian aborigines

padang – grassy area; field; also the city square

pantai – beach
pasar – market
pasar malam – night market
pelabuhan – port
penghulu – chief or village head
pengkalan – quay
perahu – sampan; small boat
Peranakan – refers to the Baba-Nonya or Straits Chinese
pulau – island

raja – prince; ruler
raja muda – crown prince; heir apparent
rakyat – common people

rattan – stems from climbing palms used for wickerwork and canes

sarong – all-purpose cloth, often sewn into a tube, and worn by women, men and children
silat – martial-arts dance form
Straits Chinese – see Baba-Nonya
sultan – ruler of one of Malaysia's nine states
sungai – river
syariah – Islamic system of law

tanjung – headland

tasik – lake
teluk – bay; sometimes spelt telok
temenggong – Malay administrator
tunku – prince

wayang – Chinese opera
wayang kulit – shadow-puppet theatre
wisma – office block or shopping centre

yang di-pertuan agong – Malaysia's head of state, or 'king'

FOOD GLOSSARY

achar – vegetable and/or fruit pickle
ais kacang – dessert of ice shavings topped with syrups, coconut milk, red beans, seeds and jelly
aloo gobi – Indian potato-and-cauliflower dish
ayam – chicken
ayam goreng – fried chicken

bak chang – rice dumpling filled with savoury or sweet meat and wrapped in leaves
bak kut teh – pork ribs and parts stewed with garlic and Chinese medicinal herbs
belacan – fermented prawn paste
belacan kangkong – water convolvulus stir-fried in prawn paste
bhindi – okra (lady's fingers)
biryani – steamed basmati rice oven-baked with spices and meat, seafood or vegetables
brinjal – aubergine (eggplant)

carrot cake – firm radish cake cubed and stir-fried with egg, garlic, chilli, soy sauce, and bean sprouts; also known as chye tow kway
cendol – dessert of shaved ice and mung-bean-flour 'pasta' doused with coconut milk and liquid palm sugar

chapati – griddle-fried whole-wheat bread
char kway teow – wide rice noodles stir-fried with cockles, prawns, Chinese sausage, eggs, bean sprouts, and soy and chilli sauces
char siew – sweet and sticky barbecued pork fillet
char yoke – crispy-skinned roasted pork fillet
chicken-rice – steamed chicken, served with rice boiled or steamed in chicken stock, slices of cucumber and a chilli-ginger sauce
chilli padi – extremely hot small chilli
choi sum – popular Chinese green vegetable, served steamed with oyster sauce
claypot rice – rice cooked in a clay pot with chicken, mushroom, Chinese sausage and soy sauce
congee – Chinese porridge

daun kunyit – turmeric leaf
daun pisang – banana leaf, often used as a plate in Malaysia
daun salam – leaves used much like bay leaves in cooking
dhal – dish of puréed lentils
dim sum – sweet and savoury minidishes served at breakfast and lunch; also known as dian xin or yum cha
dosa – large, light, crispy pancake

fish sauce – liquid made from fermented anchovies and salt
fish-head curry – head and 'shoulders' of large fish such as red snapper in curry sauce; also known as kepala ikan

gado gado – cold dish of bean sprouts, potatoes, long beans, bean curd, rice cakes and prawn crackers, topped with a spicy peanut sauce
galangal – ginger-like root used to flavour various dishes
garam masala – sweet, mild mixture of freshly ground spices
garoupa – white fish popular in Southeast Asia
ghee – clarified butter
gula jawa – brown palm-sugar sold in thin blocks

halal – food prepared according to Muslim dietary laws
hoisin sauce – thick sweet-spicy sauce made from soya beans, red beans, sugar, flour, vinegar, salt, garlic, sesame, chillies and spices
Hokkien mee – yellow noodles fried with sliced meat, boiled squid, prawns and strips of fried egg; in Penang, hot and spicy prawn and pork noodle soup

idli – steamed rice cake
ikan asam – fried fish in sour tamarind curry

ikan bilis – small, deep-fried anchovies

kangkong – water convolvulus; thick-stemmed type of spinach

kari ayam – curried chicken

kecap – soy sauce

keema – spicy minced meat

kepala ikan – fish head, usually in curry or grilled

kofta – minced-meat or vegetable ball

kopi-o – black coffee

korma – mild Indian curry with yoghurt sauce

kueh melayu – sweet pancakes with peanuts, raisins and sugar

kueh mueh – Malay cakes

kway teow – broad rice-noodles

laksa – noodles in a spicy coconut soup with bean sprouts, quail eggs, prawns, shredded chicken and dried bean curd; also called Nonya laksa to differentiate it from Penang laksa (or asam laksa), a version that has a prawn paste and tamarind-flavoured gravy

lassi – yoghurt-based drink

lombok – type of hot chilli

lontong – rice cakes in spicy coconut-milk gravy topped with grated coconut and, sometimes, bean curd and egg

lor mee – noodles with slices of meat, eggs and a dash of vinegar in a dark brown sauce

masala dosa – thin pancake rolled around spicy vegetables with rasam on the side

mee – noodles

mee goreng – fried noodles

mee pok – flat noodles made with egg and wheat

mee rebus – yellow noodles served in a thick sweetish sauce made from sweet potatoes and garnished with sliced hard-boiled eggs and green chillies

mee siam – white thin noodles in a sweet and sour gravy made with tamarind

mee soto – noodle soup with shredded chicken

murtabak – roti canai filled with pieces of mutton, chicken or vegetables

naan – tear-shaped leavened bread baked in a clay oven

nasi – rice

nasi biryani – saffron rice flavoured with spices and garnished with cashew nuts, almonds and raisins

nasi campur – buffet of curried meats, fish and vegetables, served with rice

nasi goreng – fried rice

nasi lemak – rice boiled in coconut milk, served with ikan bilis, peanuts and a curry dish

nasi padang – Malay rice and accompanying meat and vegetable dishes

pakora – vegetable fritter

pan mee – wide, thick wheat noodles tossed with dark soy and topped with ground pork, *ikan bilis* and shredded cloud ear mushrooms

pappadam – Indian cracker

phrik – chillies

pilau – rice fried in ghee and mixed with nuts, then cooked in stock

pisang goreng – banana fritter

popiah – similar to a spring roll, but not fried

pudina – mint sauce

raita – side dish of cucumber, yoghurt and mint

rasam – spicy soup

rendang – spicy coconut curry with beef or chicken

rijsttafel – literally 'rice table'; a buffet of Indonesian dishes

rogan josh – stewed mutton in a rich sauce

rojak – salad doused in a peanut-sauce dressing that may contain shrimp paste

roti – bread

roti canai – unleavened flaky bread cooked with ghee on a hotplate; eaten dipped in dhal or curry; also known as *paratha* or *roti prata*

saag – spicy chopped-spinach dish

sambal – sauce of chilli, onions and prawn paste that has been fried

sambal udang – hot curried prawns

sambar – fiery mixture of vegetables, lentils and split peas

samosa – pastry filled with vegetables or meat

santan – coconut milk

satay – pieces of chicken, beef or mutton that are skewered and grilled

Sichuan – region in south central China famous for its spicy cuisine

soto ayam – spicy chicken soup with vegetables and potatoes

steamboat – meat, seafood and vegetables cooked at the table by being dipped into a pot of boiling clear stock

tamarind – large bean from the tamarind tree with a brittle shell and a dark brown, sticky pulp; used for its sweet-sour taste

tandoori – Indian style of cooking in which marinated meat is baked in a clay oven

taro – vegetable with leaves like spinach, stalks like asparagus and a starchy root similar in size and taste to the potato

tauhu goreng – fried bean curd and bean sprouts in peanut sauce

teh tarik – tea made with evaporated milk, which is literally pulled or stretched (tarik) from one glass to another

teh-o – tea without milk

tikka – small pieces of meat or fish served off the bone and marinated in yoghurt before baking

tom yam – tomato-red hot-and-sour spicy seafood soup

umai – raw fish marinated and served with onions

won ton – mee soup dish with shredded chicken or braised beef

yong tau fu – bean curd stuffed with minced meat

yu tiao – deep-fried pastry eaten for breakfast or as a dessert

yu yuan mian – fish-ball soup

Behind the Scenes

SEND US YOUR FEEDBACK

We love to hear from travellers – your comments keep us on our toes and help make our books better. Our well-travelled team reads every word on what you loved or loathed about this book. Although we cannot reply individually to your submissions, we always guarantee that your feedback goes straight to the appropriate authors, in time for the next edition. Each person who sends us information is thanked in the next edition – and the most useful submissions are rewarded with a selection of digital PDF chapters.

Visit **lonelyplanet.com/contact** to submit your updates and suggestions or to ask for help. Our award-winning website also features inspirational travel stories, news and discussions.

Note: We may edit, reproduce and incorporate your comments in Lonely Planet products such as guidebooks, websites and digital products, so let us know if you don't want your comments reproduced or your name acknowledged. For a copy of our privacy policy visit lonelyplanet.com/privacy.

OUR READERS

Many thanks to the travellers who used the last edition and wrote to us with helpful hints, useful advice and interesting anecdotes: Tammy Bare, Ronald Beers, Jonathan Boyle, Pepe Clemente, Mat Mannion, Carolyn Oliff, Michelle Reiner, Jennifer Segail, Christopher Smith, Gemma Stewart, Nigel Teasdale, Stefan Tuchila

AUTHOR THANKS

Simon Richmond

Terima kasih to Laura at Lonely Planet HQ for commissioning me, and to my trusted friends in Malaysia, including Alex Yong, Nani Kahar, Peter Kiernan, Andrew Sebastian, Claudia Low, David Hogan Jr, Narelle Mc-Murtrie, Chris Bauer, Eddy Chew, Adly Rizal, Karl Steinberg and Chris Ong. Also thanks to Jeffrey Lim, Pakhruddin Sulaiman, Ng Seksan, Noraza Yusof, Charles Steven, Paula Conway and Grey Yeoh for assistance with research.

ACKNOWLEDGMENTS

Cover photograph: Thean Hou Temple, Gavin Hellier/AWL.

THIS BOOK

This 3rd edition of Lonely Planet's *Kuala Lumpur, Melaka & Penang* guidebook was researched and written by Simon Richmond, who also coauthored the previous edition with Celeste Brash. The 1st edition was written by Joe Bindloss and Celeste Brash. This guidebook was commissioned in Lonely Planet's Melbourne office, and produced by the following:

Commissioning Editor Laura Stansfeld

Coordinating Editors Carolyn Boicos, Erin Richards

Senior Cartographers Julie Sheridan, Diana Von Holdt

Book Designer Jessica Rose

Managing Editors Sasha Baskett, Bruce Evans

Senior Editor Catherine Naghten

Assisting Editors Katie Connolly, Kate Evans, Charlotte Orr

Assisting Cartographer Rachel Imeson

Cover Research Naomi Parker

Language Content Branislava Vladisavljevic

Thanks to Anita Banh, Ryan Evans, Larissa Frost, Genesys India, Jouve India, Indra Kilfoyle, Wayne Murphy, Chad Parkhill, Trent Paton, Martine Power, Dianne Schallmeiner

Index

See also separate subindexes for:

🍴 **EATING P241**

🍷 **DRINKING & NIGHTLIFE P242**

☆ **ENTERTAINMENT P242**

🛍 **SHOPPING P242**

🏃 **SPORTS & ACTIVITIES P243**

🛏 **SLEEPING P244**

✖ EATING

Sights 000
Map Pages 000
Photo Pages 000

SPORTS & ACTIVITIES

Kuala Lumpur Maps

Map Legend

Sights
- Beach
- Buddhist
- Castle
- Christian
- Hindu
- Islamic
- Jewish
- Monument
- Museum/Gallery
- Ruin
- Winery/Vineyard
- Zoo
- Other Sight

Eating
- Eating

Drinking & Nightlife
- Drinking & Nightlife
- Cafe

Entertainment
- Entertainment

Shopping
- Shopping

Sleeping
- Sleeping
- Camping

Sports & Activities
- Diving/Snorkelling
- Canoeing/Kayaking
- Skiing
- Surfing
- Swimming/Pool
- Walking
- Windsurfing
- Other Sports & Activities

Information
- Post Office
- Tourist Information

Transport
- Airport
- Border Crossing
- Bus
- Cable Car/Funicular
- Cycling
- Ferry
- Monorail
- Parking
- S-Bahn
- Taxi
- Train/Railway
- Tram
- Tube Station
- U-Bahn
- Underground Train Station
- Other Transport

Routes
- Tollway
- Freeway
- Primary
- Secondary
- Tertiary
- Lane
- Unsealed Road
- Plaza/Mall
- Steps
- Tunnel
- Pedestrian Overpass
- Walking Tour
- Walking Tour Detour
- Path

Boundaries
- International
- State/Province
- Disputed
- Regional/Suburb
- Marine Park
- Cliff
- Wall

Geographic
- Hut/Shelter
- Lighthouse
- Lookout
- Mountain/Volcano
- Oasis
- Park
- Pass
- Picnic Area
- Waterfall

Hydrography
- River/Creek
- Intermittent River
- Swamp/Mangrove
- Reef
- Canal
- Water
- Dry/Salt/Intermittent Lake
- Glacier

Areas
- Beach/Desert
- Cemetery (Christian)
- Cemetery (Other)
- Park/Forest
- Sportsground
- Sight (Building)
- Top Sight (Building)

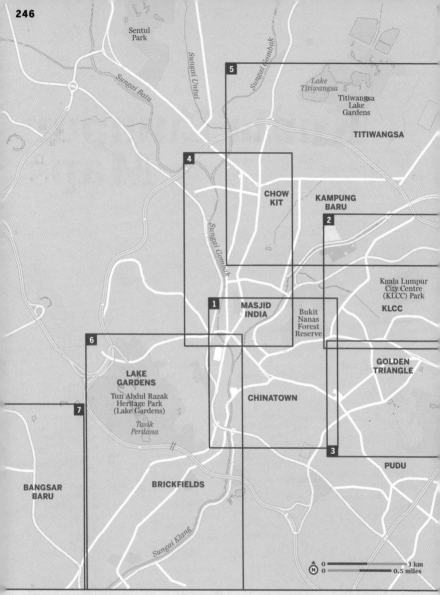

MAP INDEX

CHINATOWN & MERDEKA SQUARE

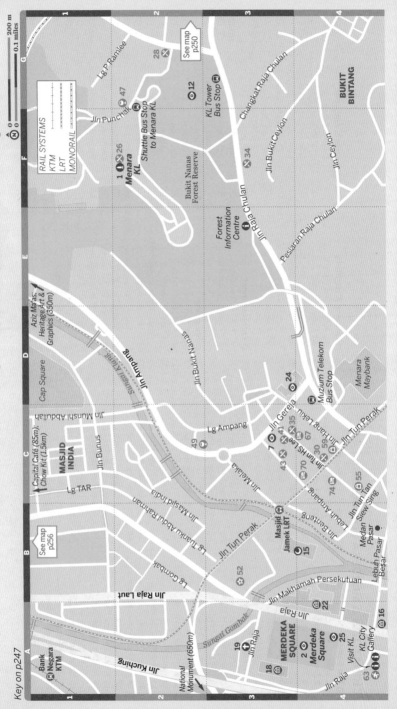

Key on p247

See map p256

See map p250

0   200 m
0   0.1 miles

RAIL SYSTEMS
KTM
LRT
MONORAIL

BUKIT BINTANG

Jln P Ramlee

Jln Punchak

Menara KL

Shuttle Bus Stop to Menara KL

KL Tower Bus Stop

Changkat Raja Chulan

Jln Bukit Ceylon

Jln Ceylon

Bukit Nanas Forest Reserve

Forest Information Centre

Jln Raja Chulan

Pesiaran Raja Chulan

Aziz Ma'ras; Heritage Art & Graphics (350m)

Cap Square

Jln Munshi Abdullah

Jln Bunus

MASJID INDIA

Lg TAR

Capital Café (85m); Chow Kit (1.5km)

Sungai Klang

Jln Ampang

Jln Bukit Nanas

Jln Bukit Nanas

Lg Ampang

Jln Gereja

Muzium Telekom Bus Stop

Menara Maybank

Jln Hang Lekiu

Jln Tun Perak

Jln Malaka

Jln HS Lee

Jln Tun HS Lee

Lg Tuanku Abdul Rahman

Jln Masjid India

Lg Gombak

Jln Tun Perak

Masjid Jamek LRT

Lebuh Ampang

Jln Tun Tan

Jln Tun Perak

Jln Benteng

Medan Siew Sing

Lebuh Pasar Besar

Jln Makhamah Persekutuan

Jln Raja Laut

National Monument (650m)

Jln Kuching

Sungai Gombak

Jln Raja

Jln Raja

Jln Raja

MERDEKA SQUARE

Merdeka Square

KL City Gallery

Visit KL

Bank Negara KTM

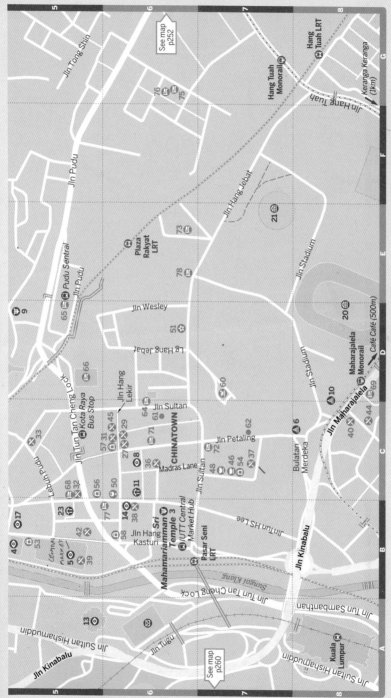

500 m
0.25 miles

RAIL SYSTEMS
KTM
LRT
MONORAIL

Jln Ampang

Jln Tun Razak

Jln U Thant

Jln Langgak Golf

Jln Tun Razak

47

46

28

40

8

13

Jln Binjai

Persiaran Stonor

Jln Stonor

4

11

Kuala Lumpur
City Centre
(KLCC) Park

Jln Ampang

16

10

9

Pesiaran KLCC

Jln Kia Peng

See map
p258

23

Jln Mayang

27

5

20

Jln Dato' Kwan Seng

KLCC
LRT

15

34

45

2

32

41

Jln Sungai Baharu

Ampang Elevated Hwy

12

25

36

1

Petronas
Towers

30

22

43

Jln Pinang

Sungai Klang

26

Jln P Ramlee

Jln Perak

39

31

24

Jln Sultan Ismail

Kampung Baru
LRT

6

42

29

33

Jln Ampang

37

Jln Perak

Jln P Ramlee

17

Pasar
Minggu
Market

Jln Raja Muda Musa

Sungai Klang

Muslim
Cemetery

See map
p258

Bukit
Nanas
Forest
Reserve

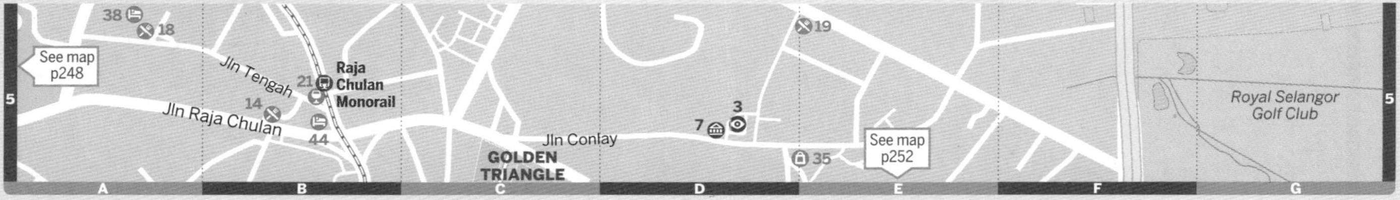

38
18
See map p248
Jln Tengah
21
Raja Chulan Monorail
14
Jln Raja Chulan
44
GOLDEN TRIANGLE
Jln Conlay
7
3
19
35
See map p252
Royal Selangor Golf Club
A
B
C
D
E
F
G
5
5

Top Sights (p50)
1 Petronas Towers B3

Sights (p52)
2 Aquaria KLCC C4
3 Badan Warisan Malaysia D5
4 Dharma Realm Guan Yin Sagely Monastery D2
Galeri Petronas .... (see 36)
5 KLCC Park C3
6 Muslim Cemetery A2
Petrosains .... (see 36)
7 Rumah Penghulu Abu Seman D5
8 Tabung Haji E2

Eating (p59)
9 Acme Bar & Coffee D2
Bisou .... (see 36)
10 Cantaloupe D2
Cilantro .... (see 46)
11 Dharma Realm Guan Yin Sagely Monastery Canteen D2
12 il Lido B2
Little Penang Kafé .... (see 36)
13 LivingFood F3
14 Marco Polo B5
15 Melur & Thyme C3
16 Nasi Kandar Pelita D2
17 Sisters Kitchen A4
Strato .... (see 10)
18 Sushi Hinata A5
19 Top Hat E5

Drinking & Nightlife (p65)
Apartment Downtown .... (see 36)
20 Butter Factory KL C4
Claret .... (see 10)
21 Heli Lounge Bar B5
22 Marini's on 57 .... B3
23 Marketplace C1
24 Neo Tamarind A4
25 RAWcoffee B2
26 Rum Jungle B3
27 Sky Bar D4
28 Tate E1
29 Zouk A3

Entertainment (p66)
30 Dewan Filharmonik Petronas C3
31 KL Live A4
32 Kuala Lumpur Convention Centre C4
33 Saloma A3
TGV Cineplex, Suria KLCC ... (see 36)
Zouk Club .... (see 29)

Shopping (p69)
Aseana .... (see 36)
Cocoa Boutique .... (see 33)
iKARRTiNi .... (see 36)
34 Kinokuniya C3
35 Kompleks Kraf Kuala Lumpur E5
Pucuk Rebung .... (see 36)
36 Suria KLCC C3
Tenmoku Pottery .... (see 36)

Sports & Activities (p219)
37 Malaysian Travel Business A3
Tour 51 Malaysia .... (see 37)

Sleeping (p131)
38 E&O Residences Kuala Lumpur A5
39 Fraser Place Kuala Lumpur B4
40 G Tower Hotel E2
41 Grand Hyatt Kuala Lumpur C4
42 Hotel Maya A2
43 Impiana B4
44 Lodge Paradize Hotel B5
45 Mandarin Oriental C3
46 MiCasa All Suite Hotel F3
Traders Hotel Kuala Lumpur (see 27)
47 Villa Samadhi G3

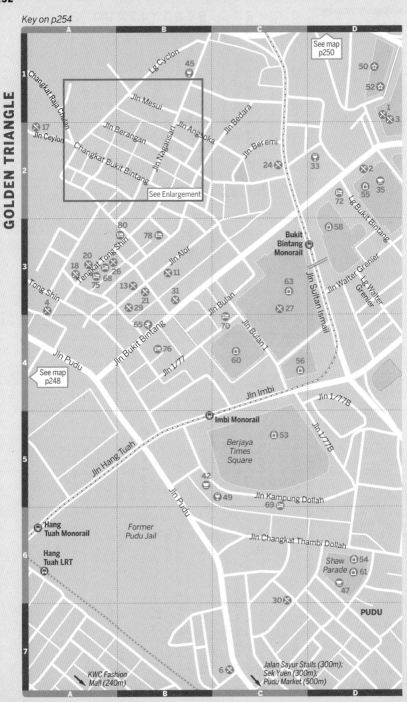

GOLDEN TRIANGLE

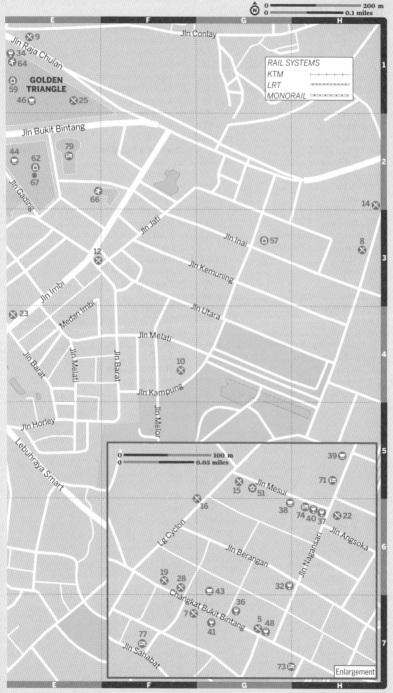

GOLDEN TRIANGLE *Map on p252*

GOLDEN TRIANGLE

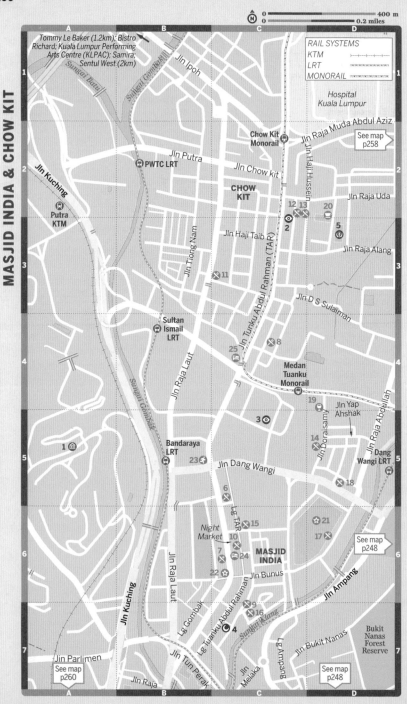

0   400 m
0   0.2 miles

RAIL SYSTEMS
KTM
LRT
MONORAIL

Tommy Le Baker (1.2km); Bistro
Richard; Kuala Lumpur Performing
Arts Centre (KLPAC); Samira;
Sentul West (2km)

Jln Ipoh

Sungai Batu

Sungai Gombak

Hospital
Kuala Lumpur

Jln Kuching

Jln Putra

PWTC LRT

Chow Kit
Monorail

Jln Raja Muda Abdul Aziz

Jln Chow kit

See map
p258

Putra
KTM

Sungai Batu

CHOW
KIT

Jln Haji Hussein

Jln Raja Uda

12 13
🍴   🍴
2

20

5

Jln Haji Taib

Jln Raja Alang

Jln Tiong Nam

11

Jln Tunku Abdul Rahman (TAR)

Jln D S Sulaiman

Sungai Gombak

Sultan
Ismail
LRT

25

8

Medan
Tuanku
Monorail

Jln Raja Laut

3

19

Jln Yap
Ahshak

Jln Raja Abdullah

1

Bandaraya
LRT

23

14

Jln Doraisamy

Dang
Wangi LRT

Jln Dang Wangi

18

6

Lg TAR

15

21

Night
Market

10

17

See map
p248

Jln Kuching

Jln Raja Laut

7 24

MASJID
INDIA

22

Jln Bunus

Lg Gombak

Lg Tuanku Abdul Rahman

9
16

Jln Ampang

4

Sungai Klang

Lg Ampang

Jln Bukit Nanas

Bukit
Nanas
Forest
Reserve

Jln Parlimen

Jln Tun Perak

Jln
Melaka

See map
p248

Jln Raja

See map
p260

MASJID INDIA & CHOW KIT

MASJID INDIA & CHOW KIT

KAMPUNG BARU & TITIWANGSA

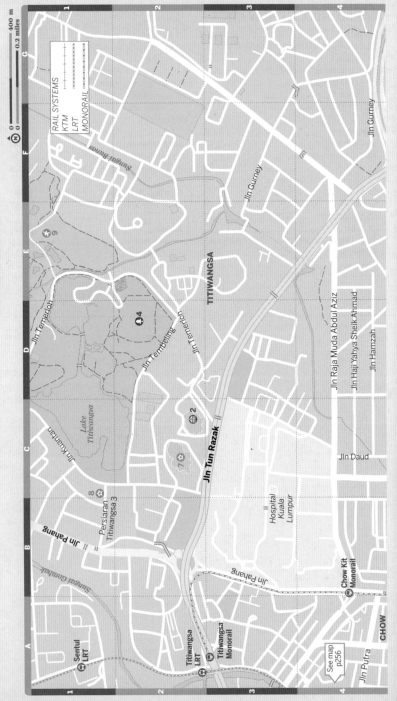

0 400 m
0 0.2 miles

RAIL SYSTEMS
KTM
LRT
MONORAIL

Sungai Batus

Jln Gurney

Jln Gurney

Jln Temeloh

TITIWANGSA

Jln Temeloh

Jln Tembeling

Jln Temeloh

Jln Raja Muda Abdul Aziz

Jln Haji Yahya Sheik Ahmad

Jln Hanzah

Lake
Titiwangsa

Jln Kuantan

Jln Tun Razak

Jln Daud

Persiaran
Titiwangsa 3

Jln Pahang

Hospital
Kuala
Lumpur

Sungai Gombak

Jln Pahang

Chow Kit
Monorail

Sentul
LRT

Titiwangsa
LRT

Titiwangsa
Monorail

CHOW

See map
p256

Jln Putra

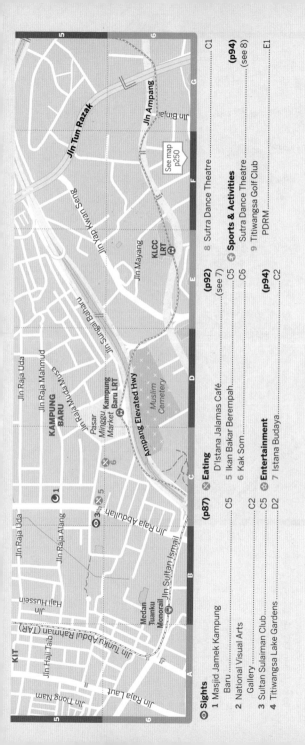

Sights (p87)

1 Masjid Jamek Kampung
   Baru C5
2 National Visual Arts
   Gallery C2
3 Sultan Sulaiman Club C5
4 Titiwangsa Lake Gardens D2

Eating (p92)

   D'Istana Jalamas Café .... (see 7)
5 Ikan Bakar Berempah C5
6 Kak Som C6

Entertainment (p94)

7 Istana Budaya C2

   Sutra Dance Theatre C1

Sports & Activities (p94)

   Sutra Dance Theatre .... (see 8)
9 Titiwangsa Golf Club E1
   PDRM C2

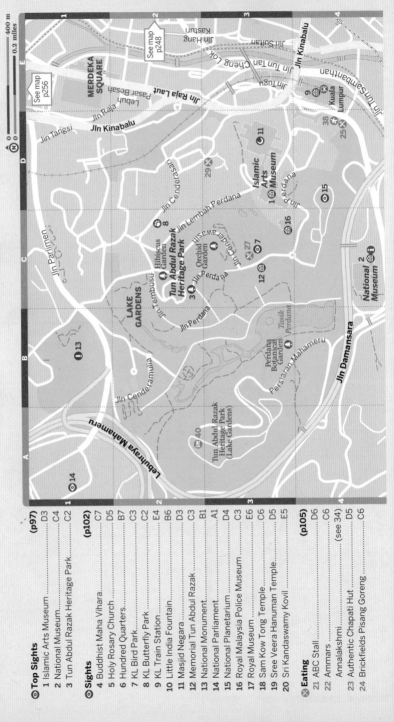

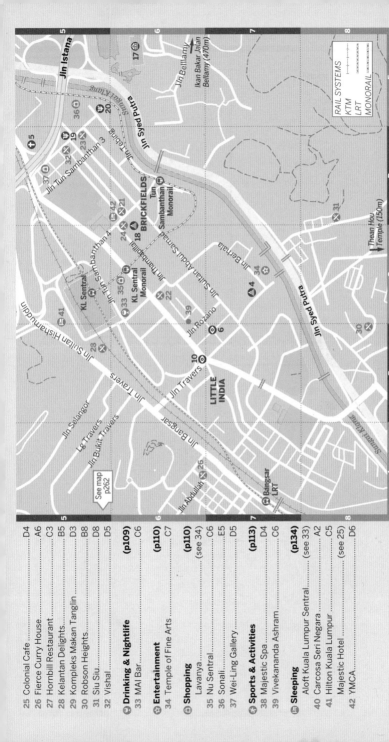

LAKE GARDENS & BRICKFIELDS

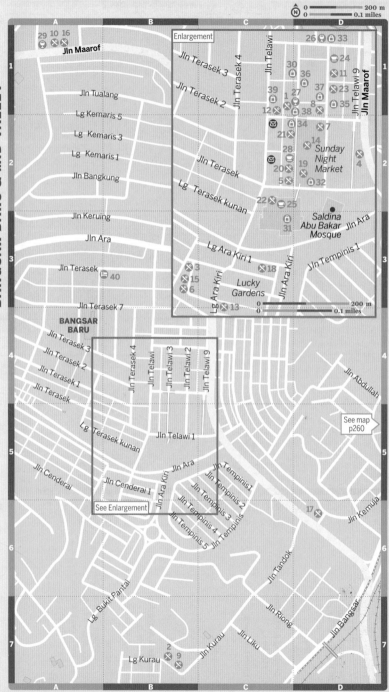

BANGSAR BARU & MID VALLEY

Enlargement

See map p260

See Enlargement

BANGSAR BARU & MID VALLEY

Our Story

A beat-up old car, a few dollars in the pocket and a sense of adventure. In 1972 that's all Tony and Maureen Wheeler needed for the trip of a lifetime – across Europe and Asia overland to Australia. It took several months, and at the end – broke but inspired – they sat at their kitchen table writing and stapling together their first travel guide, *Across Asia on the Cheap*. Within a week they'd sold 1500 copies. Lonely Planet was born.

Today, Lonely Planet has offices in Melbourne, London and Oakland, with more than 600 staff and writers. We share Tony's belief that 'a great guidebook should do three things: inform, educate and amuse'.

Our Writer

Simon Richmond

Coordinating Author Simon first started travelling in Malaysia back in the early 1990s. A lot has changed since, but the country remains among Simon's favourite destinations for its easily accessible blend of cultures, landscapes, adventure and, crucially, lip-smacking range of cuisines. This is the second time the award-winning travel writer and photographer has helmed Lonely Planet's *Kuala Lumpur, Melaka & Penang* guide. He's also the coordinating author of Lonely Planet's *Malaysia, Singapore & Brunei* guide, as well as a shelf-load of other titles for this and other publishers. Follow his travel adventures on www.simonrichmond.com.

Read more about Simon at:
lonelyplanet.com/members/simonrichmond

Published by Lonely Planet Publications Pty Ltd
ABN 36 005 607 983
3rd edition – Jun 2014
ISBN 978 1 74220 424 6
© Lonely Planet 2014   Photographs © as indicated 2014
10 9 8 7 6 5 4 3 2 1
Printed in China